This book is dedicated to my parents for putting up with me.
— ANTON POLINGER

Developing Microsoft® Media Foundation Applications

Anton Polinger

Published with the authorization of Microsoft Corporation by:
O'Reilly Media, Inc.
1005 Gravenstein Highway North
Sebastopol, California 95472

Copyright © 2011 by Anton Polinger
All rights reserved. No part of the contents of this book may be reproduced or transmitted in any form or by any means without the written permission of the publisher.

ISBN: 978-0-7356-5659-8

1 2 3 4 5 6 7 8 9 LSI 6 5 4 3 2 1

Printed and bound in the United States of America.

Microsoft Press books are available through booksellers and distributors worldwide. If you need support related to this book, email Microsoft Press Book Support at *mspinput@microsoft.com*. Please tell us what you think of this book at *http://www.microsoft.com/learning/booksurvey*.

Microsoft and the trademarks listed at *http://www.microsoft.com/about/legal/en/us/IntellectualProperty/Trademarks/EN-US.aspx* are trademarks of the Microsoft group of companies. All other marks are property of their respective owners.

The example companies, organizations, products, domain names, email addresses, logos, people, places, and events depicted herein are fictitious. No association with any real company, organization, product, domain name, email address, logo, person, place, or event is intended or should be inferred.

This book expresses the author's views and opinions. The information contained in this book is provided without any express, statutory, or implied warranties. Neither the authors, O'Reilly Media, Inc., Microsoft Corporation, nor its resellers, or distributors will be held liable for any damages caused or alleged to be caused either directly or indirectly by this book.

Acquisitions and Developmental Editor: Russell Jones
Production Editor: Teresa Elsey
Editorial Production: Online Training Solutions, Inc.
Technical Reviewers: Anders Klemets and Matthieu Maitre
Indexer: Lucie Haskins
Cover Design: Twist Creative • Seattle
Cover Composition: Karen Montgomery

Contents at a Glance

	Introduction	xiii
CHAPTER 1	Core Media Foundation Concepts	1
CHAPTER 2	TopoEdit	11
CHAPTER 3	Media Playback	23
CHAPTER 4	Transcoding	61
CHAPTER 5	Media Foundation Transforms	97
CHAPTER 6	Media Foundation Sources	139
CHAPTER 7	Media Foundation Sinks	205
CHAPTER 8	Custom Media Sessions	247
CHAPTER 9	Advanced Media Foundation Topics	287
APPENDIX A	Debugging Media Foundation Code	323
APPENDIX B	COM Concepts	331
APPENDIX C	Active Template Library Objects	339
	Index	345
	About the Author	361

Contents

Introduction . . . . *xiii*

Chapter 1   Core Media Foundation Concepts   1
Media Foundation Audio/Video Pipelines. 2
Media Foundation Components 5
    Data Flow Through a Media Foundation Pipeline 7
Media Foundation Topologies 9
Conclusion 10

Chapter 2   TopoEdit   11
Manual Topology Construction in TopoEdit 16
Capturing Data from External Sources 20
Conclusion 22

Chapter 3   Media Playback   23
Basic File Rendering with Media Sessions. 25
    Creating the Player 27
    Initializing the Media Session 28
    Media Session Asynchronous Events 31
    Event Processing and Player Behavior 34
Building the Media Pipeline 43
    Creating the Media Foundation Source. 44
    Building the Partial Topology 48
    Resolving the Partial Topology 55
Conclusion 57
    Class Listings 57

What do you think of this book? We want to hear from you!
Microsoft is interested in hearing your feedback so we can continually improve our books and learning resources for you. To participate in a brief online survey, please visit:

microsoft.com/learning/booksurvey

Chapter 4 Transcoding   61

The Transcode API. 62
    Creating a Transcode Profile 64
    The Transcoding Session. 74

Transcoding with the Source Reader. 78
    Creating a Source Reader and a Sink Writer 80
    Mapping Sink Writer Streams 81
    Intermediate Format Negotiation 84
    The Target Transcode Media Type 88
    The Source-Reader-to-Sink-Writer Loop. 92

Conclusion 94
    Class Listings. 94

Chapter 5 Media Foundation Transforms   97

MFT Architecture Overview 98

Writing a Simple MFT. 101
    Stream Configuration Functions 101
    Media Type Selection Functions 107
    MFT Data Processing. 113
    Status Query and Event Functions 119
    MFT Registration 121

Injecting Images into Video Frames 122
    Uncompressed Video Formats. 123
    RGB to YUV Image Conversion 125
    Frame Format Detection. 128
    UYVY Image Injection 130
    NV12 Image Injection 132

Conclusion 133
    Class Listings. 134

Chapter 6 Media Foundation Sources 139

    Overview. 141

    The Asynchronous Call Pattern 143

    Instantiating a Media Source 146

        The AVF Byte Stream Handler 149

    Media Foundation Events 157

    The Media Foundation Source. 159

        Initializing the Source 160

        Asynchronous Source Command Functions 171

        Starting Playback 174

        Source Media Event Functions. 178

        Sample Streaming in *AVFSource* 180

    Media Stream Objects 183

    Windows Property Handlers. 189

    Conclusion 195

        Class Listings 196

Chapter 7 Media Foundation Sinks 205

    The Sample AVI File Sink 207

    The AVI Media Sink. 210

        Media Stream Sink Control Functions 211

        Media Sink Clock Functions 216

        The Sink Data Loop 220

    The AVI Media Stream 227

        Stream Playback Control Functions 229

        Stream Sample Functions. 230

        Stream Markers. 234

    Conclusion 242

        Class Listings 242

Chapter 8 Custom Media Sessions — 247

The Custom MP3 Media Session 250

Building an MP3 Topology 251

    Negotiating Media Type 256

The Custom Session Data Pipeline. 261

    Synchronous and Asynchronous MFTs. 262

    Synchronous Media Foundation Pipeline Events 266

    MP3 Session Data Flow. 272

The Session Clock 279

Conclusion 283

    Class Listings. 283

Chapter 9 Advanced Media Foundation Topics — 287

Rendering a Player UI with the EVR Mixer 289

Streaming a Network Player 298

    Building the Network Topology 300

    The HTTP Byte Stream Activator. 305

    The HTTP Output Byte Stream 306

Conclusion 315

    Class Listings. 315

Appendix A Debugging Media Foundation Code — 323

Media Foundation Error Lookup 323

The MFTrace Tool 324

    An MFTrace Example. 326

Appendix B COM Concepts — 331

The *IUnknown* Interface. 331

COM Object Registration. 336

Appendix C Active Template Library Objects   **339**

    ATL Smart Pointers 339

    CComCritSecLock and *CComAutoCriticalSection* Thread Synchronization
        Helpers 343

Index   *345*

About the Author   *361*

Introduction

Microsoft Media Foundation (MF) is Microsoft's new media platform in Windows, introduced in Windows Vista. MF is intended as the primary media application development platform, superseding and replacing Microsoft DirectShow, Microsoft DirectX Media Objects, Microsoft Video for Windows, and all other previous media technologies. MF gives you the ability to create advanced video and audio processing applications on the Windows platform starting with Windows Vista. If you want to develop Windows media applications, you will need to use the Media Foundation platform to access various components and hardware acceleration capabilities provided with Windows.

Developing Microsoft Media Foundation Applications provides an organized walk-through of the MF system, giving the reader an overview of the core ideas necessary for designing MF applications. This book will provide you with a basic understanding of all the major components necessary to write MF applications. The samples provided with this book demonstrate the ideas discussed here and provide concrete examples of how to use the various APIs and components demonstrated in each chapter. Though the book is designed to give you a necessary grounding in the ideas required for developing Media Foundation applications, it can also be used as a Media Foundation reference.

Who Should Read This Book

This book is designed to help existing COM and C++ developers understand the core concepts of Media Foundation. The book does not assume that the reader is already familiar with other media technologies, and it gives an overview of the core concepts behind media application development. However, a grounding in the basic ideas used in DirectShow and other media platforms will be useful for the reader. Though the book is not a complete reference of MF technologies, it will also be worthwhile for experienced Media Foundation developers because it provides the background and ideas of MF at a deeper level than in many other sources.

Although an understanding of basic COM concepts is required for the book, you do not need to have extensive knowledge of related technologies such as Active Template Libraries (ATL). The examples use only a handful of ATL objects, and the book provides a quick explanation of these ATL classes and ideas.

Assumptions

Because MF uses COM extensively, this book expects that you have a basic understanding of C++ and COM technologies. If you do not yet have the knowledge of the core COM ideas and APIs, you might consider reading *Essential COM* by Don Box (Addison-Wesley Professional, 1998), or *Inside COM* by Dale Rogerson (Microsoft Press, 1997).

Though you can gain access to the MF APIs through managed wrappers and by importing various MF functions, this book contains examples only in C++. You can use managed code to access these APIs and attempt to follow along with the examples, but be aware that a layer of managed code will add an extra level of complexity to your applications and make it more difficult to apply the concepts being discussed.

Who Should Not Read This Book

Not every book is aimed at every possible audience. If you do not have basic COM and C++ experience, or if you're not aiming to gain a thorough grounding in developing media-based applications, this book is not for you.

Organization of This Book

This book is divided into nine chapters, each of which focuses on a different concept or idea within Media Foundation. Though you can read the chapters independently from each other, they gradually increase in complexity and assume a basic knowledge of the ideas previously discussed.

Chapter 1, "Core Media Foundation Concepts," and Chapter 2, "TopoEdit," provide a brief introduction to media playback technologies and an overview of basic MF concepts. These chapters do not contain any code and are intended as a starter for developers unfamiliar with the basic concepts behind MF. Chapter 3, "Media Playback," and Chapter 4, "Transcoding," provide a grounding in MF application development, demonstrating and discussing a simple media player and a transcoding application. Chapter 5, "Media Foundation Transforms," Chapter 6, "Media Foundation Sources," and Chapter 7, "Media Foundation Sinks," discuss and show the design of core Media Foundation components used in media processing pipelines. And finally, Chapter 8, "Custom Media Sessions," and Chapter 9, "Advanced Media Foundation Topics," describe more advanced concepts behind the MF platform and applications.

In addition, the book contains three appendixes that can be used as reference material. Appendix A explains how to debug asynchronous Media Foundation applications and gives a brief overview of the MFTrace debugging tool. Appendix B provides a quick refresher for basic COM concepts. Finally, Appendix C demonstrates several common ATL objects used in every sample in the book.

Finding Your Best Starting Point in This Book

The various chapters of *Developing Microsoft Media Foundation Applications* cover several objects and ideas used in MF applications. Depending on your needs and the current level of your media development experience, you can concentrate on different chapters of the book. Use the following table to determine how best to proceed through the book.

If you are	Follow these steps
New to media application development	Focus on Chapter 1, Chapter 2, and Chapter 3, or read through the entire book in order.
Familiar with core media concepts and other media platforms	Briefly skim Chapter 1 and Chapter 2 if you need a refresher on the core concepts.
	Read through Chapter 3 and Chapter 4 to gain an understanding of the asynchronous design pattern of MF applications.
	Read through Chapter 5 to get an understanding of the core media processing components most commonly developed in MF.
An experienced MF developer	Skim Chapter 5. Read through Chapter 6 and Chapter 8. Skim Chapter 7 and Chapter 9.

Most of the book's chapters include hands-on samples that let you try out the concepts just learned. No matter which sections you choose to focus on, be sure to download and install the sample applications on your system.

Conventions and Features in This Book

This book presents information using conventions designed to make the information readable and easy to follow.

- Boxed elements with labels such as "Note" and "More Info" provide additional information or more advanced ideas behind some of the concepts discussed in that section.

- At the end of most chapters, you can find the class definitions of key classes used in the examples for the chapter.

- At the beginning of most sections, you can find introductions with conceptual diagrams and brief overviews of the components discussed later in the chapter.

- Before demonstrating various MF interfaces, each chapter provides a brief overview of all the methods in the interface.

Standard Coding Practices

This book uses several standard coding practices and a specific coding style. For simplicity, it omits some of the more esoteric macros and unusual design decisions often seen in MF code on MSDN. Instead, you'll use several basic ATL and Standard Template Library (STL) objects that help streamline application design, reduce the amount of code you need to write, and eliminate some of the more common COM programming bugs.

> **More Info** For an extremely brief overview of COM and ATL, see Appendixes B and C.

Because this book uses only the simplest and most common ATL and STL constructs, prior knowledge of those libraries will be helpful but is not required.

In addition to ATL, this book uses a common error-handling *do{}while(false)* pattern to halt execution in a function if a catastrophic error occurs. Here is an example that demonstrates this idea, together with some basic *CComPtr* smart pointer usage.

```cpp
// macro that will test the passed-in value, and if the value indicates a failure
// will cause the execution path to break out of the current loop
#define BREAK_ON_FAIL(value)      if(FAILED(value)) break;

// macro that will test the passed-in value for NULL. If the value is NULL, the
// macro will assign the passed-in newHr error value to the hr variable, and then
// break out of the current loop.
#define BREAK_ON_NULL(value, newHr)   if(value == NULL) { hr = newHr; break; }

// macro that will catch any exceptions thrown by the enclosed expression and
// convert them into standard HRESULTs
#define EXCEPTION_TO_HR(expression)    \
{ \
try { hr = S_OK; expression; } \
catch(const CAtlException& e) { hr = e.m_hr; break; } \
catch(...) { hr = E_OUTOFMEMORY; break; } \
}


HRESULT SampleFunction(void)
{
  // declare the standard HRESULT result variable
  HRESULT hr = S_OK;
  CComPtr<ITestInterface> pInterfaceObj;

  // enter the do-while loop. Note that the condition in while() is "false". This
  // ensures that we go through this loop only once. Thus the purpose of the
  // do{}while(false); loop is to have something from which we can drop out
  // immediately and return a result without executing the rest of the function.
  do
  {
    // Do some operation, and receive a result. The function will initialize the
    // pInterfaceObj object.
    hr = Foo(&pInterfaceObj);

    // test the result of the function call. Break out of do-while if hr indicates
    // a failure
    BREAK_ON_FAIL(hr);

    // test the pInterfaceObj pointer, and break out of the do-while if the
    // pointer is NULL. Also assign E_UNEXPECTED error code to hr - it will be
    // returned out of the function.
    BREAK_ON_NULL(pInterfaceObj, E_UNEXPECTED);
```

```
        // Since pInterfaceObj pointer is guaranteed to not be NULL at this point, we
        // can use it safely. Store the result in the hr.
        hr = pInterfaceObj->Bar();

    }
    while(false);

    // note that we did not need to call IUnknown::AddRef() or IUnknown::Release()
    // for the pInterfaceObj pointer. That is because those calls are made
    // automatically by the CComPtr smart pointer wrapper. The CComPtr smart pointer
    // wrapper calls AddRef() during assignment, and calls Release() in the
    // destructor. As a result, smart pointers help us eliminate many of the common
    // COM reference counting issues.

    return hr;
}
```

The core idea demonstrated by this sample function concerns the *do-while* loop. Notice that the *while* condition is set to *false*. This ensures that the *do-while* loop executes only once, because the sole purpose of the *do-while* construct here is to provide a way to break out of the standard code path and interrupt the execution if an error occurs.

The preceding *SampleFunction()* contains two function calls, one of which initializes the *pInterfaceObj* pointer, and another that uses the *pInterfaceObj* pointer to call a method of that object. The idea here is that if the first *Foo()* function fails, the second function should not—and cannot—be called, because the *pInterfaceObj* will not be initialized properly. To ensure that the *pInterfaceObj->Bar()* method is not called if the *Foo()* function fails, the code uses two C++ macros: BREAK_ON_FAIL() and BREAK_ON_NULL(). The code behind those macros is extremely simple and is shown in the example as well.

As you can see, the BREAK_ON_FAIL() macro will cause the execution to break out of the *do-while* loop if the HRESULT returned from *Foo()* indicates a failure. This arrangement lets you bypass the *pInterfaceObj->Bar()* call, so you can avoid an access violation in the example. The BREAK_ON_NULL() macro functions similarly, except that it also assigns an error code to the *hr* variable, which is returned as the result of the *SampleFunction()*.

> **Note** I chose not to use the *goto* statements that developers sometimes choose to handle these sorts of error conditions, because *goto* calls in C++ confuse the compiler and break compiler optimization. The code will still work as expected, but the compiler will fail to optimize the binary properly. In addition, in my opinion, *goto* statements are ugly and should be avoided.

Although the *do{}while(false)* construct may seem to be overkill in this small example, it is extremely useful in more complex functions. For example, suppose you have a function with 10 statements, each of which should be executed if and only if all the preceding statements have succeeded. If you attempt to use nested *if()* statements, you will produce unclear and hard-to-read code, adding greatly to the complexity of the function structure. That will make your code far more confusing than it should be, and thus increase the probability of bugs in that function.

As you might have noticed, the preceding code listing also has a third macro that was not demonstrated in the example function. The *EXCEPTION_TO_HR()* macro is designed to hide the *try-catch* blocks and automatically convert any exceptions into common *HRESULT*s. This macro is needed because the internal components of Media Foundation do not catch exceptions. Therefore, if your custom MF components throw exceptions, various internal MF threads might fail and abort unexpectedly, leaving the application in an unpredictable state. As with most Windows code, Media Foundation propagates errors by returning failing *HRESULT* error codes. This macro is therefore used in the samples to convert any exceptions thrown by ATL or STL components into standard codes that can then be detected and used by MF applications.

System Requirements

You will need the following hardware and software to complete the practice exercises in this book:

- One of the following operating systems: Windows Vista, Windows 7, or Windows Server 2008
- Microsoft Visual Studio 2010, any edition (multiple downloads may be required if you are using Express Edition products)
- The Windows SDK version 7.1
- Microsoft DirectX 2010 SDK (used only in the Chapter 9 sample)
- A computer that has a 1.6-gigahertz (GHz) or faster processor (2 GHz recommended)
- 1 GB (32-bit) or 2 GB (64-bit) RAM
- 3.5 GB of available hard disk space
- A 5400 RPM hard disk drive

- A video card that supports DirectX 9 and a 1024 x 768 or higher-resolution display
- A DVD-ROM drive (if installing Visual Studio from DVD)
- An Internet connection to download software or chapter examples

Depending on your Windows configuration, you might require local administrator rights to install or configure Visual Studio and to register sample MF components.

Code Samples

Most of the chapters in this book include exercises that let you interactively try out new material learned in the main text. All sample projects can be downloaded from the following page:

http://go.microsoft.com/FWLink/?Linkid=229072

Follow the instructions to download the Media_Foundation_samples.zip file.

> **Note** In addition to the code samples, your system should have Visual Studio 2010, the Windows SDK, and the DirectX SDK installed. If available, the latest service packs for each product should also be installed.

Installing the Code Samples

Follow these steps to install the code samples on your computer so that you can use them with the exercises in this book.

1. Unzip the Media_Foundation_samples.zip file that you downloaded from the book's website.
2. If prompted, review the displayed end-user license agreement. If you accept the terms, select the Accept option, and then click Next.

> **Note** If the license agreement doesn't appear, you can access it from the same webpage from which you downloaded the Media_Foundation_samples.zip file.

Using the Code Samples

The folder structure of the files in the program contains three subfolders.

- **SampleMediaFiles**   This folder contains several video and audio files used to test the sample applications used in the book.

- **Code**   The main example projects referenced in each chapter appear in this folder. Separate folders indicate each chapter's sample code. All of the projects are complete and should compile in Visual Studio normally if the Windows and DirectX SDKs are properly installed.

- **Tools**   This folder contains several tools that are referenced in the chapters and that will be useful for debugging and testing the samples.

To examine and compile a sample, access the appropriate chapter folder in the Code folder, and open the Visual Studio solution file. If your system is configured to display file extensions, Visual Studio solution files use an .sln extension.

If during compilation you get an error indicating that a header (.h) file is not found, your project is missing the right include directories. In that case, do the following:

1. Right-click the project in the Solution Explorer and select Properties.
2. Under Configuration Properties, select the VC++ Directories node.
3. Add the SDK directory to the Include Directories field after a semicolon. If you installed the SDK in the default location, the field may contain something like "$(IncludePath);C:\Program Files\Microsoft SDKs\Windows\v7.1\Include".

If during compilation you get linker errors indicating that there are unresolved external symbols or functions, your project is missing the right library directories. In that case, do the following:

1. Right-click the project in the Solution Explorer and select Properties.
2. Under Configuration Properties, select the VC++ Directories node.
3. Add the SDK directory to the Library Directories field after a semicolon. If you installed the SDK in the default location, the field may contain something like "$(LibraryPath);C:\Program Files\Microsoft SDKs\Windows\v7.1\Lib". For x64 versions of the library files, look under Lib\x64.

All the sample code provided with this book is fully functional and compiles and works as described in the chapters.

Acknowledgments

I'd like to thank Anders Klemets and Matthieu Maitre for tech reviewing the book, and Emad Barsoum for giving me the idea to write the book, signing up to write half of it, and then running off to get married.

Errata & Book Support

We've made every effort to ensure the accuracy of this book and its companion content. Any errors that have been reported since this book was published are listed on our Microsoft Press site at oreilly.com:

http://go.microsoft.com/FWLink/?Linkid=229070

If you find an error that is not already listed, you can report it to us through the same page.

If you need additional support, email Microsoft Press Book Support at *mspinput@microsoft.com*.

Please note that product support for Microsoft software is not offered through the addresses above.

We Want to Hear from You

At Microsoft Press, your satisfaction is our top priority, and your feedback our most valuable asset. Please tell us what you think of this book at:

http://www.microsoft.com/learning/booksurvey

The survey is short, and we read every one of your comments and ideas. Thanks in advance for your input!

Stay in Touch

Let's keep the conversation going! We're on Twitter: *http://twitter.com/MicrosoftPress*.

CHAPTER 1

Core Media Foundation Concepts

Media Foundation Audio/Video Pipelines. 2
Media Foundation Components 5
Media Foundation Topologies 9

Microsoft Media Foundation (MF) applications are programs that load and use various MF components and modules to process various media data streams. Some MF applications are designed to simply play back video or audio files. Others convert the media streams between different formats, store them in different files, and even send and receive media data over the Internet. In this chapter, you will learn the basic terms and concepts used when discussing and considering Media Foundation applications.

Media Foundation applications break up the tasks necessary to process media data streams into multiple simple steps. Each step is performed by a separate MF component that is loaded into an MF application. The MF components work together to carry out various media processing tasks in an MF application. Different MF components link up together to process the data and do the work in the application.

Abstractly, you can think of MF components as a series of domino pieces loaded into the program. The domino pieces line up and connect to each other, forming chains that work together to process media data streams. Each of the dominos can connect to certain types of other dominos, based on the number of dots on each end. In other words, the dominos can connect to each other only in specific ways—other combinations are invalid and will refuse to connect.

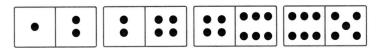

In effect, MF applications are containers for these collections of domino chains, processing media data flowing through them. Each MF application can contain any number of separate chains, and each chain (pipeline) will work on a different data stream. For example, an MF application can be used to play a video file with closed captioning data and audio. To play this type of file, such an application would need three chains of MF components: one to decode and display the video, one to decode and render the audio, and one to display the subtitle data stream.

The individual MF components cooperate and work together to process a data stream. In a video player application, one component would be responsible for loading the stream from a file, another for decoding and decompressing the stream, and yet another for presenting the video on the screen. If necessary, some of the components modify and transform the data flowing through them from the format in which it was stored or transmitted into a format that the video card will accept.

Windows includes a number of MF components that any Media Foundation program can use. In this book, you will see how to load existing MF components, create your own MF components, arrange them into chains, and use them to process media streams. By combining these MF modules, you will learn how to write applications that can play back different types of media files, and perform complex operations on media data.

Media Foundation Audio/Video Pipelines

When audio or video is digitized and stored on a computer, it is formatted and compressed in a way that significantly reduces its size on disk. This is necessary because uncompressed video takes up a lot of space; a standard uncompressed HD video stream may take up hundreds of megabytes per second and produce 5 to 15 gigabytes of data per minute, depending on the frame rate and the video resolution. Obviously this is too much data to store for normal operations. Therefore, audio and video files are compressed using various compression algorithms, reducing their size by several orders of magnitude. Furthermore, the audio and video streams are stored in different file (container) formats, to simplify video processing used for different operations. For example, some file formats are convenient for transmitting data over the network. Files in these formats are played as the data comes in, and the data stream contains error correction information. Other file formats are more suited for storage and quick access by different types of decoders and players. Consequently, to play back video, a program needs to perform a series of operations to first unpack the video from its file, then to decode (uncompress) it, and finally to display it on the screen.

To simplify these operations, media processing applications build audio/video *pipelines*. These pipelines consist of a series of MF components, each of which is responsible for an operation on or transformation of the data. You can think of the pipeline as a series of pipes with water flowing through them. Just as with water pipes, data in the A/V pipelines flows only in one direction—downstream. Each of the components in the pipeline is responsible for a specific operation on the data. As an example, here is a conceptual diagram that represents the pipeline used to play back an audio file.

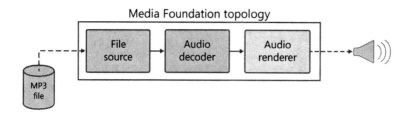

Pipeline is a generic term used for a design where a series of objects are arranged in sequence and work together to process some data flowing through them. In the image just shown, the file source object is responsible for unpacking the compressed audio data from the MP3-compressed audio file, the audio decoder decodes/decompresses the data, and the audio renderer communicates with the audio hardware on your PC to "render" the audio and produce sounds.

The arrows in the image indicate the flow of data in the pipeline—data flows from the file to the file source, from the file source to the audio decoder, from the decoder to the audio renderer, and finally from the renderer through the PC audio hardware to the actual speaker. The dashed arrows represent data flow that is outside of Media Foundation control, and are specific to the individual components. For example, the file source uses operating system calls to load the file from the disk, and the audio driver (represented by the renderer) uses internal hardware calls to send information to the audio hardware. Notice that the data all flows in one direction, like a river—from upstream to downstream.

In a media pipeline, the output of the upstream components is used as the input for some downstream components, and no chain of components contains a loop. If considered in mathematical terms, MF pipelines are *directed acyclic graphs*—the data always flows in a particular direction, and there are no cycles. When dealing with MF objects, you can also call the pipeline a *graph* or a *topology*. These terms are synonyms and can be used interchangeably.

For another MF pipeline example, consider the steps necessary to play back a video file. As mentioned above, video files are stored in an encoded, compressed format in specific file types. Therefore, a video processing pipeline needs to perform a series of very specific operations to play back the file:

1. Load the file from disk.
2. Unpack the data streams from the file.
3. Separate the audio and video streams for processing by their respective codecs.
4. Decode—decompress—the data.
    a. Decompress audio data.
    b. Decompress video data.
5. Present the uncompressed and decoded information to the user.
    a. Send the audio data to the audio hardware on the PC, and eventually the PC speakers.
    b. Send the video data to the video card, and display the video on the PC monitor.

Here is a diagram of a standard Media Foundation pipeline used to play a video stream to the user. In the diagram, steps 1, 2, and 3 from the list just shown are done by the file source, step 4 is performed by the audio and video decoders, and step 5 is done by the renderers.

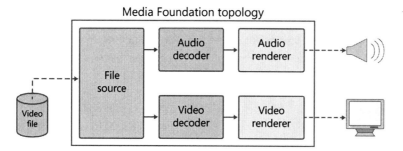

A video file usually contains both audio and video data, stored in a special file format. The audio and video information is stored in chunks, or packets. Each data packet in the pipeline is used to store either a frame, part of a frame, or a small section of the audio. Each packet also usually contains some sort of time indication that tells the decoders and renderers which video packets must be played concurrently with which audio packets.

The diagram shows several types of MF components, as well as conceptual representations of several external components. The video file connected to the source is not part of the Media Foundation pipeline—the MF source object loads the file by using standard Windows APIs. Similarly, the audio and video hardware are also separate from the MF pipeline. The connections that load the data into the MF pipeline from external entities and pass the data to external components are shown as dashed line arrows.

As you can see from the diagram, a Media Foundation pipeline consists of several standardized component types:

- **MF sources**   These are the components that load the multiplexed (intertwined) data streams from a file or the network, unpack the elementary audio or video streams from the container, and send them to other objects in the topology. In this example, the source loads data from a video file, separates (demultiplexes) the audio and video streams, and sends them to the decoders. As far as MF is concerned, sources produce data for the topology and have no input.

- **Media Foundation transforms (MFTs)**   These are components that transform the data in various ways. In the example described previously, the decoders are implemented as MFTs—they accept compressed data as input, *transform* the data by decoding it, and produce uncompressed information. All MFTs have at least one input link and at least one output link.

- **MF sinks**   These components are responsible for rendering content on the screen or to the audio card, saving data to the hard drive, or sending it over the network. Sinks are essentially the components that extract data from the topology and pass it to the external entities. The two sinks shown in this example render the video stream to the screen and the audio stream to the audio card.

The reason for these naming conventions—sources, sinks, and transforms—can be seen from the diagram. MF source components are sources of data for the MF pipeline, MF transforms modify the data, and MF sinks remove the data from an MF pipeline.

Media Foundation Components

MF data processing components—sinks, sources, and MFTs—are independent modules used to process the data flowing through the pipeline. The internal implementation of these objects is hidden from the application and the application programmer. The only way that the application and developer can communicate to the components is through well-known COM interfaces. Objects are MF components if and only if they implement specific Media Foundation interfaces. For example, MF transforms must implement the *IMFTransform* interface. Any object that implements this interface can therefore be considered an MFT.

In later chapters of this book, you will see how to implement your own custom sources, sinks, and MFTs by implementing various MF interfaces. The samples will demonstrate how each of these types of components operates and how they can be loaded, used, configured, and extended.

MF data components have no idea what application they reside in or who is calling them. They operate in isolation and separately from each other. As a result, they have no control over and no knowledge of what other components are in the pipeline with them, or who produces or consumes their data. The data processing components could even be loaded outside of an MF topology for testing or custom media handling.

The only restriction on how MF sources, sinks, and MFTs can be hooked up to each other is in the types of data they produce and consume. To go back to an earlier analogy, the domino pieces can be placed in any order, as long as the number of dots on one end of a piece matches the number of dots on the other end of the piece connected to it.

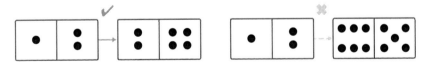

The dots in this analogy represent what's known as the media type supported by an MF component. The media type is the data type that this particular component can process and understand. For example, an MP3 audio decoder MFT is designed to decode MP3 audio. Therefore, the MP3 decoder MFT accepts as input only MP3 audio streams, and can produce only uncompressed audio. In other words, the input stream of the MP3 decoder MFT has the MP3 audio media type, and the output of the MFT has the WAV (uncompressed) audio media type. As a result, the MF component upstream of an MP3 decoder must output MP3 audio so that the decoder can consume it. Similarly, the MF component downstream of the MP3 decoder must be able to consume an uncompressed audio stream.

An MF media type object describes the type of media in a data stream that is produced or consumed by an MF component. A media type contains several values that define the data type that an MF component can produce or consume. The two most important values in a media type are the major and minor types, stored as GUIDs (unique 128-bit numbers):

- **Major type**   Defines the generic type of data handled by a component. For example, it can be audio, video, closed captioning, or custom iTV data.
- **Subtype**   Indicates the specific format of the data. Usually this value indicates the compression used in the data stream—such as MP3, MPEG2, or H.264.

> **Note**   A subtype of a media type is also sometimes known as its *minor type*.

Besides these values, a media type can also contain any number of custom data structures and parameters with specific information required to decode the data. For instance, a video media type would usually contain the frame size, sample size, pixel aspect ratio, and frame rate of the video stream, as well as any number of other parameters. These values are then used by the downstream component to properly process the passed-in data.

If you want to connect two MF components to each other, the output media type of the upstream component must match the input media type of the downstream component. If the media types do not match, you might be able to find a transform that will allow you to convert the media types and allow them to match.

> **Note**   Unlike dominos, MF objects cannot be flipped around—MFTs are only one-way components. This is where the domino analogy breaks down. For instance, you cannot use the MP3 decoder MFT to encode uncompressed audio into the MP3 format. Similarly, a source cannot be used as a sink, and a sink cannot be used as a source.

Many MF components can support several media types, and adjust to the pipeline appropriately. For example, an AVI video file source will expose the media types of the streams that are stored in the file. If the file contains DivX video and MP3 audio, the source will expose the DivX video media type on one stream and the MP3 audio media type on another. If the file contains MPEG1 video and AC3 audio, the source will expose a stream with the MPEG1 media type and a stream with the AC3 media type.

Exactly which media types are exposed by a component depends on the internal component design. When two components are being connected, a client usually goes through all of the media types exposed by the upstream and downstream objects, trying each one in turn. This media type matching procedure will be covered in more detail in Chapter 3, "Media Playback."

Data Flow Through a Media Foundation Pipeline

As mentioned earlier, data is passed between individual components in a topology in chunks or packets, usually called media samples. Each media sample is an object with a data buffer, with a small segment of the data stream and a set of information describing the data. For example, when a media sample contains a segment of an audio stream, the data buffer inside of it holds a fraction of a second of audio data. When the sample is part of the video stream, the buffer contains part of a video frame or a full frame.

Here is a graphical representation of a media sample object, as well as some information inside of it.

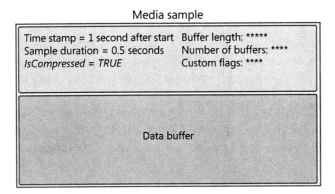

Besides a data buffer with some stream data, a media sample may also contain values and attributes that provide specific information about the sample. These values indicate exactly how many buffers are in the sample, describe custom flags, indicate when the sample should be presented or rendered, indicate the duration of the sample, and so on. Exactly what extra values are attached to each sample depends on the component that generated it and on the data in the sample.

Here is a diagram that demonstrates the operation of an MF pipeline playing an MP3 file.

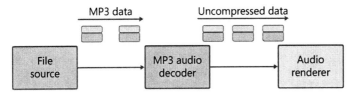

In this diagram, the file source is loading data from an MP3 file. The source therefore generates new media samples with the MP3 audio media type and sends them to the MP3 audio decoder. The samples themselves are filled with audio information compressed with the MPEG Layer 3 (MP3) encoder. This connection is of course represented by the thin arrow connecting the file source box and the audio decoder box in the diagram.

More Info Another analogy that you can use to think of Media Foundation components is bucket brigades—chains of people passing water buckets to each other. Each person in the chain represents an MF component processing data. The buckets in this analogy are media samples (packets) being passed between individual MF components. The water in the buckets is the media data.

Here is how data flows through the audio pipeline presented in the diagram:

1. The file source loads data from a file, generates a new media sample, and fills it with some of the MP3-encoded audio bits.

2. The MP3 audio decoder consumes the incoming MP3 audio samples, extracts the compressed audio data from the samples, and releases them. It then decodes (uncompresses) the audio data, generates new samples, stores the decoded audio data in them, and then sends those uncompressed samples to the audio renderer. Note that in this hypothetical example more samples are exiting the decoder than are entering—this is because the decoder uncompresses the audio information. Therefore, the data takes up more space, and more samples need to be generated. Some decoders can solve this problem by reusing the same samples but inserting more data into them.

3. The audio renderer receives the samples with uncompressed audio and holds onto them. The renderer compares the time stamps in the samples to the current time, and sends the sample data to the audio hardware (through the driver), which in turn generates the sounds. After the renderer is done with the samples, it releases them and requests the next sample from the upstream MF components.

This process, in which data flows from the source to the decoder and then to the sink, continues while the pipeline is running, and while there is data in the source file.

Note Though the media samples themselves are implemented as standard objects and are created and destroyed on demand, the media buffers inside of the samples are special. Each sample object is essentially a wrapper around the internal buffer object. To improve performance and speed up allocations, MF reuses the data buffers.

When a sample is created by the file source, it instantiates a new sample object but gets a buffer from the underlying MF system. When the MP3 audio decoder is done with the sample, the sample is released (deleted), but the media buffer is sent back to the file source for reuse. This optimization significantly reduces the number and size of the allocations that are done by MF applications during playback. This functionality is not exposed to the MF components themselves, but is instead handled by the MF system.

While the pipeline shown in the previous illustration is playing, the MP3 file samples continuously flow through it. Each sample contains a small fraction of the audio stream—for example, a sample may contain 0.25 seconds of audio. The MP3 decoder decodes the compressed data and sends it in samples to the audio renderer. The renderer in turn passes the information to the audio hardware of the computer, which plays the sounds that you hear through your speakers or headphones.

Notice that the MP3 file source cannot be connected directly to the audio renderer. The renderer expects to receive media samples with uncompressed audio information, but the MP3 file source can generate only media samples with MP3 data. In other words, the output media type of the MP3 source is MP3 audio, while the input media type of the audio renderer is uncompressed audio. The only way for them to connect is to find an intermediate MF component that can transform the data from the format of the upstream component (the source) to the format of the downstream component (the sink). In this case, the transform object is the MP3 audio decoder MFT.

Some MFTs release the samples passed in and generate new ones that are sent out. Others keep the same samples flowing to the downstream components, and simply modify some of the data inside of them. The exact behavior of the MFT depends on the purpose and design of each MFT.

Media Foundation Topologies

To build an MF media pipeline—an MF topology—applications usually use the MF topology builder components provided with Windows. Topology builders receive various hints about the topology from the application and then automatically discover which components need to be loaded to create a working pipeline. In other words, topology builders load and connect Media Foundation components in a specific order, so that each upstream component produces data in the right format for the downstream component.

To give a topology builder the information it needs to build a working topology, an application provides it with a partial topology. The partial topology usually contains only the source nodes and their corresponding sink nodes. The topology builder then searches the registry for all MF transforms, instantiates them, and attempts to insert them between the source and the sink. This continues until either the topology builder finds a transform (or a series of transforms) that can successfully convert the source media type to the sink media type, or it runs out of transforms. This is the standard mode of operation for most players.

For example, to build the MP3 player shown previously, an application would first create a source for the MP3 file, then create an audio renderer, and then instruct the topology builder to find a transform that accepts the MP3 audio on the input and produces uncompressed audio on the output. If the topology builder cannot find a single MFT that can satisfy those requirements, it tries combinations of MFTs—it attempts to find an MFT that accepts MP3 audio on the input, and produces some other, intermediate data type on the output. Then it looks for another MFT that can process that intermediate data type and produce uncompressed audio output that will be accepted by the renderer.

This type of automated topology resolution works for most basic cases where the input and output are well known and nothing special needs to happen in between. However, in some situations an application may need to modify the media stream in some special way. For example, a video encoding application may need to insert a watermark into the video itself, or an audio player may need to clean up the sound and add an echo. These types of effects are handled by custom MFTs. In this case, automatic topology resolution would not suffice, because the topology builder would not have a reason to insert such an MFT into the topology.

To instruct the topology builder to add an extra component into the pipeline, an application can insert extra MFTs into the topology between the source and the sink. The topology builder then repeats the same process as mentioned previously, but it does so twice—first it attempts to find an MFT to fit between the source and the custom effect MFT, and then it tries to find another transform that would fit between the effect MFT and the sink. Of course, if the media types of the upstream and downstream components already match, then the topology builder does not insert any intermediate MFTs.

Conclusion

In this chapter, you learned the core ideas and concepts behind Media Foundation. You have seen how MF applications build media pipelines out of separate MF components, and how data flows through those pipelines. The chapter also provided an introduction to how individual MF components connect to each other. These ideas are behind all MF applications, so you need to fully understand them to be able to comprehend how MF applications function.

In the subsequent chapters, you will see how each of the major types of MF components operates, how they process data, and how the data is passed from one component to another. You will see how to build basic and complex topologies that will be used to achieve all sorts of effects and deal with different types of media.

CHAPTER 2

TopoEdit

Manual Topology Construction in TopoEdit 16
Capturing Data from External Sources 20

One of the most important tools in the arsenal of a Microsoft Media Foundation (MF) developer is the manual topology construction tool, TopoEdit. Developers use the tool extensively for prototyping and testing while designing MF components. TopoEdit—which stands for *Topology Editor*—is a tool that allows you to manually create, examine, and modify Media Foundation topologies, controlling which MF components are placed where, and how exactly a topology is constructed.

In this chapter, you will see how to use the TopoEdit tool to build various topologies by hand. This will help you understand how to programmatically construct these same topologies and how to test individual MF components that will be written in the following chapters.

To understand what exactly TopoEdit does, you can look back at the domino analogy presented in Chapter 1, "Core Media Foundation Concepts." In that analogy, the individual MF components were presented as domino pieces connected to each other. TopoEdit allows you to actually see these domino pieces, arrange them in any order you want, and attempt to hook them up in all sorts of combinations and arrangements.

The TopoEdit tool is available as a sample application with the Windows 7 software development kit (SDK). To avoid having to build the tool, you can use the already-built version available in the files provided with this book. The TopoEdit version provided with the book also contains several minor bug fixes that are not present in the Windows 7 SDK codebase.

Note If you are using a 64-bit version of Windows, you can use either the 32-bit or the 64-bit version of the TopoEdit tool. However, if you use the 32-bit version of TopoEdit on 64-bit Windows, the tool will show you only 32-bit Media Foundation components registered on the machine. If you use a 64-bit version of TopoEdit, the tool will show you (and use) only 64-bit MF components. This is an important distinction, because you need to be aware of the version of the hosting application to expose your custom MF components to it.

To launch the tool, you can simply double-click the TopoEdit.exe executable located in the Tools folder, in the directory to which you unzipped the sample code. You can find the sample code installation instructions in the Introduction of this book. Here is the main TopoEdit UI that you will see.

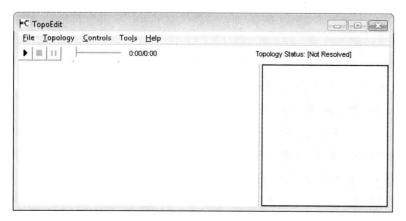

The most basic operation in the TopoEdit tool is automatically creating a topology for playback of a media file. This is known as *rendering* the media file. In this mode, TopoEdit loads an audio or video file and automatically determines which components need to be inserted into the topology to present the file to the user.

To render a media file, select File | Render Media File and choose a video or audio file from the resulting Open File dialog box. The following shows a topology that will be created by TopoEdit if you try to render the sample Wildlife.wmv file provided with this book.

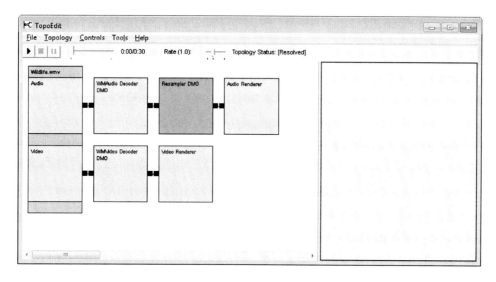

As you can see, TopoEdit generated all of the MF components needed to play the Wildlife.wmv file and displayed them as boxes in the main window. From left to right, we have the following MF components:

- **WMV source component**   The component that loads the WMV file from the disk, separates the elementary audio and video streams, and exposes them to the rest of the topology. The audio stream is represented by the top box labeled *Audio,* and the video stream is, of course, represented by the bottom box.

- **WMAudio decoder MFT**   The decoder component that decodes the audio stream in the file. The audio stream was encoded with the standard Windows Media Audio encoder (WMA encoder), which is why you need the WMA decoder to play it.

- **WMVideo decoder MFT**   The decoder that uncompresses the video stream in the WMV file. The video for this file was encoded with the Windows Media Video encoder (WMV encoder), which is why you need the WMV decoder to play it.

- **Resampler MFT**   This is an automatically inserted audio transform that is needed to re-sample the audio stream. This MFT is often necessary because the audio in the file may not exactly match the format expected by the audio renderer. For example, a file may be encoded with eight audio channels but may be played on a PC with only two speakers. The resampler adjusts the audio, mixing the individual channels to allow the user to hear everything in the stream. Most of the time, you don't need to worry about this MFT, because it will be inserted automatically by the topology builder.

- **Audio renderer sink**   The MF sink component that connects to the audio driver on the PC. This sink accepts uncompressed audio samples and sends them to the audio hardware for playback.

- **Video renderer sink**   The MF sink that connects to the video driver, which in turn displays the video on the screen.

Each of these components is represented by one or more boxes in the TopoEdit window. The boxes are all connected to each other by lines, which represent the paths over which media samples will flow through the topology. Notice that you can use your mouse to drag the components around on the screen to clarify the topology.

> **Note**   You may have noticed that many of the MFTs are marked with the *DMO* acronym. DMO stands for DirectX Media Object. A DMO is a component designed to work like an MFT or a Microsoft DirectShow filter, but uses different interfaces and a slightly different runtime model. Though DMOs do not implement the *IMFTransform* interface, they are loaded into the MF topology inside of special MFT wrapper objects. You don't need to worry about whether a component is a DMO or an MF object—Media Foundation will take care of the conversion for you.

Now that the topology has been created, you can play the video file by either clicking the Play button on the toolbar (below the menu bar) or by using the Controls | Play menu option. The video will be rendered in a small window generated by TopoEdit. You can also pause and stop the video by using appropriate buttons or control options.

To the right of the pause button is a small seek bar that you can use to skip around in the file. The seek bar indicates the current position of the playback. Note that seek functionality is implemented in the MF source being used to play back the video. Not all MF sources support seeking.

Next to the seek bar is the rate control. MF renderers support playback of content at different rates of speed— for example, you can play the video at twice the normal speed or at half speed. The exact rate supported depends on the renderer and the source.

To the right of the rate control on the toolbar is text that indicates the current topology status. If the topology status is [Resolved], then all of the MF components have been loaded into the topology and have agreed on common media types and connections. If the topology status is [Not Resolved], then the topology builder will need to negotiate some connections and possibly load some additional MFTs to make all of the components work together.

The actual rectangles in the main TopoEdit interface represent not MF components directly, but topology nodes that are a level of abstraction above the MF objects. With topology nodes, you can control how the actual objects are created without having to instantiate the actual objects directly. You will see more information about topology nodes and their relationship to the actual underlying MF objects in Chapter 3, "Media Playback."

You may have noticed an empty gray area to the right of the main MF component field. That area is used to display the current attributes of the selected object. The following shows what you can see if you click the video decoder node in the topology.

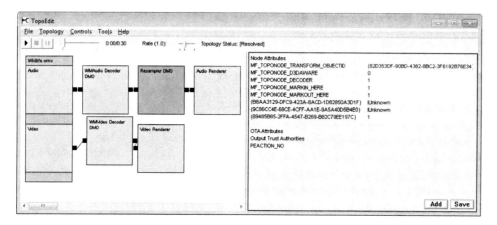

The attribute values indicate various values stored in the topology object that represents the underlying MFT. These values allow an application to configure the individual components, control their behavior, and get their status. In this screen shot, the attributes indicate the underlying object's ID, as well as several of its internal settings and parameters.

Note TopoEdit can recognize a limited list of hard-coded attributes. Each attribute is identified by a GUID, and TopoEdit has an internal mapping between the attribute GUIDs and their string representations. For example, TopoEdit knows that the GUID {c9c0dc88–3e29–8b4e–9aeb–ad64cc016b0} corresponds to the string "MF_TOPONODE_TRANSFORM_OBJECTID." Whenever TopoEdit doesn't have a matching string for an attribute GUID, it inserts the GUID itself instead of the name on the attribute pane.

The OTA attributes displayed in the previous screen shot represent the custom Output Trust Authority attributes that allow playback of protected (encrypted) content. OTA and Digital Rights Management (DRM) functionality will not be covered in this book.

In addition to the node attributes, the attribute pane of TopoEdit can display something extremely useful—the media types produced by the upstream and expected by the downstream components. To see the media types, click the link connecting two nodes to each other.

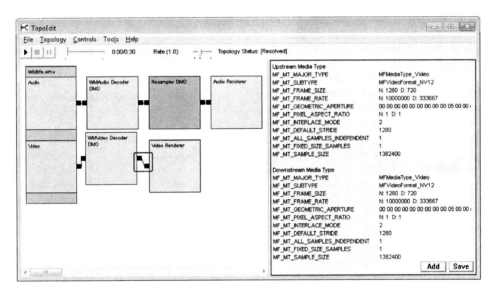

CHAPTER 2 TopoEdit **15**

The attribute pane in the image is displaying the media type that will be produced by the upstream node and the media type that is expected by the downstream node. When topology is resolved, the two media types should match, because both components have already agreed on a common data format between each other. If the topology is not resolved—if the topology builder did not have a chance to ensure that every component has agreed on a connection—the two types may differ. During the topology resolution phase, the topology builder will attempt to find an intermediate MFT that will convert the data from the upstream type into the type expected by the downstream component.

In this image, the link selected in TopoEdit is between the video decoder and the video renderer. This means that the connection—when it is resolved, as shown here—is displaying details about the uncompressed media type that will be passed to the video renderer. Here are some of the more interesting media type details about the link shown in the image:

- **Media major type** The major type of the data stream. In this case, it is a video stream.
- **Media subtype** The format of the data stream. The format used here is known as NV12—this is a common uncompressed data format. Uncompressed video types will be discussed in Chapter 5, "Media Foundation Transforms."
- **Frame size** The size of the video frame. The native resolution of this video is 720p—the height of each frame is 720 pixels, and the width is 1280 pixels.
- **Frame rate** The rate at which frames change during normal playback of the video. This value is presented as a fraction of two numbers. To get the actual number, divide the first value by the second. Therefore, 10,000,000 / 333,667 = 29.97 frames per second.

The rest of the media type parameters are more specific to the individual type and are less interesting.

Manual Topology Construction in TopoEdit

The procedure in the previous section allows you to use TopoEdit to automatically construct a topology for a specific file. However, you can also manually create the topology. This allows you to insert custom and special components into the topology that are not strictly necessary for normal file rendering. Let's now create a custom topology for playback of the sample AVI_Wildlife.avi file provided with this book.

The actual order of steps that you take to create any topology is arbitrary. For simplicity, however, this example will proceed from left to right, from source to renderer. Therefore, let's begin by inserting an MF source for the file. This is done by using the Topology | Add Source menu option. This creates the familiar Open File dialog box that allows you to choose a media file for which the source will be created.

Behind the scenes, MF uses a set of functions to automatically create an MF source from a file or a network stream. The functions open the file, determine its type, and generate the right source for the container format. You will see more examples of explicit source creation in the following chapters.

After you have created a source for the file, your topology will look something like the following.

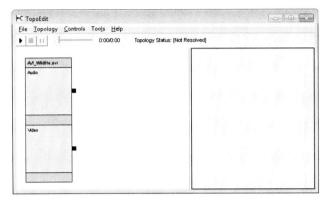

Because this file contains only two streams, the source will show only two rectangles representing the stream objects—one for audio and one for video.

Next, let's add the audio and video renderers to the topology. Unlike DirectShow, Media Foundation does not support enumeration of various sink objects. There is no single location in the registry where an application can look for all of the Media Foundation renderers available on the machine. Therefore, TopoEdit has two hard-coded renderers specified explicitly and instantiated like COM objects by their class IDs (CLSIDs)—the video renderer and the audio renderer.

The standard video renderer that can be used with MF is the EVR (which stands for *Enhanced Video Renderer*). The EVR was initially created for use with DirectShow applications but has been extended for use in MF. The EVR is an advanced rendering sink filter that employs hardware acceleration to display video on the screen and supports several advanced features and behaviors. You will learn more about the EVR's advanced features in Chapter 9, "Advanced Media Foundation Topics."

To add the EVR to the topology, you use the Topology | Add EVR option. This will add the EVR sink node. Next, let's add the standard audio renderer. Similarly, TopoEdit has a hard-coded audio sink known as the SAR (Streaming Audio Renderer). You can add it to the topology in the same way as the video renderer—by using the Topology | Add SAR menu option.

Finally, let's add the video decoder that will be used to decode the video stream for this AVI file. Though the AVI file format supports all sorts of video codecs, the file used as a sample for this book was encoded with the DivX encoder. Therefore, you need to add the MPEG43 decoder MFT. To add this MFT, select the Topology | Add Transform option, expand the Video Decoder node in the list of available MFTs, select Mpeg43 Decoder MFT from the list, and click the Add button.

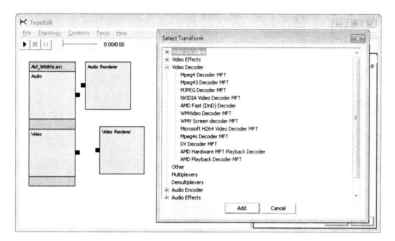

As you can see, TopoEdit provides a list of all the MFTs registered on the machine. This is done in the same way that DirectShow filter registration is done—the MFT CLSIDs are stored in a specific location in the registry. An application can enumerate them by either directly accessing that registry location or by using a helper MFT enumeration function. The MFTs are stored under different categories, which indicate their particular purpose.

Some of the MFTs—such as the NVIDIA Video Decoder MFT and the AMD Playback Decoder MFT in this screen shot —expose underlying hardware functionality, allowing direct access to the hardware. These transforms allow an MF application to pass data directly to the hardware for accelerated decoding or special processing. Because the AVI_Wildlife.avi file contains video encoded in the H.264 format, select the Microsoft H264 Video Decoder MFT decoder—this is a standard software decoder MFT provided with Windows.

After these components are added to the topology, you can start connecting them to each other. To connect two topology nodes together, you need to drag the mouse from one of the small black squares on the right of a square representing a topology node to another black square on the left side of another node.

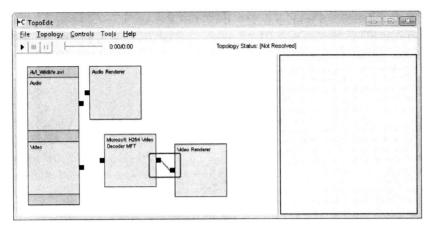

This creates a link between the two nodes. Note that if a link is invalid, you can select it with the mouse, press the Delete button on the keyboard, and remove it. Let's hook up the nodes in the following order: the video source stream to the H264 decoder MFT to the video renderer, and the audio source stream to the audio renderer. If you select the links—by clicking the little black squares—you will see only the upstream media types exposed by the source, because the topology is not yet resolved. Before the topology has been resolved, only the source knows what its output media type is going to be—at this point, no other nodes have negotiated connections with each other.

After the topology is resolved, you may see one or more extra MFTs that have been added. Usually the topology builder will add audio and video decoders and various resampler components that ensure that the output audio format is at the correct sample rate, has the right number of channels, that uncompressed video uses a supported color space, and so on.

The topology shown in the screen shot would work as is if the file used as a sample here had audio at the right sample rate. In that case, you would not need a custom audio decoder or an audio resampler. This file, however, uses audio at a different sample rate than is normally supported by audio drivers. This topology will not play as it is shown here. You can also see that the topology is not ready by looking at the topology status string on the toolbar—it indicates that the topology status is [Not Resolved], which means that the individual MF components are not connected to each other.

To explicitly resolve the topology, you can either click Play or use the Topology | Resolve Topology menu option. At that point, TopoEdit will use the default MF topology loader to negotiate the connections between all of the MF components already loaded, and add any missing MFTs necessary to convert the output media type of the upstream components to the input media type of the downstream components.

Just as you skipped adding the audio decoder to this topology and hooked up the audio source stream to the audio renderer directly, you could have also skipped the explicit creation of the video decoder transform. The topology loader would have automatically detected that the output media type exposed by the source's video stream was different from all the types that the video renderer could accept, and it would have loaded the required decoder automatically. The decoder MFT step was explicitly described here to demonstrate how you can load your own custom transforms for testing outside of any external applications.

When the topology is resolved, you can play back the file. At that point, TopoEdit has negotiated connections between all of the MF components in the topology, and you can view the upstream and downstream media types between MF sources, transforms, and sinks. Furthermore, at this point the duration of the file loaded into the source is displayed to the right of the seek bar.

Capturing Data from External Sources

In addition to building standard playback topologies that play content from a file, you can use TopoEdit to build a topology that captures and plays video from a hardware source. MF natively supports USB-based devices and standard audio drivers. Therefore, you can create a topology that gets its data from a USB webcam and the computer's input audio port, and use it to play back live video and audio.

Unlike DirectShow, MF does not have a way to enumerate all capture source components present on the machine. MF source filters are not stored in any directory in the registry. Instead, MF provides a set of enumeration and creation functions that allow you to instantiate the right component for each source type. To find available capture devices on the machine, MF uses the built-in *MFEnumDeviceSources()* function to enumerate all of the MF capture sources that are currently enabled, based on some passed-in parameters.

This functionality is exposed in TopoEdit through two menu options on the Topology menu—the Add Video Capture Source and Add Audio Capture Source options. When invoked, these menu items enumerate all of the capture sources of the specified type and present them in a list box.

Here is what this looks like if you are trying to add a video capture source.

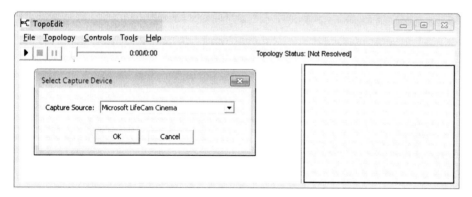

In this example, the PC has the Microsoft LifeCam Cinema USB webcam attached and enabled. You will get a similar view when adding an audio capture device.

Tip If the list box does not contain the video or audio capture device that you know is available on your machine, make sure that the device hardware is enabled and properly hooked up. For example, on many systems, the audio recorder will not be enabled by default—you need to connect an actual microphone to get this working, and make sure that the device is enabled in Windows Control Panel.

Using these options, you can create a topology with capture sources for both audio and video streams. The content in this topology will play in a synchronized fashion because, by default, all renderers in a topology share the same clock object, which tells them when to render each video and audio sample. Advanced topology clock manipulation will be covered in Chapter 8, "Custom Media Sessions."

The following screen shot demonstrates the topology that you can build to capture and render audio and video data. This topology captures video from the LifeCam USB camera, and audio from the microphone.

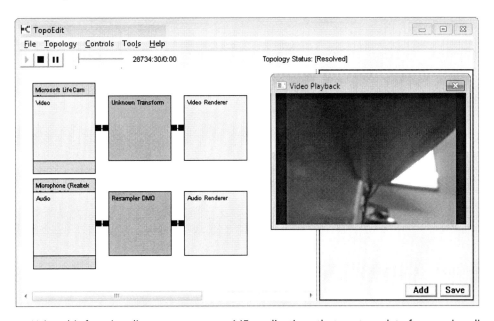

Using this functionality, you can create MF applications that capture data from various live sources. Note that most webcams are supported only because they use standard Microsoft USB drivers. TV capture cards or more esoteric capture devices might not work if they don't have MF-compatible capture drivers and source components installed.

CHAPTER 2 TopoEdit   **21**

Conclusion

In this chapter, you learned how to use the TopoEdit tool to create various MF topologies. You saw how to add various components to the topology, and then either explicitly connect all of the nodes or use the topology builder to discover and insert any missing MFTs. Though most MF applications perform these steps programmatically, it is useful to first go through them manually. This allows you to visualize and fully comprehend topology building before you write a single line of code.

In addition, TopoEdit is extremely useful for building test topologies and testing your custom MF components outside of any external applications that might add unneeded complexity. With TopoEdit, you can quickly prototype a topology with your component, and debug a problem without worrying about bugs in the hosting application. Several of the following chapters use this approach to demonstrate and test the sample MF components. They present the MF components outside of any application framework and expect you to simply load and try out the objects directly inside of TopoEdit.

CHAPTER 3

Media Playback

Basic File Rendering with Media Sessions 25
Building the Media Pipeline 43

Now that we have covered some of the basic Microsoft Media Foundation (MF) concepts, let's look at the process of writing MF applications. In this chapter, you will create a simple video file player—a Windows application that accepts a media file and plays it back in a window. This file player demonstrates the core ideas of Media Foundation. With those fundamental concepts in hand, you will be able to build more advanced applications in later chapters.

Before you begin writing Media Foundation applications, you need to have at least a basic understanding of COM APIs. COM is a Microsoft technology that was introduced in the early 1990s to enable disparate objects to link to each other. At its core, COM provides a way for various objects to interoperate with each other without knowing each other's internal structure or details.

More Info You can find a brief overview of COM in Appendix B. The overview is not meant to be a full description of COM but is designed to give you a refresher of some core COM concepts.

MF uses COM extensively but is not itself a pure COM API. A pure COM API consists of only COM objects that can be instantiated exclusively by the COM *CoCreateInstance()* function. Instead, MF uses a mix of COM and normal objects, as well as several other standard functions. For example, to instantiate an MF playback topology, you cannot create an instance of a well-known and registered class by calling *CoCreateInstance()* with the topology's class ID (CLSID) but must instead use the *MFCreateTopology()* function.

Despite that, internally MF uses some COM functionality. Therefore, at the beginning of your application you must initialize the COM system by calling the *CoInitializeEx()* function. This will initialize the COM library and prepare it for use. After the application is done executing, you should also call *CoUninitialize()* to shut down the COM library.

Note MF is a free-threaded system, which means that COM interface methods can be invoked from arbitrary threads. Therefore, when calling *CoInitializeEx()*, you must initialize COM with the apartment-threaded object concurrency by passing in the *COINIT_APARTMENTTHREADED* parameter. Your objects might also need to use synchronization primitives, such as locks, to control access to internal variables by concurrently running threads.

In most cases, you should use implementations of interfaces that are provided by Media Foundation. Some MF APIs rely on additional functionality that is only present in the MF objects that implement these interfaces. For example, if you are going to use the default media session, you should not implement your own *IMFTopology* object, but use the object returned by the *MFCreateTopology()* API.

To demonstrate some of the concepts of Media Foundation, this chapter uses and analyzes a sample player provided with the downloadable code for this book.

More Info For instructions on how to obtain and download the sample code, see the Introduction.

The player is a very simple MF application designed to play various media files using the MF components that are built into Windows Vista and Windows 7.

Background This player application started out as the BasicPlayback MSDN sample (*http://msdn.microsoft.com/en-us/library/bb970475(v=VS.85).aspx*) but has been heavily modified. The media session eventing model has been separated from the Win32 application layer, and the topology-building functions were pulled into a separate class. In addition, redundant code was removed. The purpose of these modifications was to segment various concepts of the player into self-contained classes, and thus simplify exploring them in manageable chunks.

The player is built on top of a basic Win32 application, with all its functionality encapsulated in winmain.cpp. Because the core purpose of this book is to explore Media Foundation, it does not cover the application itself.

Over the course of this chapter, you'll explore the two main classes that compose the player: *CPlayer*, which encapsulates media session behavior; and *CTopoBuilder*, which builds the media topology for the player. These two classes contain all the MF functionality of the player and abstract it from the Win32 components, thus greatly simplifying the code.

The *CPlayer* class wraps and encapsulates everything you need to do to instantiate core playback Media Foundation objects and control video playback. You can find the code for the *CPlayer* class in the Player.h and Player.cpp files in the downloadable code.

The *CTopoBuilder* class, in turn, encapsulates the functions and objects needed to create a partial Media Foundation topology. The topology is used to initialize and connect the MF objects that are actually responsible for processing media data. The *CTopoBuilder* class is separate from the *CPlayer* to simplify the code and separate each object's areas of responsibility. You will cover topology building and MF pipeline object instantiation in the second half of this chapter. The *CTopoBuilder* class is defined in the TopoBuilder.h and TopoBuilder.cpp files in the downloadable code.

Basic File Rendering with Media Sessions

Just like Microsoft DirectShow, the Media Foundation architecture uses a series of components connected to each other to process media files and display them to the user. Although these objects can be instantiated and hooked up together in various ways, one of the most common means of managing these sets of data processing components is with a media session object. By using a media session object, you can generate a media pipeline and control the playback of the content.

The media session in MF serves roughly the same purpose as the graph in DirectShow. The media session holds all of the MF components that process the data and gives you the ability to start and stop playback. During playback, the media session pulls samples from the source, passes them through the MFTs, and sends them to the renderers. At the moment, however, you can ignore all that. Internal media session functionality will be discussed in more detail in Chapter 8, "Custom Media Sessions."

> **Note** In addition to the media session, MF contains another method for building and controlling playback topologies—the *MFPlay* API. However, *MFPlay* has been deprecated and therefore will not be covered in this book.

Because the media session is a basic concept used in most Media Foundation applications, it lies at the core of the player application example. As such, the main player class—*CPlayer*—wraps and encapsulates most of the functionality exposed by the media session. The *CPlayer* class uses the media session to first build a media pipeline, then control video playback, and finally, to clean up resources on shutdown. In addition, the *CPlayer* class also wraps and hides the complexities of the MF asynchronous messaging system from the main Win32 application.

As mentioned earlier, most MF operations are asynchronous, which makes them difficult to represent graphically without resorting to Unified Modeling Language (UML). In this case, I've chosen to demonstrate the basic life cycle of the sample player as a modified UML sequence diagram. Don't worry: this book does not delve deeper into UML's complexity and uses it only sparingly.

UML sequence diagrams are well suited for demonstrating lifelines and behaviors of multiple objects. The sequence diagrams used in this book do not follow all of the UML sequence diagram conventions but are used to bring across the basic underlying ideas. The following diagram shows which object instantiates which, and the sequence of calls made by individual components. In addition, this book sometimes uses the vertical rectangles visible along some of the object lifelines to indicate the duration of various function calls. Thus the first vertical rectangle under the *Player* object indicates the duration of the *CPlayer::OpenURL()* method, and shows what calls that function makes. The vertical dimension in the diagram represents time, and subsequent calls are shown one above the other. For example, in the diagram, the Create Player call happens before the Set File URL call—which is why the first call is above the second.

Here is the basic sequence of calls in the application to start video playback:

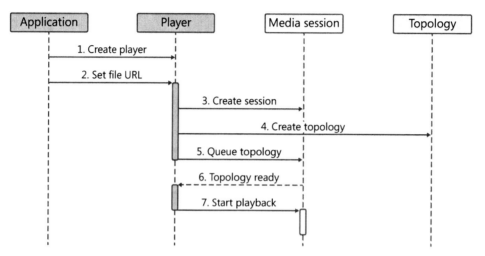

Here's a detailed description of these calls and steps:

1. The application instantiates the *CPlayer* component. In the diagram, the rectangle with the name "Player" represents the object, and the dashed vertical line underneath the rectangle indicates the lifeline of the *CPlayer* object.

2. The application sends the file URL to the player by calling the *CPlayer::OpenURL()* method. The file URL function triggers the rest of playback, shown in the subsequent steps. The application does not need to make any further calls to play the file.

3. The player instantiates the media session. During session creation, the player registers itself as the receiver for the session's asynchronous MF events by passing a pointer to itself to the *IMFMediaSession::BeginGetEvent()* method.

4. The player then instantiates the topology. Topology building in this sample is done by the *CTopoBuilder* helper class, which will be covered in the "Building the Media Pipeline" section later in this chapter.

5. The player passes the partial topology to the media session.

6. After the topology is loaded, the media session instantiates all of the components indicated in the topology and fires an asynchronous MF event indicating that the topology is ready. Because the player registered itself as the receiver of session events in step 3, it now gets called by the session with a "topology-ready" event.

7. The topology-ready event causes the player to start playback.

MF uses an asynchronous model for most operations. Internally, MF has special worker thread objects that execute scheduled asynchronous calls on separate threads, outside of the normal flow of execution that you might have seen in single-threaded applications. The asynchronous model will be covered in greater detail in Chapter 6, "Media Foundation Sources." For now you can ignore the worker thread objects, and assume that the asynchronous objects make calls of their own volition. For example, in the diagram just shown, the media session does not directly call the player's *IMFAsyncCallback::Invoke()* method, but instead schedules work with the worker thread object. The worker thread is the component that actually executes the *Invoke()* call.

More Info The asynchronous nature of MF applications makes debugging and determining the source of problems rather difficult. See Appendix A for a discussion on how to debug MF applications.

To understand how the player operates, you'll examine each of these steps in detail.

Creating the Player

Little actually occurs during player creation. Player creation involves calling the *CPlayer* constructor, which in turn initializes the MF system. Before you can start using Media Foundation calls, you need to initialize MF, which you do with the *MFStartup()* function. Here's the code for the *CPlayer* constructor.

```
//
// CPlayer constructor - instantiates internal objects and initializes MF
//
CPlayer::CPlayer(HWND videoWindow, HRESULT* pHr) :
    m_pSession(NULL),
    m_hwndVideo(videoWindow),
    m_state(Closed),
    m_nRefCount(1)
{
    HRESULT hr = S_OK;

    do
    {
        // initialize COM
        hr = CoInitializeEx(NULL, COINIT_APARTMENTTHREADED);
        BREAK_ON_FAIL(hr);
```

```
        // Start up Media Foundation platform.
        hr = MFStartup(MF_VERSION);
        BREAK_ON_FAIL(hr);

        // create an event that will be fired when the asynchronous IMFMediaSession::Close()
        // operation is complete
        m_closeCompleteEvent = CreateEvent(NULL, FALSE, FALSE, NULL);
        BREAK_ON_NULL(m_closeCompleteEvent, E_UNEXPECTED);
    }
    while(false);

    *pHr = hr;
}
```

The player constructor receives a handle to the main window as a parameter. It uses this handle when building the topology, to inform the video renderer where it should draw the video.

The player is also initializing COM by calling *CoInitializeEx()*, and MF by calling *MFStartup()*. This is necessary for MF to properly function. Each of these calls has a corresponding shutdown call that must be made when the player is finalizing. For each successful *CoInitializeEx()* call, you must make a *CoUninitialize()* call to close and unload COM; and for each successful *MFStartup()* call, you must make a corresponding *MFShutdown()* call to shut down MF. In this sample, the MF and COM shutdown functions are called from the *CPlayer* destructor.

Note Media Foundation APIs come only in the UNICODE flavor—there are no ASCII versions of Media Foundation functions.

In addition, the constructor creates a Win32 event that will be used later to signal that the session has finished closing. You'll see more about this event—and the reason for its existence—in the "Media Session Asynchronous Events" section later in this chapter.

After all of the components have been initialized, the constructor sets the output *HRESULT* parameter that returns the success or failure to the caller.

Initializing the Media Session

Most of the initialization begins only after the application tells the player which file to play. The application passes a file URL to the player (which may be either a network path or a local UNC file path). The player then uses the URL to initialize the topology that will play the content. Here is the *OpenURL()* function that initiates this work.

```
//
// OpenURL is the main initialization function that triggers building of the core
// MF components.
//
```

```cpp
HRESULT CPlayer::OpenURL(PCWSTR sURL)
{
    CComPtr<IMFTopology> pTopology = NULL;
    HRESULT hr = S_OK;

    do
    {
        // create a media session if one doesn't exist already
        if(m_pSession == NULL)
        {
            hr = CreateSession();
            BREAK_ON_FAIL(hr);
        }

        // Build the topology. Here we are using the TopoBuilder helper class.
        hr = m_topoBuilder.RenderURL(sURL, m_hwndVideo);
        BREAK_ON_FAIL(hr);

        // get the topology from the TopoBuilder
        pTopology = m_topoBuilder.GetTopology();
        BREAK_ON_NULL(pTopology, E_UNEXPECTED);

        // Add the topology to the internal queue of topologies associated with this
        // media session
        hr = m_pSession->SetTopology(0, pTopology);
        BREAK_ON_FAIL(hr);

        // If a brand new topology was just created, set the player state to "open pending"
        // - not playing yet, but ready to begin.
        if(m_state == Ready)
        {
            m_state = OpenPending;
        }
    }
    while(false);

    if (FAILED(hr))
    {
        m_state = Closed;
    }

    return hr;
}
```

As you can see, the main job of the *OpenURL()* method is to pass calls to other functions. There are three steps to player initialization:

- Creating and initializing the media session
- Building the playback topology
- Passing the topology to the session

The function responsible for creating and initializing the media session is shown here.

```
//
//  Creates a new instance of the media session.
//
HRESULT CPlayer::CreateSession(void)
{
    HRESULT hr = S_OK;

    do
    {
        // close the session if one is already created
        BREAK_ON_FAIL( CloseSession() );

        if(m_state != Closed)
        {
            hr = E_UNEXPECTED;
            break;
        }

        // Create the media session.
        BREAK_ON_FAIL( MFCreateMediaSession(NULL, &m_pSession) );

        m_state = Ready;

        // designate this class as the one that will be handling events from the media
        // session
        hr = m_pSession->BeginGetEvent((IMFAsyncCallback*)this, NULL);
        BREAK_ON_FAIL(hr);
    }
    while(false);

    return hr;
}
```

To create a media session, you need to call the *MFCreateMediaSession()* API. This function takes an optional configuration object as a parameter and returns a pointer to the new media session. After the session has been created, you need to specify a callback object that will receive asynchronous events from the session. You do that by calling the *IMFMediaEventGenerator::BeginGetEvent()* function, which notifies the media event generator (in this case, the session) that the next event should be sent to the passed-in object.

To simplify the sample code, in this case the *CPlayer* class itself is the event callback object. It implements the *IMFAsyncCallback* interface used by the event generator to pass back various events. Whenever anything of note happens in the media session, the player will be notified with a call to its *IMFAsyncCallback::Invoke()* method.

Finally, after the topology has been built by the *CTopoBuilder* class, the player passes the topology to the media session by calling the *IMFMediaSession::SetTopology()* function. The topology contains information about the MF components that the session needs to instantiate to play back the file.

The first parameter to the *IMFMediaSession::SetTopology()* function is an optional combination of the following flags:

- **MFSESSION_SETTOPOLOGY_IMMEDIATE**   Stop playback of the currently loaded media (if any) and apply the topology immediately.

- **MFSESSION_SETTOPOLOGY_NORESOLUTION**   This is a full (not partial) topology and doesn't need to be resolved. MF doesn't need to attempt to add any missing MFTs, and the session can accept the topology as is.

- **MFSESSION_SETTOPOLOGY_CLEAR_CURRENT**   If the second parameter is *NULL*, clear any topology association with the session. If the second parameter is not *NULL*, reset the session only if the passed-in topology matches the one currently associated with the session.

Passing in *0* is valid as well and indicates that no flags are specified. If the *MFSESSION_SETTOPOLOGY_IMMEDIATE* flag is not specified and a topology is already queued in the session, the new topology will be added to the queue. In that case, after the session is done playing the first topology, the second one will start. This is useful when topology resolution might take a long time and you do not want to have any gaps between playback of multiple pieces of content.

Media Session Asynchronous Events

As you may already know, all Windows applications are inherently asynchronous. Windows applications do not execute on a single thread. Instead, they have a message loop that constantly waits for events and performs different actions based on the event information. For example, each time you press a key, the system sends an event to the focused application's message loop with the key ID. The application decodes that event and performs some corresponding action.

To conform more closely to the asynchronous nature of standard Windows applications, MF uses a similar asynchronous architecture. This design choice greatly improves responsiveness of MF applications. If a Windows application directly calls a synchronous function that takes a long time to execute, the call will block the application's event loop, which causes the window to stop updating and appear to hang. As a result, the UI will freeze, and users will be unable to click buttons, resize the window, or manipulate its menus. To bypass that problem at the root—or to at least make it easier to write asynchronous applications without designing a secondary messaging system—MF also uses an asynchronous model.

In this asynchronous system, most MF functions do not directly execute any operations; instead, the calls only *schedule* the work with the main object, and return immediately. The work items themselves then execute on a background thread. After the work is completed, the objects fire events that notify the caller of the status of the scheduled work item.

To facilitate this asynchronous communication system, the media session receives a pointer to an event callback object. This callback object will be called whenever something of note happens, such as when the topology is ready for playback, when the video playback has ended, or when errors occur. This example uses the player itself as the asynchronous event callback object. The player implements the *IMFAsyncCallback* interface, registers itself with the media session in the *CPlayer::CreateSession()* method, and gets called by the session whenever something of note happens.

> **More Info** As mentioned earlier, there is actually an extra component in this system—the worker thread object. This worker thread does not drastically change the explanation but instead provides more detail and an additional level of understanding to the MF asynchronous design. For now, the worker object will be glossed over in this chapter to simplify the explanation. The worker thread will be discussed in more detail in Chapter 6.

The MF event cycle is actually fairly complex and contains several stages. The following sequence diagram demonstrates how MF events work in our sample. It shows a sequence of calls made to process an asynchronous event fired from the media session to the player object.

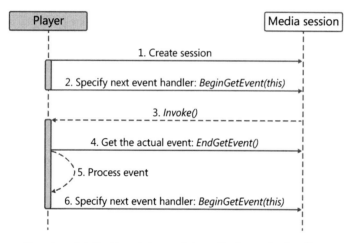

Here is a detailed breakdown of the calls shown in the diagram:

1. The player creates a new session by calling *MFCreateMediaSession()* from the *CPlayer::CreateSession()* function.

2. The player registers itself as the event handler for the next event from the media session. The player does so by passing a pointer to an *IMFAsyncCallback* object (in this case, itself) to the *IMFMediaEventGenerator::BeginGetEvent()* method. The call returns immediately. This call tells the media event generator which object it needs to call whenever an event occurs.

3. The event generator (which in this case is the session) calls *IMFAsyncCallback::Invoke()* to notify the event handler of a new event in the queue. Note that this is done from a separate thread other than the main thread—that is why this is known as an asynchronous system. Other things can be happening concurrently in the player on a different thread.

4. The event handler calls the event generator back and gets the actual event from the queue with the *IMFMediaEventGenerator::EndGetEvent()* method. This call returns immediately.

5. The event handler processes the retrieved event.

6. The player registers itself to receive the next event, the same as in step 2.

7. Go back to step 3.

By using this looping mechanism, MF ensures that events always have an object that can process them, and that responsibility for processing events can be passed smoothly between several objects. For example, an event-handling object (an implementer of the *IMFAsyncCallback* interface) can easily hand over processing of the next event to a new object by passing the new object's pointer in the next *BeginGetEvent()* call.

> **Note** You may have noticed that the *IMFAsyncCallback* interface also defines a helper *GetParameters()* method. This method is used by the media event generator to detect how the callback object will handle the calls. Most of the time, you will want to use default behavior and have the method return the *E_NOTIMPL HRESULT*.

Here is the sample player's implementation of the *IMFAsyncCallback::Invoke()* method.

```
//
// Receive asynchronous event.
//
HRESULT CPlayer::Invoke(IMFAsyncResult* pAsyncResult)
{
    CComPtr<IMFMediaEvent> pEvent;
    HRESULT hr = S_OK;

    do
    {
        CComCritSecLock<CComAutoCriticalSection> lock(m_critSec);

        BREAK_ON_NULL(pAsyncResult, E_UNEXPECTED);

        // Get the event from the event queue.
        hr = m_pSession->EndGetEvent(pAsyncResult, &pEvent);
        BREAK_ON_FAIL(hr);

        // If the player is not closing, process the media event - if it is, do nothing.
        if (m_state != PlayerState_Closing)
        {
            hr = ProcessMediaEvent(pEvent);
            BREAK_ON_FAIL(hr);
        }

        // If the media event is MESessionClosed, it is guaranteed to be the last event. If
        // the event is MESessionClosed, ProcessMediaEvent() will return S_FALSE. In that
        // case do not request the next event - otherwise tell the media session that this
```

```
            // player is the object that will handle the next event in the queue.
            if(hr != S_FALSE)
            {
                hr = m_pSession->BeginGetEvent(this, NULL);
                BREAK_ON_FAIL(hr);
            }
    }
    while(false);

    return S_OK;
}
```

> **Note** For the extraction of the asynchronous result to work correctly, you must pass exactly the same *IMFAsyncResult* object to the *IMFMediaEventGenerator::EndGetEvent()* function as the one you received in the *Invoke()* parameter.

As you can see, the *Invoke()* method does not do any processing of the event data. After the actual *IMFMediaEvent* object is retrieved from the session with the *IMFMediaSession::EndGetEvent()* call, the media event is passed to the helper *ProcessMediaEvent()* function. *ProcessMediaEvent()* parses the internal values in the media event and determines what, if anything, needs to happen. If the media event type is *MESessionClosed*, then that event is guaranteed to be the last to come from the session. In that case, *ProcessMediaEvent()* returns *S_FALSE*, which indicates that there is no need for the player to register for the next event.

Notice also the *CComCritSecLock* object instantiated in the *Invoke()* method. This object is an ATL construct that wraps around Win32 synchronization primitives. It ensures that only one thread can execute in the section locked with the same *c_critSec* critical section. For more information about ATL objects and thread synchronization, see Appendix C.

Event Processing and Player Behavior

After the *Invoke()* function has pre-processed the event, it passes control to the player event-processing function.

```
//
// Called by Invoke() to do the actual event processing, and determine what, if anything,
// needs to be done.  Returns S_FALSE if the media event type is MESessionClosed.
//
HRESULT CPlayer::ProcessMediaEvent(CComPtr<IMFMediaEvent>& pMediaEvent)
{
    HRESULT hrStatus = S_OK;            // Event status
    HRESULT hr = S_OK;
    UINT32 TopoStatus = MF_TOPOSTATUS_INVALID;
    MediaEventType eventType;
```

```cpp
    do
    {
        BREAK_ON_NULL( pMediaEvent, E_POINTER );

        // Get the event type.
        hr = pMediaEvent->GetType(&eventType);
        BREAK_ON_FAIL(hr);

        // Get the event status.  If the operation that triggered the event did
        // not succeed, the status is a failure code.
        hr = pMediaEvent->GetStatus(&hrStatus);
        BREAK_ON_FAIL(hr);

        // Check if the async operation succeeded.
        if (FAILED(hrStatus))
        {
            hr = hrStatus;
            break;
        }

        // Switch on the event type.  Update the internal state of the CPlayer as needed.
        if(eventType == MESessionTopologyStatus)
        {
            // Get the status code.
            hr = pMediaEvent->GetUINT32(MF_EVENT_TOPOLOGY_STATUS, (UINT32*)&TopoStatus);
            BREAK_ON_FAIL(hr);

            if (TopoStatus == MF_TOPOSTATUS_READY)
            {
                m_state = PlayerState_Stopped;

                hr = OnTopologyReady();
            }
        }
        else if(eventType == MEEndOfPresentation)
        {
            m_state = PlayerState_Stopped;
        }
        else if (eventType == MESessionClosed)
        {
            // signal to anybody listening that the session is closed
            SetEvent(m_closeCompleteEvent);
            hr = S_FALSE;
        }
    }
    while(false);

    return hr;
}
```

Event processing in the *CPlayer::ProcessMediaEvent()* function identifies the event and performs various operations based on the type of the event. First of all, the function extracts the type of the event—the type will be a value from the *MediaEventType* enumeration. The type provides clues about the information in the event, who fired it, and why. For example, when the topology is first set on the session, the player receives a media event with the *MESessionTopologySet* type; when the session is started, the player receives the event with the *MESessionStarted* type; and so on. This naming convention is very useful in identifying the information and context of an event.

> **More Info** The *MediaEventType* enumeration is defined in the mfobjects.h header file. If you receive a failure event of some sort, you should start by looking up the event type and using it to figure out who fired it. That will provide a clue about the error. For more information about debugging MF asynchronous failures, see Appendix A.

When the *ProcessMediaEvent()* function has identified the type of the event, it checks whether the event indicates a failure of some sort. If the *IMFMediaEvent* object was fired because of a failure, the HRESULT stored in the event object will indicate what sort of failure that is. To get the failing HRESULT, use the *IMFMediaEvent::GetStatus()* method. If the event indicates a failure, the function just exits, aborting further event processing.

If the event status does not indicate failure, *ProcessMediaEvent()* parses the event type to determine the next step. If the event type is *MESessionTopologyStatus*, and the status is that the topology is ready for playback, the function calls *OnTopologyReady()* to start playback. If the type is *MEEndOfPresentation*, indicating the end of playback, the function updates the player state to signal that the player has stopped. Finally, if the type is *MESessionClosed*, the function signals to any threads waiting for the *m_closeCompleteEvent* Win32 event that the close operation is done, and sets the return HRESULT to *S_FALSE*. This tells the caller—the *Invoke()* function—that no more new events should be requested from the session.

As you can see, the *ProcessMediaEvent()* function has special handling for the *MESessionClosed* event. This is needed to properly dispose of all the resources associated with the session. The problem with session shutdown is that you need to make sure that the closing operation is complete before you can safely dispose of the session. Because the *Close()* function is asynchronous, however, you need a synchronization mechanism that will let the thread in charge of shutting down the session (executing in the *CPlayer::CloseSession()* function) wait for the session *Close()* call to complete before proceeding with cleanup.

To solve this problem, you can use a Win32 event to synchronize individual threads responsible for the session shutdown. The main thread in the player initiates the *IMFMediaSession::Close()* call from the *CPlayer::CloseSession()* function, and then waits for the *m_closeCompleteEvent* to be set. However, calling the *Close()* function triggers a separate thread that actually performs the closing operation. That second thread does the work required to close the session, and then calls the *CPlayer::Invoke()* method. The *Invoke()* method sets the m_closeCompleteEvent, which in turn unblocks the first thread that is still waiting in the *CloseSession()* function. After the first thread resumes, it finishes the shutdown operation.

The following is a sequence diagram of these steps.

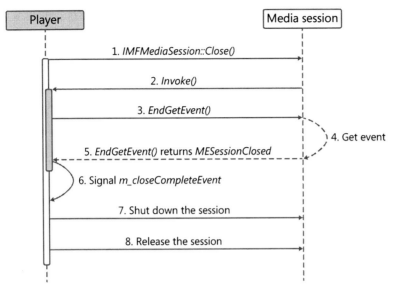

The diagram uses two vertical rectangular boxes under the *Player* object to show two threads running concurrently in two functions. The longer rectangle represents the *CPlayer::CloseSession()* method. The shorter, darker rectangle represents the player's *Invoke()* function, which is called by a different thread. Here are these steps listed in chronological order:

1. Thread 1: The *CloseSession()* thread calls *IMFMediaSession::Close()* to start session shutdown, and waits for the *m_closeCompleteEvent* to be set. The thread blocks until the *m_closeComplete-Event* event is signaled.

2. Thread 2: After the *Close()* operation completes, the media session calls *Invoke()* on a separate thread.

3. Thread 2: The *Invoke()* function calls into the session to get the actual media event by invoking its *IMFMediaEventGenerator::EndGetEvent()* method.

4. Thread 2: The *Invoke()* call thread gets the media event.

5. Thread 2: *EndGetEvent()* returns the media event with the *MESessionClosed* event type.

6. Thread 2: Because this is the *close* event and is guaranteed to be the last event from the session, *Invoke()* doesn't need to call *BeginGetEvent()* again. Instead, the thread signals the Win32 *m_closeCompleteEvent* event and exits the *Invoke()* function.

7. Thread 1: After the first thread detects that *m_closeCompleteEvent* was set, it resumes execution and calls *IMFMediaSession::Shutdown()* on the media session.

8. Thread 1: *CloseSession()* releases the media session object.

Note Again, this explanation is glossing over some details. The media session does not directly call into the player's *Invoke()* function. This is just a simplification used to describe the asynchronous operation.

Here is the code for the *CPlayer::CloseSession()* method—note that the function blocks in the middle, waiting until the *m_closeCompleteEvent* event is signaled.

```
//
// Closes the media session, blocking until the session closure is complete
//
HRESULT CPlayer::CloseSession(void)
{
    HRESULT hr = S_OK;
    DWORD dwWaitResult = 0;

    do
    {

        CComCritSecLock<CComAutoCriticalSection> lock(m_critSec);

        m_state = PlayerState_Closing;

        // release the video display object
        m_pVideoDisplay = NULL;

        // Call the asynchronous Close() method and then wait for the close
        // operation to complete on another thread
        if (m_pSession != NULL)
        {
            m_state = PlayerState_Closing;

            hr = m_pSession->Close();

            // IMFMediaSession::Close() may return MF_E_SHUTDOWN if the session is already
            // shut down. That's expected and acceptable.
            if (SUCCEEDED(hr))
            {
                // Begin waiting for the Win32 close event, fired in CPlayer::Invoke(). The
                // close event will indicate that the close operation is finished, and the
                // session can be shut down.
                dwWaitResult = WaitForSingleObject(m_closeCompleteEvent, 5000);
                if (dwWaitResult == WAIT_TIMEOUT)
                {
                    hr = E_UNEXPECTED;
                    break;
                }
            }
        }
```

```
        // Shut down the media session. (Synchronous operation, no events.)  Releases all of
        // the internal session resources.
        if (m_pSession != NULL)
        {
            m_pSession->Shutdown();
        }

        // release the session
        m_pSession = NULL;

        m_state = PlayerState_Closed;
    }
    while(false);

    return hr;
}
```

The *CPlayer::CloseSession()* method initiates session shutdown. The method first puts the player into the right state by setting the internal *m_state* variable, and then sends the *IMFMediaSession::Close()* call to the session. After that, the thread blocks, waiting for the Win32 *m_closeCompleteEvent* event to be signaled. As you saw earlier, that event is signaled from a separate thread, from the *CPlayer::ProcessMediaEvents()* method. Finally, when the close complete event has been signaled, the function sends the *Shutdown()* call to the session, releases the session by setting the *m_pSession* variable to *NULL*, and sets the *m_state* variable to indicate that the player is closed.

One possible source of confusion with the preceding description might lie in the difference between Win32 and MF events. Although both systems use the same term, the two event systems function quite differently.

You can think of MF events as conceptually "active" objects. When an MF object "fires" an event, it actively calls an event consumer and passes control over to its *IMFAsyncEvent::Invoke()* function.

Core Windows events, however, are more "passive" entities. Win32 events are actually Windows synchronization primitives used to synchronize multiple threads. Conceptually the events are similar to locks or critical sections—they are usually used to block thread execution until either the event has been signaled or some timeout expires.

Therefore, you can think of Windows events as flags rather than as execution calls. When using events, one thread sets the event "flag," while another thread waits for that flag. Unlike with MF, the execution thread that will act on the event is in a suspended wait state, passively waiting for the event to be set. After the execution thread detects that the event was set, it resumes execution, relying on the operating system to tell it when the event is signaled.

To wrap up this exploration of the player's asynchronous behavior, here's a sequence diagram that shows what happens when you schedule multiple topologies for playback with a session.

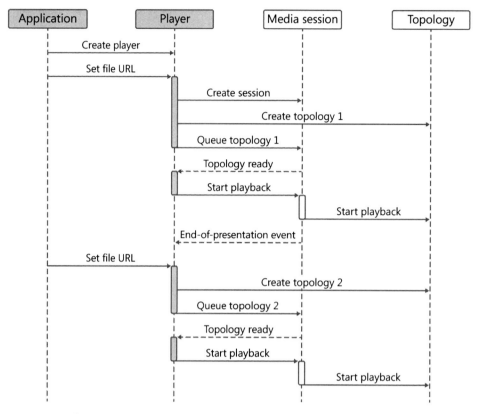

Here are the steps that the diagram demonstrates:

1. The application instantiates the player.

2. The application sets the file URL on the player object.

    a. The player creates the media session.

    b. The player creates topology 1.

    c. The player queues topology 1 with the session.

3. When the topology is ready, the session fires the topology-ready event.

4. When the player receives the topology-ready event, it tells the session to start playback.

5. The application sets a new file URL.

    a. The player creates topology 2.

    b. The player queues topology 2 with the session.

6. After topology 1 is finished playing, the media session fires the end-of-presentation event.

7. The media session gets the next topology and prepares it for playback. When topology 2 is ready, the session fires the topology-ready event again.

8. The topology-ready event tells the player to start playback.

The actual playback command to the session is triggered by the topology-ready event. To be more specific, the session calls the *CPlayer::Invoke()* function to notify the player that the topology is ready. The *Invoke()* function gets the event from the session by calling its *IMFMediaEventGenerator::End-GetEvent()* implementation. The *Invoke()* function then passes the event to the *ProcessMediaEvent()* method, which in turn starts playback. Playback is started by calling the *CPlayer::OnTopologyReady()* method.

```
//
// Handler for MESessionTopologyReady event - starts video playback.
//
HRESULT CPlayer::OnTopologyReady(void)
{
    HRESULT hr = S_OK;

    do
    {
        // release any previous instance of the m_pVideoDisplay interface
        m_pVideoDisplay.Release();

        // Ask the session for the IMFVideoDisplayControl interface. This interface is
        // implemented by the EVR (Enhanced Video Renderer) and is exposed by the media
        // session as a service. The session will query the topology for the right
        // component and return this EVR interface. The interface will be used to tell the
        // video to repaint whenever the hosting window receives a WM_PAINT window message.
        hr = MFGetService(m_pSession, MR_VIDEO_RENDER_SERVICE, IID_IMFVideoDisplayControl,
                (void**)&m_pVideoDisplay);
        BREAK_ON_FAIL(hr);

        // since the topology is ready, start playback
        hr = Play();
    }
    while(false);

    return hr;
}
```

The *OnTopologyReady()* method has two major operations inside of it:

1. When a topology is ready, the method queries the session for the *IMFVideoDisplayControl*, which is extracted from the video renderer. This interface can be used to force repainting of the video surface and control aspect ratio, video size, and more.

2. After the session fires the event indicating that the topology is ready, the method immediately starts video playback by calling the *StartPlayback()* function. *StartPlayback()* is called from within the *CPlayer::Play()* method.

The *MFGetService()* function is a generic helper subroutine used to query various components for other objects associated with them. Although in this case it's used to extract the Enhanced Video Renderer's (EVR's) *IMFVideoDisplayControl* interface, you can also pass in other flags to extract the MF source, the audio renderer, mixer components, byte streams, proxies for remote objects, and so on.

After obtaining the EVR pointer for the video-renderer control, you can start playing the video by calling the *CPlayer::StartPlayback()* method.

```
//
// Start playback from the current position.
//
HRESULT CPlayer::StartPlayback(void)
{
    HRESULT hr = S_OK;
    PROPVARIANT varStart;

    do
    {
        BREAK_ON_NULL(m_pSession, E_UNEXPECTED);

        PropVariantInit(&varStart);
        varStart.vt = VT_EMPTY;

        // If Start fails later, we will get an MESessionStarted event with an error code,
        // and will update our state.  Passing in GUID_NULL and VT_EMPTY indicates that
        // playback should start from the current position.
        hr = m_pSession->Start(&GUID_NULL, &varStart);
        if (SUCCEEDED(hr))
        {
            m_state = Started;
        }

        PropVariantClear(&varStart);
    }
    while(false);

    return hr;
}
```

To start playback, you need to use the *IMFMediaSession::Start()* method, passing in several parameters. The parameters indicate where the video should start playing—at the beginning of the piece of content or at some later point. You indicate the point at which playback should start with a *PROPVARIANT* structure, which is essentially a generic data type that can contain any value. The start position parameter can indicate that the content should start playing from an absolute position, from the current position, or even from a relative position within a playlist.

To indicate how to interpret the starting position parameter, the *IMFMediaSession::Start()* function receives a GUID as its first parameter. The GUID indicates how the method should interpret the second parameter.

Here are the possible values for the time format GUID:

- **GUID_NULL**   Indicates that the second parameter will be a *PROPVARIANT* structure set either to *VT_EMPTY*, meaning that the video should start from the current position, or to *VT_I8* (an 8-byte signed integer), meaning that the video should start this many 100-nanosecond "ticks" from the beginning of the clip. You can use this format to implement seek behavior. For example, passing in *GUID_NULL* and *VT_EMPTY* will resume playback from the position at which the video was paused. Passing in *GUID_NULL* with *VT_I8* set to 300,000,000 will start playback at 30 seconds from the beginning of the video.

- **MF_TIME_FORMAT_SEGMENT_OFFSET**   A custom format supported by the sequencer source.

> **Note** To discover the current playback position within the video, you can call the *IMFMediaSession::GetClock()* method to extract the presentation clock object for this presentation. You can then use that clock object to extract the current playback position. You will learn more about clock objects in Chapter 8.

In this case, the *Start()* method receives *GUID_NULL* as the time format, and *VT_EMPTY* as the start position, meaning that playback should start at the current position.

Building the Media Pipeline

The previous section glossed over the topology-building steps. The *CPlayer* class delegates all the work required to build the media pipeline to the . This section examines how the *CTopoBuilder* object assembles the various MF components into a structure that can be used to play content, as well as how the player uses the partial topology to build the media pipeline used to play the file.

The purpose of the *CTopoBuilder* class is to separate topology-building complexity from the main player class. This helper class takes the URL of a piece of content (usually a string containing the path to a file), creates an MF source that can load that content, and then builds a topology from it. The *CTopoBuilder* generates not a full topology but a partial one, adding only source and sink nodes and connecting them together. These source and sink nodes are the hints that the media session needs to find the rest of the components needed to play the content. Right before playing the topology, the session finds the right combination of MF transforms that can convert the source media streams into a format that the renderer sinks can process. The procedure of filling in the blanks in partial topologies is known as "resolving" or "rendering" a topology.

The following diagram shows the topology built by the *CTopoBuilder* and MF session when preparing for playback.

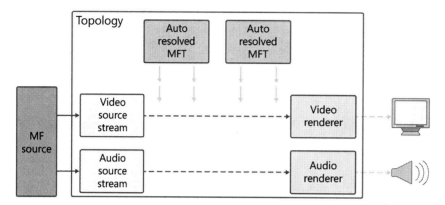

The *CTopoBuilder* class is responsible for instantiating the source nodes and the renderer nodes and connecting them to each other (in the diagram, these connections are represented by the darker dashed arrows). Later, the session will examine the data stored in the topology nodes and automatically discover ("resolve") the additional nodes needed by the topology. That process is represented by the two Auto Resolved Node boxes being directed by the series of arrows beneath the boxes.

Here are the required steps to create a media pipeline:

1. The *CTopoBuilder* class creates the MF source component. The *CTopoBuilder* needs the source to discover the type and number of streams present in the file.

2. The *CTopoBuilder* object generates a partial topology by repeating the following steps for each media stream in the file:

    a. Create a source node.

    b. Create a sink node.

    c. Connect source and sink nodes to each other.

3. Finally, after the partial topology is generated, it is given to a component that resolves the topology, finds all the missing (but implied) components, and instantiates all the objects. In this player, the media session does this job.

You'll examine these steps in more detail in the following sections.

Creating the Media Foundation Source

At the very beginning, the only thing a player application has is a file name. To be able to play that file, the application needs a component that can load the file, unwrap the data from the file container, and expose the data to the MF system. This job is done by the MF source.

To create a media source object capable of understanding the container and data format of the specified file, Media Foundation uses a built-in component called the *source resolver*. The source resolver takes the file path or stream URL and attempts to create the right media source component for that file type. Here's the *CTopoBuilder* function that calls the source resolver and asks it to create a media source for a specified file.

```
//
// Create a media source for the specified URL string.  The URL can be a path to a stream,
// or it can be a path to a local file.
//
HRESULT CTopoBuilder::CreateMediaSource(PCWSTR sURL)
{
    HRESULT hr = S_OK;
    MF_OBJECT_TYPE objectType = MF_OBJECT_INVALID;
    CComPtr<IMFSourceResolver> pSourceResolver;
    CComPtr<IUnknown> pSource;

    do
    {
        // Create the source resolver.
        hr = MFCreateSourceResolver(&pSourceResolver);
        BREAK_ON_FAIL(hr);

        // Use the synchronous source resolver to create the media source.
        hr = pSourceResolver->CreateObjectFromURL(
            sURL,                       // URL of the source.
            MF_RESOLUTION_MEDIASOURCE |
                MF_RESOLUTION_CONTENT_DOES_NOT_HAVE_TO_MATCH_EXTENSION_OR_MIME_TYPE,
                                        // indicate that we want a source object, and
                                        // pass in optional source search parameters
            NULL,                       // Optional property store for extra parameters
            &objectType,                // Receives the created object type.
            &pSource                    // Receives a pointer to the media source.
            );
        BREAK_ON_FAIL(hr);

        // Get the IMFMediaSource interface from the media source.
        m_pSource = pSource;
        BREAK_ON_NULL(m_pSource, E_NOINTERFACE);
    }
    while(false);

    return hr;
}
```

After creating the source resolver (using the appropriately named *MFCreateSourceResolver()* function), you can ask the *IMFSourceResolver* object to create an MF source. Notice that the second parameter to the *IMFSourceResolver::CreateObjectFromURL()* function is a set of flags that indicate what sort of object to create and how to search for the matching source. These flags indicate the algorithm that the source resolver uses to pick the right source for the media type—a source that can understand and parse the file in question.

The following diagram shows the logic that the source resolver follows when provided with the (ridiculously named) *MF_RESOLUTION_CONTENT_DOES_NOT_HAVE_TO_MATCH_EXTENSION_OR_MIME_TYPE* flag to discover the right source for the file.

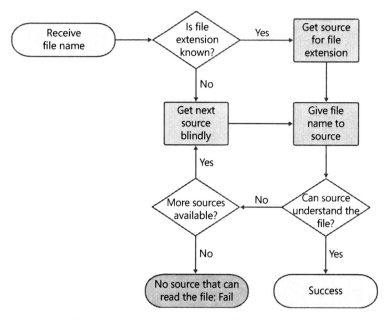

Initially, the source resolver attempts to discover the right source by looking at the file name and checking whether Windows has a source registered to handle such files. The mapping between file extensions and MF sources is stored in the Windows registry. If the resolver finds a source that claims to be able to handle files of this type, it passes the file name to the source. During construction, the source might load several megabytes of the file and double-check that the file contents are in a format that it can process. If the source returns success, the resolver is done. However, if the source fails to read the file (which can happen if a file has an incorrect extension—for example, if you rename a WMV file with an AVI extension), then the resolver tries all the sources on the machine. If none of the sources can play the file, the source resolver gives up and returns a failure.

More Info You will learn more about the source resolver and the process it uses to create media sources in Chapter 6.

Note that in this case, the code is using the synchronous *IMFSourceResolver::CreateObjectFromURL()* function. However, the source resolver also supports asynchronous methods for creating sources; for example, it also has the *BeginCreateObjectFromURL()* and *EndCreateObjectFromURL()* methods. Asynchronous object creation is useful when dealing with network streams and other data sources that can take a long time to access; asynchronous creation will not block the main application UI thread. If the operation takes too long—for example, if a network location is unreachable—the asynchronous object creation process can also be canceled.

You can use the source resolver to create not just media source objects but also *IMFByteStream* objects. Byte stream objects are responsible for actually opening the streams and passing the unparsed sequence of bytes to a source. The source then parses that stream of bytes, unwraps the actual data from the file container, separates individual elementary media streams, and presents those streams to the rest of the topology. If you use the *CreateObjectFromURL()* function to create a source directly, MF creates a matching byte stream object in the background automatically. The byte stream object will be of a type that can actually load the content. For example, if you specify a network URL (such as "http://www.contoso.com/file.wmv"), the source resolver will automatically create a network byte stream object. If you specify a file path, the source resolver will generate a byte stream that can load data from a file. Here is a conceptual diagram of how data flows through the topology and how it gets transformed by individual components.

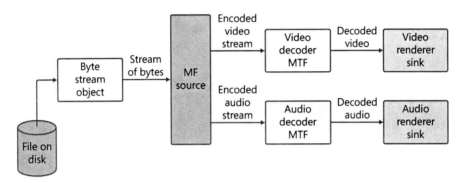

These are the individual data flow sections represented in that diagram:

1. The byte stream object loads a file from disk (or from the network, or some other location). The byte stream is responsible only for loading the bytes and giving them to the source. For example, if content is playing from a network stream, the byte stream object is responsible for accessing the network, negotiating with the server using network protocols, and presenting the source simply with byte arrays. The byte stream object does not parse the stream and has no idea what the stream contains.

2. The MF source receives a stream of bytes from the byte stream object. For example, if the source were processing a file, at this point it would receive byte arrays with file data just as it appears on disk. The byte arrays would contain a set of media streams wrapped in a media container, multiplexed (combined) together according to the file container scheme—AVI, ASF, MP4, or some other format.

3. The source unwraps the media streams from their media container, de-multiplexes them if necessary, and presents them to the topology.

4. The encoded elementary media streams go into the decoder MF transform components, which are in charge of decoding the encoded data and preparing the data for the sinks.

5. The sinks receive completely or partially decoded data and send it to their respective presentation devices.

More Info You'll see a detailed examination of MF media sources in Chapter 6.

As a result of all these operations, at the end of the *CTopoBuilder::CreateMediaSource()* method call you have a media source capable of parsing the file. At the same time, the source resolver loads the file byte stream object behind the scenes. Typically, the file byte stream and the source work seamlessly, so most of the time you won't need to care about what the byte stream object does.

Building the Partial Topology

After the *CTopoBuilder* object creates the source for the specified file, it can start building the actual topology. This entails analyzing the individual streams, creating appropriate topology source and sink nodes, and pairing the source nodes with their respective sinks. It's worth noting that the *CTopoBuilder* doesn't *create* the media source and sink objects. Instead, it generates topology nodes that serve as placeholders for those objects. After generating the nodes, the *CTopoBuilder* arranges them into a structure that can be used later to instantiate the real MF components and generate the actual media pipeline.

The topology-building steps are as follows:

1. Get the presentation descriptor from the source. The presentation descriptor lists the individual streams and their status.
2. Get a stream descriptor from the presentation descriptor.
3. Create the source node for the stream descriptor.
4. Create the sink node of the right media type for this stream.
5. Connect the source and sink nodes to each other.
6. If there are streams left to process, go back to step 2.

The following code shows the function responsible for steps 1 and 2 in the preceding list. This function creates a presentation descriptor for the stream loaded in the source, and then extracts the *stream descriptors*. Just as the name implies, stream descriptors describe the actual streams in the source. This is the main function that generates the topology.

```
//
// Create a playback topology from the media source by extracting presentation
// and stream descriptors from the source, and creating a sink for each of them.
//
HRESULT CTopoBuilder::CreateTopology(void)
{
    HRESULT hr = S_OK;

    CComPtr<IMFPresentationDescriptor> pPresDescriptor;
    DWORD nSourceStreams = 0;
```

```cpp
do
{
    // release the old topology if there was one
    m_pTopology.Release();

    // Create a new topology.
    hr = MFCreateTopology(&m_pTopology);
    BREAK_ON_FAIL(hr);

    // Create the presentation descriptor for the media source - a container object that
    // holds a list of the streams and allows selection of streams that will be used.
    hr = m_pSource->CreatePresentationDescriptor(&pPresDescriptor);
    BREAK_ON_FAIL(hr);

    // Get the number of streams in the media source
    hr = pPresDescriptor->GetStreamDescriptorCount(&nSourceStreams);
    BREAK_ON_FAIL(hr);

    // For each stream, create source and sink nodes and add them to the topology.
    for (DWORD x = 0; x < nSourceStreams; x++)
    {
        hr = AddBranchToPartialTopology(pPresDescriptor, x);

        // if we failed to build a branch for this stream type, then deselect it-
        // that will cause the stream to be disabled, and the source will not produce
        // any data for it
        if(FAILED(hr))
        {
            hr = pPresDescriptor->DeselectStream(x);
            BREAK_ON_FAIL(hr);
        }
    }
}
while(false);

return hr;
}
```

To build any topology, you first need to know what streams it will need to render—and to discover that information, you must query the source for an object known as a *presentation descriptor*, represented by the *IMFPresentationDescriptor* interface.

An MF presentation descriptor is a container object that describes what sort of streams are available for playback, and allows you to indicate which of those streams should be active and played back. For example, for a file containing two audio streams, you usually want to play only one of those streams. The presentation descriptor allows you to activate ("select") or to deactivate ("deselect") a stream using the *IMFPresentationDescriptor::SelectStream()* and *DeselectStream()* methods. If a stream is deselected, the source will not send any data to that stream. By default, all streams in a source are selected. Therefore, in cases with multiple audio streams, you must explicitly deselect the streams you do not want to play.

Note If a new stream appears somewhere in the middle of a file, the presentation descriptor will most likely not contain that information. This depends on the file format and on the design of the source itself. If the file format provides an easy way to enumerate all the streams in the file, and if the source is smart enough to discover that information, the presentation descriptor will contain the complete information. However, if this is a basic source that doesn't provide this information and an unexpected stream suddenly appears, you will need to create a brand-new presentation descriptor and regenerate the topology.

After discovering which streams are in the file, you can start building data paths for them. This entails first creating a source topology node for each stream, then creating a sink (renderer) node, and finally, connecting the two. The following conceptual diagram demonstrates a partial topology that will be generated by the *CTopoBuilder::CreateTopology()* function.

```
                    Partial topology
┌──────────────────────────────────────────────────────┐
│ Video branch                                         │
│   ┌────────┐                          ┌────────┐     │
│   │ Video  │                          │ Video  │     │
│   │ source │-------------------------→│renderer│     │
│   │ node   │                          │sink node│    │
│   └────────┘                          └────────┘     │
│ Audio branch                                         │
│   ┌────────┐                          ┌────────┐     │
│   │ Audio  │                          │ Audio  │     │
│   │ source │-------------------------→│renderer│     │
│   │ node   │                          │sink node│    │
│   └────────┘                          └────────┘     │
└──────────────────────────────────────────────────────┘
```

The topology can connect any source and sink nodes together—even if they don't expose matching media types. This is allowed because the connection is only a hint for the topology resolver. During the topology resolution step, the session tries various MF transforms until it finds a matching combination capable of consuming a media type exposed by the source node, and producing the media type expected by the sink node.

Here is the function that drives source-sink pair generation for our partial topology.

```
//
// Adds a topology branch for one stream.
//
// pPresDescriptor: The source's presentation descriptor.
// iStream: Index of the stream to render.
//
// For each stream, we must do the following steps:
//     1. Create a source node associated with the stream.
//     2. Create a sink node for the renderer.
//     3. Connect the two nodes.
// The media session will resolve the topology, inserting intermediate decoder and other
// transform MFTs that will process the data in preparation for consumption by the
// renderers.
//
```

```cpp
HRESULT CTopoBuilder::AddBranchToPartialTopology(
    IMFPresentationDescriptor* pPresDescriptor,
    DWORD iStream)
{
    HRESULT hr = S_OK;

    CComPtr<IMFStreamDescriptor> pStreamDescriptor;
    CComPtr<IMFTopologyNode> pSourceNode;
    CComPtr<IMFTopologyNode> pOutputNode;
    BOOL streamSelected = FALSE;

    do
    {
        BREAK_ON_NULL(m_pTopology, E_UNEXPECTED);

        // Get the stream descriptor for this stream (information about stream).
        hr = pPresDescriptor->GetStreamDescriptorByIndex(iStream, &streamSelected,
            &pStreamDescriptor);
        BREAK_ON_FAIL(hr);

        // Create the topology branch only if the stream is selected - in other words,
        // if the user wants to play it.
        if (streamSelected)
        {
            // Create a source node for this stream.
            hr = CreateSourceStreamNode(pPresDescriptor, pStreamDescriptor, pSourceNode);
            BREAK_ON_FAIL(hr);

            // Create the sink node for the renderer.
            hr = CreateOutputNode(pStreamDescriptor, m_videoHwnd, pOutputNode);
            BREAK_ON_FAIL(hr);

            // Add the source and sink nodes to the topology.
            hr = m_pTopology->AddNode(pSourceNode);
            BREAK_ON_FAIL(hr);

            hr = m_pTopology->AddNode(pOutputNode);
            BREAK_ON_FAIL(hr);

            // Connect the source node to the sink node. The resolver will find the
            // intermediate nodes needed to convert media types.
            hr = pSourceNode->ConnectOutput(0, pOutputNode, 0);
        }
    }
    while(false);

    return hr;
}
```

As you can see, the code is fairly straightforward. *CTopoBuilder::CreateTopology()* calls this function for each stream found in the presentation descriptor. If the passed-in stream is selected, the function generates a source and sink node pairing. The function adds a source node first, then creates the output sink node, adds both nodes to the topology, and finally, connects them to each other. This is all the information the media session requires to generate the actual MF data-processing components from the topology nodes, find any intermediate transforms that are missing, and render the stream.

Here's what you need to do to build a source node.

```cpp
//
// Create a source node for the specified stream
//
// pPresDescriptor: Presentation descriptor for the media source.
// pStreamDescriptor: Stream descriptor for the stream.
// pNode: Reference to a pointer to the new node - returns the new node.
//
HRESULT CTopoBuilder::CreateSourceStreamNode(
    IMFPresentationDescriptor* pPresDescriptor,
    IMFStreamDescriptor* pStreamDescriptor,
    CComPtr<IMFTopologyNode> &pNode)
{
    HRESULT hr = S_OK;

    do
    {
        BREAK_ON_NULL(pPresDescriptor, E_UNEXPECTED);
        BREAK_ON_NULL(pStreamDescriptor, E_UNEXPECTED);

        pNode = NULL;

        // Create the topology node, indicating that it must be a source node.
        hr = MFCreateTopologyNode(MF_TOPOLOGY_SOURCESTREAM_NODE, &pNode);
        BREAK_ON_FAIL(hr);

        // Associate the node with the source by passing in a pointer to the media source
        // and indicating that it is the source
        hr = pNode->SetUnknown(MF_TOPONODE_SOURCE, m_pSource);
        BREAK_ON_FAIL(hr);

        // Set the node presentation descriptor attribute of the node by passing
        // in a pointer to the presentation descriptor
        hr = pNode->SetUnknown(MF_TOPONODE_PRESENTATION_DESCRIPTOR, pPresDescriptor);
        BREAK_ON_FAIL(hr);

        // Set the node stream descriptor attribute by passing in a pointer to the stream
        // descriptor
        hr = pNode->SetUnknown(MF_TOPONODE_STREAM_DESCRIPTOR, pStreamDescriptor);
        BREAK_ON_FAIL(hr);
    }
    while(false);

    // if failed, clear the output parameter
    if(FAILED(hr))
        pNode = NULL;

    return hr;
}
```

As mentioned earlier, topology nodes are not the actual objects that perform the work in a media pipeline. Instead, the node objects hold a set of attributes that describe settings for the MF components that will process the data. These attributes are used during the topology rendering phase to instantiate and initialize the MF components. Therefore, the code in the *CTopoBuilder::CreateSourceStreamNode()* is again relatively simple. All this function does is instantiate the node for the source stream and set various attributes on it by using the nodes' *IMFAttributes* interface.

Creating the sink nodes is slightly more complex. You need to figure out what type of stream this is, create a controller object for the right type of renderer, and store that controller in the sink node. Here is the code for the function that creates sink nodes.

```
//
// This function creates an output node for a stream (sink).
//
HRESULT CTopoBuilder::CreateOutputNode(
    IMFStreamDescriptor* pStreamDescriptor,
    HWND hwndVideo,
    CComPtr<IMFTopologyNode> &pNode)
{
    HRESULT hr = S_OK;
    CComPtr<IMFMediaTypeHandler> pHandler;
    CComPtr<IMFActivate> pRendererActivate;

    GUID majorType = GUID_NULL;

    do
    {
        BREAK_ON_NULL(pStreamDescriptor, E_UNEXPECTED);

        // Get the media type handler for the stream, which will be used to process
        // the media types of the stream. The handler stores the media type.
        hr = pStreamDescriptor->GetMediaTypeHandler(&pHandler);
        BREAK_ON_FAIL(hr);

        // Get the major media type (e.g. video or audio)
        hr = pHandler->GetMajorType(&majorType);
        BREAK_ON_FAIL(hr);

        // Create an IMFActivate controller object for the renderer, based on the media type
        // The activation objects are used by the session in order to create the renderers
        // only when they are needed - i.e., only right before starting playback. The
        // activation objects are also used to shut down the renderers.
        if (majorType == MFMediaType_Audio)
        {
            // if the stream major type is audio, create the audio renderer.
            hr = MFCreateAudioRendererActivate(&pRendererActivate);
        }
        else if (majorType == MFMediaType_Video)
        {
            // if the stream major type is video, create the video renderer, passing in the
            // video window handle - that's where the video will be playing.
            hr = MFCreateVideoRendererActivate(hwndVideo, &pRendererActivate);
        }
        else
```

```
            {
                // fail if the stream type is not video or audio. For example, fail
                // if we encounter a CC stream.
                hr = E_FAIL;
            }

            BREAK_ON_FAIL(hr);

            pNode = NULL;

            // Create the node that will represent the renderer
            hr = MFCreateTopologyNode(MF_TOPOLOGY_OUTPUT_NODE, &pNode);
            BREAK_ON_FAIL(hr);

            // Store the IActivate object in the sink node - it will be extracted later by the
            // media session during the topology render phase.
            hr = pNode->SetObject(pRendererActivate);
            BREAK_ON_FAIL(hr);
        }
        while(false);

        // if failed, clear the output parameter
        if(FAILED(hr))
            pNode = NULL;

        return hr;
    }
```

Here's a breakdown of the steps this function takes, and an analysis of its responsibilities:

1. Get the *IMFMediaTypeHandler* object for the stream. The media type handler stores all of the stream media types and has functions for comparing and matching media types.

2. Extract the major media type for the stream. The major type indicates whether the stream contains video data, audio data, or some other information.

    a. If the major type is audio, create an activator object for an audio renderer using the *MFCreateAudioRendererActivate()* function.

    b. If the major type is video, create an activator for the video renderer using the *MFCreateVideoRendererActivate()* function. Note that this function receives the handle to the target video window.

    c. If the stream contains any other type of data, exit the function and return the generic *E_FAIL* error code. The failure will cause this stream to be de-selected in the *CTopoBuilder::CreateTopology()* function, and will allow the rest of the streams to play normally.

3. Create the topology node, passing in the *MF_TOPOLOGY_OUTPUT_NODE*, indicating that you want to create a sink node.

4. Store the activation object created in step 2 inside the output node.

In step 2, the function does not actually create the renderers themselves; to save resources, renders are not created until the moment they are needed. Instead, it creates an activator controller object for the renderer (an object that implements the *IMFActivate* interface). These activator objects are used later by the media session to instantiate the renderers, and to shut them down after playback is complete.

> **Important** If in another application you bypass the media session and call the *IMFActivate::ActivateObject()* function directly, do not forget to call *IMFActivate::ShutdownObject()* function after you are done with the renderer. Failure to do so will cause your application to leak resources. However, if you let the session handle the renderer activation, then it calls the shutdown when necessary, and you don't need to worry about this step.

After completing all of these operations, you are left with source and sink node pairs—or "branches." These branches encompass what is known as a partial topology—they do not contain all the final components needed to stream the data, but instead provide hints for the final topology resolver. As demonstrated here, the nodes themselves contain only the information required to instantiate various objects and build the full topology. After *CTopoBuilder* is done, you have only a partial topology. In the sample player application, the media session does the job of resolving the topology and adding the missing-but-implied components.

Resolving the Partial Topology

During the rendering phase of the topology-building operation—right before playback—the media session instantiates a topology loading object. The topology loading object (which implements the *IMFTopoLoader* interface) is a COM object that accepts a partial topology and resolves it, activating internal components and adding any missing components. Here are the steps involved in resolving a partial topology:

1. The session activates components that the nodes represent. In the simple topology shown here, the session needs to instantiate only the audio and video renderers, because the source is already active and available.

2. The media session searches for the MF transforms or combination of transforms needed to convert data from the media type produced by the source into the media type expected by the renderer. For the partial topology shown just previously, the session finds and adds video and audio decoder transforms.

The algorithm used by the default topology loader to "render" a partial topology is in many ways similar to the one used by the source resolver to find the right source. The session loads various MF transforms and keeps trying different ones until it either succeeds or runs out of possible transform combinations. The following flowchart demonstrates the algorithm used by the media session to resolve a partial topology and to find a combination of transforms between a source and a sink that will successfully convert the data.

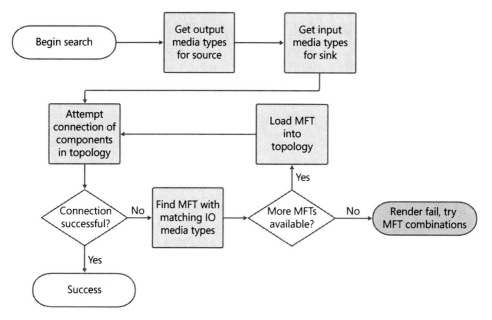

This algorithm is robust, and it's guaranteed to find a set of MFTs that will transform the data in the ways necessary to connect the source and sink nodes. The steps are as follows:

1. Begin processing.

2. Get the output media types exposed by the source.

3. Get the input media types expected by the sink.

4. Attempt to connect the components in the topology. Check to see if they can all agree on the media for input and output types. Even if all the components claimed that they can handle the media types at registration time, they may not all agree on a connection at this time.

5. If the connection succeeded, and all components agree on the media types, you are done.

6. If the connection failed, try to find an MFT registered with matching input and output media types.

7. If an MFT is found, add it to the topology between the source and sink, and go to step 4.

8. If an MFT is not found, then the first pass at building this branch of the topology has failed. Go back to step 3, but this time try combinations of several MFTs at once instead of just one.

This loop repeats until the session either finds a combination of MFTs that can all agree to connect or it runs out of untried MFT combinations. You'll see more about connections and media type negotiation in Chapter 5, "Media Foundation Transforms."

Note If you want to use a more intelligent or custom algorithm for topology building, you can tell the media session to use a custom topology loader object. To do this, you set a configuration parameter during the *MFCreateMediaSession()* function call and pass in the COM CLSID of your private topology loader, which must implement the *IMFTopoLoader* interface. This custom topology loader will receive partial topologies from the session and will be asked to resolve them into full topologies.

Note that the media session and the default topology loader use the same logic as the DirectShow graph builder. The DirectShow graph builder loads the file in a source filter, discovers how many streams it contains, and then attempts to use the filters registered on the machine to build a pipeline that can render those streams.

The main difference between the DirectShow and MF pipeline generation systems is that, by default, the DirectShow graph builder assumes that you want to display the content. As a result the DirectShow graph builder adds the renderers to the graph automatically. Media Foundation, on the other hand, requires you to tell it the final destination for each stream. This simplifies cases in which you want to create custom pipelines for advanced scenarios, such as transcoding and stream analysis, albeit at the cost of making the video playback scenario slightly more complex.

Conclusion

This chapter covered several core Media Foundation ideas that are required to build an MF player. You were introduced to the media session, examined some of its internal functionality, and looked at how you can use the media session to control playback of a topology. You saw the basic concepts of Media Foundation asynchronous event handling and analyzed how that affects the structure of the sample program.

In addition, you looked at partial topology-building concepts, examined the structure of a topology, and looked at the algorithms needed to render it.

Using these concepts, you can start building more advanced MF applications that can handle all sorts of content types and produce various effects.

Class Listings

For reference and to simplify your reading of this chapter, here are the class definitions of the core classes presented in this chapter.

The *CPlayer* class allows the main application to control the player. The *CPlayer* class wraps around the media session and hides all of the session asynchronous implementation details. Therefore, *CPlayer* implements the *IMFAsyncCallback* interface. This interface is used by the session to call the player whenever session events occur.

In addition, this listing presents the *PlayerState* enumeration used in the player to indicate its current state.

```
enum PlayerState
{
    PlayerState_Closed = 0,     // No session.
    PlayerState_Ready,          // Session was created, ready to open a file.
    PlayerState_OpenPending,    // Session is opening a file.
    PlayerState_Started,        // Session is playing a file.
    PlayerState_Paused,         // Session is paused.
    PlayerState_Stopped,        // Session is stopped (ready to play).
    PlayerState_Closing         // Application has closed the session, but is waiting for
                                // MESessionClosed.
};

//
// The CPlayer class wraps MediaSession functionality and hides it from a calling
// application.
//
class CPlayer : public IMFAsyncCallback
{
    public:
        CPlayer(HWND videoWindow, HRESULT* pHr);
        ~CPlayer();

        // Playback control
        HRESULT     OpenURL(PCWSTR sURL);
        HRESULT     Play();
        HRESULT     Pause();
        PlayerState GetState() const { return m_state; }

        // Video functionality
        HRESULT     Repaint();
        BOOL        HasVideo() const { return (m_pVideoDisplay != NULL); }

        //
        // IMFAsyncCallback implementation.
        //
        // Skip the optional GetParameters() function - it is used only in advanced players.
        // Returning the E_NOTIMPL error code causes the system to use default parameters.
        STDMETHODIMP GetParameters(DWORD *pdwFlags, DWORD *pdwQueue)   { return E_NOTIMPL; }

        // Main MF event handling function
        STDMETHODIMP Invoke(IMFAsyncResult* pAsyncResult);

        //
        // IUnknown methods
        //
        STDMETHODIMP QueryInterface(REFIID iid, void** ppv);
        STDMETHODIMP_(ULONG) AddRef();
        STDMETHODIMP_(ULONG) Release();

    protected:
```

```cpp
    // internal initialization
    HRESULT Initialize();

    // private session and playback controlling functions
    HRESULT CreateSession();
    HRESULT CloseSession();
    HRESULT StartPlayback();

    // MF event handling functionality
    HRESULT ProcessMediaEvent(CComPtr<IMFMediaEvent>& mediaEvent);

    // Media event handlers
    HRESULT OnTopologyReady(void);

    volatile long m_nRefCount;          // COM reference count.
    CComAutoCriticalSection m_critSec;       // critical section

    CTopoBuilder m_topoBuilder;

    CComPtr<IMFMediaSession> m_pSession;
    CComPtr<IMFVideoDisplayControl> m_pVideoDisplay;

    HWND m_hwndVideo;         // Video window.
    PlayerState m_state;              // Current state of the media session.

    HANDLE m_closeCompleteEvent;    // event fired when session close is complete
};
```

The *CTopoBuilder* class is used to construct the playback topology. This class hides the complexity of creating the source and adding the source and sink nodes to the topology.

```cpp
//
//  The CTopoBuilder class wraps constructs the playback topology.
//
class CTopoBuilder
{
    public:
        CTopoBuilder(void)  {};
        ~CTopoBuilder(void) { ShutdownSource(); };

        // create a topology for the URL that will be rendered in the specified window
        HRESULT RenderURL(PCWSTR sURL, HWND videoHwnd);

        // get the created topology
        IMFTopology* GetTopology(void) { return m_pTopology; }

        // shutdown the media source for the topology
        HRESULT ShutdownSource(void);

    private:
        CComQIPtr<IMFTopology> m_pTopology;                 // the topology itself
        CComQIPtr<IMFMediaSource> m_pSource;                // the MF source
        CComQIPtr<IMFVideoDisplayControl> m_pVideoDisplay;  // the EVR
        HWND m_videoHwnd;                                   // the target window
```

```cpp
    HRESULT CreateMediaSource(PCWSTR sURL);
    HRESULT CreateTopology(void);

    HRESULT AddBranchToPartialTopology(
        IMFPresentationDescriptor* pPresDescriptor,
        DWORD iStream);

    HRESULT CreateSourceStreamNode(
        IMFPresentationDescriptor* pPresDescr,
        IMFStreamDescriptor* pStreamDescr,
        CComPtr<IMFTopologyNode> &ppNode);

    HRESULT CreateOutputNode(
        IMFStreamDescriptor* pStreamDescr,
        HWND hwndVideo,
        CComPtr<IMFTopologyNode> &pNode);
};
```

CHAPTER 4

Transcoding

The Transcode API 62
Transcoding with the Source Reader. 78

One of the most powerful features offered by Microsoft Media Foundation (MF) is simple and high-performance transcoding. The term *transcoding* refers to transforming an existing video or audio stream from one format to another. This can be as simple as unwrapping the stream from one container (file) type and rewrapping it in another, or as complex as completely decoding the data and then re-encoding it using a different codec.

Previously, to change the encoding of a video stream, you had to jump through numerous hoops and deal with various stream synchronization problems that often arise during independent stream processing operations; now, MF provides greatly simplified APIs for transcoding and gives developers several powerful ways to build the necessary topology. You'll examine these methods in this chapter, which introduces several useful APIs along the way.

In addition to the new and simplified APIs, MF opens up hardware transcoding possibilities. MF supports the creation of hardware-backed transcoding transforms that offload their work to either the graphics processing unit (GPU) or to special CPU components.

Here's a conceptual diagram of a generic transcoding topology. The source component is responsible for loading the data, decoders decode the data into some common format, encoders re-encode the data into the target format, and the sink wraps the data into a container. The source and sink for transcoding are usually files.

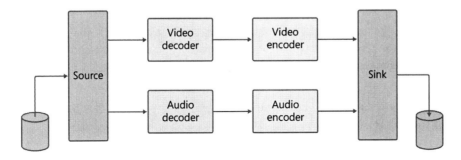

MF provides three ways of generating such topologies: you can construct a topology manually, you can use the transcoding API, or you can create a source reader combined with a sink writer. Each approach has some advantages and limitations, so be sure to select the right solution for your particular scenario.

- **Manual topology building**   This is the process of manually assembling of all the MF components into a topology. You saw this approach in Chapter 3, "Media Playback," while building a playback topology. Although this approach is the most flexible, because you can configure each component independently, it is also the most complex.

- **The transcode API**   This API is a set of functions introduced in Windows 7 intended to simplify the most common transcode scenario—transcoding from one file to another. The transcode API functions are designed to simplify the process of generating a transcode topology. Everything else is identical to the manual transcoding process.

- **Source reader and sink writer transcoding**   This approach provides intermediate flexibility between manual topology building and the transcode API. It allows you to configure the source and sink components, but automates the creation and configuration of the encoders and decoders.

The following sections demonstrate the transcode API and source reader approaches to transcoding. Manual topology transcoding is omitted, because you already learned about manual topology building in Chapter 3.

The TranscodeApp sample application provided with this book demonstrates transcoding methods. The application includes two separate implementations of the transcoding algorithm—one based on the transcode API, and the other on the source reader/sink writer. The ReaderWriterTranscoder.* files contain the source reader and sink writer transcoder, and the TranscodeApi*.* files contain the transcode API implementation. This chapter relies on this sample application to provide examples of the key mechanisms of the various transcoding approaches.

The Transcode API

The transcode API was introduced in Windows 7 to simplify the job of building a transcoding topology. This API automates the most common tasks—selection of the right combination of decoders and encoders needed to transcode a file.

Because the transcode API is designed for the most common tasks, it is unsuitable for use in many scenarios. For example, the transcode API cannot build topologies for variable-bit-rate (VBR) and multipass encoding, it can't handle files with multiple audio and/or video streams, and it has difficulty with custom Digital Rights Management (DRM) formats.

More Info See the transcode API documentation on MSDN for a full list of supported transcoding scenarios.

The transcode API does the same job that the *CTopoBuilder* class did in Chapter 3. It takes certain configuration parameters and builds the right topology to transform the provided content. Using the transcode parameters, you can specify target audio and video formats, as well as the file container type.

The process of running the topology is nearly identical to that presented for the player application in Chapter 3—you load the topology into a session, start playback, and wait for completion.

Therefore, the process for transcoding a file with the transcode API follows these steps:

1. Create an MF source for the file.

2. Create a transcode profile containing the transcoding parameters you want.

    a. Specify the video format you want.

    b. Specify the audio format you want.

    c. Specify the file container type you want.

3. Call the transcode API to build the topology.

4. Load the topology in a media session.

5. Play the media session and wait for completion.

The following function demonstrates how these steps are triggered in our sample application.

```
//
// Create a topology object for transcoding the specified input file and storing it in a
// file with the provided filename.
//
HRESULT CTranscodeApiTopoBuilder::CreateTranscodeTopology(PCWSTR pszInput, PCWSTR pszOutput)
{
    HRESULT hr = S_OK;

    do
    {
        // standard media source creation
        hr = CreateMediaSource(pszInput);
        BREAK_ON_FAIL(hr);

        // if the transcode profile has not been set yet, create a default transcode profile
        // for WMA v8 audio, WMV3 video, and ASF
        if(m_pTranscodeProfile == NULL)
        {
            hr = SetTranscodeProfile(
                MFAudioFormat_WMAudioV8,            // WMA v8 audio format
                MFVideoFormat_WMV3,                 // WMV9 video format
                MFTranscodeContainerType_ASF);      // ASF file container
            BREAK_ON_FAIL(hr);
        }
```

```
            // create the actual transcode topology based on the transcode profile
            hr = MFCreateTranscodeTopology(
                m_pSource,                    // the source of the content to transcode
                pszOutput,                    // output filename
                m_pTranscodeProfile,          // transcode profile to use
                &m_pTopology);                // resulting topology
            BREAK_ON_FAIL(hr);
    }
    while(false);

    return hr;
}
```

The first step is to create an MF source that will load the specified file. The procedure for creating a source for transcoding is identical to that of creating a source for playback. Playback source creation was shown in Chapter 3 and is therefore omitted here.

After you have created a source, the *CTranscodeApiTopoBuilder::CreateTranscodeTopology()* function generates a new transcode profile with default settings, if one has not been created already. Finally, after creating the transcode profile, you can use the *MFCreateTranscodeTopology()* function to generate a transcode topology.

The most complicated part of creating a topology with the transcode API is generating and configuring the transcode profile. The following sections demonstrate the key steps used in this process. Note that some of the functions are omitted, either because they are fairly simple, or because they are identical to the functions demonstrated in earlier chapters.

Creating a Transcode Profile

A transcode profile is essentially a property bag that holds all the transcode configuration values. Just as with many other objects in MF, you initialize the profile object by setting its various attributes. Specifically, you need to use the *IMFTranscodeProfile* methods *SetVideoAttributes()*, *SetAudioAttributes()*, and *SetContainerAttributes()* to configure the target video, audio, and container formats.

The following list shows the general steps required to configure a transcode profile:

1. Create an *IMFTrancodeProfile* object.

2. To transcode audio, specify the audio attributes of the transcode profile.

3. To transcode video data, initialize the video attributes of the transcode profile.

4. Finally, you must always specify the container (file) type, because the transcode API can transcode only to a file.

Here is a function that creates the transcode profile and initiates the other configuration steps:

```
//
// Create a transcode profile for the specified target video, audio, and container types
//
HRESULT CTranscodeApiTopoBuilder::SetTranscodeProfile(
    const GUID& audioFormat,        // target audio format
    const GUID& videoFormat,        // target video format
    const GUID& containerType)      // target file container type
{
    HRESULT hr = S_OK;

    do
    {
        // create a new transcode profile
        hr = MFCreateTranscodeProfile(&m_pTranscodeProfile);
        BREAK_ON_FAIL(hr);

        // set the audio attributes on the transcode profile
        hr = SetAudioAttributes(audioFormat);
        BREAK_ON_FAIL(hr);

        // set the video attributes on the transcode profile
        hr = SetVideoAttributes(videoFormat);
        BREAK_ON_FAIL(hr);

        // set the container attributes indicating what type of file to create
        hr = SetContainerAttributes(containerType);
        BREAK_ON_FAIL(hr);
    }
    while(false);

    return hr;
}
```

Most of the preceding function is self-explanatory—it creates a transcode profile object using the *MFCreateTranscodeProfile()* method. After that, it calls the internal functions that initialize the various attribute stores in the transcode profile. These internal functions are described in the following sections.

Configuring Target Audio Settings

The following code block demonstrates the internal workings of the *SetAudioAttributes()* function. As the name implies, this function sets the transcode profile's audio attributes.

```
//
// Initialize target audio attributes
//
HRESULT CTranscodeApiTopoBuilder::SetAudioAttributes(const GUID& audioFormat)
{
    HRESULT hr = S_OK;
    CComPtr<IMFCollection> pAudioTypeCollection;
    CComPtr<IMFAttributes> pAudioAttrs;
```

```
    do
    {
        // verify that the transcode profile is available
        BREAK_ON_NULL(m_pTranscodeProfile, E_UNEXPECTED);

        // Construct the flags that will be used during enumeration of all the encoder MFTs
        // on the machine.  The flags object will be passed into the MFTEnumEx() function
        // internally.
        DWORD dwFlags =
            (MFT_ENUM_FLAG_ALL & (~MFT_ENUM_FLAG_FIELDOFUSE))
            | MFT_ENUM_FLAG_SORTANDFILTER;


        // enumerate all of the audio encoders that match the specified parameters and
        // find all audio types that can be generated
        hr = MFTranscodeGetAudioOutputAvailableTypes(
            audioFormat,                    // specify the requested audio format
            dwFlags,                        // get all MFTs except for the FOU, and sort
            NULL,                           // no custom attributes
            &pAudioTypeCollection);         // store result in specified collection
        BREAK_ON_FAIL(hr);

        // get the first element from the collection of media types, copy all the
        // information of the first type into a new attribute collection, and return that
        //   attribute collection
        hr = GetTypeAttributesFromTypeCollection(pAudioTypeCollection, 0, pAudioAttrs);
        BREAK_ON_FAIL(hr);

        // set the audio attributes on the transcode profile
        hr = m_pTranscodeProfile->SetAudioAttributes(pAudioAttrs);
        BREAK_ON_FAIL(hr);
    }
    while(false);

    return hr;
}
```

This function sets the target audio format on the transcode profile. The audio portion of a transcode profile controls which audio encoder is loaded by the transcode API.

In this case, you are using the *MFTranscodeGetAudioOutputAvailableTypes()* function to find the available MF audio media types and get a list of the types matching the requested format. After that, you can pick the first audio type from the returned collection of available types and give it to the transcode profile.

Internally, the *MFTranscodeGetAudioOutputAvailableTypes()* function operates by calling the *MFTEnumEx()* function, enumerating all the encoder MFTs available on the machine, and extracting a list of all the output formats that the encoders support. In other words, the function receives search parameters and returns a list of types output by the matching encoders. The "Determining the Target Transcode Format" section later in this chapter describes a version of this function that produces video output formats.

This approach—searching through all available output types—may not work in all cases. Individual encoders may behave differently—and expose different types—depending on the initialization attributes passed in to their activators. For example, audio encoders default to producing constant-bitrate (CBR) audio. Therefore, media types returned by the *MFTranscodeGetAudioOutputAvailableTypes()* function may not work with VBR content.

For completeness, here is the listing for the *GetTypeAttributesFromTypeCollection()* function that extracts a single media type from the media type collection and returns the type attributes.

```
//
// Get information about a media type with the specified index from the type collection.
//
HRESULT CTranscodeApiTopoBuilder::GetTypeAttributesFromTypeCollection(
    CComPtr<IMFCollection>& pTypeCollection,        // collection of media types
    int typeIndex,                                   // index of the type to extract
    CComPtr<IMFAttributes>& pAttrCollection)        // return information on that type
{
    HRESULT hr = S_OK;
    CComQIPtr<IMFMediaType> pType;
    CComPtr<IUnknown> pUnknown;

    do
    {
        // Get the first IUnknown object from the collection
        hr = pTypeCollection->GetElement(typeIndex, &pUnknown);
        BREAK_ON_FAIL(hr);

        // implicitly Query pUnknown for the IMFMediaType interface during assignment of
        // the CComQIPtr object
        pType = pUnknown;
        BREAK_ON_NULL(pType, E_NOINTERFACE);

        // create a new attribute collection for the type extracted
        hr = MFCreateAttributes(&pAttrCollection, 0);
        BREAK_ON_FAIL(hr);

        // copy the information from the extracted type into the new attribute collection
        hr = pType->CopyAllItems(pAttrCollection);
        BREAK_ON_FAIL(hr);
    }
    while(false);

    return hr;
}
```

This function first extracts the element with the specified index from the provided collection of media types. It then casts that type into the *IMFMediaType* object by assigning it to the *CComQIPtr* smart pointer with the *IMFMediaType* template. Finally, it creates a new attribute collection for the media type information and copies all of the values from the media type into this new collection.

Configuring Target Video Settings

The following function demonstrates how to configure the video portion of the transcoding profile. Though this is not the simplest way of setting video attributes, it allows you to examine some of the inner workings of MF transcode API functions.

```
//
// Initialize target video attributes
//
HRESULT CTranscodeApiTopoBuilder::SetVideoAttributes(const GUID& videoFormat)
{
    HRESULT hr = S_OK;
    CComPtr<IMFCollection> pVideoTypeCollection;
    CComPtr<IMFAttributes> pVideoAttrs;

    DWORD dwFlags = 0;

    do
    {
        // verify that the transcode profile is available
        BREAK_ON_NULL(m_pTranscodeProfile, E_UNEXPECTED);

        // Construct the flags that will be used during enumeration of all the encoder MFTs
        // on the machine.  The flags object will be passed into the MFTEnumEx() function
        // internally.
        dwFlags =  (MFT_ENUM_FLAG_ALL & (~MFT_ENUM_FLAG_FIELDOFUSE))
                | MFT_ENUM_FLAG_SORTANDFILTER;

        // enumerate all of the video encoders that match the specified parameters and
        // find all video types that can be generated
        hr = GetVideoOutputAvailableTypes(
            videoFormat,                    // specify the requested video format
            dwFlags,                        // get all MFTs except for the FOU, and sort
            pVideoTypeCollection);          // return result in specified collection
        BREAK_ON_FAIL(hr);

        // get the first element from the collection, copy all the information into an
        // attribute collection, and return that attribute collection
        hr = GetTypeAttributesFromTypeCollection(pVideoTypeCollection, 0, pVideoAttrs);
        BREAK_ON_FAIL(hr);


        // set custom MF video information specific to what you want to do

        // Set the frame size as two numbers stored as a packed 64-bit value
        hr = MFSetAttributeSize(
            pVideoAttrs,            // target attribute collection
            MF_MT_FRAME_SIZE,       // attribute ID GUID
            720, 576);              // two 32-bit integers to be packed as a 64-bit value
        BREAK_ON_FAIL(hr);
```

```
        // Set the frame rate as a fraction of two numbers
        hr = MFSetAttributeRatio(
            pVideoAttrs,              // target attribute collection
            MF_MT_FRAME_RATE,         // attribute ID GUID
            30000, 1001);             // two 32-bit integers to be packed as a 64-bit value
        BREAK_ON_FAIL(hr);

        // set the target average bitrate of the video
        hr = pVideoAttrs->SetUINT32(MF_MT_AVG_BITRATE, 1000000);
        BREAK_ON_FAIL(hr);

        // store the video attributes in the transcode profile
        hr = m_pTranscodeProfile->SetVideoAttributes(pVideoAttrs);
        BREAK_ON_FAIL(hr);
    }
    while(false);

    return hr;
}
```

The steps to initialize video attributes are similar to those to initialize the transcode audio. You call the *GetVideoOutputAvailableTypes()* function to enumerate all the available output types, selecting one of those types. In this case, the function also updates the default type exposed by the encoder, which allows you to set the output video bitrate, frame size, and so on. The MF transcode API uses all these video parameters to find and initialize the video encoder used by the transcode process.

Note that to configure video, you would usually manually construct a media type by creating a new media type object, and storing various configuration attributes inside of it. This ensures that the media type does not have any conflicting and incompatible values or parameters. However, one of the purposes of the *GetVideoOutputAvailableTypes()* is to demonstrate some interesting MFT enumeration concepts. Therefore, you are using a video version of the *MFTranscodeGetAudioOutputAvailableTypes()* function mentioned earlier.

By enumerating the available MF encoders, you gain the ability to load any nonstandard video encoders that have been installed on the machine, including those by a third party. Microsoft-provided video profiles account for only the formats supported by the encoders that come with Windows.

The method presented here will not work with all encoders, because some of the values stored in the media type might be incompatible with the extra attributes added by the *SetVideoAttributes()* function. It works in this case because the *CTranscodeApiTopoBuilder* class is creating a video type based on the well-known WMV9 format, and the capabilities of the WMV codec are known in advance. However, if you were to create media types for other formats, the media type you select might have values that clash with other values already present in the media type, such as the frame rate, frame size, or bitrate specified here. For example, if the first media type found in the collection was for interlaced video or had a non-square pixel aspect ratio, the specified frame size would not match. In that case, the video encoder would not accept the proposed media type, and the transcode topology would fail to render, returning the *MF_E_INVALIDMEDIATYPE* error code.

Configuring the Target Container

The last step in defining a transcoding profile is to specify the target file format. The file format section of a transcode profile informs the transcode API which file sink to load into the transcode topology. MF is natively capable of generating several file formats—ASF, MP4 (MPEG4), MP3 (MPEG Layer 3), and 3GP (3GPP). The following code shows how to store the transcoded video in ASF files.

```
//
// Initialize target container attributes
//
HRESULT CTranscodeApiTopoBuilder::SetContainerAttributes(const GUID& containerType)
{
    HRESULT hr = S_OK;
    CComPtr<IMFAttributes> pContainerAttributes;

    do
    {
        // verify that the transcode profile is available
        BREAK_ON_NULL(m_pTranscodeProfile, E_UNEXPECTED);

        // create an attribute collection for one element
        hr = MFCreateAttributes(&pContainerAttributes, 1);
        BREAK_ON_FAIL(hr);

        // store an attribute that indicates that you want to write to a file with the
        // specified container type
        hr = pContainerAttributes->SetGUID(
            MF_TRANSCODE_CONTAINERTYPE,           // attribute ID GUID - container type
            containerType);                        // generate the specified container
        BREAK_ON_FAIL(hr);

        // store the container attributes in the transcode profile
        hr = m_pTranscodeProfile->SetContainerAttributes(pContainerAttributes);
        BREAK_ON_FAIL(hr);
    }
    while(false);

    return hr;
}
```

The *SetContainerAttributes()* function simply creates an attribute collection for the container values and stores the *MF_TRANSCODE_CONTAINERTYPE* attribute inside of it. The container type attribute contains a GUID that identifies the container type. After you have configured the transcode profile, you are ready to use the transcoding API to create a topology.

Determining the Target Transcode Format

Before building a transcode topology—by whatever means—the first thing you need to decide is what format you want to transcode the content into. For example, to transcode an A/V file or stream, you first need to decide what format the resulting audio and video should be.

There are several ways to make such decisions. One of the more common methods is to construct a media format by reading configuration settings from some sort of storage or file. This approach is especially useful when you want to transcode content with the intent of transferring the result to a compatible device such as a cell phone or a media player. For example, if the target phone has an 800 x 600 screen, then there is not much point in producing 1080p video. The target device may impose other physical limitations as well.

Another approach is to enumerate all the formats that the MF transforms on the PC can produce, and pick one from that list. Yet a third approach is to load an existing baseline format provided by MF and modify it as necessary. Media Foundation contains several target video formats that you can load and use for transcoding content. This chapter examines the first two approaches—constructing a predefined format, and creating and configuring a new format object.

The following function demonstrates a search through the available encoders on the machine for those that match a specified video subtype. The function then returns a list of compatible formats that can be selected by the caller.

This function operates in the same way as the MF-supplied *MFTranscodeGetAudioOutputAvailableTypes()* function—it first enumerates all the encoders that match some specified parameters, and then it extracts all possible output formats. Therefore, examining this function will help you understand the inner workings of the audio enumeration function.

```
HRESULT CTranscodeApiTopoBuilder::GetVideoOutputAvailableTypes(
    GUID videoSubtypeGuid,
    DWORD flags,
    CComPtr<IMFCollection>& pTypeCollection)
{
    HRESULT hr = S_OK;
    IMFActivate** pActivateArray = NULL;
    MFT_REGISTER_TYPE_INFO outputType;
    UINT32 nMftsFound = 0;

    do
    {
        // create the collection in which you will return the types found
        hr = MFCreateCollection(&pTypeCollection);
        BREAK_ON_FAIL(hr);

        // initialize the structure that describes the output streams that the encoders must
        // be able to produce.  In this case you want video encoders - so major type is
        // video, and you want the specified subtype
        outputType.guidMajorType = MFMediaType_Video;
        outputType.guidSubtype = videoSubtypeGuid;

        // get a collection of MFTs that fit the requested pattern - video encoders,
        // with the specified subtype, and using the specified search flags
        hr = MFTEnumEx(
            MFT_CATEGORY_VIDEO_ENCODER,     // type of object to find - video encoders
            flags,                          // search flags
            NULL,                           // match all input types for an encoder
            &outputType,                    // get encoders with specified output type
            &pActivateArray,
            &nMftsFound);
        BREAK_ON_FAIL(hr);
```

The first part of this function creates an MF collection object (basically an MF-supplied vector of *IUnknown* objects) and enumerates the available MFTs on the machine. The MFTs are enumerated by the appropriately named *MFTEnumEx()* function. This function goes through every MFT on the machine, and loads those that match some specified parameters. In addition, the *MFTEnumEx()* function also takes a series of flags that control the various types of MFTs returned, as well as their sorting order. For example, this function can be set to enumerate only DRM-capable MFTs that match specified input and output media types, prioritizing for components backed by hardware.

> **Background** Both NVIDIA and AMD ship encoder and decoder MFTs with their drivers. These encoders are exposed to the MF architecture so that applications can offload most of the computations to the video card. As a result, most video conversion work can be done by the GPU. This greatly speeds up the transcoding process, which in extreme cases can take many times longer than the duration of the video itself.

The preceding example requests all encoder MFTs on the machine that match the passed-in flags. The enumeration function call also does not specify any input types. Therefore, the transforms are not filtered by potential input type, and *MFTEnumEx()* returns all possible encoders with the specified flags and the provided output format. The result of the *MFTEnumEx()* function is an array of *IMFActivate* objects that you can use to initialize and instantiate the underlying MF encoders.

The next step of the *GetVideoOutputAvailableTypes()* function is to go through each of the *IMFActivate* objects, use them to instantiate a new MFT, and get all the supported output types from that MFT.

```
// now that you have an array of activation objects for matching MFTs, loop through
// each of those MFTs, extracting all possible and available formats from each of
// them
for(UINT32 x = 0; x < nMftsFound; x++)
{
    CComPtr<IMFTransform> pEncoder;
    UINT32 typeIndex = 0;

    // activate the encoder that corresponds to the activation object
    hr = pActivateArray[x]->ActivateObject(IID_IMFTransform,
        (void**)&pEncoder);

    // while you don't have a failure, get each available output type for the MFT
    // encoder you keep looping until there are no more available types. If there
    // are no more types for the encoder, IMFTransform::GetOutputAvailableTypes[]
    // will return MF_E_NO_MORE_TYPES
    while(SUCCEEDED(hr))
    {
        CComPtr<IMFMediaType> pType;

        // get the available type for the type index, and increment the typeIndex
        // counter
        hr = pEncoder->GetOutputAvailableType(0, typeIndex++, &pType);
        if(SUCCEEDED(hr))
```

```
                    {
                        // store the type in the IMFCollection
                        hr = pTypeCollection->AddElement(pType);
                    }
                }
            }
        }
        while(false);

        // possible valid errors that may be returned after the previous for loop is done
        if(hr == MF_E_NO_MORE_TYPES  ||  hr == MF_E_TRANSFORM_TYPE_NOT_SET)
            hr = S_OK;

        // if you successfully used MFTEnumEx() to allocate an array of the MFT activation
        // objects, then it is our responsibility to release each one and free up the memory
        // used by the array
        if(pActivateArray != NULL)
        {
            // release the individual activation objects
            for(UINT32 x = 0;  x < nMftsFound;  x++)
            {
                if(pActivateArray[x] != NULL)
                    pActivateArray[x]->Release();
            }

            // free the memory used by the array
            CoTaskMemFree(pActivateArray);
            pActivateArray = NULL;
        }

        return hr;
}
```

The rest of the function is fairly straightforward. You first enumerate the *IMFActivate* objects that you got from the *MFTEnumEx()* function and use them to activate (instantiate) the MFTs associated with those activators. Then you ask the MFTs for their available output types by calling the *IMFTransform::GetOutputAvailableType()* method and going through each of the types. These types are then stored in the *IMFCollection* object passed into the function.

Note that you are instantiating the encoders with default parameters. You are not passing in any configuration values, and you are relying on default settings internal to the encoders. As a result, the output media types they produce might be affected. For example, some encoders may expose additional media types depending on the input media type and the attributes passed to their activators. The default settings of each encoder are dependent on its implementation.

In addition, MFTs often rely on the input data type to create output types. For example, a decoder can provide an output media type with a 1280 x 768 frame size only after it receives a media type with that frame size on the input. Some encoder implementations do not expose all their output media types until they are actually instantiated and connected in a topology. This is why *GetVideoOutputAvailableTypes()* disregards the possible *MF_E_TRANSFORM_TYPE_NOT_SET* error—that error might be returned by a transform that is still waiting for somebody to set its input media type. That is a legitimate error that does not indicate a failure—other MFTs might provide useful media types.

Therefore, this error code is ignored and skipped. Similarly, *MF_E_NO_MORE_TYPES* is the error code returned by MFTs when they have returned all the media types they support, and it does not indicate a failure.

To be fair, this is a somewhat contrived example, because in this case you are getting very little information from this exercise. The example extracts the MF types, but each type contains very little information that you can't get through other means. Specifically, you could just as easily construct the target media type manually with a set of well-known attribute values. You'll see this alternative approach in "The Target Transcode Media Type" later in this chapter.

The Transcoding Session

After you have constructed a partial transcoding topology with the transcode API, you can pass the topology to an MF session and start the actual transcode process. The behavior of the transcode session is identical to that of a playback session. As a result, the code required to run it is also nearly identical to the session used in the player shown in Chapter 3 and is omitted here.

There is one difference from a basic player topology—a transcode topology is much more likely to fail during the topology resolution phase than a player is during playback. Remember that a topology is not the actual MF components that process the data. A topology instead consists of an incomplete set of activation objects that initialize and instantiate the actual source, MFTs, and sink. This partial topology constructed by the transcode API may fail to render for several reasons. For instance, during the topology resolution phase, MF may fail to find an MFT to transform the source content into the requested output format. Also remember that the *SetVideoAttributes()* function shown previously sets several attributes on the video media type. Topology resolution may therefore also fail if the output video media type set on the transcode profile is somehow inconsistent, and is not accepted by any encoders.

Just as with the player shown in Chapter 3, most of the communication between various components happens asynchronously, through the *IMFAsyncCallback* interface implemented by the *CTranscodeApi* class. Here is how the transcode API class implements the core *IMFAsyncCallback::Invoke()* method.

```
//
// IMFAsyncCallback::Invoke implementation.  This is the function called by the media
// session whenever anything of note happens or an asynchronous operation is complete.
//
HRESULT CTranscodeApi::Invoke(IMFAsyncResult* pAsyncResult)
{
    CComPtr<IMFMediaEvent> pEvent;
    HRESULT hr = S_OK;
    MediaEventType eventType;
```

```
    do
    {
        // Get the event from the event queue.
        hr = m_pSession->EndGetEvent(pAsyncResult, &pEvent);
        BREAK_ON_FAIL(hr);

        // Get the event type.
        hr = pEvent->GetType(&eventType);
        BREAK_ON_FAIL(hr);

        // parse the media event stored in the asynchronous result
        hr = ParseMediaEvent(pEvent);
        BREAK_ON_FAIL(hr);

        // If this is not the final event, tell the media session that this player is
        // the object that will handle the next event in the queue.
        if(eventType != MESessionClosed)
        {
            hr = m_pSession->BeginGetEvent(this, NULL);
            BREAK_ON_FAIL(hr);
        }
    }
    while(false);

    return S_OK;
}
```

The *CTranscodeApi::Invoke()* function is fundamentally very similar to the *IMFAsyncCallback::Invoke()* implementation shown in Chapter 3. The function gets the event from the passed-in *IMFAsyncResult* object, parses that event, and begins to get the next event if the session is not closing. And just like in the player code, the actual event parsing of the media event information is moved to a helper function.

Here is the helper *CTranscodeApi::ParseMediaEvent()* function that processes media events asynchronously passed to the *CTranscodeAPI* class.

```
//
// Parse a media event passed in asynchronously
//
HRESULT CTranscodeApi::ParseMediaEvent(IMFMediaEvent* pEvent)
{
    HRESULT hr = S_OK;

    MediaEventType eventType;
    HRESULT topologySetStatusHr = S_OK;

    do
    {
        BREAK_ON_NULL(pEvent, E_UNEXPECTED);
```

```
    // Get the event type.
    hr = pEvent->GetType(&eventType);
    BREAK_ON_FAIL(hr);


    if(eventType == MESessionEnded)
    {
        // if the session is ended, close it
        hr = m_pSession->Close();
        BREAK_ON_FAIL(hr);
    }
    else if (eventType == MESessionClosed)
    {
        // MESessionClosed event is guaranteed to be the last event fired by the session
        // Fire the m_closeCompleteEvent to let the player know that it can safely shut
        // down the session and release resources associated with the session.
        SetEvent(m_closeCompleteEvent);
    }
    else if(eventType == MESessionTopologySet)
    {
        // get the result of the topology set operation
        hr = pEvent->GetStatus(&topologySetStatusHr);
        BREAK_ON_FAIL(hr);

        // if topology resolution failed, then the returned HR will indicate that
        if(FAILED(topologySetStatusHr))
        {
            // store the failure for future reference
            m_sessionResult = topologySetStatusHr;

            // close the session
            m_pSession->Close();
        }
    }
  }
  while(false);

  return hr;
}
```

The *ParseMediaEvent()* method first gets the media event type from the *IMFMediaEvent* object, and then it processes the rest of the information based on the type of event. Here is what this method does based on the different media event types that it can receive:

- **MESessionEnded event type**   Indicates that the session has finished running. The session can now be closed and finalized. *ParseMediaEvent()* calls the *IMFMediaSession::Close()* method to begin the asynchronous finalization process.

- **MESessionClosed event type**   Indicates that the session finalization is complete. This causes the *ParseMediaEvent()* method to notify any waiting threads that the session is done, and any related resources can be released. This notification is actually received by the *CTranscodeApi:: WaitUntilCompletion()* method shown later in this section.

- ***MESessionTopologySet* event type**   This event is fired immediately after the session resolves a new topology. Therefore, when the session has queued multiple topologies, this event gets fired several times—once per topology. The event contains a *PROPVARIANT* object that holds the *IUnknown* pointer to the topology that was just resolved and set.

> **Background**   A *PROPVARIANT* object is a structure that can take just about any possible value supported by the language. This structure has a way internally to become a 32-bit integer, an *IUnknown* pointer, a character, an unsigned 64-bit integer, and so on. This structure is commonly used in COM code to pass variable data types around. Conceptually, *PROPVARIANT* is somewhat similar to the *void* pointer in C++, except that the structure also contains the information on what is stored inside of the memory blob being passed around.

To discover the status of the topology resolution—to determine whether all the components were added and connected successfully—you need to check the *HRESULT* stored in the *IMFMediaEvent* object by calling *IMFMediaEvent::GetStatus()*.

If the *ParseMediaEvent()* function detects that the topology was not properly resolved, it stops the session and signals a failure. To signal a failure, the function stores a failure *HRESULT* in a class member variable. The main thread then queries that member variable to detect the transcode session status.

Here's a function used by the sample application to wait for transcoding to complete. It then signals the result of the transcoding session.

```
//
// The WaitUntilCompletion() function blocks and doesn't return until the session is
// complete.  This function returns the HRESULT that indicates the session transcode
// status.
//
HRESULT CTranscodeApi::WaitUntilCompletion(void)
{
    // block waiting for the session closing completed event
    WaitForSingleObject(m_closeCompleteEvent, INFINITE);

    // shut down the session resource - the source and the session itself
    m_topoBuilder.ShutdownSource();
    m_pSession->Close();

    // return the result of the session
    return m_sessionResult;
}
```

The main application thread calls the *WaitUntilCompletion()* function after it has built the transcode topology and started the session. This function is necessary in the transcode application because this application is console based. As a result—unlike the player application from Chapter 3—this program does not wait for user input to exit. Instead, it exits as soon as its *main()* function completes—which happens when transcoding is complete. Note that if you interrupt the application and cause it to exit prematurely, the output file may become truncated and some of the content may not be transcoded.

Transcoding with the Source Reader

Many media applications do not need to be part of a media pipeline. For example, if you are writing a network streaming application—an application that loads a media file from the hard drive and streams it over the network in some form—you don't really care how it is decoded.

To simplify media stream processing, MF introduced the concept of a *source reader* object. A source reader allows an application to directly access media data without worrying about building a topology, creating a session, running a session, and so on. The source reader provides direct synchronous access to a media file, while requiring only minimal knowledge of MF from the user. You can use source readers for various media processing applications, including transcoding.

Besides the source reader, MF also has the ability to create *sink writer* objects. Sink writers are mirror images of source readers—they allow the application to write to a media file without worrying about which encoders to load or which sessions, topologies, or even programming models are involved.

To clearly understand the inner workings of a source reader and sink writer, consider the following transcoder application diagram.

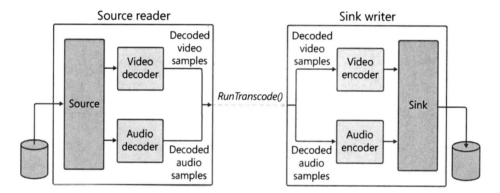

The diagram represents a conceptual data flow of the media data through a source reader–based transcoding application. The source reader is presented to the application as a "black box" that produces media samples (usually with audio or video data inside of them). The sink writer is another "black box" that accepts media samples and writes them to a target media sink. The application configures the source reader and sink writer, and then pulls samples from the reader and pushes them into the writer.

The operation of the reader is also fairly simple—to get a sample from the reader, you need to call the *IMFSourceReader::ReadSample()* function. This function causes the source reader to extract one sample from one of the media streams in the source file and return it in some requested format. The sink writer has an equivalent function that writes data synchronously using the sink writer. That function is *IMFSinkWriter::WriteSample()*.

Background The source reader and sink writer actually can function in asynchronous mode. This means that calls to their core functions return immediately, and the results arrive on a separate thread when they are ready. To set up the asynchronous mode, you need to create the *IMFSourceReaderCallback* and *IMFSinkWriterCallback* objects and pass them to the reader and writer. To set the callback objects, you need to set the *MF_SOURCE_READER_ASYNC_CALLBACK* and *MF_SINK_WRITER_ASYNC_CALLBACK* attributes on the reader and writer.

The asynchronous behavior can be useful in situations in which you have to deal with a user interface and are not certain how quickly a media sample can be read or written. For example, if you are reading from the network, you won't know exactly when a sample will arrive—but you may still need to update the UI. However, this sample application has no user interface, so you can safely use the synchronous *IMFSourceReader::ReadSample()* and *IMFSinkWriter::WriteSample()* methods.

As you can see in the preceding diagram, the source reader and sink writer components in the sample application are connected via the *RunTranscode()* function. This function pulls samples from the source reader and pushes them into the sink writer. As a result, in many ways it serves the same purpose as the media session in the preceding transcode API example.

The following sections examine several aspects of a transcoding application based on the source reader and sink writer. To transcode a file with these objects, you need to implement the following steps:

1. Create the source reader and sink writer objects.
2. Hook up the source reader and sink writer to each other.
   a. Decide which individual streams in the source file you want to transcode, and inform the source reader that you want to process data from those streams.
   b. Create corresponding streams in the sink writer.
   c. Negotiate compatible media types between corresponding source reader and sink writer streams.
3. Pull individual samples from the source reader and examine them.
4. Send individual samples into the sink writer, while handling various stream events and conditions.

Although looking at a second implementation of a transcode application may seem redundant, it allows you to gain a deeper understanding of the complexities involved when connecting components to an MF source. It will also help you better understand the processes that happen in *all* transcoding applications, including those built with the transcode API introduced earlier in this chapter.

In addition, the source reader/sink writer transcoding approach is far more flexible than the one the transcode API provides. Using the reader and writer, you can select individual streams and configure the MF source and sink objects that are inside the source reader and sink writer, which gives you more granular control over the transcoding process. With this transcode method, you can create an application capable of handling multiple audio and video streams in a file, deal with streams other than audio and video, transcode unusual media types, and even modify the data being transcoded. One example would be an application that injects a watermark into a video being transcoded.

In addition, the source reader and sink writer objects are useful for other tasks. You can easily use the reader in media-related applications that do not require playback. For instance, the source reader is a fully implemented frame grabber object. It can extract individual frames from a file for later analysis.

Creating a Source Reader and a Sink Writer

The procedure to create a source reader and a sink writer is quite straightforward, now that you have experience in creating standard sources. You can create these source and sink objects by using several standard MF functions.

```
//
// Main transcoding function that triggers the transcode process:
// 1. Create stream reader and sink writer objects.
// 2. Map the streams found in the source file to the sink.
// 3. Run the transcode operation.
//
HRESULT CReaderWriterTranscoder::Transcode(LPCWSTR source, LPCWSTR target)
{
    HRESULT hr = S_OK;
    CComPtr<IMFAttributes> pConfigAttrs;

    do
    {
        // you want to set only a single attribute - you want to make sure that both the
        // source reader and the sink writer load any hardware transforms that they can,
        // since that will greatly speed up the transcoding process. Therefore create
        // an attribute store and add the MF_READWRITE_ENABLE_HARDWARE_TRANSFORMS
        // property to it.

        // create an attribute store
        hr = MFCreateAttributes(&pConfigAttrs, 1);
        BREAK_ON_FAIL(hr);

        // set MF_READWRITE_ENABLE_HARDWARE_TRANSFORMS property in the store
        hr = pConfigAttrs->SetUINT32(MF_READWRITE_ENABLE_HARDWARE_TRANSFORMS, TRUE);
        BREAK_ON_FAIL(hr);

        // create a source reader
        hr = MFCreateSourceReaderFromURL(source, pConfigAttrs, &m_pSourceReader);
        BREAK_ON_FAIL(hr);
```

```cpp
        // create a sink writer
        hr = MFCreateSinkWriterFromURL(target, NULL, pConfigAttrs, &m_pSinkWriter);
        BREAK_ON_FAIL(hr);

        // map the streams found in the source file from the source reader to the
        // sink writer, while negotiating media types
        hr = MapStreams();
        BREAK_ON_FAIL(hr);

        // run the transcode loop
        hr = RunTranscode();
        BREAK_ON_FAIL(hr);
    }
    while(false);

    return hr;
}
```

The preceding function demonstrates how to create the source reader and sink writer. Most of the function calls in it are quite self explanatory. The *CReaderWriterTranscoder::Transcode()* function drives the transcoding process of the sample application. When you are creating the source and sink objects, you pass in an attribute store with configuration properties. These configuration properties give you some measure of control over the internal components loaded into the source reader and sink writer.

One interesting difference between this transcode implementation and the transcode API version is that here you cannot explicitly configure the file container. The *MFCreateSinkWriterFromURL()* function accepts the file name but does not give you the ability to select the file format. Instead, the function parses the target file name string and derives the requested container format from the file extension.

Internally, *MFCreateSinkWriterFromURL()* has a hard-coded mapping between various standard file extensions and container types. For example, the mapping indicates that if the file has an ASF, WMV, WMA, or WM extension, then the function must use the ASF container format. This means that if you use the *MFCreateSinkWriterFromURL()* function, you cannot provide file formats or container types other than those known by the function. You can only use the ASF, MP3, MPEG4, or 3GPP file containers and specify one of their standard extensions in the target URL parameter.

After initializing the source reader and sink writer objects, this function calls the functions that map individual streams from source to sink and do the actual job of pulling data from the reader and pushing it into the writer.

Mapping Sink Writer Streams

Now that you have created the source reader and sink writer objects, you need to specify the target media types that the sink uses when encoding content to the target file. You must determine which media streams you want to modify and which should remain unchanged from the source file.

In this case, the sample application modifies only the audio and video media types. The video streams are encoded in H.264 format and the audio in AAC format. All other stream types remain unchanged.

The following function triggers the mapping of all the source reader streams to their sink writer counterparts and the negotiation of media types used to convert the content between the two components.

```
//
// Map each source reader output stream to an input stream of the sink writer, deciding
// on the target format. Audio and video stream formats are modified to AAC and H.264
// respectively, but other target formats remain unchanged.
//
HRESULT CReaderWriterTranscoder::MapStreams(void)
{
    HRESULT hr = S_OK;
    BOOL isStreamSelected = FALSE;
    DWORD sourceStreamIndex = 0;
    DWORD sinkStreamIndex = 0;
    GUID streamMajorType;
    CComPtr<IMFMediaType> pStreamMediaType;

    do
    {
        m_nStreams = 0;

        while(SUCCEEDED(hr))
        {
            // check whether you have a stream with the right index - if you don't, the
            // IMFSourceReader::GetStreamSelection() function will fail, and you will drop
            // out of the while loop
            hr = m_pSourceReader->GetStreamSelection(sourceStreamIndex, &isStreamSelected);
            if(FAILED(hr))
            {
                hr = S_OK;
                break;
            }

            // count the total number of streams for later
            m_nStreams++;

            // get the source media type of the stream
            hr = m_pSourceReader->GetNativeMediaType(
                sourceStreamIndex,          // index of the stream you are interested in
                0,                          // index of the media type exposed by the
                                            //   stream decoder
                &pStreamMediaType);         // media type
            BREAK_ON_FAIL(hr);

            // extract the major type of the source stream from the media type
            hr = pStreamMediaType->GetMajorType(&streamMajorType);
            BREAK_ON_FAIL(hr);

            // select a stream, indicating that the source should send out its data instead
            // of dropping all of the samples
            hr = m_pSourceReader->SetStreamSelection(sourceStreamIndex, TRUE);
            BREAK_ON_FAIL(hr);
```

```cpp
        // if this is a video or audio stream, transcode it and negotiate the media type
        // between the source reader stream and the corresponding sink writer stream.
        // If this is a some other stream format (e.g. subtitles), just pass the media
        // type unchanged.
        if(streamMajorType == MFMediaType_Audio || streamMajorType == MFMediaType_Video)
        {
            // get the target media type - the media type into which you will transcode
            // the data of the current source stream
            hr = GetTranscodeMediaType(pStreamMediaType);
            BREAK_ON_FAIL(hr);

            // add the stream to the sink writer - i.e. tell the sink writer that a
            // stream with the specified index will have the target media type
            hr = m_pSinkWriter->AddStream(pStreamMediaType, &sinkStreamIndex);
            BREAK_ON_FAIL(hr);

            // hook up the source and sink streams - i.e. get them to agree on an
            // intermediate media type that will be used to pass data between source
            // and sink
            hr = ConnectStream(sourceStreamIndex, streamMajorType);
            BREAK_ON_FAIL(hr);
        }
        else
        {
            // add the stream to the sink writer with the exact same media type as the
            // source stream
            hr = m_pSinkWriter->AddStream(pStreamMediaType, &sinkStreamIndex);
            BREAK_ON_FAIL(hr);
        }

        // make sure that the source stream index is equal to the sink stream index
        if(sourceStreamIndex != sinkStreamIndex)
        {
            hr = E_UNEXPECTED;
            break;
        }

        // increment the source stream index, so that on the next loop you are analyzing
        // the next stream
        sourceStreamIndex++;

        // release the media type
        pStreamMediaType = NULL;
    }

    BREAK_ON_FAIL(hr);

    }
    while(false);

    return hr;
}
```

The *CReaderWriterTranscoder::MapStreams()* function goes through each stream in the source file and examines the media type of that stream. If the media type is audio or video, it passes the media type to the *GetTranscodeMediaType()* function for modification. After determining the target media type of each source stream, the function creates a corresponding stream on the sink writer by calling *IMFSinkWriter::AddStream()*, passing in the requested type.

If the target stream media type differs from the source stream type, then the sink writer needs to transcode the data into a new format. This means that the data of that stream must first be decoded by the source reader and then re-encoded by the sink writer. To connect the decoder and encoder, the application needs to negotiate an intermediate format used between the two MF components. This will cause the source reader to create a decoder, which will decode a stream into a format that the sink writer can understand and re-encode into the target format.

The negotiation of the intermediate format needed to transcode the content is done by the *CReaderWriterTranscoder::ConnectStream()* function. Therefore, the *MapStreams()* function calls *ConnectStream()* for every audio and video stream—in other words, for every stream that is modified and transcoded.

Intermediate Format Negotiation

After creating the source reader and hooking it up to the source file, you need to enumerate all of its streams. For each stream, you must determine whether you want to copy its data to the new file without any changes or whether it should be transcoded. Finally, if you want to transcode a stream, you need to make sure that the data can be converted from the format produced by the source reader into the format supported by the sink writer.

One way to easily convert a stream from one format into another is to decode it completely into its most basic format and then re-encode it from scratch into a new format. For example, you can decode a video into uncompressed frames and then re-encode it into a new format. Though this approach is not the most efficient, it is the simplest for a transcode scenario.

The function shown here demonstrates how you can negotiate the uncompressed data formats that are acceptable both to the decoder and to the encoder.

```
// All video decoders and encoders support at least one of these video formats - basically
// decoded frames (in some cases variants of bitmaps)
static GUID intermediateVideoFormats[] =
{
    MFVideoFormat_NV12,
    MFVideoFormat_YV12,
    MFVideoFormat_YUY2,
    MFVideoFormat_RGB32
};
int nIntermediateVideoFormats = 4;
```

```cpp
// audio stream formats that every audio decoder and encoder should
// be able to agree on - uncompressed audio data
static GUID intermediateAudioFormats[] =
{
    MFAudioFormat_Float,
    MFAudioFormat_PCM,
};
int nIntermediateAudioFormats = 2;
```

Here you can see a list of acceptable formats for uncompressed audio and video streams. The array of video GUIDs indicates four of the more common encodings for uncompressed video. All decoders and encoders will be able to agree on at least one of these uncompressed formats. The array of audio GUIDs contains the two standard formats for uncompressed audio.

The function that does the actual negotiation between individual source reader and sink writer streams is given here.

```cpp
//
// Attempt to find an uncompressed media type for the specified stream that both the source
// and sink can agree on
//
HRESULT CReaderWriterTranscoder::ConnectStream(DWORD dwStreamIndex,
    const GUID& streamMajorType)
{
    HRESULT hr = S_OK;

    CComPtr<IMFMediaType> pPartialMediaType;
    CComPtr<IMFMediaType> pFullMediaType;

    BOOL fConfigured = FALSE;
    GUID* intermediateFormats = NULL;
    int nFormats = 0;

    do
    {
        // create a media type container object that will be used to match stream input
        // and output media types
        hr = MFCreateMediaType( &pPartialMediaType );
        BREAK_ON_FAIL(hr);

        // set the major type of the partial match media type container
        hr = pPartialMediaType->SetGUID( MF_MT_MAJOR_TYPE, streamMajorType );
        BREAK_ON_FAIL(hr);

        // Get the appropriate list of intermediate formats - formats that every decoder and
        // encoder of that type should agree on. Essentially these are the uncompressed
        // formats that correspond to decoded frames for video, and uncompressed audio
        // formats
        if(streamMajorType == MFMediaType_Video)
        {
            intermediateFormats = intermediateVideoFormats;
            nFormats = nIntermediateVideoFormats;
        }
```

```cpp
        else if(streamMajorType == MFMediaType_Audio)
        {
            intermediateFormats = intermediateAudioFormats;
            nFormats = nIntermediateAudioFormats;
        }
        else
        {
            hr = E_UNEXPECTED;
            break;
        }


        // loop through every intermediate format that you have for this major type, and
        // try to find one on which both the source stream and sink stream can agree on
        for( int x = 0; x < nFormats; x++ )
        {
            // set the format of the partial media type
            hr = pPartialMediaType->SetGUID( MF_MT_SUBTYPE, intermediateFormats[x] );
            BREAK_ON_FAIL(hr);

            // set the partial media type on the source stream
            hr = m_pSourceReader->SetCurrentMediaType(
                dwStreamIndex,                  // stream index
                NULL,                           // reserved - always NULL
                pPartialMediaType );            // media type to try to set

            // if the source stream (i.e. the decoder) is not happy with this media type -
            // if it cannot decode the data into this media type, restart the loop in order
            // to try the next format on the list
            if( FAILED(hr) )
            {
                hr = S_OK;
                continue;
            }

            // if you got here, the source stream is happy with the partial media type set
            // - extract the full media type for this stream (with all internal fields
            // filled in)
            hr = m_pSourceReader->GetCurrentMediaType( dwStreamIndex, &pFullMediaType );

            // Now try to match the full media type to the corresponding sink stream
            hr = m_pSinkWriter->SetInputMediaType(
                dwStreamIndex,              // stream index
                pFullMediaType,             // media type to match
                NULL );                     // configuration attributes for the encoder

            // if the sink stream cannot accept this media type - i.e. if no encoder was
            // found that would accept this media type - restart the loop and try the next
            // format on the list
            if( FAILED(hr) )
            {
                hr = S_OK;
                continue;
            }
```

```
            // you found a media type that both the source and sink could agree on - no need
            // to try any other formats
            fConfigured = TRUE;
            break;
        }
        BREAK_ON_FAIL(hr);

        // if you didn't match any formats return an error code
        if( !fConfigured )
        {
            hr = MF_E_INVALIDMEDIATYPE;
            break;
        }

    }
    while(false);

    return hr;
}
```

First, the function determines which elementary stream type it is being called for and stores a pointer to the uncompressed format array in a holding object (shown just previously). Then it goes through every format and checks whether both source reader and sink writer agree to respectively produce and consume data in this format. If either the source reader output stream or sink writer input stream cannot work with the proposed media type, the loop continues and tries the next format on the list.

Background As mentioned earlier, decompressing the content completely and then re-encoding it is one way to transcode between two different data encodings. This method is extremely flexible, but it is not the fastest option. Substantial information is lost and then must be regenerated when data is re-encoded. For example, when you are converting between VC1 video and H.264, much of the information can be reused, because the two compression formats are closely related. But when MF decodes content into an uncompressed form, it loses things such as video motion vectors, which must then be regenerated by the encoder.

On the other hand, a smart converter can reuse the motion vectors and quantizers of the source encoding to calculate new values for the transcoded content. As a result, the system needs far less processing power and can transcode content much faster. Unfortunately, these types of MFTs are extremely rare, because they require in-depth understanding of both source and target formats, as well as foreknowledge of the scenario being addressed. These sorts of transcoders are most commonly used to reduce the bitrate of existing content without changing the format of the data.

The negotiation procedure shown here is similar to the one that happens during the connection of any two components in an MF pipeline. An upstream component is capable of producing data in a several formats. The downstream component has a list of formats that it can consume. If the two components can agree on one of the formats, or if an intermediate component exists that can convert data between the two, the topology renders properly. When they can't agree, a mismatch occurs and you get a topology rendering failure.

Note that when setting the input media type on a sink writer stream, you can specify additional attributes that configure the encoder for that stream. These configuration properties provide much more granular control of the transcoding process than the transcode API. The exact encoder parameters you would use depend on the encoder loaded into the sink writer and on what parameters that particular object supports.

The Target Transcode Media Type

To initialize the sink writer input streams, you need to decide on and specify the individual stream formats. Obviously, the formats depend on the corresponding streams coming out of the stream reader: If the stream reader produces a video stream, the sample application tries to convert it into H.264 format; if the output stream is audio, the sample converts it into AAC audio. In all other cases—closed captioning, embedded data, and so forth—the sample retains the format of the output stream, passing it through unchanged.

The function shown in this section selects the media for the stream writer streams. This function demonstrates an alternative to the approach shown in the transcode API section of the application. Rather than searching for all available media types exposed by the encoders, this function directly constructs the media types. Typically, in applications such as this, you would load the format settings from a file or use dynamically specified values, but for simplicity, this example uses hard-coded and well-known formats.

```
//
// Set the target audio and video media types to hard-coded values.  In this case you
// are setting audio to AAC, and video to 720p H.264
//
HRESULT CReaderWriterTranscoder::GetTranscodeMediaType(
    CComPtr<IMFMediaType>& pStreamMediaType)
{
    HRESULT hr = S_OK;
    GUID streamMajorType;

    do
    {
        // extract the major type of the source stream from the media type
        hr = pStreamMediaType->GetMajorType(&streamMajorType);
        BREAK_ON_FAIL(hr);

        // if this is an audio stream, configure a hard-coded AAC profile.  If this is a
        // video stream, configure an H.264 profile
        if(streamMajorType == MFMediaType_Audio)
        {
            hr = GetTranscodeAudioType(pStreamMediaType);
        }
```

```cpp
            else if(streamMajorType == MFMediaType_Video)
            {
                hr = GetTranscodeVideoType(pStreamMediaType);
            }
        }
    }
    while(false);

    return hr;
}
```

The *GetTranscodeMediaType()* method constructs the target transcode media type by figuring out whether the requested type is audio or video and then passing the *IMFMediaType* pointer to a helper function. The helper functions in turn add the various attributes and parameters to configure the AAC media type for audio or the H.264 media type for video.

Here is the function that constructs the audio media type by configuring the passed-in *IMFMediaType* object with the parameters for the AAC format.

```cpp
//
// Get the target audio media type - use the AAC media format.
//
HRESULT CReaderWriterTranscoder::GetTranscodeAudioType(
    CComPtr<IMFMediaType>& pStreamMediaType)
{
    HRESULT hr = S_OK;

    do
    {
        BREAK_ON_NULL(pStreamMediaType, E_POINTER);

        // wipe out existing data from the media type
        hr = pStreamMediaType->DeleteAllItems();
        BREAK_ON_FAIL(hr);

        // reset the major type to audio since we just wiped everything out
        pStreamMediaType->SetGUID(MF_MT_MAJOR_TYPE, MFMediaType_Audio);
        BREAK_ON_FAIL(hr);

        // set the audio subtype
        hr = pStreamMediaType->SetGUID(MF_MT_SUBTYPE, MFAudioFormat_AAC);
        BREAK_ON_FAIL(hr);

        // set the number of audio bits per sample
        hr = pStreamMediaType->SetUINT32(MF_MT_AUDIO_BITS_PER_SAMPLE, 16);
        BREAK_ON_FAIL(hr);

        // set the number of audio samples per second
        hr = pStreamMediaType->SetUINT32(MF_MT_AUDIO_SAMPLES_PER_SECOND, 44100);
        BREAK_ON_FAIL(hr);

        // set the number of audio channels
        hr = pStreamMediaType->SetUINT32(MF_MT_AUDIO_NUM_CHANNELS, 2);
        BREAK_ON_FAIL(hr);
```

```cpp
        // set the Bps of the audio stream
        hr = pStreamMediaType->SetUINT32(MF_MT_AUDIO_AVG_BYTES_PER_SECOND, 16000);
        BREAK_ON_FAIL(hr);

        // set the block alignment of the samples
        hr = pStreamMediaType->SetUINT32(MF_MT_AUDIO_BLOCK_ALIGNMENT, 1);
        BREAK_ON_FAIL(hr);
    }
    while(false);

    return hr;
}
```

Because the function is reusing the existing *IMFMediaType* object, it must first wipe out any data that is stored in the media type. If any old data remains, the values could clash with the attributes that will be inserted by the function. Therefore, the *GetTranscodeAudioType()* function first deletes all data in the media type and then sets the major type to audio.

CReaderWriterTranscoder is designed to encode audio in AAC format—therefore, the function sets the minor media type (sometimes known as the subtype) to *MFMediaType*_AAC. After that, the *GetTranscodeAudioType()* method sets several other standard audio values necessary to create a consistent media type configuration.

Here is the corresponding *GetTranscodeVideoType()* function that configures a passed-in video media type object.

```cpp
//
// Get the target video media type - use the H.264 media format.
//
HRESULT CReaderWriterTranscoder::GetTranscodeVideoType(
    CComPtr<IMFMediaType>& pStreamMediaType)
{
    HRESULT hr = S_OK;

    do
    {
        BREAK_ON_NULL(pStreamMediaType, E_POINTER);

        // wipe out existing data from the media type
        hr = pStreamMediaType->DeleteAllItems();
        BREAK_ON_FAIL(hr);

        // reset the major type to video since we just wiped everything out
        pStreamMediaType->SetGUID(MF_MT_MAJOR_TYPE, MFMediaType_Video);
        BREAK_ON_FAIL(hr);

        // set the video subtype
        hr = pStreamMediaType->SetGUID(MF_MT_SUBTYPE, MFVideoFormat_H264);
        BREAK_ON_FAIL(hr);
```

```
        // set the frame size to 720p as a 64-bit packed value
        hr = MFSetAttributeSize(
            pStreamMediaType,           // attribute store on which to set the value
            MF_MT_FRAME_SIZE,           // value ID GUID
            1280, 720);                 // frame width and height
        BREAK_ON_FAIL(hr);

        // Set the frame rate to 30/1.001 - the standard frame rate of NTSC television - as
        // a 64-bit packed value consisting of a fraction of two integers
        hr = MFSetAttributeRatio(
            pStreamMediaType,           // attribute store on which to set the value
            MF_MT_FRAME_RATE,           // value
            30000, 1001);               // frame rate ratio
        BREAK_ON_FAIL(hr);

        // set the average bitrate of the video in bits per second - in this case 10 Mbps
        hr = pStreamMediaType->SetUINT32(MF_MT_AVG_BITRATE, 10000000 );
        BREAK_ON_FAIL(hr);

        // set the interlace mode to progressive
        hr = pStreamMediaType->SetUINT32(MF_MT_INTERLACE_MODE,
            MFVideoInterlace_Progressive );
        BREAK_ON_FAIL(hr);

        // set the pixel aspect ratio to 1x1 - square pixels
        hr = MFSetAttributeSize(pStreamMediaType, MF_MT_PIXEL_ASPECT_RATIO, 1, 1 );
        BREAK_ON_FAIL(hr);
    }
    while(false);

    return hr;
}
```

Just like with the audio media type, the function first resets all of the internal values of the media type. This ensures that no attributes remain in the type attribute collection that could clash with the selected H.264 video format. After that, the function specifies the video encoding in the subtype attribute and sets several standard video format configuration attributes.

Note that the function uses the 30000/1001 fraction for the frame rate for NTSC TV, which is a more accurate frame rate representation than the commonly cited 29.97. This ability to specify a value as a fraction allows you to store more accurate information without resorting to a huge double-precision floating-point number. In this case, a more accurate frame rate value will reduce the number of adjustments that the video renderer will need to make during video playback to match the source frame rate and the frame rate supported by the display.

The Source-Reader-to-Sink-Writer Loop

After all the individual streams are hooked up to each other, you can start pulling samples from the source and pushing them into the sink. The process is quite straightforward: While data exists in the source streams, get a sample from the source and send it to the sink. Repeat until the source has no more samples.

The following code block demonstrates this procedure.

```
//
// Main transcoding loop.  The loop pulls a sample from the source, pushes
// it into the sink, and repeats until all of the data is sent through.
//
HRESULT CReaderWriterTranscoder::RunTranscode(void)
{
    HRESULT hr = S_OK;

    DWORD streamIndex;
    DWORD flags = 0;
    LONGLONG timestamp = 0;
    int nFinishedStreams = 0;
    CComPtr<IMFSample> pSample;

    do
    {
        // initialize target file and prepare for writing
        hr = m_pSinkWriter->BeginWriting();
        BREAK_ON_FAIL(hr);

        // loop while there is any data in the source streams
        while( nFinishedStreams < m_nStreams )
        {
            // pull a sample out of the source reader
            hr = m_pSourceReader->ReadSample(
                (DWORD)MF_SOURCE_READER_ANY_STREAM,  // get a sample from any stream
                0,                                   // no source reader controller flags
                &streamIndex,                        // get index of the stream
                &flags,                              // get flags for this sample
                &timestamp,                          // get the timestamp for this sample
                &pSample );                          // get the actual sample
            BREAK_ON_FAIL(hr);

            // The sample can be null if we've reached the end of stream or encountered a
            // data gap (AKA a stream tick).  If we got a sample, send it on.  Otherwise,
            // if we got a stream gap, send information about it to the sink.
            if( pSample != NULL )
            {
                // push the sample to the sink writer
                hr = m_pSinkWriter->WriteSample( streamIndex, pSample );
                BREAK_ON_FAIL(hr);
            }
```

```cpp
        else if( flags & MF_SOURCE_READERF_STREAMTICK )
        {
            // signal a stream tick
            hr = m_pSinkWriter->SendStreamTick( streamIndex, timestamp );
            BREAK_ON_FAIL(hr);
        }

        // if a stream reached the end, notify the sink, and increment the number of
        // finished streams
        if(flags & MF_SOURCE_READERF_ENDOFSTREAM)
        {
            hr = m_pSinkWriter->NotifyEndOfSegment(streamIndex);
            BREAK_ON_FAIL(hr);

            nFinishedStreams++;
        }

        // release sample
        pSample = NULL;
    }

    // check if we have encountered a failure in the loop
    BREAK_ON_FAIL(hr);

    // flush all the samples in the writer, and close the file container
    hr = m_pSinkWriter->Finalize();
    BREAK_ON_FAIL(hr);
    }
    while(false);


    return hr;
}
```

This function first extracts a media sample from the source reader by calling the *IMFSourceReader::ReadSample()* method. Note that the sample pointer returned may be *NULL* if the source data stream contains a gap or has no more data. In that case, the *ReadSample()* function sends out one of several possible signals by setting values in the flag variable. If the loop has encountered a gap in the source data stream, it needs to signal that information to the sink. If, however, the sample was extracted properly, the loop passes that sample to the sink writer's *WriteSample()* method. The sink writer then re-encodes the sample and writes it to the target file.

After all the streams have run out of data, the loop ends, and the function instructs the sink writer to finalize. During finalization, the sink writer flushes any buffered data, writes it to the file, and closes the file.

Conclusion

This chapter presented two examples that transcode content from one format to another. Though these approaches produce the same results in basic scenarios, they provide different capabilities in more complex situations. The transcode API is designed to quickly create a transcode topology and convert data from one file format to another. It embodies a simplified approach to the transcoding problem, which you can use when you don't care about variable bitrates, multipass encoding, multiple streams in the file, or live transcoding situations.

On the other hand, the source reader approach is far more flexible. With this approach, you can individually control the behavior of each stream and handle multiple streams, dynamic format changes, and variable bitrates. However, because the source reader and sink writer were designed for generic media access, they do lack some of the advantages of the dedicated transcoding approach. For example, the transcode API was designed from the ground up to avoid stream synchronization issues. The transcode API can handle cases where small differences in time stamps between two streams add up over time, causing the audio and video to gradually get out of sync.

Neither the transcode API nor the source reader/sink writer approach provides a panacea for all transcoding situations. In many cases, you may want even more control over the transcode process and may require direct access to MF components in a transcode topology. In those cases, you will be forced to manually create the transcode topology. Though that process can be cumbersome, it does provide far more flexibility when designing your transcode process.

In the end, the transcode method that you use in your application is a decision you should make based on what you need the application to do and what scenarios you expect to encounter. More esoteric problems require more complicated solutions. Higher and more complex requirements lead to more complex approaches in design.

Class Listings

For reference and to simplify your reading of this chapter, here are the class definitions of the core classes presented in this chapter.

As you have seen, the transcode API functionality is encapsulated in two classes—*CTranscodeApi*, which deals with the transcode session, and *CTranscodeApiTopoBuilder*, which constructs the partial transcode topology with the help of the transcode API.

Here is the *CTranscodeApi* class. This class is called from the main function to initiate transcoding.

```
class CTranscodeApi : public IMFAsyncCallback
{
    public:
        CTranscodeApi(void);
        ~CTranscodeApi(void);

        // transcode the file
        HRESULT TranscodeFile(PCWSTR pszInput, PCWSTR pszOutput);
```

```cpp
    // IMFAsyncCallback implementation.
    STDMETHODIMP GetParameters(DWORD *pdwFlags, DWORD *pdwQueue)    { return E_NOTIMPL; }
    STDMETHODIMP Invoke(IMFAsyncResult* pAsyncResult);

    // IUnknown methods - required for IMFAsyncCallback to function
    STDMETHODIMP QueryInterface(REFIID iid, void** ppv);
    STDMETHODIMP_(ULONG) AddRef();
    STDMETHODIMP_(ULONG) Release();

    // block waiting for the transcode to complete
    HRESULT WaitUntilCompletion(void);

private:
    volatile long m_nRefCount;                              // COM reference count.

    CTranscodeApiTopoBuilder m_topoBuilder;

    CComPtr<IMFMediaSession> m_pSession;

    HANDLE m_closeCompleteEvent;     // event fired when transcoding is complete
    HRESULT m_sessionResult;         // result of transcode process

    // helper function called from Invoke()
    HRESULT ParseMediaEvent(IMFMediaEvent* pEvt);
};
```

Here is the helper *CTranscodeApiTopoBuilder* class. This is the class that actually uses the transcode API to build the transcoding topology.

```cpp
class CTranscodeApiTopoBuilder
{
public:
    CTranscodeApiTopoBuilder(void);
    ~CTranscodeApiTopoBuilder(void);

    // create the transcode topology
    HRESULT CreateTranscodeTopology(PCWSTR pszInput, PCWSTR pszOutput);

    // create the transcode profile based on the specified formats
    HRESULT SetTranscodeProfile(const GUID& audioFormat, const GUID& videoFormat,
        const GUID& containerType);

    // get the topology
    IMFTopology* GetTopology(void) { return m_pTopology; }

    // shut down the source
    void ShutdownSource(void) { if(m_pSource != NULL) m_pSource->Shutdown(); }

private:
    CComPtr<IMFTranscodeProfile>    m_pTranscodeProfile;
    CComQIPtr<IMFMediaSource>       m_pSource;         // pointer to the MF source
    CComPtr<IMFTopology>            m_pTopology;
```

```cpp
    // get all possible output types for all encoders
    HRESULT GetVideoOutputAvailableTypes(const GUID& videoSubtypeGuid, DWORD flags,
        CComPtr<IMFCollection>& pTypeCollection);

    // helper functions that deal with collections
    HRESULT GetTypeAttributesFromTypeCollection(CComPtr<IMFCollection>& pTypeCollection,
        int typeIndex, CComPtr<IMFAttributes>& pAttrCollection);
    HRESULT GetCollectionElement(CComPtr<IMFCollection>& pCollection, int index,
        CComQIPtr<IUnknown>& pObject);

    // configure the transcode profile attributes
    HRESULT SetAudioAttributes(const GUID& audioFormat);
    HRESULT SetVideoAttributes(const GUID& videoFormat);
    HRESULT SetContainerAttributes(const GUID& containerType);

    // create the media source
    HRESULT CreateMediaSource(PCWSTR sURL);
};
```

The source reader/sink writer transcoder is defined in a separate class—in the *CReaderWriterTranscoder*. This class is responsible for constructing the source reader and sink writer, configuring them, and passing the samples between the reader and writer.

```cpp
class CReaderWriterTranscoder
{
    public:
        CReaderWriterTranscoder(void);
        ~CReaderWriterTranscoder(void);

        // Start the transcode
        HRESULT Transcode(LPCWSTR source, LPCWSTR sink);

    private:
        CComPtr<IMFSourceReader> m_pSourceReader;
        CComPtr<IMFSinkWriter> m_pSinkWriter;
        int* m_streamMap;
        int m_nStreams;

        // map individual streams
        HRESULT MapStreams(void);

        // figure out the target media types
        HRESULT GetTranscodeMediaType(CComPtr<IMFMediaType>& pStreamMediaType);
        HRESULT GetTranscodeVideoType(CComPtr<IMFMediaType>& pStreamMediaType);
        HRESULT GetTranscodeAudioType(CComPtr<IMFMediaType>& pStreamMediaType);

        // connect the streams
        HRESULT ConnectStream(DWORD dwStreamIndex, const GUID& streamMajorType);

        // do the actual transcode.
        HRESULT RunTranscode(void);
};
```

CHAPTER 5
Media Foundation Transforms

MFT Architecture Overview 98
Writing a Simple MFT 101
Injecting Images into Video Frames 122

Microsoft Media Foundation transforms (MFTs) are COM objects that process data that flows through them. All MFTs have one or more input data streams and produce one or more output data streams. The input data is manipulated and transformed inside of the MFT, and the output data streams are usually simply modified versions of the input streams. For example, video decoder MFTs consume a stream of video samples in a compressed format and produce the same video data, but in raw, uncompressed form. Other MFTs may accept a color video stream, remove the color component, and produce a black-and-white video stream. You can use MFTs to implement decoders, encoders, multiplexers, de-multiplexers, or any other type of digital signal processing (DSP).

In most respects, MFTs are equivalent to standard Microsoft DirectShow filters. They consume samples with data on the input stream, process the information in the samples, and return the modified data from an output stream. One of the advantages of MFTs over DirectShow filters is that MFTs are isolated components that don't know anything about their environment. This allows you to load and use an MFT outside of MF topology and can be extremely useful if you want to create unit tests or write a generic media-processing unit. In such a situation, an application or MFT client can use the MFT as a basic COM object. Therefore, this chapter uses the term *client* interchangeably with MF topology.

In this chapter, you will examine the architecture of a basic MFT. To demonstrate the behavior of a standard MFT, the chapter presents an example transform that adds images to a video. In other words, the transform accepts a stream of video frames on the input, modifies those video frames, and returns them on the output. This is a relatively simple MFT that allows you to examine the basics of MFT design without delving immediately into more esoteric concepts.

In addition, this chapter contains a brief discussion of uncompressed video encoding formats. You need this information to understand how the sample MFT injects an image into a video frame. This video encoding section is optional and can be omitted if you want to focus solely on the concepts specific to Media Foundation (MF).

MFT Architecture Overview

MFTs serve the same purpose in MF topologies as DirectShow filters in DirectShow graphs. MFTs are the signal processing components designed to process or manipulate streams of data samples flowing through them. Just like in DirectShow, data flowing through MFTs is split into media sample objects, each of which contains a piece of the data that the MFT needs to process.

Every MFT must implement the *IMFTransform* interface. This interface defines how a client can communicate with the MFT. Although the *IMFTransform* interface is fairly large, you don't need to implement every single function in it. Some of the functions can be left unimplemented, and return the standard *E_NOTIMPL* error code. Simpler MFTs have no need for some methods of the interface, because the methods can be redundant.

To load and use an MF transform object, you first need to go through several steps to initialize it before you can start sending it data. The following diagram shows the sequence of steps necessary to initialize an MFT and send data through it.

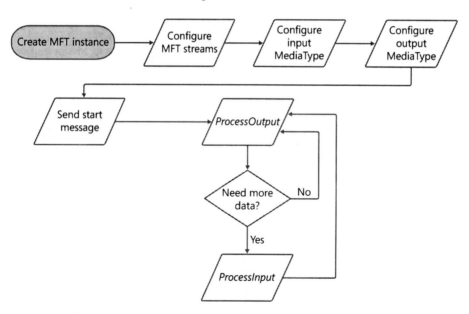

Here are the actual MFT life cycle steps in more detail:

1. The MFT is instantiated either as a standard COM object or by the *MFTEnum()* function.
2. The MFT is queried for the number of streams it supports—the number of inputs and outputs.

3. The caller configures the input media types of the MFT on every input stream.

4. The caller configures the output media types of the MFT on every output stream.

5. The caller sends a start message to the MFT indicating that it is about to start receiving data.

6. The client calls *ProcessOutput()* to get output data from the MFT.

    a. If *ProcessOutput()* returns an error indicating that it needs more data, the client calls *ProcessInput()* on the MFT.

    b. If the MFT has data to return, it returns that data, and *ProcessOutput()* is called again.

7. The client passes data to the MFT with the *ProcessInput()* call.

8. Go back to step 6.

This diagram shows behavior specific to only some clients. Due to the nature of MF, it is impossible to predict in what order every client will call the transform. Some clients, for example, might first pass input data to the MFT and then request output. Others might configure input and output streams in pairs, or attempt to set up output stream media types before input stream types. In addition, MFTs can be designed with two behavior models—synchronous and asynchronous. This chapter focuses on the more common synchronous model; asynchronous MFTs will be discussed in Chapter 8, "Custom Media Sessions."

More Info For simplicity, this description omits the drain step. The drain step tells the MFT not to accept any more input until all of the pending output and buffered information has been processed, dropping any buffered data that it cannot use to produce a complete output sample. After the drain step, the MFT will be completely empty of any buffered data.

To demonstrate the internal design of MF transforms, this chapter examines the implementation of a basic MFT with a single input stream and a single output stream. The sample MFT loads an image from a file and injects that image into video that is passing through it. Because this MFT operates on uncompressed video frames, this chapter also gives a brief overview of uncompressed video formats. In addition, the chapter also demonstrates how to register an MFT so that it can be discovered and used by other MF applications.

The sample MFT is broken up into three classes:

- The *CImageInjectorMFT* class contains the *IMFTransform* implementation of the MFT. This class contains all of the code that the MFT needs to operate in an MF topology.

- The *CFrameParser* class is used by the MFT to parse the actual uncompressed video frames and inject images into them.

- *CBmpFile* is a basic utility class used to load a 24-bit BMP image file and do some color conversion preprocessing that the *CFrameParser* needs to efficiently inject the images. Most of this class is omitted from this chapter because it does not directly apply to Media Foundation or video processing.

The sample MFT must be registered on the machine before you can use it. Therefore, after compiling the MFT, you need to use the regsvr32.exe utility from an elevated command prompt to register the MFT as a COM component, and to store its class ID (CLSID) and MF information in the Windows registry.

Here is a conceptual diagram demonstrating the topology that will be used with the image injector MFT. In the topology, the MFT is inserted between the video decoder and the video renderer. Therefore, it processes uncompressed video frames that flow between the two MF components.

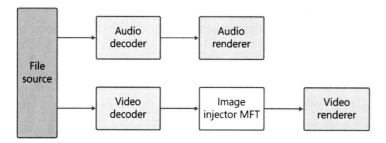

The simplest way to try out the sample MFT is to build it, register it on the machine, and then load it into the TopoEdit tool. Here are the steps that you can use to try out the MFT:

1. Build the MFT sample.

2. Register the MFT by calling *regsvr32.exe ImageInjectorMFT.dll* from a command prompt running in the administrator context.

3. Start TopoEdit.

4. Create an initial topology into which the MFT will be loaded. Select File | Render File, and choose a video file to render. This will automatically create a playback topology for the video.

5. Delete the link between the video renderer and the decoder.

6. Load the sample MFT by selecting Topology | Add Transform. Select the MFT under Video Effects—it will have the friendly name Image Injector MFT. Click the Add button to load the MFT into the topology.

7. Connect the output of the video decoder to the new image injector MFT, and the output of the MFT to the video renderer.

8. Click the play button to start video playback.

The MFT is designed to load an image from the image.bmp file in its local folder and add it to the upper-left corner of every frame of the video. If the image injector fails to find a file with this file name, the video stream will be left unmodified, and the MFT will behave as a pass-through component.

> **Note** If you are using a 64-bit version of TopoEdit, you need to compile and register a 64-bit version of the sample MFT. TopoEdit cannot load MF components compiled for a different architecture.

The following sections discuss the internal workings of a basic MFT and demonstrate the implementation of the image injector sample.

Writing a Simple MFT

As mentioned earlier, every MFT must implement the *IMFTransform* interface. The interface contains quite a few functions, but many of those functions are not required and may be left unimplemented. MF components support different ways for getting the same information about the status of an MFT, which leads to some redundancy in the methods of the *IMFTransform* interface. In addition, some functions are not necessary for many basic MFTs, and thus will be skimmed over in this chapter.

Conceptually, the methods specified in the *IMFTransform* interface can be split up into four categories:

- **Stream configuration and handling functions**   These functions allow an MFT client to add, remove, and configure the number of input and output streams supported by the transform.

- **Media type configuration functions**   These functions are used to configure an MFT and negotiate the connection with other components in the topology.

- **Data processing and messaging functions**   The data functions are used to send data for processing to the MFT. The messaging functions are used by the client to send various commands and status messages to MFTs.

- **Status query and event functions**   These functions are used by the clients to get the capabilities and custom behaviors exposed by the MFT.

The following sections describe each of these function categories. Note that the implementations of many of the functions are omitted—either because they are not implemented in the sample MFT, or because they are self evident. For example, this chapter does not show the implementation of the *IUnknown* interface, because it is nearly identical to the implementation used by all standard non-aggregating COM objects.

Stream Configuration Functions

Each entry point into the MFT where the component can receive a stream of samples is known as an *input stream*. Each exit point is known as an *output stream*. Although MF streams are not implemented as separate objects, conceptually they are equivalent to DirectShow pins.

An MF stream represents the flow of objects that are used by two MF components to pass data from one to the other. Each of these data flows moves only one way, and passes from an upstream MF component to a downstream component. In the conceptual diagram shown here, there are two sample streams, represented by the arrows that connect the MF source object to the MFT and the MFT to the sink object.

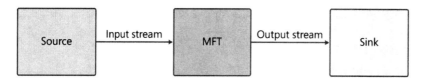

MFTs can support one or more input streams and one or more output streams. The exact number of streams is determined by the purpose and implementation of the MF transform. Some MFTs can dynamically change the number of input or output streams based on internal logic. For example, a standard T-splitter filter—a filter that duplicates its inputs—supports one input stream and a dynamic number of output streams. A multiplexing filter, in contrast, usually can support several audio and video input streams but only one output stream, with the input data combined and multiplexed into a new stream format.

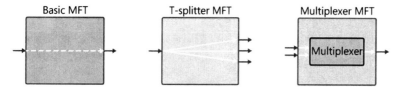

Each stream is identified by an integer value set by the MFT itself, and described by a media type. The media type is used to negotiate the format of the data flowing between the two MF components that the stream connects. In addition, some MF transforms allow non-standard configuration of individual streams by allowing a client to set stream attribute values. The attribute values can then be used by the MFT to tune and customize its behavior for the stream.

Because the image injection filter discussed in this chapter supports only one input stream and one output stream, the implementations of the stream configuration functions is rather obvious and unexciting. Most of the stream functions either return a series of flags to the MFT client or are left unimplemented.

Note MF allows you to leave many of the functions listed in an interface unimplemented. To indicate that a function is not implemented and should not be used by a client, the function should return the standard COM error code *E_NOTIMPL*.

Here is a list of all the stream-related functions specified by the *IMFTransform* interface:

- ***IMFTransform::GetStreamLimits()***   Required function shown later in this section. Returns the minimum and maximum number of input and output streams that the MFT supports.

- ***IMFTransform::GetStreamCount()***   Required function described later in this section. Returns the current number of input and output streams.

- ***IMFTransform::GetInputStreamInfo()***   Required function shown later in this section. Returns the sample buffer requirements and various attributes of a specific input stream.

- **IMFTransform::GetOutputStreamInfo()**   Required function shown later in this section. Returns the sample buffer size and various attributes of a specific output stream.

- **IMFTransform::GetStreamIDs()**   Optional function for MFTs with a fixed number of streams or for MFTs with consecutively numbered streams. Returns the IDs of the streams of the MFT. This method is left unimplemented by the image injector MFT.

- **IMFTransform::GetInputStreamAttributes()**   Optional function for MFTs that do not support input stream custom configuration parameters. Returns an object that can be used to store and configure a specified input stream. This method is left unimplemented by the image injector MFT.

- **IMFTransform::GetOutputStreamAttributes()**   Optional function for MFTs that do not support output stream custom configuration parameters. Returns an object that can be used to store and configure a specified output stream. This method is left unimplemented by the image injector MFT.

- **IMFTransform::AddInputStreams()**   Optional function for MFTs with a fixed number of input streams. Adds an input stream to the MFT. This method is left unimplemented by the image injector MFT.

- **IMFTransform::DeleteInputStream()**   Optional function for MFTs with a fixed number of input streams. Removes an input stream from the MFT. This method is left unimplemented by the image injector MFT.

For an example of an optional function, consider the *IMFTransform::GetStreamIDs()* method. This method is not needed because the image injector MFT supports only a fixed number of streams—one input stream and one output stream. Therefore, clients of the MFT can use the ID of 0 to identify the input and output streams. As a result, the *GetStreamIDs()* function is left unimplemented, and only returns the *E_NOTIMPL* error code.

```
//
// Get IDs for the input and output streams.  This function doesn't need to be implemented in
// this case because the MFT supports only a single input stream and a single output stream,
// and we can set its ID to 0.
//
HRESULT CImageInjectorMFT::GetStreamIDs(
    DWORD    dwInputIDArraySize,
    DWORD    *pdwInputIDs,
    DWORD    dwOutputIDArraySize,
    DWORD    *pdwOutputIDs)
{
    return E_NOTIMPL;
}
```

Although some stream configuration functions can be left unimplemented, others are always necessary. These stream functions allow an MFT to report the number of streams to the client and to expose the capabilities of the input and output streams. For instance, the *IMFTransform::GetStreamLimits()* method is used to identify the minimum and maximum number of input and output streams supported by the MFT. Even an MFT with a fixed number of streams is required to report to its client how many streams it actually supports.

```
//
// Get the maximum and minimum number of streams that this MFT supports.
//
HRESULT CImageInjectorMFT::GetStreamLimits(
    DWORD    *pdwInputMinimum,
    DWORD    *pdwInputMaximum,
    DWORD    *pdwOutputMinimum,
    DWORD    *pdwOutputMaximum)
{
    if (pdwInputMinimum == NULL ||
        pdwInputMaximum == NULL ||
        pdwOutputMinimum == NULL ||
        pdwOutputMaximum == NULL)
    {
        return E_POINTER;
    }

    // This MFT supports only one input stream and one output stream.
    // There can't be more or less than one input or output streams.
    *pdwInputMinimum = 1;
    *pdwInputMaximum = 1;
    *pdwOutputMinimum = 1;
    *pdwOutputMaximum = 1;

    return S_OK;
}
```

As you can see, this function is very simple, because the number of input and output streams supported by this MFT is always one. The implementation of *IMFTransform::GetStreamCount()*—the method responsible for returning the current number of input and output streams—is nearly identical. Because the number of input and output streams for the image injector MFT cannot change, its *GetStreamCount()* implementation always indicates that it has only one input stream and one output stream.

Other stream reporting functions are slightly more complex, because they report the stream configuration information to the caller. These functions return a series of flags and values that a client can use to properly format input data, and to determine the expected format of the output sample buffers used to pass data between components. This information is independent and separate from the media types of the individual streams. The following code block demonstrates the *IMFTransform::GetInputStreamInfo()* function.

```
//
// Get a structure with information about an input stream with the specified index.
//
HRESULT CImageInjectorMFT::GetInputStreamInfo(
    DWORD                      dwInputStreamID,   // stream being queried.
    MFT_INPUT_STREAM_INFO*     pStreamInfo)       // stream information
{
    HRESULT hr = S_OK;
```

```
do
{
    // lock the MFT - the lock will disengage when autoLock goes out of scope
    CComCritSecLock<CComAutoCriticalSection> lock(m_critSec);
    BREAK_ON_NULL(pStreamInfo, E_POINTER);

    // This MFT supports only a stream with ID of zero
    if (dwInputStreamID != 0)
    {
        hr = MF_E_INVALIDSTREAMNUMBER;
        break;
    }

    // The dwFlags variable contains the required configuration of the input stream. The
    // flags specified here indicate:
    //     - MFT accepts samples with whole units of data. In this case this means that
    //       each sample should contain a whole uncompressed frame.
    //     - The samples returned will have only a single buffer.
    pStreamInfo->dwFlags = MFT_INPUT_STREAM_WHOLE_SAMPLES |
        MFT_INPUT_STREAM_SINGLE_SAMPLE_PER_BUFFER ;

    // maximum amount of input data that the MFT requires to start returning samples
    pStreamInfo->cbMaxLookahead = 0;

    // memory alignment of the sample buffers
    pStreamInfo->cbAlignment = 0;

    // maximum latency between an input sample arriving and the output sample being
    // ready
    pStreamInfo->hnsMaxLatency = 0;

    // required input size of a sample - 0 indicates that any size is acceptable
    pStreamInfo->cbSize = 0;
}
while(false);

return hr;
}
```

The *GetInputStreamInfo()* function fills the passed-in *MFT_INPUT_STREAM_INFO* structure with information about the input stream with the specified ID. This information is then used by the caller of the MFT to correctly format data samples that it will be sending to the *IMFTransform::ProcessInput()* function. The *MFT_INPUT_STREAM_INFO* structure can hold several pieces of information.

- ***dwFlags*** Contains a combination of flags that indicate the behavior of the input stream. In this case, the MFT uses two flags: *MFT_INPUT_STREAM_WHOLE_SAMPLES*, indicating that each sample should contain a whole unit of information (a single frame for video); and the *MFT_INPUT_STREAM_SINGLE_SAMPLE_PER_BUFFER* flag, indicating that the input stream samples should have only one buffer per sample.

- ***cbMaxLookahead*** Contains the number of bytes the MFT needs to process before it is ready to return data.

- **cbAlignment** The memory alignment of sample buffers. MFTs can use this structure field to request that the sample buffers have a specific byte alignment in memory for more efficient operation.

- **cbSize** The minimum size of the input samples.

Before performing any operations, the function uses the *CComCritSecLock* Active Template Library (ATL) critical section to ensure that no other thread is operating inside of the MFT. This is necessary to ensure that the MFT does not change its behavior while the *IMFTransform::GetInputStreamInfo()* function is being queried, thus causing a race condition and returning inconsistent settings.

More Info The *CComCritSecLock* class is a wrapper around a basic Win32 critical section. The wrapper serves the same purpose as the COM smart pointers introduced in the earlier chapters—it ensures that the critical section is properly exited when it is no longer needed. The *CComCritSecLock* class is discussed in more detail in Appendix C.

The corresponding *GetOutputStreamInfo()* method functions in an identical manner, returning a structure with the output stream configuration information.

```
//
// Get information about the specified output stream.  Note that the returned structure
// contains information independent of the media type set on the MFT, and thus should always
// return values indicating its internal behavior.
//
HRESULT CImageInjectorMFT::GetOutputStreamInfo(
    DWORD                      dwOutputStreamID,
    MFT_OUTPUT_STREAM_INFO*    pStreamInfo)
{
    HRESULT hr = S_OK;

    do
    {
        // lock the MFT - the lock will disengage when autoLock goes out of scope
        CComCritSecLock<CComAutoCriticalSection> lock(m_critSec);

        BREAK_ON_NULL(pStreamInfo, E_POINTER);

        // The MFT supports only a single stream with ID of 0
        if (dwOutputStreamID != 0)
        {
            hr = MF_E_INVALIDSTREAMNUMBER;
            break;
        }

        // The dwFlags variable contains a set of flags indicating how the MFT behaves.  The
        // flags shown below indicate the following:
        //    - MFT provides samples with whole units of data.  This means that each sample
        //      contains a whole uncompressed frame.
        //    - The samples returned will have only a single buffer.
```

```
    //    - All of the samples produced by the MFT will have a fixed size.
    //    - The MFT provides samples and there is no need to give it output samples to
    //      fill in during its ProcessOutput() calls.
    pStreamInfo->dwFlags =
        MFT_OUTPUT_STREAM_WHOLE_SAMPLES |
        MFT_OUTPUT_STREAM_SINGLE_SAMPLE_PER_BUFFER |
        MFT_OUTPUT_STREAM_FIXED_SAMPLE_SIZE |
        MFT_OUTPUT_STREAM_PROVIDES_SAMPLES;

    // the cbAlignment variable contains information about byte alignment of the sample
    // buffers, if one is needed. Zero indicates that no specific alignment is needed.
    pStreamInfo->cbAlignment = 0;

    // Size of the samples returned by the MFT. Since the MFT provides its own samples,
    // this value must be zero.
    pStreamInfo->cbSize = 0;
    }
    while(false);

    return hr;
}
```

The main difference between the *GetInputStream()* and *GetOutputStream()* functions is in the flags returned in their corresponding parameter structures. The *GetOutputStream()* function contains some extra flags:

- **MFT_OUTPUT_STREAM_FIXED_SAMPLE_SIZE**   This flag indicates, appropriately enough, that every sample will have a fixed size.

- **MFT_OUTPUT_STREAM_PROVIDES_SAMPLES**   This flag tells the caller that the structure will provide its own samples on the output. The "MFT Data Processing" section later in this chapter provides additional details about this flag.

The other members of *MFT_OUTPUT_STREAM_INFO* contain the same information as the members of the corresponding *MFT_INPUT_STREAM_INFO* structure shown previously. If there is an incompatibility between the output buffer format produced by the upstream MF component and the input buffer format expected by the downstream MF component, the client will either manipulate the samples to try to make the components work together, or attempt to find an intermediate MFT to make the conversion.

Media Type Selection Functions

When the MFT client has determined the expected input and output stream behaviors, it is ready to start media type negotiation. The negotiation process is part of the topology building needed to allow neighboring MF components to connect to each other. In other words, the upstream MF component needs to agree with the downstream component on a common media format. The upstream component must produce data in a format that the downstream component can understand. If the two MF components can't agree on a media type, the client will insert various other MFTs between them, attempting to find an MFT that can do an acceptable conversion between the media types.

The *IMFTransform* interface contains several functions that can be used by a client to discover which media types are supported and to establish the connection:

- **GetInputAvailableType() and GetOutputAvailableType()**   Used to extract a list of media types available on the input and output of a specified stream of the MFT. The two functions are nearly identical, and only one will be shown as an example in this text.

- **SetInputType() and SetOutputType()**   Used to actually set the input and output types of the MFT. These functions also accept a flag that allows the caller to test whether a media type is acceptable to the MFT on the specified stream. This gives the caller the ability to ask the MFT to only verify the media type, but not to actually set it. These two functions are also nearly identical, and only one will be shown as an example in this chapter.

- **GetInputCurrentType() and GetOutputCurrentType()**   Used to get the currently set media types from the MFT. The two functions are nearly identical, and only one is shown here.

In many ways, *CImageInjectorMFT* is a pass-through component—it does not make any fundamental changes to the data passing through it, but is instead only changing several bytes of each frame. Therefore, the corresponding sets of input and output configuration functions have very similar implementations. Thus, the *GetInputAvailableType()* and *GetOutputAvailableType()* methods return the same set of media types by calling the internal *CImageInjectorMFT::GetSupportedMediaType()* helper function. Similarly, the *SetInputType()* and *SetOutputType()* methods use the internal *CImageInjectorMFT::CheckMediaType()* function to verify that that the passed-in media type is acceptable.

If you have used the DirectShow *CBasePin::GetMediaType()* function, then the *IMFTransform::GetInputAvailableType()* and *IMFTransform::GetOutputAvailableType()* methods should look familiar. They operate on exactly the same principle—you call the function to get a media type, passing in a zero-based media type index. You can then keep calling the function with monotonously increasing indexes extracting other supported media types until you receive an error code indicating that you have reached the end of the list. The only difference is that the MF functions are exposed off the MFT instead of the DirectShow pin, and thus require you to pass in the ID of the stream that you are interested in.

The following code shows how the *IMFTransform::GetInputAvailableType()* is implemented in the sample MFT.

```
//
// Return one of the preferred input media types for this MFT, specified by
// media type index and by stream ID.
//
HRESULT CImageInjectorMFT::GetInputAvailableType(
    DWORD           dwInputStreamID,
    DWORD           dwTypeIndex,
    IMFMediaType    **ppType)
{
    HRESULT hr = S_OK;
    CComPtr<IMFMediaType> pmt;
```

```cpp
    do
    {
        CComCritSecLock<CComAutoCriticalSection> lock(m_critSec);

        BREAK_ON_NULL(ppType, E_POINTER);

        // only a single stream is supported
        if (dwInputStreamID != 0)
        {
            hr = MF_E_INVALIDSTREAMNUMBER;
            BREAK_ON_FAIL(hr);
        }

        // If the output is not set, then return one of the supported media types.
        // Otherwise return the media type previously set.
        if (m_pOutputType == NULL)
        {
            hr = GetSupportedMediaType(dwTypeIndex, &pmt);
            BREAK_ON_FAIL(hr);

            // return the resulting media type
            *ppType = pmt.Detach();
        }
        else if(dwTypeIndex == 0)
        {
            // return the set output type
            *ppType = m_pOutputType.Detach();
        }
        else
        {
            // if the output type is set, the MFT supports only one input type, and the
            // index cannot be more than 0
            hr = MF_E_NO_MORE_TYPES;
        }
    }
    while(false);

    if(FAILED(hr) && ppType != NULL)
    {
        *ppType = NULL;
    }

    return hr;
}
```

To operate as a pass-through component and use the same media type on the input and output streams, the *GetInputAvailableType()* function returns the output media type if output has already been selected. At the same time, the *GetOutputAvailableType()* function returns the input media type if the input has already been set. Other than that, the two functions have an identical implementation—both check the stream ID, and both call the helper *CImageInjectorMFT::GetSupportedMediaType()* function if the input or output media type have not already been set.

The *GetSupportedMediaType()* function operates just as you would expect it to—it constructs a new partial media type object based on the passed-in index, and returns that object to its caller. Because the image injector MFT deals only with video, the function generates a video media type, and chooses the subtype based on the index of the type requested.

```
//
// Construct and return a partial media type with the specified index from the list of media
// types supported by this MFT.
//
HRESULT CImageInjectorMFT::GetSupportedMediaType(
    DWORD            dwTypeIndex,
    IMFMediaType**   ppMT)
{
    HRESULT hr = S_OK;
    CComPtr<IMFMediaType> pmt;

    do
    {
        // create a new media type object
        hr = MFCreateMediaType(&pmt);
        BREAK_ON_FAIL(hr);

        // set the major type of the media type to video
        hr = pmt->SetGUID(MF_MT_MAJOR_TYPE, MFMediaType_Video);
        BREAK_ON_FAIL(hr);

        // set the subtype of the video type by index. The indexes of the media types
        // that are supported by this filter are:  0 - UYVY, 1 - NV12
        if(dwTypeIndex == 0)
        {
            hr = pmt->SetGUID(MF_MT_SUBTYPE, MEDIASUBTYPE_UYVY);
        }
        else if(dwTypeIndex == 1)
        {
            hr = pmt->SetGUID(MF_MT_SUBTYPE, MEDIASUBTYPE_NV12);
        }
        else
        {
            // if we don't have any more media types, return an error signifying
            // that there is no media type with that index
            hr = MF_E_NO_MORE_TYPES;
        }
        BREAK_ON_FAIL(hr);

            // detach the underlying IUnknown pointer from the pmt CComPtr without
            // releasing the pointer so that we can return that object to the caller.
            *ppMT = pmt.Detach();
        }
    }
    while(false);

    return hr;
}
```

The *CImageInjectorMFT::GetSupportedMediaType()* method is capable of returning one of two partial media types, depending on the requested index. If the caller asked for the first media type (with the index 0), then the function returns the video media type with the UYUV uncompressed format. If the caller asks for the second type (with the index 1), then the function returns the NV12 uncompressed video type. For any other index, the function returns *MF_E_NO_MORE_TYPES*.

The two setter functions that tell the MFT which media type it should use are also alike. The setter functions first do several checks to ensure that the passed-in parameters are acceptable, that the MFT is in a state where it can accept a new media type, and that the input media type matches the output media type. Because this MFT is a pass-through, the two media types must be identical. After that, if the passed-in media type is deemed acceptable, the functions store it for future use.

```
//
// Set, test, or clear the input media type for the MFT.
//
HRESULT CImageInjectorMFT::SetInputType(DWORD dwInputStreamID, IMFMediaType* pType,
    DWORD dwFlags)
{
    HRESULT hr = S_OK;
    CComPtr<IMFAttributes> pTypeAttributes = pType;

    do
    {
        // lock the MFT - the lock will disengage when autoLock goes out of scope
        CComCritSecLock<CComAutoCriticalSection> lock(m_critSec);

        // this MFT supports only a single stream - fail if a different stream value is
        // suggested
        if (dwInputStreamID != 0)
        {
            hr = MF_E_INVALIDSTREAMNUMBER;
            BREAK_ON_FAIL(hr);
        }

        // verify that the specified media type is acceptible to the MFT
        hr = CheckMediaType(pType);
        BREAK_ON_FAIL(hr);

        // If the MFT is already processing a sample internally, fail out, since the MFT
        // can't change formats on the fly.
        if (m_pSample != NULL)
        {
            hr = MF_E_TRANSFORM_CANNOT_CHANGE_MEDIATYPE_WHILE_PROCESSING;
            BREAK_ON_FAIL(hr);
        }

        // Make sure that the input media type is the same as the output type (if the
        // output is set).  If the type passed in is NULL, skip this check since NULL
        // clears the type.
        if (pType != NULL && m_pOutputType != NULL)
```

```
        {
            BOOL result = FALSE;
            hr = pType->Compare(pTypeAttributes, MF_ATTRIBUTES_MATCH_INTERSECTION, &result);
            BREAK_ON_FAIL(hr);

            // if the types don't match, return an error code
            if(!result)
            {
                hr = MF_E_INVALIDMEDIATYPE;
                break;
            }
        }

        // If we got here, then the media type is acceptable - set it if the caller
        // explicitly tells us to set it, and is not just checking for compatible
        // types.
        if (dwFlags != MFT_SET_TYPE_TEST_ONLY)
        {
            m_pInputType = pType;

            // send the frame type into the frame parser, so that the parser knows how to
            // disassemble and modify the frames
            hr = m_frameParser.SetFrameType(m_pInputType);
        }
    }
    while(false);

    return hr;
}
```

SetInputType() first does some checks, verifies that the media type is acceptable, and then stores it internally. If the media type pointer passed in was *NULL*, then the function clears the internally stored media type. If it is not *NULL*, and the output media type is set, then the function checks the media type against the output type. Note that the function uses the *IMFAttributes::Compare()* method to compare the two media types, instead of the *IMFMediaType::IsEqual()*. This is done because the *IsEqual()* method has some peculiarities and might reject a valid media type.

If the media type is accepted and set on the MFT, then the input function also passes this type into the frame parser object. The frame parser needs the media type information to know the sizes and arrangements of the uncompressed frame buffers. The uncompressed frame formats are discussed in more detail in the next section of this chapter.

The caller of the function might pass in the *MFT_SET_TYPE_TEST_ONLY* flag in the *dwFlags* parameter. This flag indicates that the caller does not actually want to set this media type on the MFT, but is only verifying that the media type is acceptable.

After the media type is set on the MFT, the client will periodically call the corresponding "get current type" function. Due to the logging implementation in the Windows 7 codebase, a standard playback topology will call the *IMFTransform::GetInputCurrentType()* once for every input sample, and the *IMFTransform::GetOutputCurrentType()* once for every output sample. This operation is computationally very cheap, because the functions simply get a pointer to the current media type and return it to the caller.

```cpp
//
// Get the current input media type.
//
HRESULT CImageInjectorMFT::GetInputCurrentType(
    DWORD           dwInputStreamID,
    IMFMediaType**  ppType)
{
    HRESULT hr = S_OK;

    do
    {
        // lock the MFT
        CComCritSecLock<CComAutoCriticalSection> lock(m_critSec);

        BREAK_ON_NULL(ppType, E_POINTER);

        if (dwInputStreamID != 0)
        {
            hr = MF_E_INVALIDSTREAMNUMBER;
        }
        else if (m_pInputType == NULL)
        {
            hr = MF_E_TRANSFORM_TYPE_NOT_SET;
        }
        else
        {
            *ppType = m_pInputType;
            (*ppType)->AddRef();
        }
    }
    while(false);

    return hr;
}
```

The *IMFTransform::GetOutputCurrentType()* is implemented in the same way, except that it returns the *m_pOutputType* set during the *SetOutputType()* call, instead of the *m_pInputType*.

If you want to debug or examine the MFT connection steps, you can use the MFTrace tool. MFTrace allows you to see the connection process in detail, examine the proposed media types, and see how the topology is built. Appendix A describes the MFTrace tool and some basic MF debugging procedures.

MFT Data Processing

After the media types are agreed upon by all members of the topology, the client starts pumping data through the MFT. At this point, our synchronous MFT should always be either ready to receive new data or ready to transmit its internally queued data.

Note Unlike synchronous MFTs, asynchronous transforms can both receive and transmit data at the same time. This is useful in scenarios where the MFT is processing internal data by utilizing several processing threads. However, because the asynchronous MFT processing model is more complex, it is not covered in this chapter.

In contrast to DirectShow filters, MFTs do not expose methods that allow a client to control them. There are no explicit *Run()* or *Flush()* methods in the *IMFTransform* interface. Instead, MF clients send command events to all of the components in the topology. These commands tell the individual components that they should start processing data, stop, flush, and so on.

MFTs accept commands through the *IMFTransform::ProcessMessage()* function. The function receives the message type and a *void* pointer with any additional information that can be sent with that message. In general, MF sends data through the MFT in the order shown in the following illustration.

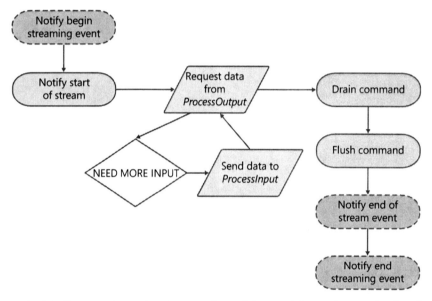

In this diagram, the optional events that might or might not be sent by the client have dashed outlines. Here is a detailed description of the steps shown:

1. The MFT receives the *MFT_MESSAGE_NOTIFY_BEGIN_STREAMING* event. This event is optional and might not be sent. The event indicates that the topology has transitioned to the run state and that the MFT is about to start receiving data.

2. The MFT receives the *MFT_MESSAGE_NOTIFY_START_OF_STREAM* event. Synchronous MFTs can ignore this message, but for asynchronous MFTs the start of stream event indicates that they can start asking for data. Synchronous and asynchronous MFTs will be discussed in Chapter 8.

3. The MFT gets the *ProcessOutput()* call asking for processed data. Because the MFT doesn't have any data to return yet, it must respond with the *MF_E_TRANSFORM_NEED_MORE_INPUT* error code.

4. The MFT gets the *ProcessInput()* call with new data. The MFT must respond with *S_OK* if it can process the passed-in sample.

5. The client goes back to step 3 (while there is data to send).

6. The MFT gets the *MFT_MESSAGE_COMMAND_DRAIN* event, indicating that it should start sending any samples and data queued internally.

7. The MFT gets the *MFT_MESSAGE_COMMAND_FLUSH* message, indicating that it should discard any data it has stored internally.

8. The MFT receives the *MFT_MESSAGE_NOTIFY_END_OF_STREAM* message, indicating that the stream or the stream segment has ended. If the client sends any additional data to the MFT, the first sample of the new data stream must have the discontinuity flag. This message is optional and is not always sent by clients.

9. The MFT receives the *MFT_MESSAGE_NOTIFY_END_STREAMING* event, indicating that it is done streaming. This message is optional and is not always sent by clients.

The order of steps 3 through 5 (the data processing loop) might be different, depending on the implementation of the client. For example, some users of the MFT might first send data to it with the *ProcessInput()* function, and only then ask for output.

The following code section shows the implementation of the *ProcessMessage()* function in the *CImageInjectorMFT* class.

```
//
// Receive and process a message or command to the MFT, specifying a
// requested behavior.
//
HRESULT CImageInjectorMFT::ProcessMessage(
    MFT_MESSAGE_TYPE    eMessage,
    ULONG_PTR           ulParam)
{
    HRESULT hr = S_OK;

    CComCritSecLock<CComAutoCriticalSection> lock(m_critSec);

    if(eMessage == MFT_MESSAGE_COMMAND_FLUSH)
    {
        // Flush the MFT - release all samples in it and reset the state
        m_pSample = NULL;
    }
    else if(eMessage ==  MFT_MESSAGE_COMMAND_DRAIN)
    {
        // The drain command tells the MFT not to accept any more input until
        // all of the pending output has been processed. That is the default
        // behavior of this MFT, so there is nothing to do.
    }
```

```
        else if(eMessage == MFT_MESSAGE_NOTIFY_BEGIN_STREAMING)
        {
        }
        else if(eMessage == MFT_MESSAGE_NOTIFY_END_STREAMING)
        {
        }
        else if(eMessage == MFT_MESSAGE_NOTIFY_END_OF_STREAM)
        {
        }
        else if(eMessage == MFT_MESSAGE_NOTIFY_START_OF_STREAM)
        {
        }

        return hr;
}
```

As you can see, this function does very little, because the image injector MFT has very simple behavior and does not need to do much when various messages come in. The only message the MFT needs to care about is the flush command. When the MFT is ordered to flush, it needs to discard any internally queued data—in this case, to release the internally queued sample by setting the *m_pSample* pointer to *NULL*.

After a client sends the start-of-stream signal, it begins sending data to the MFT by calling its *IMFTransform::ProcessInput()* method.

```
//
// Receive and process an input sample.
//
HRESULT CImageInjectorMFT::ProcessInput(
    DWORD               dwInputStreamID,
    IMFSample*          pSample,
    DWORD               dwFlags)
{
    HRESULT hr = S_OK;
    DWORD dwBufferCount = 0;

    do
    {
        // lock the MFT
        CComCritSecLock<CComAutoCriticalSection> lock(m_critSec);

        BREAK_ON_NULL(pSample, E_POINTER);

        // This MFT accepts only a single output sample at a time, and does not accept any
        // flags.
        if (dwInputStreamID != 0 || dwFlags != 0)
        {
            hr = E_INVALIDARG;
            break;
        }

        // Both input and output media types must be set in order for the MFT to function.
        BREAK_ON_NULL(m_pInputType, MF_E_NOTACCEPTING);
        BREAK_ON_NULL(m_pOutputType, MF_E_NOTACCEPTING);
```

```cpp
        // The MFT already has a sample that has not yet been processed.
        if(m_pSample != NULL)
        {
            hr = MF_E_NOTACCEPTING;
            break;
        }

        // Store the sample for later processing.
        m_pSample = pSample;
    }
    while(false);

    return hr;
}
```

The *ProcessInput()* function of the image injection MFT performs very little work. Its primary responsibility is to validate the right format and state of the MFT, and to store the sample for later processing. The actual frame processing is done inside of the helper *CFrameParser* class and is triggered by the *ProcessOutput()* function.

```cpp
//
// Get an output sample from the MFT.
//
HRESULT CImageInjectorMFT::ProcessOutput(
    DWORD                   dwFlags,
    DWORD                   cOutputBufferCount,
    MFT_OUTPUT_DATA_BUFFER* pOutputSampleBuffer,
    DWORD*                  pdwStatus)
{
    HRESULT hr = S_OK;

    do
    {
        // lock the MFT
        CComCritSecLock<CComAutoCriticalSection> lock(m_critSec);

        BREAK_ON_NULL(pOutputSampleBuffer, E_POINTER);
        BREAK_ON_NULL(pdwStatus, E_POINTER);

        // This MFT accepts only a single output sample at a time, and does
        // not accept any flags.
        if (cOutputBufferCount != 1  ||  dwFlags != 0)
        {
            hr = E_INVALIDARG;
            break;
        }

        // If we don't have an input sample, we need some input before
        // we can generate any output - return a flag indicating that more
        // input is needed.
        BREAK_ON_NULL(m_pSample, MF_E_TRANSFORM_NEED_MORE_INPUT);

        // Pass the frame to the parser and have it grab the buffer for the frame
        hr = m_frameParser.LockFrame(m_pSample);
        BREAK_ON_FAIL(hr);
```

```
        // draw the specified bitmap on the frame
        hr = m_frameParser.DrawBitmap(m_pBmp);
        BREAK_ON_FAIL(hr);

        // tell the parser that we are done with this frame
        hr = m_frameParser.UnlockFrame();
        BREAK_ON_FAIL(hr);

        // Detach the output sample from the MFT and put the pointer for
        // the processed sample into the output buffer
        pOutputSampleBuffer[0].pSample = m_pSample.Detach();

        // Set status flags for output
        pOutputSampleBuffer[0].dwStatus = 0;
        *pdwStatus = 0;
    }
    while(false);

    return hr;
}
```

The client calls the *IMFTransform::ProcessOutput()* function to pull any internal data from the MFT. The *ProcessOutput()* function shown here has several responsibilities. First, it verifies that the MFT is in the right state (in other words, that it has a buffer that it can process) and that the parameters of the call are what was expected. Then it passes the internally queued sample and an image to the *CFrameParser* frame processing class. Finally, it returns the sample in the passed-in *MFT_OUTPUT_DATA_BUFFER* structure. If the MFT returns the *MF_E_TRANSFORM_NEED_MORE_INPUT* error code, the client needs to give it more data before expecting to receive any samples.

An output stream of an MFT can operate in several different modes. It can generate brand-new samples and return them in the passed-in *MF_OUTPUT_DATA_BUFFER* structure. It can populate samples passed inside of the structure with brand-new data. It can discard samples when it runs out of space and when additional data is passed in, and so on.

The exact mode in which an MFT output stream operates is specified and returned to the client in the *IMFTransform::GetOutputStreamFormat()* method that was discussed earlier in the chapter. Remember that the *GetOutputStreamFormat()* function returns a set of flags indicating various MFT behaviors. Here are the flags that tell the MFT user what to expect and what it needs to send to the MFT in the *ProcessOutput()* function parameters:

- **MFT_OUTPUT_STREAM_PROVIDES_SAMPLES**   Indicates that the stream either generates brand-new samples or that it will pass through the samples sent in with the *ProcessInput()* function. When the MFT returns this flag, the client must set the *pSample* pointer in the *MFT_OUTPUT_DATA_BUFFER* parameter to *NULL*, because that value will be replaced with a pointer to the returned sample.

- **MFT_OUTPUT_STREAM_CAN_PROVIDE_SAMPLES**   Indicates that the MFT can either provide its own samples or populate the passed-in sample. If neither this flag nor the *MFT_OUTPUT_STREAM_PROVIDES_SAMPLES* flag is set on the *GetOutputStreamFormat()* call, the client must provide a sample in the *MFT_OUTPUT_DATA_BUFFER* structure. The MFT will then fill in the sample during the *ProcessOutput()* call.

- **MFT_OUTPUT_STREAM_LAZY_READ**   Indicates that the client will discard internal samples and data if it runs out of space and the *ProcessInput()* function keeps getting called. An MFT running in this mode will thus never return *MF_E_NOTACCEPTING* from *ProcessInput()* when it is full, and will instead just throw away extra data.

These are the main operating modes of MFTs, although there are other, more esoteric types of MFT behavior. As shown in the earlier section, the image injector MFT provides samples in the *ProcessOutput()* calls. To be more specific, the injector MFT rewrites the information in the samples sent in *ProcessInput()* calls, and returns those same samples in *ProcessOutput()*.

Status Query and Event Functions

Besides the generic configuration and data processing functions listed in the previous section, the *IMFTransform* interface also exposes several methods used to query it for status and to send events. These functions can be used by custom clients to interrogate the MFT's data processing status and to send it in-band events.

- **GetAttributes()**   Exposes the MFT capabilities and custom information to the client.

- **GetInputStatus()**   Allows the client to detect whether the MFT is ready to receive input without allocating a sample. Rarely used.

- **GetOutputStatus()**   Allows the client to detect whether the MFT is ready to send out data without allocating a sample. Optional method, rarely used.

- **ProcessEvent()**   Used by the client to send in in-band events. Optional method, almost never used.

- **SetOutputBounds()**   Allows a client to specify the range of time stamps it needs. Optional method, almost never used.

As you can see, the list indicates that some of these functions are optional and are almost never used. These functions are almost superfluous due to the behavior of other existing functions. For example, although the *IMFTransform::GetInputStatus()* method must be implemented, the current Windows 7 default topology implementation will not call it. This function makes sense if it is very computationally expensive to create and send in a new sample into the *ProcessInput()* method only to have the method return the *MF_E_NOTACCEPTING* error. In that case, a client might want to call this function to ensure that the MFT is ready to accept new data.

```cpp
//
// Check to see if the MFT is ready to accept input samples
//
HRESULT CImageInjectorMFT::GetInputStatus(
    DWORD           dwInputStreamID,
    DWORD*          pdwFlags)
{
    CComCritSecLock<CComAutoCriticalSection> lock(m_critSec);

    if (pdwFlags == NULL)
    {
        return E_POINTER;
    }

    // the MFT supports only a single stream.
    if (dwInputStreamID != 0)
    {
        return MF_E_INVALIDSTREAMNUMBER;
    }

    // if there is no sample queued in the MFT, it is ready to accept data.  If there already
    // is a sample in the MFT, the MFT can't accept any more samples until somebody calls
    // ProcessOutput to extract that sample, or flushes the MFT.
    if (m_pSample == NULL)
    {
        // there is no sample in the MFT - ready to accept data
        *pdwFlags = MFT_INPUT_STATUS_ACCEPT_DATA;
    }
    else
    {
        // a value of zero indicates that the MFT can't accept any more data
        *pdwFlags = 0;
    }

    return S_OK;
}
```

The *IMFTransform::GetInputStatus()* function is itself quite simple. All it does is return a flag that indicates whether the MFT is ready for more data. The corresponding *GetOutputStatus()* is optional and can simply return the *E_NOTIMPL* error code.

The *IMFTransform::GetAttributes()* function allows the client to send custom commands and parameters that are not supported by the *IMFTransform* interface to the MFT. The *GetAttributes()* method allows the client to get the *IMFAttributes* interface, which provides a generic method for passing any kind of data types between the client and the MFT. The client can send information into the MFT by setting an attribute on the *IMFAttributes* interface, and it can query information from the MFT by calling one of the attribute getter methods.

For example, the client can detect whether MFT supports dynamic format changes by getting the *IMFAttributes* collection and checking for the presence of the *MFT_SUPPORT_DYNAMIC_FORMAT_CHANGE* Boolean value. If the MFT supports dynamic format changes, the attribute collection will return the Boolean value *TRUE* when queried with the *MFT_SUPPORT_DYNAMIC_FORMAT_CHANGE*

GUID. Similarly, if the client wants to signal to the MFT that it can support and understand an asynchronous processing model, it can set the *MF_TRANSFORM_ASYNC_UNLOCK* attribute on the attribute collection.

The *IMFTransform::GetAttributes()* method is also optional, and the image injector MFT does not implement it.

MFT Registration

As mentioned earlier, MFTs are implemented as classic COM objects. MFT clients create the MFTs by calling the COM *CoCreateInstance()* function. However, remember that at run time the MF topology needs to discover which MFT it must load to transform data from one format to another. The topology and the other MFT clients need to know which MFTs can decode H.264 video, which MFTs can deal with audio, and which deal with subtitles. This information is necessary to speed up the load process and streamline discovery of the MFTs by various clients.

The MFT discovery functionality is implemented in the *MFTEnum()* function discussed in Chapter 4, "Transcoding." The *MFTEnum()* function uses information in the registry to discover individual MFTs. The registry contains a list of MFTs, their categories, preferred input media types, preferred output media types, and various flags.

> **Background** The *MFTEnum()* functions can also detect locally registered MFTs. A locally registered MFT is one that is registered only for the running process. This is useful if you want to use an MFT during automatic topology resolution, but make it available only to the running application. Local MFT information is stored in process memory and not in the registry. This means that, to be discoverable, a local MFT will need to be re-registered when a process is restarted. To register an MFT locally, you can use the *MFTRegisterLocal()* and *MFTRegisterLocalByCLSID()* functions.

The following code segment contains the function that is called when you call the regsvr32.exe registration utility to register the image injector MFT. The *DllRegisterServer()* function is the standard entry point into DLLs containing COM objects.

```
//
// Function exposed out of the DLL used for registration of the COM object in
// the DLL using regsvr32 (e.g. "regsvr32 filename.dll")
//
STDAPI DllRegisterServer(void)
{
    HRESULT hr = S_OK;

    do
    {
        // Register the COM object CLSID so that CoCreateInstance() can be called to
        // instantiate the MFT object.
        hr = RegisterCOMObject(IMAGE_INJECTOR_MFT_CLSID_STR, L"Image Injector MFT");
        BREAK_ON_FAIL(hr);
```

```
            // register the COM object as an MFT - store its information in the location that
            // the MFTEnum() and MFTEnumEx() functions search, and put it under the right MFT
            // category.
            hr = MFTRegister(
                CLSID_CImageInjectorMFT,     // CLSID of the MFT to register
                MFT_CATEGORY_VIDEO_EFFECT,   // Category under which the MFT will appear
                L"Image Injector MFT",       // Friendly name
                MFT_ENUM_FLAG_SYNCMFT,       // this is a synchronous MFT
                0,                           // zero pre-registered input types
                NULL,                        // no pre-registered input type array
                0,                           // zero pre-registered output types
                NULL,                        // no pre-registered output type array
                NULL);                       // no custom MFT attributes (used for merit)
        }
        while(false);

        return hr;
    }
```

The most interesting function in this code section is *MFTRegister()*, provided by MF. *MFTRegister()* performs the actual registration of the MF component and stores the CLSID, friendly name, category, and other information about the MFT. The MFT must already be registered as a COM object—that task is performed by the *RegisterCOMObject()* function.

In this case, the image injection MFT is stored under the video effect category. Categories are used as hints to the *MFTEnum()* and *MFTEnumEx()* functions and simplify MFT discovery. Note that the image injection MFT does not register support for any specific input and output media types. Consequently, *MFTEnum()* function will not pick up this MFT unless it is told to enumerate components with *NULL* input and output media types. This is allowed because this MFT is optional and does not need to be loaded during topology resolution—it is not going to be required to connect any two MF objects to each other.

Injecting Images into Video Frames

To inject an image into video frames, the MFT first needs to load the data and then convert it into the format of the frame. To simplify the scenario, the sample MFT is designed to decode only one of the simplest image formats—uncompressed 24-bit BMP files. The 24-bit BMP files store the image data for each pixel as red, green, and blue (RGB) values.

Uncompressed frame formats and injection of images is not specific to Media Foundation. These concepts are generic and are used throughout video applications. Therefore, if you are interested only in MF transforms, you can skip this section.

The process of injecting an image into a video frame consists of several stages. First, the image is converted from its native 24-bit RGB format into the color format used by the video. Then the image color data is reduced to match the color compression format of the video frames. And finally, each of the image pixels is drawn into every frame of video.

These operations are done by two classes in the code provided with this chapter. Image loading and processing is done by the *CBmpFile* class. The actual injection of the image data into the frame is done by the *CFrameParser* class.

More Info Because the code required to load the BMP file is fairly simple and has little to do with Media Foundation and video images, it will be omitted from this chapter. The only truly interesting parts of the *CBmpFile* class have to do with conversion of the BMP files between different color formats and palettes—these functions are described in the following sections.

Uncompressed Video Formats

After the image is loaded into memory, it then needs to be converted into the format of the video frames in the stream. Uncompressed video frames can be stored in several formats. All of these formats use various methods to reduce the size of the image of the data without noticeably decreasing the video quality. One of the most common image reduction methods is known as *chroma subsampling*. The idea behind this format is to separate the image into its color and black-and-white components, and then reduce the resolution of the color section. This does not produce a noticeable reduction in image quality because the human eye is much more sensitive to brightness than to color differences. This color and brightness format is usually represented by three values—brightness, shown as *Y*; and two color values, shown as *Cr* and *Cb*.

Note *Cb* and *Cr* values can be thought of as coordinates in a color plane that contains all of the combinations of primary colors. In other words, if you arrange all possible colors on a plane, you can reference any color by its *x* and *y* coordinates in that plane. The color plane is also known as the *U-V plane*, and correspondingly, the YCbCr format is often also called the *YUV* format. The rest of this chapter uses the two names for the chrominance format interchangeably.

As a first step in conversion from the RGB format into the YCbCr format, the RGB data for each pixel is separated into the brightness value (known as *luma*) and two color values (known as *chrominance* or *chroma*). The luma component can be viewed as the black-and-white version of the image, and the chroma can be viewed as the color version, but with all of the colors at maximum brightness. When the two images are combined, the resulting frame looks nearly identical to the naked eye, although some minor blurring may be detected around the edges of different colors.

In order for us to inject an image into the video stream, we need to convert it from the source format into the target format—or the output format of the video frames. This filter supports two uncompressed video formats, NV12 and UYVY. These two formats are very common and are used in this chapter to demonstrate how uncompressed images are stored in memory. The NV12 uncompressed format is what is known as a "planar" media format—the luma is stored as a single array of data in memory and is followed by another array containing the chroma values. The UYVY format demonstrates the interleaved format, where the chroma and luma values are interleaved with each other in a single large array.

The following diagram graphically demonstrates how the pixel data is stored in memory.

Planar format

Y	Y	Y	Y	Y	Y	Y	Y
Y	Y	Y	Y	Y	Y	Y	Y
Y	Y	Y	Y	Y	Y	Y	Y
Y	Y	Y	Y	Y	Y	Y	Y
Y	Y	Y	Y	Y	Y	Y	Y
Y	Y	Y	Y	Y	Y	Y	Y
Y	Y	Y	Y	Y	Y	Y	Y
Y	Y	Y	Y	Y	Y	Y	Y

U	V	U	V	U	V	U	V
U	V	U	V	U	V	U	V
U	V	U	V	U	V	U	V
U	V	U	V	U	V	U	V

Interleaved format

U	Y	V	Y	U	Y	V	Y
U	Y	V	Y	U	Y	V	Y
U	Y	V	Y	U	Y	V	Y
U	Y	V	Y	U	Y	V	Y
U	Y	V	Y	U	Y	V	Y
U	Y	V	Y	U	Y	V	Y
U	Y	V	Y	U	Y	V	Y
U	Y	V	Y	U	Y	V	Y

The image on the left represents the NV12 format, where the chroma image is at half the resolution of the luma. As a result, although the planar array has 8 x 8 pixels, the chroma array consists of only 4 x 4 chroma pairs. The interleaved image, in turn, represents the UYVY format, where the horizontal dimension of the chroma sample is still half that of the luma, but the vertical dimension is the same. Therefore, each row of pixels in the interleaved image has two chroma pairs and four luma pairs. Other interleaved and planar formats have different chroma to luma ratios.

The NV12 type is often described as a 4:2:0 format. The three numbers describe how the color information of each frame is reduced. This value represents the number of bytes needed to encode a 4 x 2 block of pixels. The first number indicates the number of bytes used for the luma—4 bytes in this case, because the brightness information is almost never reduced. The second value, 2, indicates the number of color samples used to store the data about the first row of four pixels of the image—in this case, two. This means that we use two pairs of U and V values to store the color information of the first row of four pixels. The last number indicates the number of color samples used for the second row of four pixels. In this case, the value is 0, which means that each block of four-pixel squares uses a single color sample. As a result, in a 4:2:0 reduced frame, the vertical and horizontal resolutions of the color component of the image are half that of the resolution of the brightness component.

The UYVY format is described with a similar value, 4:2:2. This indicates that although all of the brightness data is preserved, every two pixels on each line share a color sample value. In other words, the color component of the image is horizontally reduced by half, while retaining the same resolution vertically as the brightness component. The following diagram shows how the individual color components are combined to produce the final image.

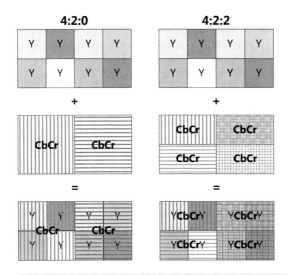

Note Because this book is printed just in black, the colors in the preceding diagram are presented as different types of shading patterns. Each different pattern corresponds to a different color. The image demonstrates how the luma and chroma values are added up in the 4:2:0 arrangement (for example, in NV12) and in the 4:2:2 arrangement (for example, UYVY).

RGB to YUV Image Conversion

To inject the image into frames encoded in the NV12 or UYVY format, you need to convert the images themselves into that format and then set the corresponding pixel values in each frame. Because you don't want to recalculate the image values for each frame, the image is converted once and then reused during processing of each frame.

Image conversion into the formats presented in the previous section is a two-step process. First, the image's RGB pixels are converted into their corresponding YUV values, and then the chroma values of corresponding pixels are blended together to achieve either the 4:2:0 or 4:2:2 chroma sampling.

The following function demonstrates how the RGB values are converted to YUV. For simplicity, the YUV information is stored in the same array as the original RGB data, replacing the stored information.

```
//
// Convert all of the RGB pixels in the image into the YUV format
//
void BmpFile::ConvertToYuv(void)
{
    if( m_width == 0 || m_height == 0 || m_pBmp == NULL )
        return;

    // explicitly cast the array into YUVTRIPLE items in order to make sure we never
    // mix up Y, U, and V order in the array. The order is arbitrary, as long as everyone
    // uses it in the same way - while setting, and while reading the values.
    YUVTRIPLE** pYuv = (YUVTRIPLE**)m_pBmp;

    for(DWORD y = 0; y < m_height; y++)
    {
        for(DWORD x = 0; x < m_width; x++)
        {
            // store the RGB data in temporary variables since it will be modified
            short R = m_pBmp[y][x].rgbtRed;
            short G = m_pBmp[y][x].rgbtGreen;
            short B = m_pBmp[y][x].rgbtBlue;

            // use integer calculations to derive the Y, U, and V values for the
            // YUV format of every single pixel.  This essentially converts the
            // data from 4:4:4 RGB to 4:4:4 YUV
            pYuv[y][x].Y = ( (  66 * R + 129 * G +  25 * B + 128) >> 8) +  16;
            pYuv[y][x].U = ( ( -38 * R -  74 * G + 112 * B + 128) >> 8) + 128;
            pYuv[y][x].V = ( ( 112 * R -  94 * G -  18 * B + 128) >> 8) + 128;
        }
    }
}
```

To simplify conversion of the YUV pixels, each of the three-byte sections of the array representing a pixel has two pointers to it—a pointer to an *RGBTRIPLE* structure, and another pointer to the same memory location as the *YUVTRIPLE* structure. This is useful because it allows us to standardize on which of the three bytes represents which value.

The conversion from RGB to YUV can be done in one of two ways: with a floating-point formula that is easy for humans, or with the integer-based formula presented in the function just shown. The function uses the integer formula because its performance is better on most CPUs.

Background To convert from RGB to YUV by using floating-point math, you can also use the following set of formulas:

```
Y =  0.299   * R + 0.587   * G + 0.114   * B
U = -0.14713 * R - 0.28886 * G + 0.436   * B
V =  0.615   * R - 0.51499 * G - 0.10001 * B
```

These floating-point formulas produce the same result as the integer calculations presented in the function just shown. Note that the formulas used here apply only to conversion from RGB into the NTSC color spectrum (a standard TV image format). The high-definition ATSC format (a digital TV signal format) uses a slightly different color palette, and the color conversion coefficients are different in ATSC color conversion functions. In a real-world application, you can also use multi-threading and some SSE (streaming SIMD Extensions) multimedia instructions to improve performance.

After the image pixels have been converted into the YUV format, you can move to the second step and smooth out the chroma between samples. This is needed to make a smoother transition between individual colors in an image. To do this, you need to average out the chroma values between individual pixels that share a chroma sample. The code block here demonstrates how you can smooth out chroma for the 4:2:2 format.

```
//
// Smooth out chroma for 4:2:2 format
//
void BmpFile::PrecalcChroma_422(void)
{
    if( m_width == 0 || m_height == 0 || m_pBmp == NULL )
        return;

    // explicitly cast the array into YUVTRIPLE items in order to make sure we never
    // mix up Y, U, and V order in the array. The order is arbitrary, as long as everyone
    // uses it in the same way - while setting, and while reading the values.
    YUVTRIPLE** pYuv = (YUVTRIPLE**)m_pBmp;

    for(DWORD y = 0; y < m_height; y++)
    {
        for(DWORD x = 0; x < (m_width - 1); x+=2)
        {
            float uSum = 0;
            float vSum = 0;

            // add up the U and V portions of every pixel
            uSum = pYuv[y][x].U + pYuv[y][x+1].U;
            vSum = pYuv[y][x].V + pYuv[y][x+1].V;
```

```
            // Since a single chroma value for 4:2:2 format represents four pixels
            // at once (the same color is used for every four pixels) set the chroma
            // values of all of the pixels to the calculated average.
            pYuv[y][x].U = pYuv[y][x+1].U = (char)(uSum / 2);
            pYuv[y][x].V = pYuv[y][x+1].V = (char)(vSum / 2);
        }
    }
}
```

As you can see, the procedure for smoothing out the chroma values is fairly straightforward. The function extracts the *U* and *V* values for two adjacent pixels, averages them out, and stores them back into these same pixels. Either one of those two pixels can now be used by the image injection function, because both contain identical chroma values.

> **Note** Chroma smoothing for the 4:2:0 format is nearly identical to that of the 4:2:2 smoothing, and is thus omitted from this chapter.

Frame Format Detection

Before the frame parser can start modifying the frames, it first needs to discover the format in which the frames are encoded. This means that the frame parser needs to determine whether the media type has a UYVY or NV12 subtype, as well as the dimensions of each frame.

The following function is called from the *CImageInjector::SetInputType()* function whenever the MFT user sets the input media type.

```
//
// Set the frame media type and stride, and precalculate the chroma values for the frame
//
HRESULT CFrameParser::SetFrameType(IMFMediaType* pType)
{
    HRESULT hr = S_OK;
    LONG lStride = 0;

    do
    {
        // reset the frame size information
        m_imageWidthInPixels = 0;
        m_imageHeightInPixels = 0;

        // if the media type is NULL, it means that the type is being cleared - reset
        // internal variables.
        if(pType == NULL)
        {
            m_stride = 0;
            m_subtype = GUID_NULL;
        }
```

```cpp
// get the frame width and height in pixels from the media type
hr = MFGetAttributeSize(pType, 
                        MF_MT_FRAME_SIZE, 
                        &m_imageWidthInPixels, 
                        &m_imageHeightInPixels);
BREAK_ON_FAIL(hr);

// image dimensions must be divisible by 2
if( m_imageWidthInPixels % 2 != 0 || m_imageHeightInPixels % 2 != 0)
{
    hr = E_UNEXPECTED;
    break;
}

// Try to get the default stride from the media type.  A stride is the length of a
// single scan line in a frame in bytes - i.e. the number of bytes per pixel times the
// width of a frame.
hr = pType->GetUINT32(MF_MT_DEFAULT_STRIDE, (UINT32*)&m_stride);

// if we failed to get the stride from the media type, we will try to get it by
// looking at the subtype
if(FAILED(hr))
{
    m_stride = 0;
}

// Get the subtype from the media type.  The first 4 bytes of the subtype GUID will
// be the FOURCC code for this video format.
hr = pType->GetGUID(MF_MT_SUBTYPE, &m_subtype);
BREAK_ON_FAIL(hr);

// precalculate the chroma values for the media type
if(m_pBmp != NULL && m_pBmp->ImageLoaded())
{
    m_pBmp->ConvertToYuv();

    if(m_subtype == MEDIASUBTYPE_UYVY)
    {
        m_pBmp->PrecalcChroma_422();
    }
    else if(m_subtype == MEDIASUBTYPE_NV12)
    {
        m_pBmp->PrecalcChroma_420();
    }
    else
    {
        hr = MF_E_INVALIDMEDIATYPE;
        break;
    }
}

// if m_stride is zero, then we failed to get the stride from the media type.  In
// that case use the frame FOURCC type and width to calculate the expected stride
// (length of each pixel line).
```

```
            if(m_stride == 0)
            {
                hr = MFGetStrideForBitmapInfoHeader(m_subtype.Data1, m_imageWidthInPixels,
                    &lStride);
                BREAK_ON_FAIL(hr);
            }
        }
        while(false);

        return hr;
    }
```

The *SetFrameType()* function is responsible for extracting information about the frame from the passed-in media type. The frame parser needs three things from the media type: the dimensions of each frame, frame stride, and frame encoding. Frame encoding tells the parser whether it needs to process the samples as UYVY encoded images or as NV12 encoded images. This information is represented by the media subtype and is guaranteed to be stored in the media type. After the function determines the media subtype, it calls the appropriate chroma precalculation method on the *CBmpFile* with the image.

Frame dimensions tell the parser the width and height of each frame in pixels. Frame stride is the length of each pixel line in the image in bytes. These two pieces of information tell the parser how many bytes are in each line of pixels of a frame. This information is necessary to navigate among the pixels of each frame. Even though we know the frame encoding and dimensions, the stride is not guaranteed, because some decoder implementations might add extra padding bytes to the frame sample buffers. This padding can speed up processing of each frame.

The *SetFrameType()* method first tries to get the *MF_MT_DEFAULT_STRIDE* attribute directly from the media type object. However, frame padding is not guaranteed to be available in a media type—some components might use the default padding usually used with a particular encoding format. Therefore, if the *MF_MT_DEFAULT_STRIDE* attribute is not set on the media type, the *SetFrameType()* method falls back on the helper *MFGetStrideForBitmapInfoHeader()* function. This function calculates the default stride by looking at the number of bits per pixel, expected alignment of the format, and whether the format is planar or interleaved, as well as other information known about this subtype.

UYVY Image Injection

After the image has been converted into the needed format, you can start modifying the video and inserting the image pixels into each frame. The following function demonstrates how the image is injected into a UYVY-encoded frame.

```
// A struct representing a single UYVY format macropixel. The macropixel describes
// two pixels in the final frame. Each pixel has its own luma value (Y1 and Y2), but
// both share the same chroma (U and V).
struct UYVY_MACRO_PIXEL
{
    BYTE U;
    BYTE Y1;
    BYTE V;
    BYTE Y2;
};
```

```cpp
//
// Inject the specified image into the current UYVY-encoded frame.
//
HRESULT CFrameParser::DrawBitmap_UYVY(BmpFile* pBmp)
{
    HRESULT hr = S_OK;
    UYVY_MACRO_PIXEL* lineStart = NULL;
    DWORD imageWidthInMacroPixels = 0;

    do
    {
        lineStart = (UYVY_MACRO_PIXEL*)m_pScanline0;

        // each macro pixel represents two actual pixels on the screen, with two
        // luma samples (Y1 and Y2), and one chroma sample (U + V). Therefore,
        // each line of the image array will contain widthInPixels/2 macropixels
        imageWidthInMacroPixels = m_imageWidthInPixels / 2;

        for(DWORD y = 0; y < pBmp->Height() && y < m_imageHeightInPixels; y++)
        {
            for(DWORD x = 0; x < (pBmp->Width() - 1) && x < imageWidthInMacroPixels; x+=2)
            {
                // extract two YUV pixels of the image
                YUVTRIPLE* yuvImagePixel1 = pBmp->GetYUVPixel(x, y);
                YUVTRIPLE* yuvImagePixel2 = pBmp->GetYUVPixel(x+1, y);

                // extract a single macropixel from the frame
                UYVY_MACRO_PIXEL* framePixel = &(lineStart[x/2]);

                // set the luma pixel values in the frame pixel
                framePixel->Y1 = yuvImagePixel1->Y;
                framePixel->Y2 = yuvImagePixel2->Y;

                // set the chroma values in the frame pixel
                framePixel->U = yuvImagePixel1->U;
                framePixel->V = yuvImagePixel1->V;
            }

            // the stride is specified in bytes - but we made the lineStart an array of
            // macropixels. Therefore we need to figure out by how many macropixels we
            // need to move the lineStart pointer in order to point to the next line of
            // pixels in the frame.
            lineStart += (m_stride / sizeof(UYVY_MACRO_PIXEL));
        }
    }
    while(false);

    return hr;
}
```

Just as with the color conversion functions presented earlier, the *CFrameParser::DrawBitmap_UYVY()* function uses a special structure to pinpoint the individual values in memory. In this case, the function uses the *UYVY_MACRO_PIXEL* structure, which allows you to easily identify which byte has which value. Because the UYVY format uses the 4:2:2 subsampling, the structure describes two on-screen pixels that consist of two luma values and a single chroma value.

The function operates by walking through all relevant pixels in the frame and replacing them with the pixels from the image. The inner loop operates on the pixels in the single line of the image, while the outer loop moves the operation to the next line. Note that because the strides are in bytes, whereas our line array consists of four-byte *UYVY_MACRO_PIXEL* structures, you need to modify the stride necessary to transition from one line of the frame to the next.

NV12 Image Injection

As mentioned earlier, the internal organization of NV12 frames is rather different from the UYVY frames. As a result, the function that injects an image into an NV12 frame is more complicated than the UYVY version. The main difference arises from the fact that the NV12 format uses 4:2:0 subsampling, and the function must set the corresponding chroma pixel once for every four pixels, on two separate lines.

```
//
// Inject the specified image into the current NV12 encoded frame.
//
HRESULT CFrameParser::DrawBitmap_NV12(BmpFile* pBmp)
{
    HRESULT hr = S_OK;
    BYTE* lumaLineStart = m_pScanline0;
    NV12_CHROMA* chromaLineStart = NULL;
    DWORD chromaStride = 0;

    do
    {
        // in NV12 the chroma is stored as interleaved U and V values in an array
        // immediately following the array of Y values. Therefore, to get to the UV array
        // we need to skip past the Y array - i.e. width of each pixel line (m_stride) times
        // the number of pixel lines in the image (m_imageHeightInPixels)
        chromaLineStart = (NV12_CHROMA*)(lumaLineStart + (m_stride*m_imageHeightInPixels));

        // Because NV12 is a 4:2:0 format, the chroma is at half of the vertical resolution
        // of the luma, and at half of the horizontal resolution of the luma. This means that
        // the chroma stride is half of the luma stride. Note that this is still true
        // despite the values being stored in two-byte U,V pairs, because the chroma is
        // treated as an array of two-byte variables.
        chromaStride = m_stride / 2;

        // iterate through every pixel of the image/frame as long as we are not outside
        // the bounds of the frame or of the image
        for(DWORD y = 0; y < pBmp->Height() && y < m_imageHeightInPixels; y++)
        {
            for(DWORD x = 0; x < pBmp->Width() && x < m_imageWidthInPixels; x++)
            {
                // extract the YUV pixel of the image
                YUVTRIPLE* yuvPixel = pBmp->GetYUVPixel(x, y);

                // set the luma of the target pixel
                lumaLineStart[x] = yuvPixel->Y;
```

```
            // Because the chroma is at half vertical and horizontal resolution of the
            // luma, we need to set the chroma pixels only for every 2 vertical and 2
            // horizontal pixels. Therefore set the chroma only if the x and y
            // coordinates of the pixel are not divisible by 2.
            if(x%2 == 0  &&  y%2 == 0)
            {
                chromaLineStart[x / 2].U = yuvPixel->U;
                chromaLineStart[x / 2].V = yuvPixel->V;
            }
        }

        // go to the next line in the luma array
        lumaLineStart += m_stride;

        // go to the next line of the chroma array if we need to
        if(y%2 == 0)
        {
            chromaLineStart += chromaStride;
        }
    }
}
while(false);

return hr;
}
```

The first thing the function does is locate the start of the luma and chroma arrays, and store them in the *lumaLineStart* and *chromaLineStart* variables. These variables are then used during the function run time to transition between individual pixel lines of the frame. For simplicity, the chroma values are cast as a two-byte *NV12_CHROMA* structure. This allows you to directly address the U and V components of each chroma pixel.

Because the resolution of the luma is not modified, the process of setting the luma values of the pixel is very straightforward: each luma value of the frame is replaced with a luma value of the replacement image. Chroma is a little bit more complicated, however, because its resolution is half that of the luma. As a result, the chroma values are extracted from the source image and overridden in the target frame at half the rate of the luma. In other words, the chroma values are set only when the *x* and *y* coordinates of the pixel are cleanly divisible by two (x%2 = 0 and y%2 = 0).

Conclusion

In this chapter, you have covered the basics of synchronous MFT design. With this knowledge, you can now write MF components that give your applications the ability to process media data streams. Though the sample MFT presented in this chapter is fairly simple, on the basis of this knowledge you can write very advanced data processing components capable of a variety of different behaviors.

In addition, this chapter presented the core concepts of uncompressed video formats, allowing you to modify video streams at will. Even though the sample in this chapter only places the injected image in the upper-left corner of the video frame, you can extend this example to all sorts of video data processing scenarios.

Class Listings

For reference and to simplify your reading of this chapter, here are the class definitions of the main classes used in the examples in this chapter.

The core class of the sample MFT presented in this chapter is *CImageInjectorMFT*. This class obviously contains all of the MFT functions and is exposed to the MF applications. Most of the image processing is done in several helper classes.

```
class CImageInjectorMFT :
    public IMFTransform
{
    public:
        CImageInjectorMFT(void);
        ~CImageInjectorMFT(void);

        //
        // IMFTransform stream handling functions
        STDMETHODIMP GetStreamLimits( DWORD* pdwInputMinimum, DWORD* pdwInputMaximum,
            DWORD* pdwOutputMinimum, DWORD* pdwOutputMaximum );

        STDMETHODIMP GetStreamIDs( DWORD dwInputIDArraySize, DWORD* pdwInputIDs,
            DWORD dwOutputIDArraySize, DWORD* pdwOutputIDs );

        STDMETHODIMP GetStreamCount( DWORD* pcInputStreams, DWORD* pcOutputStreams );
        STDMETHODIMP GetInputStreamInfo( DWORD dwInputStreamID,
            MFT_INPUT_STREAM_INFO* pStreamInfo );
        STDMETHODIMP GetOutputStreamInfo( DWORD dwOutputStreamID,
            MFT_OUTPUT_STREAM_INFO* pStreamInfo );
        STDMETHODIMP GetInputStreamAttributes( DWORD dwInputStreamID,
            IMFAttributes** pAttributes );
        STDMETHODIMP GetOutputStreamAttributes( DWORD dwOutputStreamID,
            IMFAttributes** pAttributes );
        STDMETHODIMP DeleteInputStream( DWORD dwStreamID );
        STDMETHODIMP AddInputStreams( DWORD cStreams, DWORD* adwStreamIDs );

        //
        // IMFTransform mediatype handling functions
        STDMETHODIMP GetInputAvailableType( DWORD dwInputStreamID, DWORD dwTypeIndex,
            IMFMediaType** ppType );
        STDMETHODIMP GetOutputAvailableType( DWORD dwOutputStreamID, DWORD dwTypeIndex,
            IMFMediaType** ppType );
        STDMETHODIMP SetInputType( DWORD dwInputStreamID, IMFMediaType* pType,
            DWORD dwFlags );
        STDMETHODIMP SetOutputType( DWORD dwOutputStreamID, IMFMediaType* pType,
            DWORD dwFlags );
        STDMETHODIMP GetInputCurrentType( DWORD dwInputStreamID, IMFMediaType** ppType );
        STDMETHODIMP GetOutputCurrentType( DWORD dwOutputStreamID, IMFMediaType** ppType );

        //
        // IMFTransform status and eventing functions
        STDMETHODIMP GetInputStatus( DWORD dwInputStreamID, DWORD* pdwFlags );
        STDMETHODIMP GetOutputStatus( DWORD* pdwFlags );
        STDMETHODIMP SetOutputBounds( LONGLONG hnsLowerBound, LONGLONG hnsUpperBound);
        STDMETHODIMP ProcessEvent( DWORD dwInputStreamID, IMFMediaEvent* pEvent );
        STDMETHODIMP GetAttributes( IMFAttributes** pAttributes );
```

```cpp
//
// IMFTransform main data processing and command functions
STDMETHODIMP ProcessMessage( MFT_MESSAGE_TYPE eMessage, ULONG_PTR ulParam );
STDMETHODIMP ProcessInput( DWORD dwInputStreamID, IMFSample* pSample, DWORD dwFlags);

STDMETHODIMP ProcessOutput( DWORD dwFlags, DWORD cOutputBufferCount,
    MFT_OUTPUT_DATA_BUFFER* pOutputSamples, DWORD* pdwStatus);

//
// IUnknown interface implementation
//
virtual HRESULT STDMETHODCALLTYPE QueryInterface(REFIID riid, void **ppvObject);
virtual ULONG STDMETHODCALLTYPE AddRef(void);
virtual ULONG STDMETHODCALLTYPE Release(void);

private:

    volatile long m_cRef;                     // ref count
    CComAutoCriticalSection m_critSec;        // critical section for the MFT

    CComPtr<IMFSample>   m_pSample;           // Input sample.
    CComPtr<IMFMediaType> m_pInputType;       // Input media type.
    CComPtr<IMFMediaType> m_pOutputType;      // Output media type.

    CFrameParser m_frameParser;               // frame parsing and image injection object

    // private helper functions
    HRESULT GetSupportedMediaType(DWORD dwTypeIndex, IMFMediaType** ppmt);
    HRESULT CheckMediaType(IMFMediaType *pmt);
};
```

The *CFrameParser* class is a helper component that processes passed-in uncompressed frames and actually copies a bitmap onto them.

```cpp
//
// Helper class that processes passed-in uncompressed frames and draws bitmaps on them.
//
class CFrameParser
{
    public:
        CFrameParser(void);
        CFrameParser(WCHAR* filename);
        ~CFrameParser(void);

        // Set the media type which contains the frame format.
        HRESULT SetFrameType(IMFMediaType* pMT);

        // Pass in the sample with the video frame to modify.
        HRESULT LockFrame(IMFSample* pSmp);
        HRESULT UnlockFrame(void);

        // Draw the bitmap on the passed-in frame.
        HRESULT DrawBitmap(void);
```

```cpp
        // Load the bitmap from the file.
        HRESULT SetBitmap(WCHAR* filename);

    private:
        CComPtr<IMFMediaBuffer> m_pMediaBuffer;
        CComQIPtr<IMF2DBuffer> m_p2dBuffer;

        BYTE* m_pScanline0;
        GUID m_subtype;
        LONG m_stride;
        UINT32 m_imageWidthInPixels;
        UINT32 m_imageHeightInPixels;

        CBmpFile* m_pBmp;           // The bitmap to inject.

        HRESULT DrawBitmap_NV12(CBmpFile* pBmp);    // Draw bitmap on an NV12 frame.
        HRESULT DrawBitmap_UYVY(CBmpFile* pBmp);    // Draw bitmap on a UYVY frame.
};
```

Finally, here is the *CBmpFile* class, which loads the bitmap and converts it into the requested chroma format. Note that the file does not do a full conversion—the byte array holds many copies of the chroma information. This is done to simplify image processing by the *CFrameParser*.

```cpp
// Helper structure defining the YUV format and byte positioning.
struct YUVTRIPLE
{
    BYTE Y;
    BYTE U;
    BYTE V;
};

//
// Helper class that holds the bitmap and converts the bitmap into a common format.
//
class CBmpFile
{
    public:
        CBmpFile(WCHAR* filename);
        ~CBmpFile(void);

        bool ImageLoaded(void) { return m_pBmp != NULL; };

        // Get an RGB pixel from the specified coordinates.
        inline RGBTRIPLE* GetRgbPixel(DWORD x, DWORD y)
        {
            if(x < 0 || x >= m_width)
                return NULL;
            if(y < 0 || y >= m_width)
                return NULL;

            return &(m_pBmp[y][x]);
        }
```

```cpp
    // Get a YUV pixel from the specified coordinates.
    inline YUVTRIPLE* GetYUVPixel(DWORD x, DWORD y)
    {
        if(x < 0 || x >= m_width)
            return NULL;
        if(y < 0 || y >= m_width)
            return NULL;

        return (YUVTRIPLE*)(&(m_pBmp[y][x]));
    }

    // Convert file into one format and precalculate the chroma.
    void ConvertToYuv(void);
    void PrecalcChroma_420(void);
    void PrecalcChroma_422(void);

    // Get image dimensions.
    inline DWORD Width(void) { return m_width; }
    inline DWORD Height(void) { return m_height; }

private:
    RGBTRIPLE** m_pBmp;
    DWORD m_width;
    DWORD m_height;

    HRESULT ReadFile(WCHAR* filename);
    void ClearData(void);
};
```

CHAPTER 6

Media Foundation Sources

Overview 141

The Asynchronous Call Pattern 143

Instantiating a Media Source 146

Media Foundation Events 157

The Media Foundation Source 159

Media Stream Objects 183

Windows Property Handlers. 189

As you saw earlier in this book, Microsoft Media Foundation (MF) uses media sources to deliver media data into MF topologies. Media sources abstract the actual origin and container format of data so that media can be streamed from a file on the hard drive, from a network endpoint, from a capture device, or even from a synthetic, dynamically generated media stream. After creating an MF topology around a particular media source, MF controls the flow of data by pulling samples from the media source as needed. This behavior is different than in Microsoft DirectShow, where most source filters push data to the graph.

Media sources expose a set of stream objects, each of which has a media type that describes the type of data it contains. For example, if an application is processing data from a video file, then the corresponding media source might expose three data streams: one for video, one for audio, and one for closed captions. Each of the data streams will be exposed through its own media stream object. A source may expose multiple streams with the same media type, for cases where the file or network endpoint contains multiple data streams of the same type. For instance, some files contain multiple audio data streams, each in a different language.

The following illustration is a conceptual diagram that demonstrates how media stream objects relate to the data streams and to the media source.

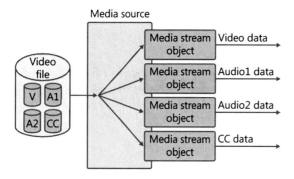

In the diagram, a media source is processing a file with four internal data streams—one video, two audio, and a closed-captioning data stream. The media source loads the file and de-multiplexes (separates) the individual data streams. It then sends each of the data streams to its own media stream object, which actually delivers that data to the topology.

Media Foundation provides a set of interfaces to activate (select) and deactivate (deselect) streams, as well as the ability to dynamically change the number of available stream objects at any given time. These APIs provide great flexibility and allow you to perform advanced operations on complex media files, such as playback of files with multiple video streams, files with streams that dynamically change media type in the middle of a file, and files with sparse data streams.

Most of the time, applications will ask Media Foundation to automatically load the right media source object for a file or a network endpoint. To match the container format with a correct media source, MF maintains entries in the registry that associate specific file extensions and protocols with special handler objects. These handler objects are responsible for instantiating media sources. In this chapter, you will learn about these helper objects and see the implementation of one for a sample media source.

Because one of the purposes of media source components is to analyze and preprocess data streams, media sources are usually also responsible for extracting file metadata. This metadata can include things such as frame rate, audio bit rate, title, artist, and genre of the media. The metadata is then used by various applications to display information about media files. For example, the Windows Shell uses metadata to populate the Details property page for media files, whereas Windows Media Player uses it to classify audio files and store them in the media library for sorting and later retrieval.

In this chapter, you will see a detailed overview of several media source concepts and learn how to design and implement your own custom media source. You will also see how to expose metadata from the source to the Windows Shell. For simplicity, the source is designed to parse AVI files. However, to bypass the Microsoft AVI handler, the source is instead registered as a parser for files with the made-up .avf extension.

Overview

MF media sources are COM objects that must expose at least two interfaces: *IMFMediaSource* and *IMFMediaEventGenerator*. The *IMFMediaSource* interface allows an application to control the source, and the media generator interface is used by the source to signal various states and operations. Media sources can expose one or more output media stream objects and no input media stream objects. Conceptually, an MF media source is equivalent to a DirectShow source filter, and each media stream object serves the same purpose as a DirectShow output pin. Each media stream object is responsible for delivering one elementary stream with a specific data type, such as video, audio, interactive TV data, or captions. If the file contains multiple elementary streams of the same type, the source will usually expose multiple stream objects—one per elementary stream. For example, if a file contains two audio tracks, the source will expose two media stream objects that deliver audio data to the topology—one for each stream.

As discussed in previous chapters, the Media Foundation pipeline uses a "pull" architecture, where the media session (acting as the controller) pulls samples from each node as needed. During playback, the media session will request data from each of the selected media stream objects. Conversely, the media session will not request any data from inactive (deselected) streams.

The reason that you might want to select or deselect a specific data stream is because media files often contain multiple data streams of the same type. For example, a movie may contain three separate audio tracks (each for a different language), as well as three subtitle tracks. Because you want to play and display information associated with only a single language, you can deselect unneeded streams.

Each media stream object is associated with one or more media types that describe the types of media that can flow from this object. The MF topology builder needs this information to know which MFT or sink is compatible with a particular output stream object.

The following diagram demonstrates the major classes that comprise the AVF Source sample shown in this chapter.

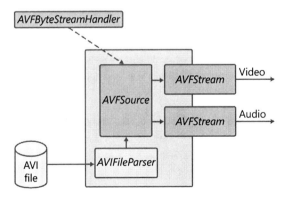

The conceptual diagram shows the data flow between individual components of the source. The sample consists of four major new classes:

- **AVFByteStreamHandler**   This is the class that instantiates the source. The byte stream handler serves as a class factory for the media source and is registered and invoked for files with the .avf extension.

- **AVFSource**   This class contains most of the driving functionality of the source. *AVFSource* loads the samples from helper classes, instantiates output stream objects, and passes samples to them.

- **AVIFileParser**   This is the AVI file-handling helper class. This class is responsible for actually parsing the AVI file, reading its header, detecting data types in the file, and creating the media samples returned by the media source.

- **AVFStream**   This is the *IMFMediaStream* implementation used by the AVF media source sample. Each media stream object represents an individual data stream in the file and allows the media source to pass data to MFTs connected to it.

Together the *AVFSource*, *AVIFileParser*, and *AVFStream* classes make up the source object that parses the files. This source can handle AVI files as long as they are renamed with the .avf extension.

This chapter omits a lot of the helper methods that are part of the *AVFSource* and *AVFStream* classes. These helper methods are either extremely simple, and thus not worth exploring in detail here, or are fairly self-explanatory. In addition, the chapter does not explain the *AVIFileParser* helper class. Though that class is interesting, its implementation is not specific to MF, and is not very advanced. *AVIFileParser* uses the in-box Microsoft Video for Windows (VFW) interfaces to parse the AVI file header and extract individual samples from the file. The only MF-related activity in the file parser is the creation of media types and the generation of new MF samples.

> **Note** The VFW AVI parsing functionality is not very robust and fails to properly parse some AVI audio headers. As a result, the VFW sample parser will fail to load audio samples from some files, which will result in video that plays while the audio remains silent. Unfortunately, the only way to correct this problem is to implement a custom AVI file parser, which is far beyond the topics covered in this chapter. However, this is another reason to not cover the *AVIFileParser* class here—this parser (or the MF wrapper around the VFW parser) is not a definitive implementation and cannot be used in many real-world scenarios.

To test AVF Source, you need to register it and load it with TopoEdit. You cannot use Windows Media Player because it contains a custom source resolution mechanism that will detect that an .avf file is actually an AVI file in disguise and automatically load the default AVI parser instead of the AVF

Source. For testing, you can use the AVI_Wildlife.avi sample file provided with the sample code—this file is guaranteed to work with the source. To instantiate an *AVFSource*, simply rename AVI_Wildlife.avi to AVI_Wildlife.avf, and open it with TopoEdit. TopoEdit will automatically load the right MF source.

> **Important** Because the Windows Explorer process loads avfsource.dll, the file cannot be recompiled, changed, or deleted while you are viewing the properties of an .avf file. You need to close that window and wait for the explorer process to be unloaded from memory before you can manipulate avfsource.dll. If you are still having trouble, consider using the free SysInternal Process Explorer tool (available from *http://technet.microsoft.com/en-us /sysinternals/bb896653.aspx*) to find the processes that are holding on to the DLL.

Most media source implementations abstract the actual source of the data and separate the object that loads the data from the media source. These MF sources use *IMFByteStream* objects to load the data from the network, from a file, or from a dynamically generated stream. These byte stream objects load the data directly and send it as byte arrays to the media source object, which parses the data. In such implementations, the MF source objects are unaware of the original location of the data that they are processing. However, for simplicity, the example presented in this chapter uses a more basic version of the source, one that accesses files directly and is incapable of parsing data streams from other locations. This is necessary because all of the AVI file parsing in the AVF Source sample is done by the VFW interfaces, which are designed to access the disk, load the AVI file, parse the AVI headers, and extract individual samples. This makes it impossible to separate the file loading functionality that would usually go into an *IMFByteStream* object from the file parsing functionality usually found in a media source object.

The Asynchronous Call Pattern

One of the major differences between Media Foundation and DirectShow is that most MF calls are asynchronous. This requires a bit of learning and getting used to. You already saw a simplified explanation of the MF asynchronous calls in Chapter 3, "Media Playback." Although that explanation was sufficient for the samples in the previous chapters, AVF Source uses more advanced asynchronous functionality. Therefore, here is a more involved description of the asynchronous mechanism used in MF.

Unlike some other implementations, the MF system provides its own worker thread for all MF-related asynchronous calls. Your components do not need to explicitly create separate threads to execute work concurrently. Instead, they can rely on the helper worker thread queues and worker thread objects provided for you. Here is a modified sequence diagram of a standard asynchronous call in MF, together with the worker thread object.

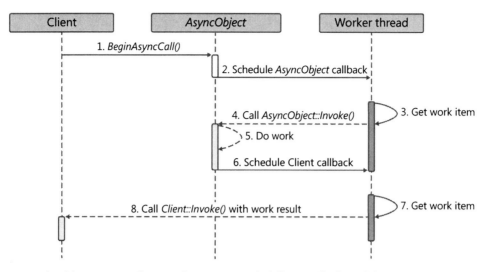

Again, this sequence diagram does not exactly follow Unified Modeling Language (UML) conventions, but it will help you understand the sequence of steps taken during asynchronous calls. Just as in previous sequence diagrams, the thin vertical rectangles represent the lifetime of individual function calls.

The diagram shows the three major actors in a hypothetical asynchronous operation. The *Client* object is some component that makes an asynchronous work request on the asynchronous object. *AsyncObject* is an MF component that implements the asynchronous functionality. And finally, the *WorkerThread* object is an internal MF component that stores various asynchronous requests in an internal queue and executes the requests on the actual worker thread by calling the asynchronous object's *Invoke()* method. Both *Client* and *AsyncObject* implement the *IMFAsyncCallback* interface because they both will need to be called asynchronously by the worker thread at some point.

Here are the steps that are shown in this diagram:

1. The client object calls an asynchronous object, beginning the asynchronous operation. In this example, the client calls *AsyncObject::BeginAsyncCall()*. The rectangle representing the *BeginAsyncCall()* function is very short, because the function executes quickly and immediately returns. During the *BeginAsyncCall()* call, the client object passes in an *IMFAsyncCallback* pointer to itself so that it can be notified when the asynchronous operation is complete (in step 8).

2. The *AsyncObject* schedules work on itself from within the *AsyncObject::BeginAsyncCall()* method. Essentially this entails pushing a work request onto a work queue stored in the worker thread object. The work request contains a pointer to the *IMFAsyncCallback* interface exposed by the *AsyncObject*. After scheduling is complete, the *BeginAsyncCall()* method immediately returns, and the thread executing in the *Client* object becomes idle (or is allowed to do other work).

3. While this is happening, the worker thread is waiting for a new work request to arrive in its work queue. When the worker thread finds that it has work to do, it gets the work item and processes it.

4. The worker thread extracts the *AsyncObject*'s *IMFAsyncCallback* interface pointer from the work item and calls the *AsyncObject::Invoke()* function.

5. The *AsyncObject::Invoke()* call starts executing—that's the longer rectangle on the *AsyncObject* lifeline. This rectangle represents the time that it takes the asynchronous object to do all of its work. Notice that the work is done on the worker thread—not on the main thread that came from the *Client* object.

6. After the work is complete, *AsyncObject* schedules another work request with the worker thread. Because this time *AsyncObject* needs to return the result of the operation, it creates an *IMFAsyncResult* object from the client's *IMFAsyncCallback* pointer that it received from the client in step 1. The work item this time contains the callback pointer to the client, and when the worker thread picks up the work item, it will call the *Client::Invoke()* function.

7. Again, the worker thread finds a work request on its work queue. When the worker thread finds that it has work to do, it gets the work item and processes it.

8. This time, the work request contains a pointer to the *Client*'s *IMFAsyncCallback* interface, which means that this time, the worker thread calls the *Client::Invoke()* method with the result of the work done in step 4.

Note Sometimes there is an additional step to the asynchronous operations. To extract advanced status information—something beyond an *HRESULT*—the asynchronous object may require the client to call a function such as *AsyncObject::EndAsyncCall()*. This call was omitted from this example for simplicity.

You need to make sure that both *Client* and *AsyncObject* are thread safe. Multiple threads will be executing inside of these components and will most likely be modifying various internal class variables. To avoid a race condition, you need to use some sort of thread synchronization mechanisms inside of the various functions of these classes. The sample functions shown in this chapter use the Active Template Library (ATL) synchronization mechanisms described in Appendix C.

This asynchronous pattern is used throughout the MF codebase. Though the pattern is more complex than basic synchronous calls, it is also far more useful in situations in which an operation can take significant time to complete. You will see several variations of this pattern later in this chapter.

Instead of manually doing the above steps each time, you can wrap them into a class or use one of the helper classes provided in MF. However, the classes in the AVF Source sample explicitly implement this functionality to demonstrate all of the intricacies of this pattern. For example, the *AVFSource* class uses this pattern to implement its play, pause, stop, and seek call behaviors.

Instantiating a Media Source

MF contains several mechanisms for discovering and instantiating a media source. Each of these methods is applicable and useful in different scenarios. The creation is broken out into several objects, each of which is responsible for a different stage of identifying the source of the data (for example, file versus HTTP stream), identifying the container format of the data stream, and instantiating the media source.

The actual process of creating a media source consists of several stages and varies depending on the actual capabilities of the source.

Some media sources receive their data from an intermediate byte stream object that abstracts the location and media loading details of the media data. Other sources load their data directly from some location or data stream, bypassing the need for a byte stream component. The actual steps and objects used to instantiate a source depend on the implementation of the specific source, and on the initial information or objects available.

Here are the methods that an MF application can use to instantiate a media source:

- Create an *IMFByteStream* object that loads the media data, and use the source resolver's *CreateObjectFromByteStream()* method to generate a source for that byte stream object.

- Use the source resolver's *CreateObjectFromURL()* method to parse a URL and figure out the URL scheme (protocol) specified in it. Internally, *CreateObjectFromURL()* creates a byte stream object and generates a source for it.

- Instantiate the media source directly as a well-known class or a COM component.

Most applications use the *IMFSourceResolver::CreateObjectFromURL()* function to create media sources. This function uses a several-stage process that creates the media source. The application creates a source resolver, and the source resolver creates a handler object for the protocol scheme specified in the URL, the protocol (scheme) handler object. The scheme handler instantiates an *IMFByteStream* object and creates a byte stream handler object, and that handler object finally creates the source. Here is a graphical representation of these steps.

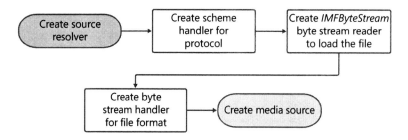

As an example, consider the algorithm used to instantiate a source for a file, given the following URL: *file:///C:/temp/AVF_wildlife.avf*.

1. The application instantiates a source resolver and passes the URL to its *CreateObjectFromURL()* method.

2. The source resolver parses the URL to discover the scheme (protocol) specified in it. For the file, the scheme will be *file:*.

3. The source resolver finds the class ID (CLSID) of the scheme handler object that knows about this protocol. Scheme handlers are objects that implement the *IMFSchemeHandler* interface and can create components for dealing with specific protocols—for example, for the http: protocol, the https: protocol, or the rtsp: protocol. Scheme-handler CLSIDs are stored in the registry under *HKLM\SOFTWARE\Microsoft\Windows Media Foundation\SchemeHandlers*.

4. The source resolver instantiates the scheme handler object with the CLSID found in the previous step and passes the URL to it.

5. The file scheme handler parses the URL and creates an *IMFByteStream* byte stream reader object for that file. This object will be used to load the file from disk.

6. The file scheme handler finds the CLSID for the byte stream handler that understands the file extension specified in the URL. Byte stream handlers are objects that implement the *IMFByteStreamHandler* interface—they can create sources for specific container formats such as .avi files, .mov files, .mp3 files, and so on. Their CLSIDs are stored in the registry under *HKLM\SOFTWARE\Microsoft\Windows Media Foundation\ByteStreamHandlers*.

7. The file scheme handler instantiates the byte stream handler object with the CLSID found in the previous step and passes it the byte stream object from step 5, as well as the file URL.

8. The byte stream handler instantiates and initializes a source that can handle the specified file.

In this section, you will see the implementation of a custom byte stream handler object registered for the .avf file extension. The custom byte stream handler is used by MF to discover the AVF media source and is required to instantiate a media source with the source resolver. Strictly speaking, you could avoid implementing the byte stream handler for your source by using applications that explicitly instantiate the AVF source. However, without a byte stream handler, only applications that are aware of the AVF files and know the CLSID of the AVF source will be able to instantiate this sample media source. Existing applications that use the source resolver will not be able to instantiate the media source.

Note The chapter does not show an implementation of scheme handlers, because conceptually they are nearly identical to byte stream handlers. The only time you would need to create a custom scheme handler is if you want to add support for a new protocol or a custom URL scheme. However, if you use a custom scheme handler, it could conceivably instantiate a source directly, removing the need for a byte stream handler.

CHAPTER 6   Media Foundation Sources   **147**

As previously mentioned, a byte stream handler is an object that implements the *IMFByteStreamHandler* interface and knows how to instantiate a source for a specific file extension or Multipurpose Internet Mail Extension (MIME) type. To associate a byte stream handler with a file extension, you need to add a registry entry that creates a mapping between the CLSID of the byte stream handler COM component and the file extension (or the MIME type) that the corresponding source can understand and process. The mappings between file extensions and byte stream handlers are stored in the standard MF registry location, in the *ByteStreamHandler* key. Therefore, to register the AVF byte stream handler to process .avf files, you must store its CLSID in the following location:

[HKEY_LOCAL_MACHINE\SOFTWARE\Microsoft\Windows Media Foundation\ByteStreamHandlers
\.avf]"{65085DC5-EB10-421B-943A-425F0CADBD0B}"="AVF Byte Stream Handler"

The handler registered here has the friendly name "AVF Byte Stream Handler," but this string is never used.

Tip Byte stream handlers are standard globally registered COM objects, and their CLSIDs need to be stored in the registry. MF needs this information to know which DLL file it has to load for the byte stream handler. Just like with the MFT shown in Chapter 5, "Media Foundation Transforms," to register the COM object in the AvfSource.dll, you can use the Windows regsvr32 utility from a command prompt running in the administrator context.

The main purpose of the byte stream handler is to create a media source object that understands and can parse some type of data stream. In essence, the byte stream handler is a class factory for your media source.

The source resolver looks for byte stream handlers and scheme handlers in the registry in the standard MF locations. There are actually two places where each handler can be registered—under *HKEY_CURRENT_USER\SOFTWARE\Microsoft\Windows Media Foundation* and under *HKEY_LOCAL_MACHINE\SOFTWARE\Microsoft\Windows Media Foundation*. The first location registers the handlers per user, and the second registers the handlers for all users on the machine.

The registry entries for scheme handlers are identical to the entries for the byte stream handlers. The key name for a scheme handler represents the scheme itself, and the CLSID of the scheme handler is stored under that key. For example, here are the registry entries for two *shttp:* scheme handlers—the source resolver will try first one and then the other handler if it encounters a URL with the secure HTTP protocol.

[HKEY_LOCAL_MACHINE\SOFTWARE\Microsoft\Windows Media Foundation\SchemeHandlers\shttp:]
"{CLSID1}"="Scheme Handler Description 1"
"{CLSID2}"="Scheme Handler Description 2"

Byte stream handlers must also verify that the data stream is actually in the expected format before returning a source. For instance, if the user renames an MP4 file, and gives it the .asf extension, the default ASF media source will not be able to parse the MP4 container format. The byte stream handler must detect that the stream is not in the expected container and return an error when asked to create a source for such a file. To do this, byte stream handlers preload several hundred bytes of the data stream and verify it, usually by sending it to their corresponding media source. If the media source does not return an error, the byte stream handler can be certain that the media source can parse this data. This functionality is essential if the user passes in the (ridiculously named) *MF_RESOLUTION_CONTENT_DOES_NOT_HAVE_TO_MATCH_EXTENSION_OR_MIME_TYPE* flag to the source resolver. In this case, the scheme handler will keep trying to find a source that will be happy with the data stream by passing it to every byte stream handler it finds under the *ByteStreamHandlers* registry key. The scheme handler will iterate through all of the byte stream handlers and ask them one by one if they understand this format. The first handler that claims to understand the file format will be returned by the source resolver.

> **Note** If a byte stream handler does not support the verification of the file format, then it will break the source resolver content resolution behavior. The source resolver relies on the byte stream handlers to notify it if the file they are given is not supported. If one of the byte stream handlers blindly accepts all file formats, then the source resolver will stop iterating through byte stream handlers early and will not try any others. In such a case, MF might stop working for many of the files with unexpected file extensions.

Unlike DirectShow source filters and MF hardware decoders, MF sources do not have merit values. Though you can have multiple byte stream handlers registered for the same extension or MIME type, you cannot specify which handler should be tried first. The only preference used with Media Foundation is that Microsoft media sources will always be tried first.

The AVF Byte Stream Handler

As mentioned earlier, the AVF source needs its own byte stream handler to allow the source resolver to create a source for AVF files. Each byte stream handler must implement the *IMFByteStreamHandler* interface. This interface is used to instantiate an MF source capable of parsing the data delivered by the passed-in byte stream.

In this case, the byte stream handler is ignoring the passed-in *IMFByteStream* object and relies instead on the URL parameter. This may fail in some situations, however, because the URL parameter is present mainly for information purposes, and can in fact be NULL. The actual behavior depends on the caller of the byte stream handler—the source resolver. This particular implementation will work with the default file scheme handler but may fail in other scenarios. Unfortunately, because this source does not use its own implementation of the AVI file parser the source relies on the VFW functions and needs a file URL to function. Therefore, this presents a special case that will not function with some other scheme handlers and applications that do not use scheme handlers and call the *IMFSourceResolver:: CreateObjectFromByteStream()* function directly.

As with most MF objects, the byte stream handler interface supports asynchronous instantiation. This is especially useful for creating sources for media that can block or take a long time to load. For example, if you are instantiating a source that will stream data from a network location, and the network suddenly becomes unavailable, source creation operation might not complete for a long time.

To handle these types of blocking conditions, *IMFByteStreamHandler* has the *BeginCreateObject()* and *EndCreateObject()* methods. The first one obviously begins object creation, and the second ends object creation and returns either a failure or the new source object. An application can therefore call the first method from the UI thread. After the source is created, the MF worker thread will call the *IMFAsyncCallback::Invoke()* method implemented by the byte stream handler, which will in turn cause the client of the byte stream handler to call the *EndCreateObject()* method.

Similarly, the *AVFSource* class also uses the asynchronous model to open the underlying file. Therefore, the client asynchronously creates the object with the byte stream handler, and the byte stream handler asynchronously opens the source.

Here is a diagram of the full source creation process. Of course, it skips most of the internal initialization of the source itself, but this should give you a better understanding of *AVFByteStreamHandler*'s asynchronous gyrations.

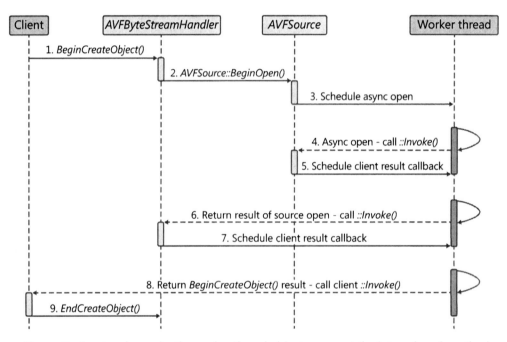

The vertical rectangles under the worker thread object represent the internal work method running in the worker thread. Here are all of these steps in more detail:

1. The client calls *BeginCreateObject()* on the byte stream handler.

2. The byte stream handler stores the client's *IMFAsyncCallback*, creates a new instance of an uninitialized *AVFSource* object, and calls the source's *BeginOpen()* method, passing in its own *IMFAsyncCallback* pointer. This way, when the media source is done opening, it will call back the byte stream handler.

3. *AVFSource::BeginOpen()* schedules work on itself, passing in a special operations object with the byte stream handler's *IMFAsyncCallback* pointer, as well as the URL of the file to open.

The operations object is part of the AVF Source sample and will be discussed in the following sections.

4. The worker thread discovers that it has work to do and calls the media source's *Invoke()* method, passing in the operations object created in step 3. The *AVFSource::Invoke()* method extracts the file URL from the passed-in operations object and opens a file. This is done on a separate thread in case the file open call blocks.

5. After the file open operation is completed, the *AVFSource::Invoke()* method gets the *AVFByteStreamHandler*'s *IMFAsyncCallback* pointer from the operations object and invokes it, scheduling callback to the byte stream handler.

6. The worker thread discovers that it has work to do, and calls the byte stream handler's *Invoke()* method. The *Invoke()* method gets the result of the media source's open operation. Note that the operation may have failed if the source received a path to a file that is not in the AVI format.

7. The *AVFByteStreamHandler::Invoke()* method extracts a locally saved pointer to its caller's *IMFAsyncCallback* interface and invokes it, to notify its client that the open operation is complete.

8. The worker thread discovers that it has work to do and calls the client's *Invoke()* method.

9. The client calls the *IMFByteStreamHandler::EndCreateObject()* to get the created media source.

As you can see, the byte stream handler implements the asynchronous pattern demonstrated in the earlier section. This asynchronous pattern is used twice here—first to call the byte stream handler asynchronously, and second to asynchronously open the underlying file specified by the URL. The second asynchronous operation is needed in case the open call blocks.

Here is the *AVFByteStreamHandler* implementation of the *BeginCreateObject()* function.

```
//
// Begin asynchronously creating and initializing the IMFByteStreamHandler object.
//
HRESULT AVFByteStreamHandler::BeginCreateObject(IMFByteStream *pByteStream, LPCWSTR pwszURL,
    DWORD dwFlags, IPropertyStore *pProps, IUnknown **ppIUnknownCancelCookie,
    IMFAsyncCallback *pCallback, IUnknown *punkState)
{
    HRESULT hr = S_OK;
    CComCritSecLock<CComAutoCriticalSection> lock(m_critSec);

    do
    {
        // Sanity check input arguments.
        BREAK_ON_NULL (pByteStream, E_POINTER);
        BREAK_ON_NULL (pCallback, E_POINTER);
        BREAK_ON_NULL (pwszURL, E_POINTER);

        // At this point the source should be NULL - otherwise multiple clients are trying
        // to create an AVFSource concurrently with the same byte stream handler - that is
        // not supported.
        if( m_pAVFSource != NULL)
```

```cpp
        {
            hr = E_UNEXPECTED;
            break;
        }

        // Verify that the caller is requesting the creation of a MediaSource object -
        // the AVFByteStreamHandler doesn't support other object types.
        if ((dwFlags & MF_RESOLUTION_MEDIASOURCE) == 0)
        {
            hr = E_INVALIDARG;
            break;
        }

        // Create an asynchronous result that will be used to indicate to the caller that
        // the source has been created.  The result is stored in a class member variable.
        hr = MFCreateAsyncResult(NULL, pCallback, punkState, &m_pResult);
        BREAK_ON_FAIL(hr);

        // New object - creation was not canceled, reset the cancel flag.
        m_objectCreationCanceled = false;

        // just return a pointer to the byte stream handler as the cancel cookie object
        if (ppIUnknownCancelCookie != NULL)
        {
            hr = this->QueryInterface(IID_IUnknown, (void**)ppIUnknownCancelCookie);
            BREAK_ON_FAIL(hr);
        }

        // create the main source worker object - the AVFSource
        hr = AVFSource::CreateInstance(&m_pAVFSource);
        BREAK_ON_FAIL(hr);

        // Begin source asynchronous open operation - tell the source to call this object
        // when it is done
        hr = m_pAVFSource->BeginOpen(pwszURL, this, NULL);
        BREAK_ON_FAIL(hr);
    }
    while(false);

    // if something failed, release all internal variables
    if(FAILED(hr))
    {
        SafeRelease(m_pAVFSource);
        m_pResult = NULL;
    }

    return hr;
}
```

This function demonstrates the implementation of *AsyncObject::BeginAsyncWork()* from the abstract example shown in the "The Asynchronous Call Pattern" section and corresponds to steps 1 and 2 shown in the diagram.

More Info The *CComPtr* object used here is a smart COM pointer defined in the ATL libraries. You can see a brief description of ATL in Appendix C. Similarly, the *CComCritSecLock* object is an ATL implementation of a smart critical section and is also described in Appendix C.

The function first checks some input parameters, stores some parameters given to it in internal variables, and creates an *IMFAsyncResult* object. This is the object that will be used later to notify the caller of the byte stream handler that the asynchronous operation is complete. The asynchronous result object is stored in the byte stream handler's member variable, which consequently means that the handler supports only one client at a time—it can notify only a single client that its work is complete.

After the parameters are all stored for later use, the *BeginCreateObject()* method creates an instance of the *AVFSource* class and tells it to start asynchronously opening the file specified in the URL. This is done by calling the *AVFSource::BeginOpen()* function. Note that *BeginOpen()* receives not just the URL but also a pointer to the byte stream handler's *IMFAsyncCallback* interface—this tells the media source who it should call when it is done opening the file.

The *BeginCreateObject()* method contains another parameter—the *ppIUnknownCancelCookie* pointer. This output parameter can be used to abort the creation operation. You might want to cancel the media source creation if the operation is taking a long time—for example, if this is a network source, and the network connection is down. By canceling the source creation, the caller application can avoid hanging. The caller application can call the *IMFByteStreamHandler::CancelObjectCreation()* method and pass in the same cookie that was returned from the *BeginCreateObject()* call, which serves as the ID of the creation operation. However, because *AVFByteStreamHandler* does not support concurrent clients, and each instance can create only a single media source at a time, the actual cookie value is not used in the handler.

After the media source is done opening the passed-in URL, it puts a new work item in the worker thread's queue with the passed-in *IMFAsyncCallbackPointer*. As soon as the worker thread detects a new work item on its queue, it calls the *Invoke()* method of the corresponding *IMFAsyncCallback* object—the *AVFByteStreamHandler*.

```
//
// Asynchronous worker function - called when the source has finished initializing.
//
HRESULT AVFByteStreamHandler::Invoke(IMFAsyncResult* pResult)
{
    HRESULT hr = S_OK;
    CComCritSecLock<CComAutoCriticalSection> lock(m_critSec);

    do
    {
        BREAK_ON_NULL(m_pResult, E_UNEXPECTED);

        // If object creation was canceled, just delete the AVFSource, and return E_ABORT.
        if(m_objectCreationCanceled)
```

```
        {
            m_objectCreationCanceled = false;
            hr = E_ABORT;

            // release the source - it will not be needed now
            m_pAVFSource->Release();
            m_pAVFSource = NULL;
        }
        else
        {
            // Call EndOpen to finish asynchronous open operation, and check for errors
            // during parsing.  If this failed, the HR will be stored in the result.
            hr = m_pAVFSource->EndOpen(pResult);
        }

        // Store the result of the operation.
        m_pResult->SetStatus(hr);

        // Call back the caller with the result.
        hr = MFInvokeCallback(m_pResult);

        // Release the result for the client - it has been used and is no longer needed.
        m_pResult = NULL;
    }
    while(false);

    return hr;
}
```

The code section just shown demonstrates the *Invoke()* implementation of an asynchronous object. It is equivalent to steps 4 and 5 as described in "The Asynchronous Call Pattern" earlier in this chapter.

The *Invoke()* method of most objects may be called for a number of reasons and needs to be able to do different things, depending on the parameters passed in and on the state of the object. For example, the *Invoke()* method of an object may be called to do asynchronous work inside of the object itself, or it may be called upon completion of some asynchronous request called on a different object. In this case, *AVFByteStreamHandler::Invoke()* will be called only after the media source is finished opening the underlying file. At this point, the asynchronous creation of the source is complete, and the *Invoke()* method is being called to notify the byte stream handler of the creation result.

As you can see, the *AVFByteStreamHandler::Invoke()* method first checks the *m_objectCreation-Canceled* member variable. This variable is set if the client called the *IMFByteStreamHandler::Cancel-ObjectCreation()* function to cancel the creation of the media source. If this Boolean variable is TRUE, the created media source is discarded. However, if it is not TRUE—if creation has not been canceled—then the byte stream handler gets the result of the open operation and schedules a call on its client. The byte stream uses the *MFInvokeCallback()* function to tell the worker thread to call the *IMFAsyncCallback* pointer stored in the *IMFAsyncResult* object that was created in *AVFByteStream-Handler::BeginCreateObject()*. This means that the worker thread will next call the client that originally initiated the *BeginCreateObject()* call. When the client is notified that the object has been created, it will call the *AVFByteStreamHandler::EndObjectCreation()* method to extract the source object created by the byte stream handler.

The following is the *AVFByteStreamHandler::EndObjectCreation()* function. This function is called by the byte stream handler's client to get the created media source—or to get the error code if media source creation failed.

```
//
// End asynchronously creating and initializing the IMFByteStreamHandler object
//
HRESULT AVFByteStreamHandler::EndCreateObject(IMFAsyncResult* pResult,
                                              MF_OBJECT_TYPE* pObjectType,
                                              IUnknown** ppObject)
{
    HRESULT hr = S_OK;

    do
    {
        CComCritSecLock<CComAutoCriticalSection> lock(m_critSec);

        // Sanity checks input arguments.
        BREAK_ON_NULL (pResult, E_POINTER);
        BREAK_ON_NULL (pObjectType, E_POINTER);
        BREAK_ON_NULL (ppObject, E_POINTER);
        BREAK_ON_NULL (m_pAVFSource, E_UNEXPECTED);

        // initialize output parameters - the object has not been created yet, so if there
        // is an error these output parameters will contain the right values
        *pObjectType = MF_OBJECT_INVALID;
        *ppObject = NULL;

        // Check to see if there is an error.
        hr = pResult->GetStatus();

        if(SUCCEEDED(hr))
        {
            // if we got here, result indicated success in creating the source - therefore
            // we can return a flag indicating that we created a source
            *pObjectType = MF_OBJECT_MEDIASOURCE;

            // Since the handler just created a media source, get the media source interface
            // from the underlying AVFSource helper object.
            hr = m_pAVFSource->QueryInterface(IID_IMFMediaSource, (void**)ppObject);
        }

        // whatever happens, make sure the source is in a good state by resetting internal
        // variables
        SafeRelease(m_pAVFSource);
        m_pResult = NULL;
        m_objectCreationCanceled = false;
    }
    while(false);

    return hr;
}
```

The operation of this function is fairly self explanatory. The function first checks the passed-in *IMFAsyncResult* object for an error. This is the same *IMFAsyncResult* that was sent over from the *AVFByteStreamHandler::Invoke()* function and contains the final result of the source open operation. Then, if the source creation succeeded, the function gets an *IUnknown* pointer to the source and stores it in the *ppObject* out parameter. Finally, the function releases and clears the internal variables of the byte stream handler.

The source creation can and must fail if the passed-in file is not in the AVI format. This is required to enable the source resolver to find the right media source for files with invalid or unexpected extensions.

Remember that *AVFByteStreamHandler* allows you to cancel object creation. A client can do that by calling the byte stream handler's *CancelObjectCreation()* method and passing in the special cookie object returned during the *BeginObjectCreation()* call. Here is the *AVFByteStreamHandler::CancelObjectCreation()* method implementation.

```
//
// Cancel the asynchronous object creation operation.
//
HRESULT AVFByteStreamHandler::CancelObjectCreation(IUnknown* pIUnknownCancelCookie)
{
    CComCritSecLock<CComAutoCriticalSection> lock(m_critSec);

    // if m_pResult is NULL, nobody is trying to create an object, and there is nothing to
    // cancel - return an error.  Otherwise, store the cancellation command.
    if(m_pResult == NULL)
    {
        return E_UNEXPECTED;
    }
    else
    {
        m_objectCreationCanceled = true;
        return S_OK;
    }
}
```

Though in some respects the *AVFByteStreamHandler:: CancelObjectCreation()* function is not very interesting, it is shown here for completeness. All this function does is store the intended cancellation in the *m_objectCreationCanceled* Boolean member variable. The *Invoke()* method will check this variable and either abandon the just-created media source or continue with the source creation, notifying the caller that the source is ready.

The *CancelObjectCreation()* function does not actually cancel anything, because the AVF Source uses the VFW interfaces to open the file. The VFW functions are synchronous and do not allow you to cancel the open operation. In other implementations, this method might actually stop or abort some asynchronous operation.

Media Foundation Events

Because of the asynchronous nature of Media Foundation, events play a crucial role in MF. The status of most asynchronous operations is reported through events. For example, if an *Invoke()* call fails for some reason, it usually signals its state in a standard *MEError* event sent through the *IMFMediaEventGenerator* interface. This event is then received by all objects registered to receive events from the media event generator object.

Any component that wants to send events inside of an MF topology needs to implement the *IMFMediaEventGenerator* interface. Because the source has a lot of events that it needs to fire—stream discovery, start and stop operations, end of stream—both the *IMFMediaSource* and *IMFMediaStream* interfaces inherit from the media event generator interface.

IMFMediaEventGenerator acts as an aggregator and sender of events. Some component stores events in the event generator queue, and the event generator pulls events from the queue and sends them to any consumers registered with it. Here is the list of key methods in the *IMFMediaEventGenerator* interface.

- **QueueEvent()**   The function that is used by various components to schedule events for transmission.
- **BeginGetEvent()**   The function used by clients to register for event receiving. You can see an example of the use of this function in Chapter 3.
- **EndGetEvent()**   The function used by clients to extract an event from the media event generator's queue. You can also see an example of the use of this function in Chapter 3.
- **GetEvent()**   This is a synchronous version of the *BeginGetEvent()* and *EndGetEvent()* functions. *GetEvent()* blocks and does not return until an event is available.

When some component wants to fire an event, it calls the media event generator's *QueueEvent()* method.

```
HRESULT QueueEvent(
        MediaEventType met,             // media event type
        REFGUID guidExtendedType,       // GUID_NULL or an extension GUID
        HRESULT hrStatus,               // status of the operation
        const PROPVARIANT* pvValue)     // a VARIANT with custom event value or NULL
```

Media events are often used to signal the result of some operation. In such a case, the *MediaEventType* parameter would contain the operation completion event, and the *hrStatus* would hold the result of the operation. If you use the event to signal some other conditions, just set the *hrStatus* parameter to S_OK. The *IMFMediaEventGenerator::QueueEvent()* method can also accept additional information in the *guidExtendedType* value to extend the event type, and the *pvValue* parameter with some extra pertinent information.

IMFMediaEventGenerator has three very similar methods for retrieving information from the event queue—*GetEvent()*, *BeginGetEvent()*, and *EndGetEvent()*. The *GetEvent()* method is a synchronous event extraction function, whereas the *BeginGetEvent()*, and *EndGetEvent()* methods pop an event from the queue asynchronously. Both of the event retrieval methods get an event from the event queue and return an *IMFMediaEvent* object.

```
//
// Begin processing an event from the event queue asynchronously
//
HRESULT MFMediaEventGenerator::BeginGetEvent(
        IMFAsyncCallback* pCallback,    // callback of the object interested in events
        IUnknown* punkState)            // an optional custom state object
{
    ...
}


//
// Complete asynchronous event processing
//
HRESULT MFMediaEventGenerator::EndGetEvent(
        IMFAsyncResult* pResult,        // asynchronous result received in invoke
        IMFMediaEvent** ppEvent)        // event to be extracted from the queue
{
    ...
}


//
// Synchronously retrieve the next event from the event queue
//
HRESULT MFMediaEventGenerator::GetEvent(
        DWORD dwFlags,                  // flag with the event behavior
        IMFMediaEvent** ppEvent)        // event extracted from the queue
{
    ...
}
```

BeginGetEvent() signals an event generator that a component wants to receive event notifications. Note that this function passes to the event generator the *IMFAsyncCallback* pointer to the object that is interested in events—this callback will be used to notify that object that a new event is ready. The function also receives a custom state object that can be any object implementing the *IUnknown* interface. This state object is associated with the event and can be retrieved by the caller of *BeginGetEvent()* after the *Invoke()* function has been called.

The *EndGetEvent()* function is the asynchronous counterpart of the *BeginGetEvent()* function. This is the actual function that retrieves the event from the event generator. This function passes in the *IMFAsyncResult* received as a parameter by the consumer's *::Invoke()* method and retrieves a pointer to the actual *IMFMediaEvent* object.

In essence, the media event generator operates in a similar manner to the *IMFByteStreamHandler* shown previously. It has a begin operation function that gives the worker object a callback to the client, and it has an end operation function that retrieves the result of the operation. Unlike the byte stream handler, however, the *IMFMediaEventGenerator* interface also supports synchronous operations. It exposes the synchronous *GetEvent()* method that allows the client to either try to get an event from the generator if one is available, or block waiting for the next event. This behavior is controlled by the *GetEvent()* parameter *dwFlags*. This parameter supports two values—if *dwFlags* is set to 0 (zero), then *GetEvent()* will block and will not return until the event generator has the next event. If the *dwFlags* parameter is set to *MF_EVENT_FLAG_NO_WAIT*, then the method will return immediately, either with the event or with the *MF_E_NO_EVENTS_AVAILABLE* error.

Most of the time, you won't need to implement your own event generator. Instead, you can use an event generator provided by MF, and pass all the calls to an *IMFEventGenerator* object created by the *MFCreateEventQueue()* function.

Additional details about the MF event system are provided in the "Source Media Event Functions" section later in this chapter.

The Media Foundation Source

As you saw in the diagram at the beginning of this chapter, the AVF source object consists of three major parts—the *AVFSource* object, which implements the *IMFMediaSource* interface; the helper *AVIFileParser* class, which parses the files and extracts individual samples from them; and a set of *AVFStream* objects that pass the actual samples to any connected MF components. The main driving component of that ensemble is the *AVFSource* object. This is the component that initializes the file parser and the stream objects and passes the samples from the parser to the stream objects. It also exposes methods that allow MF to control the media source, passing it commands such as start, stop, and pause.

The following list breaks down all of the major functions of the *AVFSource* object by category. First are the command functions exposed by the *IMFMediaSource* interface. These functions are used to start and control playback of the source.

- **IMFMediaSource::Start()**   The function that starts playback. This function receives the presentation descriptor that describes which streams should be active, as well as the starting point within the file where the media source should start playing. This method also allows you to seek within the file by pausing playback and passing a new start position with the *Start()* method.

- **IMFMediaSource::Pause()**   The function that pauses playback.

- **IMFMediaSource::Stop()**   The function that stops playback.

Next are the functions that allow you to initialize and shut down the source:

- **IMFMediaSource::CreatePresentationDescriptor()**   Used to create an object that describes the data streams in the file. The presentation descriptor can also be used to indicate which of the streams should be active during playback. This is the same object that needs to be passed into the *Start()* method mentioned previously.

- **IMFMediaSource::GetCharacteristics()**   Retrieves a set of flags that provide the characteristics and capabilities of the source.

- **IMFMediaSource::Shutdown()**   Gracefully shuts down the source.

The *IMFMediaSource* interface inherits from the *IMFMediaEventGenerator* interface. The source needs the event generator interface to send out events signaling the state of the playback. Here are the media event generator functions implemented by the source:

- **IMFMediaEventGenerator::BeginGetEvent()**   Starts asynchronous event retrieval

- **IMFMediaEventGenerator::EndGetEvent()**   Ends asynchronous event retrieval and returns a new event

- **IMFMediaEventGenerator::GetEvent()**   Synchronously retrieves an event from the media event generator

- **IMFMediaEventGenerator::QueueEvent()**   Used to add a new event to the queue that will later be sent out to the clients of the media event generator

The *AVFSource* object contains many other internal functions, but these are the major public methods that are exposed to the clients of the source. The following sections will examine these methods in greater detail, thereby giving you a greater understanding of the source functionality.

Initializing the Source

During playback, the MF session requests samples from the individual *IMFMediaStream* objects, which in turn get their samples from *IMFMediaSource*. Before that can happen, however, the source needs to be initialized—it must discover the underlying elementary data streams in the file and instantiate the corresponding stream objects that implement the *IMFMediaStream* interface. For example, if the file has one video and two audio streams, the source needs to instantiate and expose three media stream objects to the session.

AVFSource performs this initialization inside of the asynchronous *OnParseHeader()* function that is triggered from the source's *BeginOpen()* method. *BeginOpen()* is in turn called by the byte stream handler as part of the creation of the source itself. The *BeginOpen()* function is not very interesting, because all it does is trigger work on the main object by calling the *MFPutWorkItem()* method and passing it a pointer to the *AVFSource* object.

```
//
// Begin the asynchronous open operation
//
HRESULT AVFSource::BeginOpen(LPCWSTR pwszURL, IMFAsyncCallback* pCallback,
    IUnknown* pUnkState)
{
    HRESULT hr = S_OK;
    CComCritSecLock<CComAutoCriticalSection> lock(m_critSec);
    CComPtr<IMFAsyncResult> pResult;
    CComPtr<ISourceOperation> pOperation;

    do
    {
        // Pack the needed arguments into an AsyncResult object
        hr = MFCreateAsyncResult(NULL, pCallback, pUnkState, &pResult);
        BREAK_ON_FAIL(hr);

        // create a new SourceOperation object with the Open command
        pOperation = new (std::nothrow) SourceOperation(SourceOperationOpen, pwszURL,
                pResult);
        BREAK_ON_NULL (pOperation, E_OUTOFMEMORY);

        // Submit the request into the background thread
        hr = MFPutWorkItem(MFASYNC_CALLBACK_QUEUE_STANDARD, this, pOperation);
        BREAK_ON_FAIL(hr);
    }
    while(false);

    return hr;
}
```

AVFSource::BeginOpen() is a fairly simple function—it creates an *IMFAsyncResult* object that hold the caller's *IMFAsyncCallback* interface, creates a special *SourceOperation* object that holds the open parameters, and then schedules work on the *AVFSource* object, with the operation object as a state variable. The *SourceOperation* class is simply a COM object that holds several variables used to pass information and commands between threads. You can think of it as a structure with values inside of it—a structure that just happens to also implement a COM interface.

> **Note** The *new (std::nothrow)* operator shown here is used to ensure that the *new* operation does not throw an exception. This greatly simplifies the code and allows you to check for *NULL* instead of setting up *try-catch* blocks and dealing with exceptions. In addition, MF is not designed to work with exceptions and will not be able to gracefully handle exceptions thrown during execution. MF does not catch exceptions and will unexpectedly fail if an exception is thrown and not caught by the component.

Here is the corresponding *AVFSource::Invoke()* function that's called when the worker thread needs to perform some work on the source.

```cpp
//
// Do an asynchronous task - execute a queued command (operation).
//
HRESULT AVFSource::Invoke(IMFAsyncResult* pResult)
{
    HRESULT hr = S_OK;
    CComPtr<IMFAsyncResult> pAsyncResult = pResult;
    CComPtr<IMFAsyncResult> pCallerResult;
    CComPtr<ISourceOperation> pCommand;
    CComPtr<IUnknown> pState;

    do
    {
        CComCritSecLock<CComAutoCriticalSection> lock(m_critSec);

        // Get the state object associated with this asynchronous call
        hr = pAsyncResult->GetState(&pState);
        BREAK_ON_FAIL(hr);

        // QI the IUnknown state variable for the ISourceOperation interface
        hr = pState->QueryInterface(IID_ISourceOperation, (void**)&pCommand);
        BREAK_ON_FAIL(hr);

        // Make sure the source is not shut down - if the source is shut down, just exit

        hr = CheckShutdown();
        BREAK_ON_FAIL(hr);

        // figure out what the requested command is, and then dispatch it to one of the
        // internal handler objects
        switch (pCommand->Type())
        {
            case SourceOperationOpen:
                hr = InternalOpen(pCommand);
                break;
            case SourceOperationStart:
                hr = InternalStart(pCommand);
                break;
            case SourceOperationStop:
                hr = InternalStop();
                break;
            case SourceOperationPause:
                hr = InternalPause();
                break;
            case SourceOperationStreamNeedData:
                hr = InternalRequestSample();
                break;
            case SourceOperationEndOfStream:
                hr = InternalEndOfStream();
                break;
        }
    }
    while(false);

    return hr;
}
```

Because the *Invoke()* function can be called for all sorts of reasons, it needs a way to figure out why it was called. In this case, the reason for the call—the command that the *Invoke()* function is supposed to execute—is stored in a state object attached to the passed-in *IMFAsyncResult* object.

> **Note** The *SourceOperation* class is a helper COM object that is used to pass different variables between threads. The object is a very basic container that has very little functionality. The class implements the COM *IUnknown* interface and the *ISourceOperation* interface that extracts the variables stored in the object. It has to be a COM object because it must be passed inside of *IMFAsyncResult* objects. You can see a readout of the *SourceOperation* class and the *ISourceOperation* interface at the end of this chapter.

Therefore, the *Invoke()* function extracts the *SourceOperation* object from *IMFAsyncResult*, figures out the operation type, and calls the appropriate helper function. If the command asks to start the source, the *Invoke()* method calls *AVFSource::InternalStart()*. If the command asks to pause the source, the *Invoke()* method calls *AVFSource::InternalPause()*.

> **Note** As you may have noticed, the *Invoke()* method calls the *CheckShutdown()* helper function. This function is used to verify that the source is in a good state—it simply verifies that the *AVFSource::m_state* member variable is not set to *SourceStateShutdown*.

During initialization, the command will hold the *SourceOperationOpen* enumeration value—this will cause the *Invoke()* method to call the *InternalOpen()* helper method.

```
//
// Initialize the underlying AVFFileParser, and open the file in the operation object.
//
HRESULT AVFSource::InternalOpen(ISourceOperation* pOp)
{
    HRESULT hr = S_OK;
    CComCritSecLock<CComAutoCriticalSection> lock(m_critSec);
    WCHAR* pUrl = NULL;
    CComPtr<ISourceOperation> pOperation = pOp;
    CComPtr<IMFAsyncResult> pCallerResult;

    do
    {
        BREAK_ON_NULL(pOperation, E_UNEXPECTED);

        // Get the async result that will be sent once the open operation is complete.
        hr = pOperation->GetCallerAsyncResult(&pCallerResult);
        BREAK_ON_FAIL(hr);
        BREAK_ON_NULL(pCallerResult, E_UNEXPECTED);

        // get the file URL from the operation
        pUrl = pOperation->GetUrl();
        BREAK_ON_NULL(pUrl, E_UNEXPECTED);
```

```
            // Create the AVI parser
            hr = AVIFileParser::CreateInstance(pUrl, &m_pAVIFileParser);
            BREAK_ON_FAIL(hr);

            // parse the file header and instantiate the individual stream objects
            hr = ParseHeader();
        }
        while(false);

        // return the result whether we succeeded or failed
        if(pCallerResult != NULL)
        {
            // Store the result of the initialization operation in the caller result.
            pCallerResult->SetStatus(hr);

            // Notify the caller of the BeginOpen() method that the open is complete.
            MFInvokeCallback(pCallerResult);
        }

        return hr;
    }
```

As you saw earlier, the *AVFSource::BeginOpen()* method stores the file URL in the *SourceOperation* object. That object is passed through the worker thread to the *Invoke()* method, which in turn sends it to the *InternalOpen()* method. *InternalOpen()* extracts that URL and passes it to the helper *AVFFileParser* class. This is done on a separate thread in case the open operation takes too long and blocks for some reason.

After the *InternalOpen()* method is done with initialization, it stores the result of the operation in the *IMFAsyncResult* object for the client and invokes the callback.

Finally, when the client receives a notification that the media source has been created, it calls the *AVFSource::EndOpen()* method.

```
//
// End the asynchronous open operation
//
HRESULT AVFSource::EndOpen(IMFAsyncResult* pAsyncResult)
{
    HRESULT hr = S_OK;

    do
    {
        BREAK_ON_NULL (pAsyncResult, E_POINTER);

        hr = pAsyncResult->GetStatus();
    }
    while(false);

    return hr;
}
```

EndOpen() simply gets the result of the operation that was stored in the asynchronous result by the *InternalOpen()* method. This step is, strictly speaking, not necessary, but it follows the asynchronous method convention, again demonstrating the asynchronous pattern.

Finally, here is the *AVFSource::ParseHeader()* method that is called from the *InternalOpen()* function. This helper method calls several private functions needed to initialize the media stream objects.

```
//
// Parse the file header of the current file
//
HRESULT AVFSource::ParseHeader(void)
{
    HRESULT hr = S_OK;

    do
    {
        // Sanity checks against input arguments.
        BREAK_ON_NULL (m_pAVIFileParser, E_UNEXPECTED);

        // Parse the AVI file header.
        hr = m_pAVIFileParser->ParseHeader();
        BREAK_ON_FAIL(hr);

        // Create the individual streams from the presentation descriptor
        hr = InternalCreatePresentationDescriptor();
        BREAK_ON_FAIL(hr);
    }
    while(false);

    // if the header was successfully parsed, and if the streams have been created,
    // update the internal state variables
    if (SUCCEEDED(hr))
    {
        m_state = SourceStateStopped;
    }

    return hr;
}
```

The *ParseHeader()* method first tells the *AVIFileParser* to scan through the AVI header of the file and determine the number and type of elementary streams in the file. Then, after the parser has determined the structure of the AVI file, the source generates the individual *IMFMediaStream* objects for the audio and video streams in the file. This is done in the *AVFSource::InternalCreatePresentationDescriptor()* function.

Creating a Presentation Descriptor

In Media Foundation, data streams that should be rendered at the same time are grouped together into an object called a *presentation*. A presentation is an object that describes a set of data streams with the same presentation time that must be synchronized among each other. Presentation information is stored in objects that implement the *IMFPresentationDescriptor* interface. *IMFPresentationDescriptor* offers the ability to select (activate) or deselect (deactivate) streams, extract the number of streams in a presentation, and access individual streams.

The presentation descriptor object contains several stream descriptor objects—one for each media stream object. The stream descriptor objects implement the *IMFStreamDescriptor* interface that allows client applications and components to determine the media type for the stream. Here is a diagram that shows the relationship between the presentation descriptor, the stream descriptors, and the media stream objects.

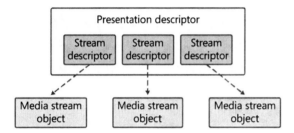

The stream descriptors are stored in the presentation descriptor. Each stream descriptor is associated with a media stream object.

A media source can have only one presentation at a time; however, presentations can change during playback. To change the current presentation while the media is playing, the media source needs to do the following:

1. Send the *MEEndOfStream* event for each stream in the current presentation.
2. Send the *MEEndOfPresentation* event to signal the end of the current presentation.
3. Create a new presentation with all of its streams.
4. Send the *MENewPresentation* event for the new presentation to notify MF that a new presentation is available.

The *InternalCreatePresentationDescriptor()* function shown in this section serves two purposes—it initializes the individual media stream objects that will provide data to the rest of the MF topology, and it creates a presentation that describes those stream objects. As a result, this function is quite large and will be shown in two parts.

The first part of the *AVFSource::InternalCreatePresentationDescriptor()* function validates the state of the source, creates the audio and video stream descriptors, and constructs the presentation descriptor itself. The second part of the function initializes the media stream objects and configures the presentation descriptor.

Here is the first section of the *InternalCreatePresentationDescriptor()* method.

```cpp
//
// Create the presentation descriptor object
//
HRESULT AVFSource::InternalCreatePresentationDescriptor(void)
{
    HRESULT hr = S_OK;
    CComCritSecLock<CComAutoCriticalSection> lock(m_critSec);

    IMFStreamDescriptor* streamDescriptors[2];

    do
    {
        BREAK_ON_NULL (m_pAVIFileParser, E_POINTER);

        // make sure this is a supported file format
        if (!m_pAVIFileParser->IsSupportedFormat())
        {
            hr = MF_E_INVALID_FORMAT;
            break;
        }

        // create a video stream descriptor if there is video in the file
        hr = CreateVideoStream(&(streamDescriptors[m_mediaStreams.size()]));
        BREAK_ON_FAIL(hr);

        // create an audio stream descriptor if there is audio in the file
        hr = CreateAudioStream(&(streamDescriptors[m_mediaStreams.size()]));
        BREAK_ON_FAIL(hr);

        // if we got here, we have successfully created at a stream descriptor for the audio
        // stream (if there is one), and a video stream (if the file has video).  Now create
        // the presentation descriptor which will hold the stream descriptors.
        hr = MFCreatePresentationDescriptor(
                    (DWORD)m_mediaStreams.size(),     // number of streams created
                    streamDescriptors,                // array of stream descriptors
                    &m_pPresentationDescriptor);      // get the presentation descriptor
        BREAK_ON_FAIL(hr);
```

The audio and video stream objects, as well as their corresponding stream descriptors, are created in the *CreateVideoStream()* and *CreateAudioStream()* helper functions. These functions will be covered in the next section. After the streams are initialized—and their stream descriptors are stored in the *streamDescriptors* array—the function creates the presentation descriptor. The presentation descriptor combines all of the stream descriptors in a single package that will later be used by the *AVFSource* client. The presentation descriptor is, of course, created by calling the appropriately named *MFCreatePresentationDescriptor()* function.

Because *AVFSource* is designed to play only one video stream and one audio stream, the function uses a single two-member array of stream descriptor pointers—*streamDescriptors*. The indexes into the stream array are always dynamic, however, and correspond to the number of media stream objects that have been created and stored in the *m_mediaStreams* vector. Both *CreateVideoStream()* and *CreateAudioStream()* methods add the newly created streams into the *m_mediaStreams* vector.

Therefore, there is always a one-to-one correlation between stream descriptors and media stream objects, and *m_mediaStreams.size()* will have the same value as the index of the next stream to be inserted into the array.

After the *InternalCreatePresentationDescriptor()* function has created the stream descriptors, it initializes the presentation descriptor and activates all of the streams.

```
        // activate all of the streams in the beginning - that's their default state
        for (DWORD i = 0; i < m_mediaStreams.size(); i++)
        {
            hr = m_pPresentationDescriptor->SelectStream(i);
            BREAK_ON_FAIL(hr);
        }
        BREAK_ON_FAIL(hr);

        // get the duration of the file from the AVI file parser
        LONGLONG fileDuration = m_pAVIFileParser->Duration();

        // set the file duration on the presentation descriptor - length of the file
        // in 100-ns units
        hr = m_pPresentationDescriptor->SetUINT64(MF_PD_DURATION, (UINT64)(fileDuration));
    }
    while(false);

    // all of the stream descriptors have now been stored in the presentation descriptor -
    // therefore release all of the stream descriptor pointers we have left over
    for (DWORD i = 0; i < m_mediaStreams.size(); i++)
    {
        SafeRelease(streamDescriptors[i]);
    }

    return hr;
}
```

This code section shows how the *InternalCreatePresentationDescriptor()* function marks all of the streams in the presentation descriptor as active. This is done by going through a loop and calling *IMFPresentationDescriptor::SelectStream()* with an index of each of the streams. The index corresponds to how the individual streams are stored internally in the presentation descriptor. The last part of the presentation descriptor creation is initialization of the file duration attribute stored in the presentation descriptor. The function gets the file duration from the AVI file parser and stores it in the presentation descriptor under the *MF_PD_DURATION* attribute GUID.

Creating Media Stream Objects

AVFSource creates several *IMFMediaStream* objects during initialization. These objects are used to pipe samples from the file into the MF components connected to the source. AVFSource uses two helper functions to perform the stream creation and initialization: *AVFSource::CreateVideoStream()* and *AVFSource::CreateAudioStream()*. These functions are virtually identical to each other, differing only by a couple of internal calls.

Here is the *CreateVideoStream()* helper function.

```cpp
//
// Create the video stream and return the corresponding stream descriptor
//
HRESULT AVFSource::CreateVideoStream(IMFStreamDescriptor** ppStreamDescriptor)
{
    HRESULT hr = S_OK;

    IMFMediaType* pMediaType = NULL;
    AVFStream* pAVFStream = NULL;

    do
    {
        // if the file has a video stream, create an AVFStream object and a stream
        // descriptor for it
        if (m_pAVIFileParser->HasVideo())
        {
            CComPtr<IMFMediaTypeHandler> pHandler;

            // get the media type for the video stream
            hr = m_pAVIFileParser->GetVideoMediaType(&pMediaType);
            BREAK_ON_FAIL(hr);

            // create the stream descriptor
            hr = MFCreateStreamDescriptor(
                    m_mediaStreams.size()+1,   // stream ID
                    1,                         // number of media types
                    &pMediaType,               // media type for the stream
                    ppStreamDescriptor);       // get the descriptor
            BREAK_ON_FAIL(hr);

            // get a media type handler for the stream
            hr = (*ppStreamDescriptor)->GetMediaTypeHandler(&pHandler);
            BREAK_ON_FAIL(hr);

            // set current type of the stream visible to source users
            hr = pHandler->SetCurrentMediaType(pMediaType);
            BREAK_ON_FAIL(hr);

            // Create AVFStream object that is implementing the IMFMediaStream interface
            hr = AVFStream::CreateInstance(&pAVFStream, this, *ppStreamDescriptor);
            BREAK_ON_FAIL(hr);

            // tell the AVFStream object that it's a video stream
            pAVFStream->SetVideoStream();

            // store the stream in a vector for later reuse
            EXCEPTION_TO_HR( m_mediaStreams.push_back(pAVFStream) );          }
    }
    while(false);

    SafeRelease(pMediaType);

    return hr;
}
```

The *CreateVideoStream()* function queries *AVIParser* for the information about the video stream and initializes its corresponding stream descriptor and *AVFStream* object. The main piece of information extracted from the parser is the media type of the data stream. *AVIParser* parses this information out of the AVI file header. After the method discovers the media type, it creates the stream descriptor with the provided media type as one of the supported stream media types. Remember that some sources and MFTs can support multiple output media types. This is, of course, not true in this scenario, because AVFSource cannot transcode the video data on the fly, which is why the stream descriptor is initialized with only one media type.

After creation of the stream descriptor, the *CreateVideoStream()* method instantiates the *IMFMediaStream* object that will be used to actually pass data to MFTs connected to the source. The *AVFStream* object is initialized with its corresponding stream descriptor, after which the object is stored in the internal *AVFSource::m_mediaStreams* vector.

Note Some applications are written to be independent from Media Foundation source implementation and assume that media stream object IDs are equivalent to the IDs of data streams in source files. For example, some applications assume that the media stream with an ID of 0 coming from an ASF file will contain ASF file metadata. For that reason, it is a good idea to ensure that media stream object IDs are never 0, and instead begin with 1. That is why the *CreateVideoStream()* method adds a 1 to *m_mediaStreams.size()* when creating a new stream descriptor by calling the *MFCreateStreamDescriptor()* function.

After *AVFSource* has instantiated all of the stream objects and initialized the presentation descriptor, its initialization is complete. When the presentation descriptor and stream construction functions return and control reverts back to the *Invoke()* method, the source signals its client (the byte stream handler) that the creation is complete.

Note The function uses the *EXCEPTION_TO_HR()* macro to wrap a *try-catch* block. This block is necessary because *m_mediaStreams* is a Standard Template Library (STL) vector, and can therefore throw exceptions. The macro catches the exceptions and converts them to *HRESULT* values.

The only difference between the *CreateVideoStream()* and *CreateAudioStream()* functions is in the media types of the streams they create. *CreateVideoStream()* uses the *AVIFileParser::GetVideoMediaType()* method to extract the video media type and the *AVFStream::SetVideoMediaType()* method to set that media type on the stream object that will deliver video samples. Similarly, *CreateAudioStream()* uses the *AVIFileParser::GetAudioMediaType()* method to extract the audio media type and the *AVFStream::SetAudioMediaType()* method to set that media type on the audio stream object. Because these two functions are so similar, the *CreateAudioStream()* method will not be shown in this chapter.

Asynchronous Source Command Functions

Like most MF operations, the main command functions in the *AVFSource* class are asynchronous. The *AVFSource* command functions operate on the same principle as the byte stream handler shown previously. They queue work events and rely on the worker thread to do the actual work by calling the source's *Invoke()* function.

As you saw earlier when we discussed the media source open operation, *AVFSource* uses a special state object that can be inserted into *IMFAsyncResult* to indicate the asynchronous command. The *AVFSource::Invoke()* function extracts the command from the passed-in asynchronous result object, parses the command, and executes it.

All of the media source control functions are also implemented as asynchronous commands. For example, here is the *IMFMediaSource::Pause()* implementation in *AVFSource*.

```
//
// Pause the source
//
HRESULT AVFSource::Pause()
{
    HRESULT hr = S_OK;
    CComCritSecLock<CComAutoCriticalSection> lock(m_critSec);
    CComPtr<ISourceOperation> pOperation;

    do
    {
        // make sure the source is not shut down
        hr = CheckShutdown();
        BREAK_ON_FAIL(hr);

        // create a new SourceOperationType command
        pOperation = new (std::nothrow) SourceOperation(SourceOperationPause);
        BREAK_ON_NULL (pOperation, E_OUTOFMEMORY);

        // put the command on the work queue
        hr = MFPutWorkItem(
            MFASYNC_CALLBACK_QUEUE_STANDARD,          // work queue to use
            this,                                      // IMFAsyncCallback object to call
            static_cast<IUnknown*>(pOperation));       // state variable - the command
        BREAK_ON_FAIL(hr);
    }
    while(false);

    return hr;
}
```

This public *Pause()* method does very little because it is only an external asynchronous trigger for an internal version of the pause function. In effect, it is equivalent to the *AsyncObject::BeginAsyncCall()* shown previously in the "The Asynchronous Call Pattern" section. As such, the function executes very quickly and returns to the caller—usually the application UI—without holding up the process.

As you can see, *Pause()* first checks to make sure that the source is not shut down, and then it queues an operation object on the work queue. *SourceOperation* is simply a COM object that serves as a container for various commands and parameters that need to be passed to the internal asynchronous function. In this case, the operation object is initialized with the *SourceOperationPause* enumeration constant—this tells the *AVFSource::Invoke()* function that it needs to call the internal version of the pause method. After the operation object has been instantiated, it is then put on the work queue with the now-familiar *MFPutWorkItem()* function.

As soon as the worker thread detects that there is a new work item on the worker queue, it calls the corresponding *IMFAsyncCallback* method. The *Pause()* function passed in *this* as the *IMFAsyncCallback* pointer—therefore, the worker thread calls the *AVFSource::Invoke()* method.

Because the original source command queued was *SourceOperationPause*, *Invoke()* calls the *InternalPause()* method.

```
//
// Internal implementation of the pause command - needed to asynchronously handle pause
//
HRESULT AVFSource::InternalPause(void)
{
    HRESULT hr = S_OK;

    do
    {
        // if the source is not started, it cannot be paused
        if (m_state != SourceStateStarted)
        {
            hr = MF_E_INVALID_STATE_TRANSITION;
            break;
        }

        // go through every stream, and if it is active, send a pause command to it
        for (DWORD x = 0; x < m_mediaStreams.size(); x++)
        {
            AVFStream* pStream = NULL;

            pStream = m_mediaStreams[x];
            BREAK_ON_FAIL(hr);
            BREAK_ON_NULL(pStream, E_UNEXPECTED);

            if (pStream->IsActive())
            {
                hr = pStream->Pause();
                BREAK_ON_FAIL(hr);
            }
        }
        BREAK_ON_FAIL(hr);

        // update the internal state variable
        m_state = SourceStatePaused;
    }
```

```
    while(false);

    // fire an event indicating status of the operation
    m_pEventQueue->QueueEventParamVar(MESourcePaused, GUID_NULL, hr, NULL);

    return hr;
}
```

Conceptually, *InternalPause()* is not complicated. It goes through every stream that is currently active in the source and passes it the *Pause()* command. Because all streams are stored in the *m_mediaStreams* Standard Template Library (STL) vector, this operation is identical to enumerating through an array of *AVFStream* pointers. When all of the streams have been paused, the method sets the internal source state to *SourceStatePaused* and fires an event to any listeners indicating that the paused state has been reached.

Background The STL vector is a helper object that is part of the Standard Template Library. This object is essentially a dynamic array implementation. The vector has methods that allow you to quickly add and remove items to it, without worrying about reallocation of the underlying data type. The vector object also overloads the array subscript operator (opening and closing brackets, []), which gives you the ability to treat the vector as a smart array. *AVFSource* uses the vector to hold the list of the streams exposed by the source.

The following illustration is a conceptual diagram of this chain of calls that is used to trigger an asynchronous command.

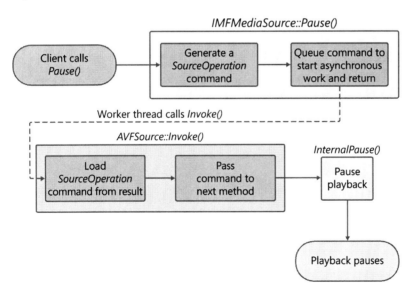

The asynchronous command dispatch steps are as follows:

1. A client calls the *IMFMediaSource::Pause()* method in *AVFSource*.

2. The *Pause()* method generates a new *SourceOperation* object with the pause command inside of it.

3. The *Pause()* method queues a work request together with the *SourceOperation* command object. This triggers an asynchronous call to the *AVFSource::Invoke()* method. The asynchronous call is represented by the arrow with a dashed line.

4. The *Invoke()* method loads the *SourceOperation* object back from the *IMFAsyncResult* it receives as a parameter.

5. The *Invoke()* method calls *AVFSource::InternalPause()*.

6. *InternalPause()* pauses playback.

This long 6-step procedure is necessary to asynchronously trigger various behaviors in the source. The other asynchronous command methods of *AVFSource* are implemented identically—they instantiate a new *SourceOperation* object, add any pertinent parameters to it, and then fire the event that triggers asynchronous operation together with the command object.

The only difference between the sequence of calls made to pause the source and to stop it is in the function names, and in the function call being passed to each individual stream in the source. Whereas the pause command sends *AVFStream::Pause()* calls to each of the active streams, stop sends *AVFStream::Stop()* calls to the active streams. Therefore, because the implementation of *AVFStream::Stop()* is nearly identical to *Pause()*, it is omitted from this text.

Starting Playback

The source's *IMFMediaSource::Start()* implementation is slightly more complicated, however. The public version of the method differs primarily in the fact that the start command requires several extra parameters. This means that these extra parameters must be inserted into the source command object before the command is placed on the work queue.

```
//
// Start playback at the specified time
//
HRESULT AVFSource::Start(IMFPresentationDescriptor* pPresentationDescriptor,
            const GUID* pguidTimeFormat,            // format of the following time variable
            const PROPVARIANT* pvarStartPosition)   // stream time where to start playback
{
    HRESULT hr = S_OK;
    bool isSeek = false;
    CComPtr<ISourceOperation> pOperation;
```

```cpp
do
{
    CComCritSecLock<CComAutoCriticalSection> lock(m_critSec);

    BREAK_ON_NULL (pvarStartPosition, E_INVALIDARG);
    BREAK_ON_NULL (pPresentationDescriptor, E_INVALIDARG);

    // The IMFMediaSource::Start() function can support various time formats for input,
    // but this implementation supports only the default version - time indicated in
    // 100-ns units
    if ((pguidTimeFormat != NULL) && (*pguidTimeFormat != GUID_NULL))
    {
        hr = MF_E_UNSUPPORTED_TIME_FORMAT;
        break;
    }

    // make sure we have the start time in the pvarStartPosition PROPVARIANT structure
    if ((pvarStartPosition->vt != VT_I8) && (pvarStartPosition->vt != VT_EMPTY))
    {
        hr = MF_E_UNSUPPORTED_TIME_FORMAT;
        break;
    }

    // make sure the source is not shut down
    hr = CheckShutdown();
    BREAK_ON_FAIL(hr);

    // make sure the source is initialized
    hr = IsInitialized();
    BREAK_ON_FAIL(hr);

    // figure out whether the caller is trying to seek or to just start playback
    if (pvarStartPosition->vt == VT_I8)
    {
        if (m_state != SourceStateStopped)
        {
            isSeek = true;
        }
    }

    // create the new command that will tell us to start playback
    pOperation = new (std::nothrow) SourceOperation(
        SourceOperationStart,               // store command type - start command
        pPresentationDescriptor);           // store presentation descriptor param
    BREAK_ON_NULL(pOperation, E_OUTOFMEMORY);

    // set the internal information in the new command
    hr = pOperation->SetData(*pvarStartPosition, isSeek);
    BREAK_ON_FAIL(hr);
```

```
        // queue the start command work item
        hr = MFPutWorkItem(
            MFASYNC_CALLBACK_QUEUE_STANDARD,        // work queue to use
            this,                                    // IMFAsyncCallback object to call
            static_cast<IUnknown*>(pOperation));    // state variable - the command
        BREAK_ON_FAIL(hr);
    }
    while(false);

    return hr;
}
```

This code sample demonstrates how the *Start()* method operates. The *IMFMediaSource::Start()* function first checks to see if this is a seek command or if the caller wants to start playback. If the *AVFSource* object is stopped, then the caller is trying to start playback. If the source is not stopped, then this must be a seek request.

After the function determines the type of request, it again constructs a *SourceOperation* object that will hold information about the command. In this case, the command object contains not just the command type—*SourceOperationStart*—but also the passed-in presentation descriptor, the start position, and a Boolean variable indicating whether this is a seek request. The presentation descriptor passed into the *Start()* method tells the source which streams must be activated, and the start position indicates where to start playback relative to the beginning of the stream. The start position is given inside the *PROPVARIANT* structure, in 100-nanosecond time units.

> **Note** A *PROPVARIANT* is a structure that can contain virtually any type of variable—from a character to a 64-bit integer. This structure is often used in COM to pass around values of unknown size and type. In this case, the *PROPVARIANT* is supposed to contain a VT_I8 (variable-type integer of 8 bytes); this way the variable is large enough to contain 100-nanosecond intervals without overflowing.
>
> The *IMFMediaSource::Start()* interface function allows you to pass in parameters in all sorts of formats by using the *PROPVARIANT* data type together with the time-format GUID parameter. The GUID can identify the time format, and the *PROPVARIANT* can contain any data type needed for that format. However, the *AVFSource* implementation of the *Start()* function supports only the default time format in 100-nanosecond units.

When the *Invoke()* function receives the command object with the *SourceOperationStart* value, it calls the *AVFSource::InternalStart()* method. The start method initializes the streams based on the information in the passed-in *ISourceOperation* object, sets the offset value, and sends the start event.

```
//
// Start playback or seek to the specified location.
//
HRESULT AVFSource::InternalStart(ISourceOperation* pCommand)
{
    HRESULT hr = S_OK;
    CComPtr<IMFPresentationDescriptor> pPresentationDescriptor;
```

```cpp
do
{
    // get the presentation descriptor from the start operation
    hr = pCommand->GetPresentationDescriptor(&pPresentationDescriptor);
    BREAK_ON_FAIL(hr);

    // activate the streams associated with the presentation descriptor
    hr = SelectStreams(pPresentationDescriptor, pCommand->GetData(),
        pCommand->IsSeek());
    BREAK_ON_FAIL(hr);

    // set the start position in the file
    hr = m_pAVIFileParser->SetOffset(pCommand->GetData());
    BREAK_ON_FAIL(hr);

    // update the internal state variable
    m_state = SourceStateStarted;

    // we have just started - which means that none of the streams have hit the
    // end of stream indicator yet.  Once all of the streams have ended, the source
    // will stop.
    m_pendingEndOfStream = 0;

    // if we got here, then everything succeed.  If this was a seek request, queue the
    // result of the seek command.  If this is a start request, queue the result of the
    // start command.
    if (pCommand->IsSeek())
    {
        hr = m_pEventQueue->QueueEventParamVar(
                    MESourceSeeked,              // seek result
                    GUID_NULL,                   // no extended event data
                    S_OK,                        // succeeded
                    &pCommand->GetData());       // operation object
    }
    else
    {
        hr = m_pEventQueue->QueueEventParamVar(
                    MESourceStarted,             // start result
                    GUID_NULL,                   // no extended event data
                    S_OK,                        // succeeded
                    &pCommand->GetData());       // operation object
    }
}
while(false);

// if we failed, fire an event indicating status of the operation - there is no need to
// fire status if start succeeded, since that would have been handled above in the while
// loop
if (FAILED(hr))
{
    m_pEventQueue->QueueEventParamVar(MESourceStarted, GUID_NULL, hr, NULL);
}

return hr;
}
```

Just like *InternalOpen()*, the *InternalStart()* method requires extra parameters to be stored and transmitted in the command object. Therefore, the *InternalStart()* method receives a pointer to the *ISourceOperation* object, extracts the presentation descriptor, and uses it to activate individual streams exposed by the media file.

After all of the initializations are complete, *InternalStart()* fires the *MESourceStarted* media event indicating that playback has started. This event is later received by the MF session, which starts pulling data from the streams. The stream objects in turn start requesting samples from the source, which pulls them out of the *AVIFileParser*. This streaming process will be covered later in this chapter, in the "Media Stream Objects" section.

Source Media Event Functions

The *IMFMediaSource* and *IMFMediaStream* interfaces inherit from the *IMFMediaEventGenerator* interface. Therefore, both *AVFSource* and *AVFStream* classes need to implement all the methods from this interface.

Because the *IMFMediaEventGenerator* interface implementation is identical in both *AVFSource* and *AVFStream*, this chapter will describe only the *AVFSource* version. Luckily, the *IMFMediaEventGenerator* implementation is easy, with the helper classes and objects provided by Media Foundation. Instead of implementing an event queue together with various worker and helper methods, *AVFSource* and *AVFStream* objects instantiate an MF event queue object by calling the *MFCreateEventQueue* function.

```
//
// Constructor
//
AVFSource::AVFSource(HRESULT* pHr) :
    m_cRef(1),
    m_pAVIFileParser(NULL),
    m_state(SourceStateUninitialized),
    m_pendingEndOfStream(0)
{
    // Initialize the event queue that will execute all of the source's
    // IMFEventGenerator duties.
    *pHr = MFCreateEventQueue(&m_pEventQueue);
}
```

After the queue is created, all of the *IMFMediaEventGenerator* function calls are passed to the event queue for execution. For example, here is the source implementation of the *IMFMediaEventGenerator::BeginGetEvent()* method.

```
//
// Begin processing an event from the event queue asynchronously
//
HRESULT AVFSource::BeginGetEvent(
            IMFAsyncCallback* pCallback,    // callback of the object interested in events
            IUnknown* punkState)            // some custom state object returned with event
```

```cpp
{
    HRESULT hr = S_OK;

    // make sure the queue is not released prematurely by another thread
    CComPtr<IMFMediaEventQueue> pLocQueue = m_pEventQueue;

    do
    {
        CComCritSecLock<CComAutoCriticalSection> lock(m_critSec);

        // make sure the source is not shut down
        hr = CheckShutdown();
        BREAK_ON_FAIL(hr);

        // get the next event from the event queue
        hr = pLocQueue->BeginGetEvent(pCallback, punkState);
    }
    while(false);

    return hr;
}
```

As you can see, this method simply passes all of the function parameters to the event queue's *IMFMediaEventQueue::BeginGetEvent()* method. *EndGetEvent()* and *QueueEvent()* use the same type implementation and will therefore be skipped here.

One interesting feature in the *GetEvent()* function, however, is that it handles synchronization in a special manner. Because the *GetEvent()* function can block, you need to make sure that the source is not locked to other threads during the *GetEvent()* method execution. Therefore, the *GetEvent()* method ensures that the critical section is released by the time the underlying blocking function is called.

```cpp
//
// Synchronously retrieve the next event from the event queue
//
HRESULT AVFSource::GetEvent(
        DWORD dwFlags,              // flag with the event behavior
        IMFMediaEvent** ppEvent)    // event extracted from the queue
{
    HRESULT hr = S_OK;
    CComPtr<IMFMediaEventQueue> pLocQueue = m_pEventQueue;

    do
    {
        // Check whether the source is shut down but do it in a separate locked section-
        // GetEvent() may block, and we don't want to hold the critical section during
        // that time.
        {
            CComCritSecLock<CComAutoCriticalSection> lock(m_critSec);

            hr = CheckShutdown();
            BREAK_ON_FAIL(hr);
        }
```

```
        // Get the event from the queue - note, may block!
        hr = pLocQueue->GetEvent(dwFlags, ppEvent);
        BREAK_ON_FAIL(hr);
    }
    while(false);

    return hr;
}
```

As usual, the *AVFSource::GetEvent()* method checks whether the source is shut down in a separate locked area. Notice that because the *pLocQueue->GetEvent()* call may block, that call is made outside of the locked section. Therefore, if the call blocks, clients can still use other *AVFSource* methods.

Sample Streaming in *AVFSource*

The standard MF source architecture does not specify how samples flow through the source components. They can come from a custom parser, they can be generated in the *IMFMediaSource* object, or they can be created directly in the *IMFMediaStream* implementations. The only requirement is that a source must expose one or more *IMFMediaStream* objects, and the samples must exit the source through the streams.

As you saw in the diagram at the beginning of this chapter, the *AVFSource* object in this design is responsible for loading samples from the *AVIFileParser* and passing them to the individual streams. Specifically, the source pulls individual samples from the parser whenever it receives a request for additional data and passes those samples to the individual stream objects.

The data requests arrive at the source as asynchronous work item events, in exactly the same manner as start, stop, and pause commands. Whenever one of the streams needs another sample, it queues a work item event against the source. The work item contains a *SourceOperation* object with the *SourceOperationStreamNeedData* command. Just as with the *Pause()* and *Stop()* commands, the worker thread passes the *SourceOperation* object to the *AVFSource::Invoke()* method, which in turn detects the *SourceOperationStreamNeedData* value in the *ISourceOperation* container object and calls a corresponding function. For the data request, the *Invoke()* method calls the appropriately named *InternalRequestSample()* method.

The operation of the *InternalRequestSample()* function is fairly simple. All it does is iterate through the list of available streams and check whether they need samples. If a stream needs data, the function sends it a sample. The request-sample function keeps looping through that procedure until all of the streams are satisfied, after which it exits.

```
//
// Handle the request sample command - pull out a sample of the right type from the
// underlying AVI file parser, and send it to the stream
//
HRESULT AVFSource::InternalRequestSample(void)
{
    bool needMoreData = false;
    HRESULT hr = S_OK;
```

```cpp
    do
    {
        needMoreData = false;

        // go through each of the streams, figure out if they need data, pull out a sample
        // from the underlying AVI file parser, and deliver it to the right stream
        for (DWORD x = 0; x < m_mediaStreams.size(); x++)
        {
            AVFStream* pStream = NULL;

            pStream = m_mediaStreams[x];
            BREAK_ON_FAIL(hr);
            BREAK_ON_NULL(pStream, E_UNEXPECTED);

            // if the current stream needs more data, process its requests
            if (pStream->NeedsData())
            {
                // store a flag indicating that somebody did need data
                needMoreData = true;

                // call a function to send a sample to the stream
                hr = SendSampleToStream(pStream);
                BREAK_ON_FAIL(hr);
            }
        }

        BREAK_ON_FAIL(hr);

        // loop while some stream needs more data - stop only once none of the streams are
        // requesting more samples
    }
    while (needMoreData);

    if(FAILED(hr))
    {
        QueueEvent(MEError, GUID_NULL, hr, NULL);
    }

    return hr;
}
```

Note that, unlike other methods, *InternalRequestSample()* checks a variable in the *while* condition—this *while* loop is actually used as a loop, and not as something to break out of if an error is encountered. The *while* loop keeps executing while the *needMoreData* variable is *true*. The *needMoreData* variable indicates that at least one of the streams requested data—when both of the streams stop requesting data, the function exits the *while* loop and returns.

Furthermore, notice that *InternalRequestSample()* will fire the *MEError* error event if it detects that something failed. Because this operation is asynchronous, this is the only way to deliver an error to the client. Without this event, the media source would just stop streaming data whenever a failure occurred.

The *InternalRequestSample()* method calls *AVFSource::SendSampleToStream()* to load the sample from the parser and pass it to the stream.

```cpp
//
// Load a sample of the right type from the parser and send it to the passed-in stream
//
HRESULT AVFSource::SendSampleToStream(AVFStream* pStream)
{
    HRESULT hr = S_OK;
    CComPtr<IMFSample> spSample;

    do
    {
        // if this is a video stream, then get a video sample from the AVI file parser
        // if this is an audio stream, get an audio sample
        if (pStream->IsVideoStream())
        {
            // get a video sample from the underlying AVI parser
            hr = m_pAVIFileParser->GetNextVideoSample(&spSample);
            BREAK_ON_FAIL(hr);

            // deliver the video sample
            hr = pStream->DeliverSample(spSample);
            BREAK_ON_FAIL(hr);

            // if this is the end of the video stream, tell the stream that there
            // are no more samples
            if (m_pAVIFileParser->IsVideoEndOfStream())
            {
                hr = pStream->EndOfStream();
                BREAK_ON_FAIL(hr);
            }
        }
        else if (pStream->IsAudioStream())
        {
            // get a audio sample from the underlying AVI parser
            hr = m_pAVIFileParser->GetNextAudioSample(&spSample);
            BREAK_ON_FAIL(hr);

            // deliver the audio sample
            hr = pStream->DeliverSample(spSample);
            BREAK_ON_FAIL(hr);

            // if this is the end of the audio stream, tell the stream that there
            // are no more samples
            if (m_pAVIFileParser->IsAudioEndOfStream())
            {
                hr = pStream->EndOfStream();
                BREAK_ON_FAIL(hr);
            }
        }
    }
    while(false);

    return hr;
}
```

The *SendSampleToStream()* function loads either the audio or video sample, depending on the type of stream. The sample is delivered to the *IMFMediaStream* object, after which the method checks with the parser to see whether an end of the stream was reached. If the end of the stream is detected, the function sends that information to the media stream object. The stream object needs to know that the stream is at an end to return the *MF_E_END_OF_STREAM* error the next time somebody calls its *IMFMediaStream::RequestSample()* function.

Media Stream Objects

The *IMFMediaStream*s themselves are usually fairly simple objects. In most implementations, their only responsibility is to receive requests for samples, pass those requests to the underlying source, get the samples from the source, and then send them back out. Because MF uses an asynchronous architecture, the samples themselves are delivered as media events to a client listening to the media stream's *IMFMediaEventGenerator* interface.

The *IMFMediaStream* interface exposes just four methods, three of which are described here:

- **GetMediaSource()**   Returns a pointer to the source associated with the stream.
- **GetStreamDescriptor()**   Returns a stream descriptor that exposes the media types supported by the stream and the stream ID.
- **RequestSample()**   Requests the next sample from the stream. The sample is not returned in this function call—instead, the sample is sent out as an asynchronous media event. This method is called by the media session when it is trying to pull the next sample out of the source.

Remember that the *IMFMediaStream* interface also inherits from *IMFMediaEventGenerator*. This means that besides the three methods just listed, you also must implement the four methods of the media event generator: *BeginGetEvent()*, *EndGetEvent()*, *GetEvent()*, and *QueueEvent()*. However, because the *AVFStream* class uses an implementation of this interface that is identical to that in *AVFSource*, the implementation is extremely simple and will not be discussed in this section. All you need to know about it is that the sample stream implementation, just like the source implementation, is creating and using a queue object provided by MF, and all of the media event generator calls are proxied to that queue.

The *IMFMediaStream::RequestSample()* calls do not return the actual media sample. Calling the request method is essentially equivalent to firing an event to the stream, asking it for the next sample—nothing is returned directly on the same thread. Instead, when the media stream object has the next sample, it fires the *MEMediaSample* event, with the sample attached to the event.

Here is a conceptual diagram that shows the approximate sequence of calls that are made to send out a sample.

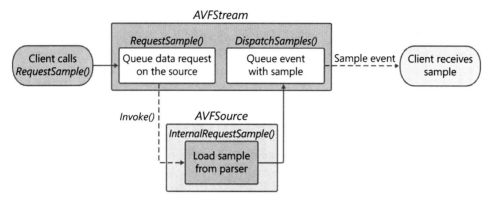

Quite a few steps are missing from this diagram—for example, neither *AVFSource::Invoke()* nor *AVFSource::SendSampleToStream()* are shown here. Nevertheless, this representation should give you a much better idea of how the samples are requested from and flow out of the source. Here is a breakdown of each of the steps in the diagram:

1. The client calls *IMFMediaStream::RequestSample()* to request a sample from the stream.

2. *AVFStream* queues an asynchronous work item with the *IMFAsyncCallback* pointer to the source, passing in *SourceOperationNeedsData* as the command parameter.

3. The worker thread detects that there is a new work item and calls *AVFSource::Invoke()*, passing in the *SourceOperationStreamNeedsData* request. This asynchronous call is represented by a dashed line.

4. The *AVFSource::Invoke()* function calls *InternalRequestSample()*, which loads a sample from the parser and sends it to *AVFStream::DeliverSample()*.

5. *AVFStream::DeliverSample()* calls *AVFSource::DispatchSamples()*, which in turn fires an *MEMediaSample* event with the sample attached.

6. The client, listening to the stream's *IMFMediaEventGenerator* interface, receives the event with the new sample.

The actual implementation in *AVFStream* is a little bit more complex, because for performance reasons the stream queues up several samples internally. This buffer is useful in cases where, due to some performance condition, the sink consumes samples faster than the source can read them from the hard drive. For example, if the hard drive is busy, the source can still load the next sample from the buffer and send it out on time, without causing a glitch due to a late frame. This is the same idea that is commonly implemented in network players—they prebuffer video data before starting playback to account for unexpected network slowdowns.

To examine the sample streaming procedure in more detail, let's start by looking at the *AVFStream* implementation of the *IMFMediaStream::RequestSample()* function.

```cpp
//
// Request the next sample from the stream.
//
HRESULT AVFStream::RequestSample(IUnknown* pToken)
{
    HRESULT hr = S_OK;

    do
    {
        CComCritSecLock<CComAutoCriticalSection> lock(m_critSec);

        // make sure the stream is not shut down
        hr = CheckShutdown();
        BREAK_ON_FAIL(hr);

        // make sure the stream is not stopped
        if (m_state == SourceStateStopped)
        {
            hr = MF_E_MEDIA_SOURCE_WRONGSTATE;
            break;
        }

        // check for the end of stream - fire an end of stream event only if there
        // are no more samples, and we received an end of stream notification
        if (m_endOfStream && m_pSampleList.IsEmpty())
        {
            hr = MF_E_END_OF_STREAM;
            break;
        }

        // Add the token to the CInterfaceList even if it is NULL
        EXCEPTION_TO_HR ( m_pTokenList.AddTail(pToken) );
        BREAK_ON_FAIL(hr);

        // increment the number of requested samples
        m_nSamplesRequested++;

        // dispatch the samples
        hr = DispatchSamples();
    }
    while(false);


    // if something failed and we are not shut down, fire an event indicating the error
    {
        CComCritSecLock<CComAutoCriticalSection> lock(m_critSec);
        if (FAILED(hr) && (m_state != SourceStateShutdown))
        {
            hr = m_pMediaSource->QueueEvent(MEError, GUID_NULL, hr, NULL);
        }
    }

    return hr;
}
```

Obviously, the *RequestSample()* function is used by the MF source clients to request new samples associated with this stream. The function can receive an *IUnknown* token object or *NULL*. The token objects (or *NULL*s) are inserted into samples as they go out, which allows the client to track individual requests, matching tokens it has sent out to the ones in the samples. It also gives the client the ability to detect whether a source dropped a request for some reason. If *AVFStream::RequestSample()* receives a token, it stores that token in a queue for later reinsertion into an outgoing sample.

The stream sends out one sample per each call of *RequestSample()*. The *AVFStream* object tracks the number of outstanding sample requests with the *m_nSamplesRequested* counter. The *RequestSample()* function increments the sample request counter once per call, and the *AVFStream::DispatchSamples()* method decrements the counter each time it sends out a sample.

After the sample request function has determined that the source is in the right state, has incremented the sample request counter, and has dealt with the token if one was passed in, it then calls *DispatchSamples()*. Unlike what you saw in the simplified diagram, *RequestSample()* does not queue a request for a new sample on the source directly. Instead, it tries to send out any samples inside of the *AVFStream* object. The *DispatchSample()* function itself will determine when to ask for more samples from the source.

```
//
// Dispatch samples stored in the stream object, and request samples if more are needed.
//
HRESULT AVFStream::DispatchSamples(void)
{
    HRESULT hr = S_OK;

    CComCritSecLock<CComAutoCriticalSection> lock(m_critSec);

    do
    {
        // if the stream is not started, just exit
        if (m_state != SourceStateStarted)
        {
            hr = S_OK;
            break;
        }

        // send out the samples
        hr = SendSamplesOut();
        BREAK_ON_FAIL(hr);

        // if there are no more samples stored in the stream, and if we have been notified
        // that this is the end of stream, send the end of stream events.  Otherwise, if
        // the stream needs more data, request additional data from the source.
        if (m_pSampleList.IsEmpty() && m_endOfStream)
```

```
    {
        // send the end of stream event to anyone listening to this stream
        hr = m_pEventQueue->QueueEventParamVar(MEEndOfStream, GUID_NULL, S_OK, NULL);
        BREAK_ON_FAIL(hr);

        // tell the source that the end of stream has been reached
        hr = m_pMediaSource->SendOperation(SourceOperationEndOfStream);
        BREAK_ON_FAIL(hr);
    }
    else if (NeedsData())
    {
        // send an event to the source indicating that a stream needs more data
        hr = m_pMediaSource->SendOperation(SourceOperationStreamNeedData);
        BREAK_ON_FAIL(hr);
    }
}
while(false);

// if there was a failure, queue an MEError event
if (FAILED(hr) && (m_state != SourceStateShutdown))
{
    m_pMediaSource->QueueEvent(MEError, GUID_NULL, hr, NULL);
}

return hr;
}
```

The first thing the *DispatchSamples()* function tries to do is actually dispatch the samples by calling the helper *SendSamplesOut()* method. After that, the dispatch method first checks for an end-of-stream notification and then checks whether the stream requires more data. If there are no more samples in the buffer (the *m_pSamples* list) and the source signaled to the stream that there are no more samples for this stream in the file, *DispatchSamples()* first sends out the *MEEndOfStream* event and then signals to the source that all of the data was delivered. The source in turn sends out the *MEEndOfPresentation* event after all of the streams that comprise the presentation have reported that all of the data was sent out.

The dispatch method requests samples when the buffer is less than full. The buffer ensures that if the source has trouble reading the next sample (for example, because the hard drive is busy), the video continues to play uninterrupted.

Note The sample buffer is actually not a basic list, but a special vector-like object designed to hold COM interfaces. The object, *CInterfaceList* is an ATL construct similar to the STL vector, except that it internally calls *AddRef()* when it receives each pointer. This ensures that the COM objects are not released and deleted prematurely, leaving you with a list of dangling pointers.

Now let's take a look at the *AVFStream::SendSamplesOut()* method that is actually firing events with samples.

```
//
// Send out events with samples
//
HRESULT AVFStream::SendSamplesOut(void)
{
    HRESULT hr = S_OK;
    CComPtr<IUnknown> pUnkSample;
    CComPtr<IMFSample> pSample;
    CComPtr<IUnknown> pToken;

    do
    {
        // loop while there are samples in the stream object, and while samples have been
        // requested
        while (!m_pSampleList.IsEmpty() && m_nSamplesRequested > 0)
        {
            // reset the pUnkSample variable
            pUnkSample = NULL;

            // get the next sample and a sample token
            EXCEPTION_TO_HR( pSample = m_pSampleList.RemoveHead() );
            BREAK_ON_FAIL(hr);

            // if there are tokens, then get one, and associate it with the sample
            if(!m_pTokenList.IsEmpty())
            {
                EXCEPTION_TO_HR( pToken = m_pTokenList.RemoveHead() );
                BREAK_ON_FAIL(hr);

                // if there is a sample token, store it in the sample
                hr = pSample->SetUnknown(MFSampleExtension_Token, pToken);
                BREAK_ON_FAIL(hr);
            }

            // get the IUnknown pointer for the sample
            pUnkSample = pSample;

            // queue an event indicating that a new sample is available, and pass it a
            // pointer to the sample
            hr = m_pEventQueue->QueueEventParamUnk(MEMediaSample, GUID_NULL, S_OK,
                pUnkSample);
            BREAK_ON_FAIL(hr);

            // decrement the counter indicating how many samples have been requested
            m_nSamplesRequested--;
        }
        BREAK_ON_FAIL(hr);
    }
    while(false);

    return hr;
}
```

Despite its length, the *SendSamplesOut()* procedure is fairly simple. The method keeps looping while there are samples in the buffer, and while there are outstanding sample requests. During each pass of the loop, the method extracts one sample, attaches a tracking token (or *NULL*) to it, and fires a *MEMediaSample* event with the sample. The event will later be received by the listener to the stream's *IMFMediaEventGenerator* interface.

If you look carefully at the function implementation, you will notice that the first time *RequestSample()* gets called, the queue will be empty. This means that the first time that the *DispatchSamples()* function is run, it cannot actually send out any samples, because the stream is still empty. Instead, all it can do is ask the source for more data and exit. The actual samples in this first pass are sent out on the code path demonstrated by the diagram at the beginning of this section. What happens is that *RequestSample()* calls *DispatchSamples()*, which in turn requests more data from the source. The source calls *AVFStream::DeliverSample()* and sends out the first data buffer. Then the *DeliverSample()* function actually calls *DispatchSamples()* again.

Here is the *DeliverSample()* function.

```
//
// Receive a sample for the stream, and immediately dispatch it.
//
HRESULT AVFStream::DeliverSample(IMFSample *pSample)
{
    HRESULT hr = S_OK;
    CComCritSecLock<CComAutoCriticalSection> lock(m_critSec);

    // store the sample in the sample list
    EXCEPTION_TO_HR( m_pSampleList.AddTail(pSample) );
    BREAK_ON_FAIL(hr);

    // Call the sample dispatching function.
    hr = DispatchSamples();

    return hr;
}
```

This method adds the new sample to the sample queue and then immediately calls *DispatchSamples()* to send it out. The dispatch method must be called as soon as possible because the sample queue may be empty at this point, and there could be an outstanding request for samples from the stream client. If there are no outstanding requests, then *DispatchSamples()* will simply exit.

Windows Property Handlers

Property handlers were introduced in Windows Vista to support adding custom metadata to any file type. Such metadata can be indexed and used in Windows Search, read and changed from Windows Explorer, or inspected and modified through APIs.

Windows Shell metadata is composed of key/value pairs that are either stored in the file or dynamically generated. For example, most video files have something like the duration property in their header table—this property indicates the length of the video clip in the file. At the same time, video thumbnails are extracted and dynamically generated by the Windows Explorer shell.

Each property can be marked as read-only or read-write. Read-write properties can be modified by the user directly from Windows Explorer. The developer of the property handler for that type of file is responsible for writing the code that will store read-write property values. In this example, all of the properties will be marked as read-only for simplicity.

A property handler can be part of a media source or can be implemented as a separate COM component. Because *AVFSource* already parses its media files, we will modify our custom media source to act as a shell property handler for AVF files.

The minimum requirement for creating a property handler is the implementation of a COM component that exposes the following two interfaces:

- **A property store initialization interface such as *IInitializeWithFile*** This interface will be used to initialize and instantiate a new property store object.

- ***IPropertyStore*** This interface is used for extracting properties from and setting properties to a property collection.

IInitializeWithFile is an interface with only one method: *IInitializeWithFile::Initialize()*. This initialization method is called by the shell and is used to initialize the property handler with the file path to the media file.

Though this example implements the *IInitializeWithFile* interface, in a real-world scenario you should try to use the equivalent interface, *IInitializeWithStream*. The stream version of the interface does exactly the same thing as the file version, except that it receives an *IStream* object as a parameter. *IInitializeWithStream* is preferable to the file version because it provides several important security and abstraction features to the property handler.

When initializing with the stream object, the shell can use process isolation to protect itself from misbehaving property handlers, use the property handler to parse streams other than files, and provide multiple applications with concurrent access to the file. For example, an *IInitializeWithStream* property handler can accept an *IStream* object created from an FTP data stream, from a normal file, or from a compressed file. Therefore, if at all possible you should try to use the stream property handler initialization interface.

Unfortunately, the AVF Source sample is again limited by the VFW interfaces. Because VFW expects to parse the file on its own and cannot receive a stream as a parameter, the *AVFByteStreamHandler* has to implement the *IInitializeWithFile* interface. Because of this limitation, Windows Explorer is forced to load the property handler directly into its process. This means that the AvfSource.dll binary will be locked while you are viewing the property of an AVF file. You will not be able to change or delete this file while the DLL is loaded. Furthermore, if the property handler crashes, it will also take down the Windows Explorer process.

Here is the implementation of the *IIinitializeWithFile::Initialize()* method by the *AVFByteStream-Handler* object.

```
//
// Initialize the IPropertyStore interface components of the AVFByteStreamHandler
//
HRESULT AVFByteStreamHandler::Initialize( LPCWSTR pszFilePath, DWORD grfMode )
{
    HRESULT hr = S_OK;
    AVIFileParser* pParser = NULL;

    do
    {
        BREAK_ON_NULL(pszFilePath, E_POINTER);

        // If the mode is trying to modify the properties, return access denied -
        // read-write properties are not supported.
        if ((grfMode & (STGM_READWRITE | STGM_WRITE)) != 0 )
        {
            hr = STG_E_ACCESSDENIED;
            break;
        }

        // Create the AVI parser
        hr = AVIFileParser::CreateInstance(pszFilePath, &pParser);
        BREAK_ON_FAIL(hr);

        // Parse the AVI file header.
        hr = pParser->ParseHeader();
        BREAK_ON_FAIL(hr);

        hr = pParser->GetPropertyStore(&m_pPropertyStore);
        BREAK_ON_FAIL(hr);
    }
    while(false);

    if(pParser != NULL)
    {
        delete pParser;
    }

    return hr;
}
```

There is very little to it. The function first instantiates the parser and then gets an instance of an *IPropertyStore* object. The property store is then stored for later reuse inside of the *AVFByteStreamHandler* object.

In addition to the property handler initialization function, you need to generate and populate a property store for the file. The property store is contained in an object that implements the *IPropertyStore* interface. This is an interface that exposes methods to add and retrieve from the property bag (essentially a container).

You can either implement your own property store by creating an object that implements the *IPropertyStore* interface, or you can instantiate a property store provided by Windows, and proxy all of the *IPropertyStore* calls sent to the byte stream handler to the methods of an already-implemented property store.

Here is the *AVIFileParser::GetPropertyStore()* function implementation that creates a property store object and populates it with the information about an AVI file.

```
//
// Create and return a new property store describing the file
//
HRESULT AVIFileParser::GetPropertyStore(IPropertyStore** ppPropertyStore)
{
    HRESULT hr = S_OK;
    CComPtr<IPropertyStore> pPropStore;
    PROPVARIANT propValue;

    do
    {
        BREAK_ON_NULL(ppPropertyStore, E_POINTER);
        BREAK_ON_NULL(m_pAviFile, E_UNEXPECTED);

        // create a new property store
        hr = PSCreateMemoryPropertyStore(IID_IPropertyStore, (void**)&pPropStore);
        BREAK_ON_FAIL(hr);

        // set the duration property
        InitPropVariantFromInt64(m_duration, &propValue);
        hr = pPropStore->SetValue(PKEY_Media_Duration, propValue);
        BREAK_ON_FAIL(hr);

        // if we got here, everything succeeded - detach and return the property store
        *ppPropertyStore = pPropStore.Detach();
    }
    while(false);

    return hr;
}
```

This function first creates an empty property store object by calling the Windows *PSCreateMemoryPropertyStore()* method. After that, the file parser populates the property store with information about the file. In this limited example, the only information added to the property store is the file duration, but other property handlers populate and generate many other key/value pairs.

As mentioned earlier, the byte stream handler can simply proxy all of the *IPropertyStore* interface calls to the object received from *AVIFileParser::GetPropertyStore()*. Here is an example for the *AVF-ByteStreamHandler::GetValue()* function.

```
HRESULT AVFByteStreamHandler::GetValue( REFPROPERTYKEY key, PROPVARIANT *pv)
{
    if(m_pPropertyStore == NULL)
        return E_UNEXPECTED;

    return m_pPropertyStore->GetValue(key, pv);
}
```

The *GetValue()* function is used by the Windows Shell to extract property information about the file from the property store. The key used for extraction of a property will be the same as the one used to add the property. In other words, to extract the duration of the file clip, you need to call *GetValue()* and pass in the *PKEY_Media_Duration* GUID.

Just like with the byte stream handler, you need to register the property handler to tell Windows which component it needs to load to extract file properties. Here is the registry entry that needs to be added to instantiate the property handler for files with the .avf extension.

```
[HKEY_LOCAL_MACHINE\SOFTWARE\Microsoft\Windows\CurrentVersion\PropertySystem\
PropertyHandlers\.avf]
@="{65085DC5-EB10-421B-943A-425F0CADBD0B}"
```

> **Note** The at sign (@) in this case indicates that the registry value name is *(Default)*. This entry tells Windows Shell that the property handler for a file with the .avf extension can be instantiated by creating a COM object with this CLSID.

In addition, because the property handler in this example implements the *IInitializeFromFile* interface and not *IInitializeFromStream*, you also need to opt out from running in an isolated process. This disables several security and protection features, and forces the property handler to run in the Windows Explorer process, with the same privileges as Windows Explorer itself. To opt out of process isolation, you need to set the key shown here.

```
[HKEY_CLASSES_ROOT\CLSID\{65085DC5-EB10-421B-943A-425F0CADBD0B}]
"DisableProcessIsolation"=dword:00000001
```

With the registry keys just shown, Windows Shell knows where to find the property handler for files with the .avf extension and is able to instantiate it. However, it also needs to know exactly which properties you want to see, and where they should be placed in the Windows Explorer UI. This information is stored in the following key.

```
[HKEY_CLASSES_ROOT\SystemFileAssociations\.avf]
"FullDetails"="prop:System.Media.Duration"
```

The *FullDetails* registry entry tells Windows Explorer that it should try to display the media duration only on the full details page of the Properties dialog box for the file. There are also registry values that correspond to other UI locations.

Here is an example of what the Windows Shell Details page in the Properties dialog box will show for a test AVF file.

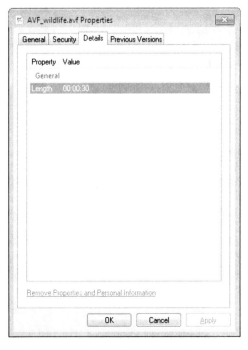

Because you have added only the *System.Media.Duration* property name to the *FullDetails* registry entry under system file associations, the Details page shows only the file length. If you want to add more properties to the Details page, you can populate the *FullDetails* registry entry with more property names, separated by semicolons. For example, you can take a look at the list of properties for files with the .avi extension under the *SystemFileAssociations* registry key.

Here is a short and incomplete table of properties that are often displayed for media files. The full list is far longer and can contain dozens of key/value pairs.

Key	Type	Shell Name
PKEY_Video_StreamNumber	VT_UI2	System.Video.StreamNumber
PKEY_Video_Compression	VT_LPWSTR	System.Video.Compression
PKEY_Video_FrameHeight	VT_UI4	System.Video.FrameHeight
PKEY_Video_FrameWidth	VT_UI4	System.Video.FrameWidth
PKEY_Video_FrameRate	VT_UI4	System.Video.FrameRate
PKEY_Video_FourCC	VT_UI4	System.Video.FourCC
PKEY_Audio_StreamNumber	VT_UI2	System.Audio.StreamNumber
PKEY_Audio_Format	VT_LPWSTR	System.Audio.Format
PKEY_Audio_SampleRate	VT_UI4	System.Audio.SampleRate
PKEY_Audio_SampleSize	VT_UI4	System.Audio.SampleSize
PKEY_Media_Duration	VT_UI8	System.Media.Duration

The Key column contains the name of the GUID for that particular property, the Type column contains the data type used for the property, and the Shell Name column is the name of the property when it is populated in the registry.

The shell name is the string in the registry that identifies the property that you want the Windows UI to display. This property information can be displayed in a tooltip, on the preview details page, or on the full details page. Where the information is displayed depends on the name of the registry value that contains the list of shell property names. For example, if you add property names to the *ExtendedTitle* registry value, the information will be displayed in a tooltip when you point to the file in Windows Explorer. If you add the property names to the *FullDetails* string, the values will be displayed on the Details page of the file's Properties dialog box.

Conclusion

In this chapter, you saw the implementation of a basic Media Foundation source object. The chapter explained the standard asynchronous pattern used throughout MF by showing MF asynchronous sequence diagrams and by showing several versions of the pattern implementation in the source. Understanding asynchronous patterns is vital to fully comprehending the Media Foundation design philosophy and most MF applications.

The chapter also touched on media event generation and handling, and provided an example of how samples flow asynchronously through the MF pipeline. The examples provided here demonstrated how samples are generated in and flow through a standard media source object. Finally, the chapter gave a brief demonstration of property handlers that allow Windows and other applications access to the internal information of media files.

These examples and ideas give you the ability to appreciate the internal workings of standard MF sources and to write your own custom MF source objects.

Class Listings

For reference and to simplify your reading of this chapter, here are the class definitions of the main *AVFSource* classes.

The *AVFByteStreamHandler* class has two main responsibilities: it instantiates the *AVFSource* object on request, and it creates a property store with the AVF file metadata. Therefore, the *AVFByteStreamHandler* implements the *IMFByteStreamHandler* and *IMFAsyncCallback* interfaces to support source creation, and the *IInitializeWithFile* and *IPropertyStore* interfaces to provide metadata to clients.

```cpp
class AVFByteStreamHandler :
    public IMFByteStreamHandler,
    public IMFAsyncCallback,
    public IInitializeWithFile,
    public IPropertyStore
{
public:
        AVFByteStreamHandler(void);
       ~AVFByteStreamHandler(void);

    // IMFByteStreamHandler interface implementation
    STDMETHODIMP BeginCreateObject(IMFByteStream* pByteStream,
                            LPCWSTR pwszURL,
                            DWORD dwFlags,
                            IPropertyStore* pProps,
                            IUnknown** ppIUnknownCancelCookie,
                            IMFAsyncCallback* pCallback,
                            IUnknown *punkState);

    STDMETHODIMP EndCreateObject(IMFAsyncResult* pResult,
                            MF_OBJECT_TYPE* pObjectType,
                            IUnknown** ppObject);

    STDMETHODIMP CancelObjectCreation(IUnknown* pIUnknownCancelCookie);
    STDMETHODIMP GetMaxNumberOfBytesRequiredForResolution(QWORD* pqwBytes);

    //
    // IMFAsyncCallback interface implementation
    STDMETHODIMP GetParameters(DWORD* pdwFlags, DWORD* pdwQueue);
    STDMETHODIMP Invoke(IMFAsyncResult* pResult);

    //
    // IUnknown interface implementation
    virtual HRESULT STDMETHODCALLTYPE QueryInterface(REFIID riid, void** ppvObject);
    virtual ULONG STDMETHODCALLTYPE AddRef(void);
    virtual ULONG STDMETHODCALLTYPE Release(void);

    //
    // IInitializeWithFile interface implementation
    STDMETHODIMP Initialize( LPCWSTR pszFilePath, DWORD grfMode );

    //
    // IPropertyStore interface implementation
    STDMETHODIMP Commit();
    STDMETHODIMP GetAt( DWORD iProp, PROPERTYKEY* pkey);
```

```cpp
        STDMETHODIMP GetCount( DWORD* cProps );
        STDMETHODIMP GetValue( REFPROPERTYKEY key, PROPVARIANT* pv);
        STDMETHODIMP SetValue( REFPROPERTYKEY key, REFPROPVARIANT propvar);

    private:
        volatile long m_cRef;                                    // ref count
        CComAutoCriticalSection m_critSec;

        AVFSource* m_pAVFSource;
        CComPtr<IMFAsyncResult> m_pResult;
        CComPtr<IPropertyStore> m_pPropertyStore;

        // holds a value indicating that the creation is being canceled
        bool m_objectCreationCanceled;
};
```

The main class used by the sample is *AVFSource*. This class contains most of the functionality required to initialize the media source and create the media stream objects that will deliver data to the topology.

```cpp
// forward declaration of the class implementing the IMFMediaStream for the AVF file.
class AVFStream;

//
// Main source class.
//
class AVFSource : public IMFMediaSource,
                  public IMFAsyncCallback
{
    public:
        static HRESULT CreateInstance(AVFSource **ppAVFSource);

        // IUnknown interface implementation
        virtual HRESULT STDMETHODCALLTYPE QueryInterface(REFIID riid, void **ppvObject);
        virtual ULONG STDMETHODCALLTYPE AddRef(void);
        virtual ULONG STDMETHODCALLTYPE Release(void);

        //
        // IMFMediaEventGenerator interface implementation
        STDMETHODIMP BeginGetEvent(IMFAsyncCallback* pCallback,IUnknown* punkState);
        STDMETHODIMP EndGetEvent(IMFAsyncResult* pResult, IMFMediaEvent** ppEvent);
        STDMETHODIMP GetEvent(DWORD dwFlags, IMFMediaEvent** ppEvent);
        STDMETHODIMP QueueEvent(MediaEventType met, REFGUID guidExtendedType,
            HRESULT hrStatus, const PROPVARIANT* pvValue);

        //
        // IMFMediaSource interface implementation
        STDMETHODIMP CreatePresentationDescriptor(
            IMFPresentationDescriptor** ppPresDescriptor);
        STDMETHODIMP GetCharacteristics(DWORD* pdwCharacteristics);
        STDMETHODIMP Start(IMFPresentationDescriptor* pPresentationDescriptor,
            const GUID* pguidTimeFormat,
            const PROPVARIANT* pvarStartPosition);
        STDMETHODIMP Stop(void);
        STDMETHODIMP Pause(void);
        STDMETHODIMP Shutdown(void);
```

```cpp
    //
    // IMFAsyncCallback interface implementation
    STDMETHODIMP GetParameters(DWORD *pdwFlags, DWORD *pdwQueue);
    STDMETHODIMP Invoke(IMFAsyncResult* pAsyncResult);

    //
    // Helper methods called by the bytestream handler.
    HRESULT BeginOpen(LPCWSTR pwszURL, IMFAsyncCallback *pCallback,
        IUnknown *pUnkState);
    HRESULT EndOpen(IMFAsyncResult *pResult);

    HRESULT CheckShutdown(void) const;       // Check if AVSource is shutting down.
    HRESULT IsInitialized(void) const;       // Check if AVSource is initialized

private:
    AVFSource(HRESULT* pHr);

    // file handling methods used to parse the file and initialize the objects
    HRESULT ParseHeader(void);
    HRESULT InternalCreatePresentationDescriptor(void);
    HRESULT CreateVideoStream(IMFStreamDescriptor** pStreamDescriptor);
    HRESULT CreateAudioStream(IMFStreamDescriptor** pStreamDescriptor);

    HRESULT SendOperation(SourceOperationType operationType);

    // internal asynchronous event handler methods
    HRESULT InternalOpen(ISourceOperation* pCommand);
    HRESULT InternalStart(ISourceOperation* pCommand);
    HRESULT InternalStop(void);
    HRESULT InternalPause(void);
    HRESULT InternalRequestSample(void);
    HRESULT InternalEndOfStream(void);

    HRESULT SendSampleToStream(AVFStream* pStream);

    HRESULT SelectStreams(IMFPresentationDescriptor *pPresentationDescriptor, const
        PROPVARIANT varStart, bool isSeek);

    ~AVFSource(void);

    friend class AVFStream;

private:
    volatile long m_cRef;                    // reference count

    size_t m_pendingEndOfStream;
    AVIFileParser* m_pAVIFileParser;
    CComAutoCriticalSection m_critSec;       // critical section

    CComPtr<IMFMediaEventQueue> m_pEventQueue;
    CComPtr<IMFPresentationDescriptor> m_pPresentationDescriptor;
```

```
        // an STL vector with media stream pointers
        vector<AVFStream*> m_mediaStreams;

        // current state of the source
        SourceState m_state;
};
```

Internally, the *AVFSource* object holds its state as a value from the *SourceState* enumeration. Here is that enumeration—it indicates all of the possible states that the source can have.

```
enum SourceState
{
    SourceStateUninitialized,
    SourceStateOpening,
    SourceStateStopped,
    SourceStatePaused,
    SourceStateStarted,
    SourceStateShutdown
};
```

Like all media sources, *AVFSource* sends data to the MF topology through media stream objects. Each of the data streams exposed by the source has a corresponding stream object. Here is the *AVFStream* class that implements the *IMFMediaStream* interface and delivers samples to the downstream components.

```
#define SAMPLE_BUFFER_SIZE 2

class AVFSource;

class AVFStream : public IMFMediaStream
{
    public:
        static HRESULT CreateInstance(AVFStream** ppMediaStream, AVFSource *pMediaSource,
            IMFStreamDescriptor *pStreamDescriptor);

        //
        // IMFMediaEventGenerator interface implementation
        STDMETHODIMP BeginGetEvent(IMFAsyncCallback* pCallback,IUnknown* punkState);
        STDMETHODIMP EndGetEvent(IMFAsyncResult* pResult, IMFMediaEvent** ppEvent);
        STDMETHODIMP GetEvent(DWORD dwFlags, IMFMediaEvent** ppEvent);
        STDMETHODIMP QueueEvent(MediaEventType met, REFGUID guidExtendedType,
            HRESULT hrStatus, const PROPVARIANT* pvValue);

        //
        // IMFMediaStream interface implementation
        STDMETHODIMP GetMediaSource(IMFMediaSource** ppMediaSource);
        STDMETHODIMP GetStreamDescriptor(IMFStreamDescriptor** ppStreamDescriptor);
        STDMETHODIMP RequestSample(IUnknown* pToken);

        //
        // IUnknown interface implementation
        virtual HRESULT STDMETHODCALLTYPE QueryInterface(REFIID riid, void **ppvObject);
        virtual ULONG STDMETHODCALLTYPE AddRef(void);
        virtual ULONG STDMETHODCALLTYPE Release(void);
```

```cpp
        //
        // Helper functions used by AVFSource
        HRESULT DeliverSample(IMFSample *pSample);
        void Activate(bool active);
        HRESULT Start(const PROPVARIANT& varStart, bool isSeek);
        HRESULT Pause(void);
        HRESULT Stop(void);
        HRESULT EndOfStream();
        bool IsActive(void) const { return m_active; }
        HRESULT Shutdown();
        void SetVideoStream(void) { m_isVideo = true; m_isAudio = false; }
        void SetAudioStream(void) { m_isVideo = false; m_isAudio = true; }
        bool IsVideoStream(void) const { return m_isVideo; }
        bool IsAudioStream(void) const { return m_isAudio; }
        bool NeedsData(void);

    private:
        AVFStream(void);
        HRESULT Init(AVFSource *pMediaSource, IMFStreamDescriptor *pStreamDescriptor);
        HRESULT CheckShutdown(void);
        HRESULT DispatchSamples(void);
        HRESULT SendSamplesOut(void);
        ~AVFStream(void);

    private:
        volatile long m_cRef;
        AVFSource* m_pMediaSource;
        bool m_active;
        bool m_endOfStream;
        bool m_isVideo;
        bool m_isAudio;
        SourceState m_state;

        volatile int m_nSamplesRequested;

        CComAutoCriticalSection m_critSec;         // critical section

        CComPtr<IMFStreamDescriptor> m_pStreamDescriptor;
        CComPtr<IMFMediaEventQueue>  m_pEventQueue;
        CInterfaceList<IMFSample> m_pSampleList;
        CInterfaceList<IUnknown, &IID_IUnknown> m_pTokenList;
};
```

Internally, the media source uses a lot of asynchronous calls. To pass command information to the media source's implementation of the *IMFAsyncCallback::Invoke()* method, *AVFSource* uses the helper *SourceOperation* class. This class is simply a COM container with several values and parameters used to send commands from one thread to another.

```cpp
// Operation type.
enum SourceOperationType
{
    SourceOperationOpen,
    SourceOperationStart,
    SourceOperationPause,
    SourceOperationStop,
    SourceOperationStreamNeedData,
    SourceOperationEndOfStream
};

// ISourceOperation COM IID.
// {35D8883D-3239-4ABE-84BD-43EAC5ED2304}
DEFINE_GUID(IID_ISourceOperation, 0x35d8883d, 0x3239, 0x4abe, 0x84, 0xbd, 0x43, 0xea, 0xc5,
    0xed, 0x23, 0x4);

// ISourceOperation COM interface
struct ISourceOperation : public IUnknown
{
    public:
        virtual HRESULT GetPresentationDescriptor(
            IMFPresentationDescriptor** ppPresentationDescriptor) = 0;
        virtual HRESULT SetData(const PROPVARIANT& data, bool isSeek) = 0;
        virtual PROPVARIANT& GetData() = 0;
        virtual bool IsSeek(void) = 0;
        virtual SourceOperationType Type(void) = 0;
        virtual WCHAR* GetUrl(void) = 0;
        virtual HRESULT GetCallerAsyncResult(IMFAsyncResult** pCallerResult) = 0;
};

// COM object used to pass commands between threads.
class SourceOperation : public ISourceOperation
{
    public:
        SourceOperation(SourceOperationType operation);
        SourceOperation(SourceOperationType operation, LPCWSTR pUrl,
            IMFAsyncResult* pCallerResult);
        SourceOperation(SourceOperationType operation,
            IMFPresentationDescriptor* pPresentationDescriptor);
        SourceOperation(const SourceOperation& operation);

        // ISourceOperation interface implementation
        virtual HRESULT GetPresentationDescriptor(
            IMFPresentationDescriptor** ppPresentationDescriptor);
        virtual PROPVARIANT& GetData();
        virtual bool IsSeek(void)  { return m_isSeek; }
        virtual SourceOperationType Type(void) { return m_operationType; }
        virtual WCHAR* GetUrl(void) { return m_pUrl; };
        virtual HRESULT GetCallerAsyncResult(IMFAsyncResult** ppCallerResult);
```

```cpp
    // IUnknown interface implementation
    virtual HRESULT STDMETHODCALLTYPE QueryInterface(REFIID riid, void **ppvObject);
    virtual ULONG STDMETHODCALLTYPE AddRef(void);
    virtual ULONG STDMETHODCALLTYPE Release(void);


    HRESULT SetData(const PROPVARIANT& data, bool isSeek);


private:
    ~SourceOperation();
    void Init(SourceOperationType operation,
        IMFPresentationDescriptor* pPresentationDescriptor);

    volatile long m_cRef;                       // reference count
    bool m_isSeek;
    SourceOperationType m_operationType;
    PropVariantGeneric m_data;
    CComPtr<IMFPresentationDescriptor> m_pPresentationDescriptor;

    // variables used during BeginOpen operation - URL of file to open and client's
    // result that will be invoked when open is complete
    CComPtr<IMFAsyncResult> m_pCallerResult;
    WCHAR* m_pUrl;
};
```

Finally, here is the AVI file parser class—this class is used by the media source to parse the AVI files. The *AVIFileParser* itself is just a wrapper around several VFW interfaces and functions provided by Windows.

```cpp
// Parse the AVI file with the VFW interfaces.
class AVIFileParser
{
    public:
        static HRESULT CreateInstance(const WCHAR* url, AVIFileParser **ppParser);

        HRESULT ParseHeader(void);
        HRESULT GetVideoMediaType(IMFMediaType** ppMediaType);
        HRESULT GetAudioMediaType(IMFMediaType** ppMediaType);
        HRESULT GetNextVideoSample(IMFSample** ppSample);
        HRESULT GetNextAudioSample(IMFSample** ppSample);
        HRESULT SetOffset(const PROPVARIANT& varStart);

        DWORD StreamCount(void) const             { return m_aviInfo.dwStreams; };
        bool IsSupportedFormat(void) const        { return true; };
        bool HasVideo(void) const                 { return (m_pVideoStream != NULL); };
        bool HasAudio(void) const                 { return (m_pAudioStream != NULL); };
        bool IsVideoEndOfStream(void) const
        { return (m_currentVideoSample >= m_videoStreamInfo.dwLength); };
        bool IsAudioEndOfStream(void) const
        { return (m_currentAudioSample >= m_audioStreamInfo.dwLength); };
        LONGLONG Duration(void) const             { return m_duration; };
```

```cpp
    ~AVIFileParser(void);

    HRESULT GetPropertyStore(IPropertyStore** ppPropertyStore);

protected:
    AVIFileParser(const WCHAR* url);
    HRESULT Init();
    HRESULT CreateVideoMediaType(BYTE* pUserData, DWORD dwUserData);
    HRESULT CreateAudioMediaType(BYTE* pUserData, DWORD dwUserData);
    HRESULT ParseVideoStreamHeader(void);
    HRESULT ParseAudioStreamHeader(void);

private:
    WCHAR* m_url;
    AVIFILEINFO m_aviInfo;
    AVISTREAMINFO m_videoStreamInfo;
    AVISTREAMINFO m_audioStreamInfo;

    BITMAPINFOHEADER m_videoFormat;
    WAVEFORMATEX m_audioFormat;

    IAVIFile* m_pAviFile;
    IAVIStream* m_pVideoStream;
    IAVIStream* m_pAudioStream;

    DWORD m_currentVideoSample;
    DWORD m_currentAudioSample;
    LONGLONG m_audioSampleTime;
    LONGLONG m_duration;

    LONG m_nextKeyframe;

    CComPtr<IMFMediaType> m_pVideoType;
    CComPtr<IMFMediaType> m_pAudioType;
};
```

CHAPTER 7

Media Foundation Sinks

The Sample AVI File Sink	207
The AVI Media Sink	210
The AVI Media Stream	227

Media sinks are objects in the Microsoft Media Foundation (MF) pipeline that receive one or more input streams but have no output streams. The purpose of most sinks in the MF pipeline is to consume all of the data and provide it to the user in some form. In an MF topology, each requested (selected) stream comes out of a media source, is processed by zero or more MFTs, and ends in the media sink.

There are three major types of media sinks: renderer, archive, and streaming sinks. A renderer sink "renders" the input data and presents it to the user. The way that a renderer sink presents the information to the user depends on the type of data. For example, the Enhanced Video Renderer (EVR) renders input video frames to the screen, whereas the Streaming Audio Renderer (SAR) sends the audio samples to an output audio device. Archive sinks save data into a media file, usually after multiplexing several data streams into one. Unlike rendering sinks, archive sinks pull data from the source as fast as it can be delivered. Finally, streaming sinks are designed for streaming network scenarios and transmit the data over the network. In some ways, streaming sinks are similar to the archive sinks—they also pull data from the source as quickly as they can. However, unlike archive sinks, streaming sinks support rate changes and seeking.

Because MF uses the pull data flow model, sinks are responsible for requesting data from the source components. To request samples, a sink fires sample request events, which are received by the sink's client. The client then requests samples from the component upstream from the sink, which in turn pulls data from its upstream component, and so on.

Unlike sources, sinks do not have dedicated creator objects. There is no equivalent to the *IMFByte-StreamHandler* object that is supposed to create a sink. Unfortunately, MF does not have a discovery system capable of automatically finding which sinks are available on the machine. There are no designated registry locations that contain available sinks and their corresponding container types.

Instead, all MF sinks are treated as pure COM objects. To instantiate a custom sink, your application needs to know its COM Class ID (CLSID) and either explicitly call *CoCreateInstance()* or pass that CLSID to a manually created activator object. If you want to instantiate one of the standard Microsoft-provided sinks, you can use one of the built-in MF sink creation functions, but these functions use hard-coded lists of internal sink objects. The functions do not dynamically discover supported sinks on the machine by looking in the registry for lists of sink CLSIDs but instantiate specific and well-known sink objects. Here is a list of MF sink creation functions provided in Windows 7:

- **MFCreate3GPMediaSink()**   Create a media sink capable of writing files and streams in 3GP format.

- **MFCreateASFMediaSink()**   Create a media sink that will encapsulate the provided data as an ASF stream and write it to a file.

- **MFCreateASFStreamingMediaSink()**   Create a version of the ASF media sink capable of streaming data over the network.

- **MFCreateMP3MediaSink()**   Create a media sink for generating MP3 files.

- **MFCreateMPEG4MediaSink()**   Create a media sink for generating files in the MPEG-4 format.

- **MFCreateAudioRenderer()**   Create the Streaming Audio Renderer sink.

- **MFCreateVideoRenderer()**   Create the Enhanced Video Renderer sink.

Each of these functions is designed to know about one type of sink, and internally simply instantiates the sink objects.

As a result of this design, you cannot browse the available sinks in the TopoEdit tool, as you did with custom MFTs and MF sources. Instead, to test a sink, you need to use the TopoEdit's Add Custom Sink menu option and specify the AVI sink's CLSID as a string, as shown in the following graphic.

This will cause TopoEdit to use *CoCreateInstance()* to create the MF sink directly. In this screen shot, the custom media sink GUID is {357a0c45-ead4-4eac-b088-54e2271e7874}, which is the class ID of the sample AVI sink shown in this chapter.

The following sections discuss a typical archival media sink designed to store data it receives in an AVI file. The archival sink is demonstrated by showing select functions of the sample *CAviSink* and the *CAviStream* classes, which make up the AVI sink.

The Sample AVI File Sink

In many ways, MF sinks are constructed like MF source objects in reverse. Instead of transmitting data from the source through individual streams, an MF sink receives data through its own streams and collects it in the sink object. Of course, data doesn't actually have to flow into the sink and can be processed inside of the stream sink objects, but this is the common design. Nevertheless, every functioning MF sink must have at least one *IMFStreamSink* object for receiving media data, along with the *IMFMediaSink* object that allows the client to send commands to the sink.

Here is a diagram that demonstrates the design of the MF sink presented as a sample in this chapter. The sample sink is designed to receive two data streams and write them to an AVI file.

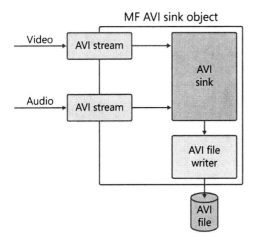

Notice the similarity in design to the diagram shown in Chapter 6, "Media Foundation Sources." The sink is almost a mirror image of the AVF file source shown there. Data flows into the two stream objects, is processed in the sink, and then is written to the AVI file through a helper AVI file writer object.

Note As mentioned earlier, there is no special construction object that will instantiate the sink. Instead, the AVI sink is treated as a pure COM component, and is instantiated with the standard *CoCreateInstance()* function. Because the sink is a COM object, it must be registered before it can be used. The sample project in this chapter again uses a series of helper registration methods to store the sink CLSID in the registry, and a version of the *ClassFactory* class to instantiate it. The code for this is nearly identical to what was used for COM objects in the previous chapters and will not be discussed here.

This sample again uses the open-source AVI format because Windows provides libraries capable of processing AVI file data. Just like the *AVFSource* from Chapter 6 used the Microsoft Video for Windows (VFW) AVI functions to read files, the AVI sink uses VFW to author AVI files.

As the diagram indicates, the individual media samples arrive through the streams. The sink is notified when a stream receives a sample. As soon as all of the streams associated with the sink have data, the sink picks the next sample according to its time stamp, and writes it to the AVI file through the helper file writer class.

The AVI sink sample thus consists of three major components:

- **CAviSink**   The main sink object that controls sink behavior, communicates with the host of the MF object, and processes individual samples.

- **CAviStream**   A stream class that receives individual samples, as well as stream-specific events. Samples are queued inside of each stream until the sink is ready to process them.

- **CAviFileWriter**   A helper class that encapsulates the VFW AVI functionality. This class is responsible for actually writing sample data to the file.

As you saw in the earlier diagram, samples flow into the individual stream sink objects, then into the sink itself, and finally into the helper file writer that actually writes the samples to the AVI file. Here is a more detailed look at how data flows between the stream objects and the sink in the AVI sink sample.

In the AVI sink architecture presented in this chapter, whenever a stream sink object receives a sample, it fires an event that notifies the sink that a new sample is available. The sink then asynchronously receives that event, pulls out the sample with the earliest time stamp, and writes it to the file. The following sequence diagram demonstrates this procedure, showing how two stream sink objects communicate with the sink and the worker thread.

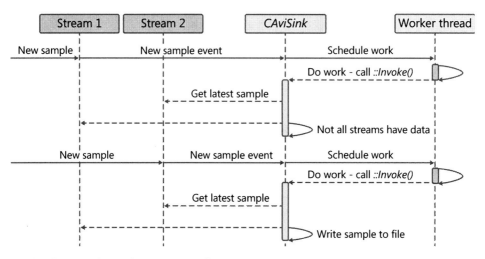

The diagram shows the sequence of events that are used to pass data through the sink. It demonstrates two passes through the loop—the first time when only one stream object has data and the other is empty, and the second when both stream sinks have data. The following is a more detailed description of these steps.

1. A new sample arrives to stream sink 1.
2. The stream object calls a method on the sink, notifying it that there is a new sample to be processed.
3. The sink schedules asynchronous work on itself with the worker thread.
4. The worker thread discovers that there is a new work item on its internal queue and calls the sink's *IMFAsyncCallback::Invoke()* method.
5. The *CAviSink::Invoke()* procedure calls several functions that eventually check all of the stream objects associated with the sink for samples.
6. To figure out which stream object has the data that needs to be written next, the sink requires all of its streams to have data. If not all of the stream objects have samples, the asynchronous operation just ends.
7. A new sample arrives—this time to stream sink 2.
8. The stream object calls the *ScheduleNewSampleProcessing()* method on the sink to notify it that there is new data.
9. The sink schedules asynchronous work with the worker thread.
10. The worker thread detects that there is a new worker item, and calls the sink's *Invoke()* method.
11. The sink compares the samples in all of the stream sink objects, pulls out the earliest one, and writes it to the file.

Of course, this is only one of many possible ways of implementing a media sink. Other methods may use synchronous communication between components, store and process all of the data inside of the stream objects instead of the sink, add extra classes for processing the data, and so on.

Just like sources, many archive sinks provided by MF receive an *IMFByteStream* object during initialization. The media sinks then write the data into the provided *IMFByteStream*, which allows the caller to isolate the media sinks from the implementation details of file writing or network streaming. However, because the AVI sink uses VFW interfaces, this type of implementation is impossible—the VFW AVI functions are designed to deal directly with the hard drive, and need to be initialized with the initial data stream media types. As a result, the AVI sink constructor receives a path to the target AVI file name. The path itself is constructed in the *ClassFactory* instantiation function. The target AVI file is therefore placed in the directory where the AviSink.dll file is located, and is always given the default test.avi file name.

Important The sample media sink was designed to work with existing AVI files—there could be problems if you attempt to process data from other file types. Therefore, for best results during testing, you should use the provided sample AVI file as a source for the media sink.

To test the AVI sink, simply create a source in TopoEdit, create the sink by passing in its CLSID, {357A0C45-EAD4-4EAC-B088-54E2271E7874}, and connect the output streams of an AVI file media source to the sink. Then click the TopoEdit play button to transfer the data into the new file.

The AVI Media Sink

As you saw in the diagram in the previous section, MF media sinks consist of two major components—media sink objects and individual stream objects that feed data into the sink. Each media sink implements the *IMFMediaSink* interface and exposes one or more stream sink objects. Each stream sink in turn implements the *IMFStreamSink* interface. This section will focus primarily on the *CAviSink* object implementing the *IMFMediaSink* interface, because that is the core object that drives the sink behavior. Furthermore, each sink object must also expose the *IMFClockStateSink* interface, which allows clients to control playback of the topology.

The *IMFMediaSink* interface exposes several methods. Most of the methods are used to dynamically discover, add, and remove stream sink objects to and from the media sink. The individual stream objects stored in the sink can be addressed by their ID, or by an index:

- **AddStreamSink()**   Add a new stream sink object to the sink object, specifying its ID and (optionally) its media type.

- **GetStreamSinkById()**   Get a stream sink object with the specified ID from the sink object.

- **GetStreamSinkByIndex()**   Get a stream sink object from the sink identified by index.

- **GetStreamSinkCount()**   Get the number of stream sink objects registered with the media sink.

- **RemoveStreamSink()**   Remove the stream sink object with the specified ID from the media sink.

Each stream sink object is responsible for receiving and processing data for one data stream. Depending on the media sink implementation, the data stream may contain only one elementary media stream, or a number of elementary data streams multiplexed together. In most standard media sink implementations, the sink itself is responsible for multiplexing data streams, and therefore each stream sink object receives a single media data stream with a specific media type.

The media type for an *IMFStreamSink* can be specified at construction time, when the stream sink object is being created with the *IMFMediaSink::AddStreamSink()* function call, or it can be given to the stream sink later on.

In addition to the stream sink control functions, the *IMFMediaSink* interface contains several methods that allow a client to get and set the presentation clock, get the characteristics of the sink, and shut down the sink.

- **GetPresentationClock()**   Get the *IMFPresentationClock* object used with this media sink.

- **SetPresentationClock()**   Set the presentation clock that the media sink will use to display the individual samples.

- **Shutdown()**   Shut down the media sink, releasing its internal resources.
- **GetCharacteristics()**   Get a series of flags describing the capabilities and characteristics of the media sink.

> **Note** The presentation clock is an object that allows a sink to schedule individual samples for display. The clock is used to synchronize sample rendering between multiple sinks (for example, to synchronize audio sample rendering in an audio sink to video sample rendering in a video renderer sink), and to control the behavior of the presentation—to start, pause, and stop playback. Presentation clocks will be discussed in more detail in the "Media Sink Clock Functions" section later in this chapter.

In addition to the *IMFMediaSink* interface, all MF sinks must also implement the *IMFClockStateSink* interface that allows a client to control the sink playback. These methods are used by the presentation clock to pass commands to the media sink:

- **OnClockStart()**   Called to start playback
- **OnClockPause()**   Called to pause playback of the media sink
- **OnClockStop()**   Called to stop playback
- **OnClockRestart()**   Called to restart playback after it was paused
- **OnClockSetRate()**   Called to set the playback rate (speed) of the media sink

The *CAviSink* object implements only a few of these functions because it is an archival media sink. As an archival sink, it is *rateless*—it pulls data from the source as fast as possible, ignoring any rate commands. This implementation also does not support *Pause()* and *Restart()* calls, because there is usually no point in pausing or restarting the process of writing to a file.

> **Note** In some rare cases, it might actually be useful to pause an archival sink—for example, if you have a long-running encoding operation and want to free up the CPU cycles. This sample sink, however, does not support this behavior.

The following sections demonstrate how the *CAviSink* class implements these two main interfaces.

Media Stream Sink Control Functions

As mentioned earlier, MF media sinks expose a series of methods that allow you to add, remove, and enumerate the stream sink objects exposed by the sink. These stream objects all implement the *IMF-StreamSink* interface and represent individual data streams that the media sink will receive.

To detect the capabilities of the media sink, a client can call the *IMFMediaSink::GetCharacteristics()* function.

```
//
// Get the characteristics of the sink
//
HRESULT CAviSink::GetCharacteristics(DWORD* pdwCharacteristics)
{
    if(pdwCharacteristics == NULL)
        return E_POINTER;

    // rateless sink with a fixed number of streams
    *pdwCharacteristics = MEDIASINK_RATELESS | MEDIASINK_FIXED_STREAMS;

    return S_OK;
}
```

The *GetCharacteristics()* function can return a combination of flags indicating several features of the sink. Here are the possible flags that can be returned by this function:

- **MEDIASINK_RATELESS**   This is an archival sink and will pull data from the source at maximum speed.

- **MEDIASINK_FIXED_STREAMS**   The sink has a fixed number of stream sink objects and does not support the *AddStreamSink()* and *RemoveStreamSink()* functions.

- **MEDIASINK_CANNOT_MATCH_CLOCK**   The media sink cannot use an external clock, but instead utilizes an internal clock object. This type of sink is usually used as the clock source, and all other sinks in the topology use it as a point of reference for playback synchronization.

- **MEDIASINK_CAN_PREROLL**   The media sink can prebuffer data to smooth out playback. A client can therefore notify the sink that it is about to start playback, which allows the sink to pull in and preprocess several samples before starting playback.

- **MEDIASINK_REQUIRE_REFERENCE_MEDIATYPE**   The first steam sink object on the sink (the one with index 0 [zero]) must have a media type set before other streams can be configured with their media types.

As you can see, the *CAviSink* object exposes two flags—one that indicates that this is an archival sink, and another that indicates that the media sink has a fixed number of stream sink objects.

Because the *CAviSink* object has a fixed number of stream sinks, it does not implement the *IMFMediaSink::AddStreamSink()* and *RemoveStreamSink()* methods. This is done primarily because the TopoEdit tool does not dynamically refresh the UI and is therefore incapable of displaying a different number of streams from the ones exposed at construction time. The implementation of these functions, however, is extremely simple, and omitting them from the design does not simplify the code to any great extent.

Internally, the AVI sink stores its individual stream sink objects in the Standard Template Library (STL) vector *m_streamSinks*. Therefore, it is very easy to extract the streams by index.

```
//
// Get stream by index
//
HRESULT CAviSink::GetStreamSinkByIndex(DWORD dwIndex, IMFStreamSink** ppStreamSink)
{
    HRESULT hr = S_OK;

    do
    {
        CComCritSecLock<CComAutoCriticalSection> lock(m_critSec);
        BREAK_ON_NULL(ppStreamSink, E_POINTER);

        // make sure the sink is in a good state
        hr = CheckShutdown();
        BREAK_ON_FAIL(hr);

        // make sure the index is in the right range
        if(dwIndex < 0 || dwIndex >= m_streamSinks.size())
        {
            hr = E_INVALIDARG;
            break;
        }

        // get the IMFStreamSink pointer for a stream with the specified index
        hr = m_streamSinks[dwIndex]->QueryInterface(IID_IMFStreamSink,
            (void**)ppStreamSink);
    }
    while(false);

    return hr;
}
```

The *CAviSink::GetStreamSinkByIndex()* function simply makes sure that the sink is in the right state, verifies passed-in parameters, and then calls *QueryInterface()* on the stream object with the specified index.

The procedure for extraction of a stream sink object by ID is also fairly self-evident.

```
//
// Get stream by sink ID
//
HRESULT CAviSink::GetStreamSinkById(DWORD dwStreamSinkIdentifier,
    IMFStreamSink** ppStreamSink)
{
    HRESULT hr = S_OK;
    DWORD streamId;
```

```
    do
    {
        BREAK_ON_NULL(ppStreamSink, E_POINTER);
        CComCritSecLock<CComAutoCriticalSection> lock(m_critSec);

        *ppStreamSink = NULL;

        hr = CheckShutdown();
        BREAK_ON_FAIL(hr);

        // go through every sink in the vector until we find one with the right ID
        for(DWORD x = 0; x < m_streamSinks.size(); x++)
        {
            // get sink ID
            hr = m_streamSinks[x]->GetIdentifier(&streamId);
            BREAK_ON_FAIL(hr);

            // if this is the right sink, remove it
            if(streamId == dwStreamSinkIdentifier)
            {
                // get the IMFStreamSink interface for this sink
                hr = m_streamSinks[x]->QueryInterface(IID_IMFStreamSink,
                    (void**)ppStreamSink);
                break;
            }
        }
        BREAK_ON_FAIL(hr);

        // if we did not find a matching sink, the ID must be wrong
        if(*ppStreamSink == NULL)
        {
            hr = MF_E_INVALIDSTREAMNUMBER;
        }
    }
    while(false);

    return hr;
}
```

The *CAviSink::GetStreamSinkById()* function iterates through every stream sink object in the internal vector of streams, querying each one for its ID. The ID of a stream sink can be retrieved by calling its *IMFStreamSink::GetIdentifier()* method. If a stream object with the specified ID is found, the function again calls *QueryInterface()* on the object, extracting its *IMFStreamSink* interface pointer.

The implementation of the *GetStreamSinkCount()* method is also quite simple and is thus omitted from this chapter. The two other stream control functions, *CAviSink::AddStreamSink()* and *RemoveStreamSink()*, return the *MF_E_STREAMSINKS_FIXED* error, because the number of stream sinks is fixed.

Instead of allowing the client of the media sink to specify the number of stream sinks, *CAviSink* instantiates and sets up two stream objects at construction time. The two stream sinks are sequentially numbered and are not initialized with media types.

```
//
// CAviSink constructor - create a sink for the specified file name
//
CAviSink::CAviSink(const WCHAR* pFilename, HRESULT* pHr) :
    m_pFilename(NULL),
    m_pFileWriter(NULL),
    m_pSampleData(NULL),
    m_dwSampleData(0),
    m_sinkState(SinkStopped)
{
    HRESULT hr = S_OK;
    CAviStream* pStream = NULL;

    do
    {
        BREAK_ON_NULL(pFilename, E_UNEXPECTED);

        // store the file name of the target file
        m_pFilename = new (std::nothrow) WCHAR[wcslen(pFilename) + 1];
        BREAK_ON_NULL(m_pFilename, E_OUTOFMEMORY);

        // copy the file name into an internal member variable
        StringCchCopy(m_pFilename, wcslen(pFilename)+1, pFilename);

        // create a stream and add it to the sink
        hr = CAviStream::CreateInstance(
            0,          // stream ID
            NULL,       // don't specify a media type
            this,       // store a pointer to the sink in the stream
            &pStream);  // retrieve the resulting stream
        BREAK_ON_FAIL(hr);

        // add the stream sink object to the m_streamSinks vector
        EXCEPTION_TO_HR( m_streamSinks.push_back(pStream) );

        // create a second stream
        hr = CAviStream::CreateInstance(1, NULL, this, &pStream);
        BREAK_ON_FAIL(hr);

        // add the second stream sink object to the m_streamSinks vector
        EXCEPTION_TO_HR( m_streamSinks.push_back(pStream) );
    }
    while(false);

    if(pHr != NULL)
    {
        *pHr = hr;
    }
}
```

The *CAviSink* constructor backs up the file name string in a member variable, creates two *CAvi-Stream* objects, and stores them in the internal *m_streamSinks* vector. The two sinks created in the constructor are sequentially numbered.

> **Note** The *CAviSink* uses the *new (std::nothrow)* version of the *new* C++ operator because MF components must not throw exceptions. This version of the operator will return a *NULL* value if the memory allocation fails. Similarly, the *vector::push_back()* function call may throw exceptions. To avoid that, the function call is wrapped in the *EXCEPTION_TO_HR()* macro that simply encapsulates it in a *try-catch* block.

Media Sink Clock Functions

The presentation clock is an object that controls the timing of the sink and allows synchronization between individual sinks in the topology. Internally, however, it is stored simply as a pointer to the *IMFPresentationClock* object. Therefore, the functions that get and set the clock have a very predictable implementation.

```
//
// Set the presentation clock on the sink
//
HRESULT CAviSink::SetPresentationClock(IMFPresentationClock* pPresentationClock)
{
    HRESULT hr = S_OK;

    do
    {
        CComCritSecLock<CComAutoCriticalSection> lock(m_critSec);

        hr = CheckShutdown();
        BREAK_ON_FAIL(hr);

        // If we already have a clock, remove ourselves from that clock's
        // state notifications.
        if (m_pClock != NULL)
        {
            hr = m_pClock->RemoveClockStateSink(this);
            BREAK_ON_FAIL(hr);
        }

        // Register ourselves to get state notifications from the new clock.  Note that
        // pPresentationClock can legitimately be NULL if call is made to remove the
        // existing presentation clock
```

```
        if (pPresentationClock != NULL)
        {
            hr = pPresentationClock->AddClockStateSink(this);
            BREAK_ON_FAIL(hr);
        }

        // Release the pointer to the old clock.
        // Store the pointer to the new clock.
        m_pClock = NULL;
        m_pClock = pPresentationClock;
    }
    while(false);

    return hr;
}
```

The most interesting aspect of *CAviSink::SetPresentationClock()* is that it handles both registration and unregistration of the media sink from the clock object itself. When a new presentation clock is passed into the function, the function unregisters the old clock and registers the media sink with the new clock.

A presentation clock object sends control commands to the sink by calling its *IMFClockStateSink* methods. Therefore, when a clock is removed from the sink, the clock and the sink must be disassociated—the sink must be unregistered from the clock. This is done by calling the *IMFPresentationClock::RemoveClockStateSink()* method and passing in a pointer to the sink that should be removed from a list of objects that are synchronized by the clock. Similarly, if a new clock is added to the sink, the *SetPresentationClock()* method must register the sink as a receiver of commands with the clock by calling the *IMFPresentationClock::AddClockStateSink()* method.

The *IMFMediaSink::GetPresentationClock()* method simply extracts a pointer to the presentation clock stored in the class member variable, and associated with the media sink. Therefore, the implementation of this method is self-explanatory and will not be shown in this chapter.

After the media sink is registered as a receiver of commands from the presentation clock, the clock will call the sink's *IMFClockStateSink* methods. These methods notify the media sink when it needs to start pulling data, when it should pause, and when it should stop.

Because the AVI sink does not support rate changes or pause behavior, the *CAviSink* class needs to implement only the *IMFClockStateSink::OnClockStart()* and *OnClockStop()* methods. The other three, *OnClockPause()*, *OnClockRestart()*, and *OnClockSetRate()*, simply return *S_OK*.

The architecture of the AVI sink requires the start and stop methods to do two things—pass the start and stop commands to the stream sink objects, and send control commands to the underlying file writer. The stream objects need to know when playback has started, to fire their *MEStreamSinkRequestSample* events and request samples from the upstream components in the topology. Similarly, the *CAviFileWriter* class needs to be initialized and finalized whenever the streams start and stop—it needs to open and close the AVI file to which it will be writing.

Here is the *CAviSink* implementation of the *IMFClockStateSink::OnClockStart()* method.

```cpp
//
// Called when the clock has been started
//
HRESULT CAviSink::OnClockStart(MFTIME hnsSystemTime, LONGLONG llClockStartOffset)
{
    HRESULT hr = S_OK;
    CComPtr<IMFMediaType> pMediaType;

    do
    {
        CComCritSecLock<CComAutoCriticalSection> lock(m_critSec);

        hr = CheckShutdown();
        BREAK_ON_FAIL(hr);

        // if the sink is stopped, start it
        if(m_sinkState == SinkStopped)
        {
            if(m_pFileWriter != NULL)
            {
                delete m_pFileWriter;
            }

            // create a new instance of the file writer
            m_pFileWriter = new (std::nothrow) CAviFileWriter(m_pFilename);
            BREAK_ON_NULL(m_pFileWriter, E_OUTOFMEMORY);

            // go through every stream, initialize the file writer with these streams, and
            // send the start command to each of the streams
            for(DWORD x = 0; x < m_streamSinks.size(); x++)
            {
                pMediaType = NULL;
                CAviStream* pStream = m_streamSinks[x];

                // get the stream media type - it should be known by this point
                hr = pStream->GetCurrentMediaType(&pMediaType);
                BREAK_ON_FAIL(hr);

                // add a new stream to the file writer, initializing it with the stream ID
                // and the media type
                hr = m_pFileWriter->AddStream(pMediaType, x);
                BREAK_ON_FAIL(hr);

                // pass the start command to the stream
                hr = pStream->OnStarted();
            }
            BREAK_ON_FAIL(hr);
        }

        m_sinkState = SinkStarted;
    }
    while(false);

    return hr;
}
```

As mentioned earlier, the start method has two jobs—it initializes the file writer class, and it passes the start commands to the stream objects associated with this media sink. File writer initialization consists of creating a new instance of the *CAviFileWriter* class. After that, the function loops through every stream sink object in the *m_streamSinks* stream vector and adds the data stream to the file writer by passing in the stream ID and media type. The file writer needs to know the format of the data streams that will be written to the file to initialize the AVI file headers.

In addition, the function calls the *CAviStream::OnStarted()* helper methods of each of the streams. This method causes the stream objects to fire sample request events and therefore start pulling in data through the topology.

The *IMFClockStateSink::OnClockStop()* method implementation is nearly identical, but in reverse. The function passes the stop command to each of the streams and deletes the file writer, which causes its finalization in the class destructor.

```
//
// Called when the clock has been stopped
//
HRESULT CAviSink::OnClockStop(MFTIME hnsSystemTime)
{
    HRESULT hr = S_OK;

    do
    {
        CComCritSecLock<CComAutoCriticalSection> lock(m_critSec);

        hr = CheckShutdown();
        BREAK_ON_FAIL(hr);

        // if the sink is stopped, do nothing - otherwise shut down
        if(m_sinkState != SinkStopped)
        {
            // Stop all of the stream sinks
            for(DWORD x = 0; x < m_streamSinks.size(); x++)
            {
                m_streamSinks[x]->OnStopped();
            }

            // delete the file writer finalizing the AVI file
            delete m_pFileWriter;
            m_pFileWriter = NULL;

            m_sinkState = SinkStopped;
        }
    }
    while(false);

    return hr;
}
```

The individual stream sink objects need to know when the stop has occurred to fire the *MEStreamSinkStopped* event. This event lets all sink clients know that the sink has stopped requesting and consuming. The function also deletes the file writer object, which causes it to finalize. Finalization for the *CAviFileWriter* object consists of writing the final version of the AVI file headers to the file and closing the file.

The Sink Data Loop

The AVI sink is designed to interleave individual samples based on their presentation time. Each sample is written to the file in the order in which it should to be rendered and presented. The earlier sample is stored first, no matter what stream it comes from. This is not a requirement of the AVI file implementation, but it will greatly reduce the initialization time of some players when they are attempting to play an AVI file authored by the sink.

> **Background** Even though AVI stands for *Audio Video Interleaved*, the actual audio and video samples do not have to be interleaved in the file. AVI files contain an index with the locations of all of the samples for each stream. Therefore, any AVI file parser is capable of finding the location of the next sample fairly quickly, and in theory you could first write all of the video samples to the file, and then all of the audio samples.
>
> This is not ideal, however, because during playback the application playing back this file will need to seek back and forth between the beginning and end of the file to load audio and video samples that go together. Seeking back and forth takes additional time and puts extra strain on non–solid-state hard drives. In addition, files that are not interleaved cannot be played back while they are being progressively downloaded—a network client application would need to receive the entire file before it could start playing a non-interleaved AVI file.

The AVI sink presented in this chapter is designed to write files to the presentation order, on each pass writing only the earliest sample from each of the streams to the file. This requires a nontrivial algorithm, however. Before examining the individual helper and parsing functions that are used for the sample processing in *CAviSink*, let's look at an abstract, bird's-eye view of the algorithm itself.

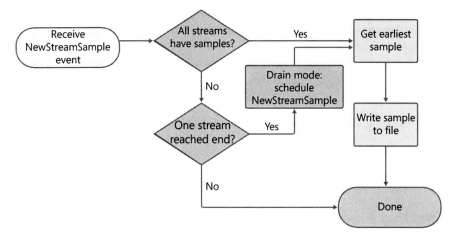

Here are the steps of this algorithm:

1. The *CAviSink* object receives an asynchronous work item indicating that one of the stream sink objects has received a new sample.

2. The media sink goes through all of the stream objects, checking whether all of them have a sample. This is necessary because the media sink requires all of the stream sink objects to have at least one sample to figure out which of these streams has the earliest sample.

    a. If one or more of the streams doesn't have samples, but an end-of-stream event has not yet been received, the function exits. The sink will be called again when another stream has received a sample, but for now there is nothing to do.

    b. If one of the streams is at an end and will not receive any more samples, then the sink enters "drain" mode. In this mode, it keeps pulling samples out of all the streams that are left by scheduling the work while any of the streams still have samples left over.

3. If all of the stream sink objects have data or if the media sink is in the drain mode, the sink extracts the earliest sample.

4. The media sink writes the earliest sample to the file.

5. The function exits and the asynchronous operation is complete.

As you can see, this is a somewhat complex procedure requiring the sink to first pull out samples in order, and second, keep extracting samples while any data is left. This algorithm ensures that all of the data that can be written to the file is written, even if one of the streams comes to the end prematurely, seconds before the other.

The key to the *CAviSink* work loop is again asynchronous operation. Consequently, *CAviSink* implements the *IMFAsyncCallback* interface. The callback interface is used by various components to notify the sink that one of the streams has a new sample. However, because this is the only event that the sink can receive, the corresponding *IMFAsyncCallback::Invoke()* method implementation is as small as possible, thereby conceptually simplifying the class and isolating sample processing functionality.

```
//
// Execute an asynchronous task - process samples in the streams.
//
HRESULT CAviSink::Invoke(IMFAsyncResult* pResult)
{
    return ProcessStreamSamples();
}
```

All that *Invoke()* function does is call the *ProcessStreamSamples()* helper method, which does most of the work. The *CAviSink::ProcessStreamSamples()* method drives most of the sample processing. It calls one function to extract the index of the stream with the earliest sample, and then calls another function to actually get the sample from that stream and write it to the file.

```
//
// Process samples contained in the streams, extracting the next pending sample and writing
// it to the AVI file.
//
HRESULT CAviSink::ProcessStreamSamples(void)
{
    HRESULT hr = S_OK;
    int nEarliestSampleStream = 0;

    do
    {

        CComCritSecLock<CComAutoCriticalSection> lock(m_critSec);

        // if the sink is not started and we got here, ignore all pending messages
        if(m_sinkState != SinkStarted)
        {
            break;
        }

        // get a stream that has the next sample to be written - it should be the stream
        // with a sample that has the earliest time stamp
        hr = GetEarliestSampleStream(&nEarliestSampleStream);

        // if not all of the streams have data, the function returns E_PENDING - in that
        // case just exit since the function will be called again for the next sample
        if(hr == E_PENDING || nEarliestSampleStream < 0)
```

```
        {
            break;
        }
        BREAK_ON_FAIL(hr);

        // call a function to extract a sample from the stream and write it to the file
        hr = WriteSampleFromStream(nEarliestSampleStream);
    }
    while(false);

    return hr;
}
```

Here the function first verifies that the media sink is in the started state by checking the *m_sinkState* variable. If the sink is not started, then the pending sample processing request (asynchronous call to the *CAviSink*) is discarded, and the function just exits.

If the media sink is in a good state, then *ProcessStreamSamples()* calls the *GetEarliestSampleStream()* helper method to get the index of the stream sink object with the earliest sample. *GetEarliestSampleStream()* in turn either returns *S_OK* with the index of the stream sink that has the earliest sample, or it returns *E_PENDING*, indicating that one of the streams does not have data yet. If not all of the stream objects are populated with samples, the media sink cannot determine which data stream should be written next. For example, the implementation of a topology might cause the video data stream to have a higher priority than audio, and thus to deliver all video samples before sending out any audio samples. If the media sink pulls data as fast as possible and writes the first available sample, then it may first write all video samples, and only after that all audio samples.

By selecting the stream sink object with the earliest sample, the *CAviSink* ensures that samples are written to the file in sequential order, just as they would be rendered. Therefore, if not all stream objects have data, the function exits. When the other stream object receives a sample, the function will be called again, and the earliest sample will be extracted then.

If all of the stream sink objects have samples, and the stream object with the earliest sample has been found, the *ProcessStreamSamples()* function calls *CAviSink::WriteSampleFromStream()* to actually grab the sample from the *CAviStream* object and send it to *CAviFileWriter* for writing.

```
//
// Extract a sample from the specified stream and write it to the file
//
HRESULT CAviSink::WriteSampleFromStream(DWORD nEarliestSampleStream)
{
    HRESULT hr = S_OK;
    DWORD requestedSampleSize = 0;
    bool isKeyFrame = false;
```

```
do
{
    // make sure there is enough space in the internal buffer for the next sample
    hr = CheckBufferSize(nEarliestSampleStream);
    BREAK_ON_FAIL(hr);

    // store the size of the available buffer
    requestedSampleSize = m_dwSampleData;

    // actually get the next sample from the queue of the stream selected earlier
    hr = m_streamSinks[nEarliestSampleStream]->GetNextSample(
        m_pSampleData,            // sample data buffer
        &requestedSampleSize,     // get the number of useful bytes in the buffer
        &isKeyFrame);             // a Boolean key frame flag
    BREAK_ON_FAIL(hr);

    // send the sample to the file writer
    hr = m_pFileWriter->WriteSample(
        m_pSampleData,            // data buffer to write
        requestedSampleSize,      // number of useful bytes in the buffer
        nEarliestSampleStream,    // stream ID
        isKeyFrame);              // a Boolean key frame flag
    BREAK_ON_FAIL(hr);
}
while(false);

return hr;
}
```

Here the *CheckBufferSize()* function is used to verify that the internal *m_pSampleData* buffer (a byte array that will hold the sample data) in the AVI sink is large enough for the next sample. Then the *WriteSampleFromStream()* method gets the next sample from the stream with the index derived earlier and sends that sample onward, to the AVI file writer.

Note One of the parameters getting extracted and passed on here is the *isKeyFrame* Boolean flag. This flag is not required, because AVI files don't have to have key frames marked, but it will greatly speed up seeks within the file. Without key frame flags in the AVI file, a player would have to start at the very beginning of the file and go through every frame each time it needed to seek. If you mark the key frames, however, the player simply needs to find the nearest key frame and start playback from there.

Most of the stream and sample selection logic is encapsulated in the *CAviSink::GetEarliestSampleStream()* function. The function is large because it needs to handle several edge cases, so let's break down the function into three parts: one that extracts a time stamp from each stream, one that deals with error cases where the stream doesn't have any samples, and one that makes sure that the function returns the stream ID of the stream with the earliest sample.

Here is the first part of the *GetEarliestSampleStream()* method.

```
//
// Go through every stream, and figure out which stream has the next sample we want to write
// to the file, since we want to write all samples in sequential order, arranged by the time
// they need to be rendered (earliest time stamps first).
//
HRESULT CAviSink::GetEarliestSampleStream(int* pEarliestStream)
{
    HRESULT hr = S_OK;
    int nEarliestSampleStream = -1;
    LONGLONG nextSampleTime = -1;
    bool drainMode = false;

    do
    {
        // go through every stream, and figure out which stream has the next earliest sample
        for(DWORD x = 0; x < m_streamSinks.size(); x++)
        {
            CAviStream* pStream = m_streamSinks[x];
            LONGLONG currentStreamSampleTime = 0;

            // get the time stamp of the next sample in this stream
            hr = pStream->GetNextSampleTimestamp(&currentStreamSampleTime);
```

Here the function loops through every stream, extracting the time stamp of the sample at the head of the queue in each stream. The sample time stamp is returned by the *CAviStream::GetNextSampleTimestamp()* method. The method may fail to extract the time stamp, however, if the stream doesn't have any samples for some reason. The next section of the function deals with the two cases where the stream may not have samples.

```
            // if a stream has reached the end, just ignore it.  However, if a stream does
            // not have any samples, but is not at the end, break out of the loop, because
            // we need all streams to have some data
            if(hr == S_FALSE)
            {
                // store a flag indicating that we are in drain mode and need to keep
                // pulling samples while some of the streams are empty but others are not
                drainMode = true;

                // Stream has no data and is not expecting any more soon - ignore this error
                // and this stream, and look for data in the other streams.
                continue;
            }
            else if(hr == E_PENDING)
            {
                // a stream has indicated that it doesn't have any samples yet by returning
                // E_PENDING - just break out of the loop, and return -1 which will indicate
                // that not all streams have data.
                nEarliestSampleStream = -1;
                break;
            }
            BREAK_ON_FAIL(hr);
```

The helper *CAviStream::GetNextSampleTimestamp()* method can return three *HRESULT* codes under normal conditions; *S_OK*, *S_FALSE*, and *E_PENDING*.

- **S_OK** The function completed successfully and returned a valid time stamp for the next sample in the stream.

- **E_PENDING** The function doesn't have any more samples, but more samples are expected to arrive soon. In this case, the sink abandons the current process sample request. When a sample arrives to one of the streams, the sink will be called again with another processing request.

- **S_FALSE** The stream doesn't have any samples because the data stream has reached the end. In this case, the sink ignores the empty stream and turns on drain mode. Drain mode will cause the function to schedule another sample processing request—this is needed to ensure that the last sample is drained out of the stream, even if we dropped some sample requests after receiving an *E_PENDING* error code.

After *GetEarliestSampleStream()* has extracted the time stamp of the sample in the next stream, it needs to verify that this sample is earlier than the samples in the other streams. In other words, it needs to check to see if the time stamp is smaller than the time stamps of samples from other streams.

```
            // Figure out if the next sample in this stream has an earlier time stamp than
            // the other streams we have seen in this for loop
            if(currentStreamSampleTime <= nextSampleTime || nextSampleTime == -1)
            {
                nextSampleTime = currentStreamSampleTime;
                nEarliestSampleStream = x;
            }
        }

        // if we are in the drain mode - because some of the streams are already empty but
        // the others are not - schedule another sample pass to drain out the stream
        if(drainMode && nEarliestSampleStream >= 0)
        {
            hr = ScheduleNewSampleProcessing();
        }
    }
    while(false);

    // return the stream that has a sample with the earliest time stamp
    if(SUCCEEDED(hr))
    {
        *pEarliestStream = nEarliestSampleStream;
    }

    return hr;
}
```

The time stamp comparison section is fairly self-explanatory—it compares the newest time stamp to a cached time stamp of an earlier loaded stream. If the newest time stamp is smaller than the cached one—if the sample in the current stream has an earlier presentation time than the sample in the previous examined stream—then the function will store the index of the current stream.

If *GetEarliestSampleStream()* detects that it is in drain mode and finds a nonempty stream, it returns the ID of the nonempty stream and schedules another sample processing loop by calling *ScheduleNewSampleProcessing()*. The *CAviSink::ScheduleNewSampleProcessing()* method simply schedules asynchronous work on the sink. This is the same function that is called by the stream sinks whenever they receive a sample to notify the AVI sink that it needs to process more samples.

The AVI Media Stream

As you saw earlier in the chapter, all data flows to the media sink through *IMFStreamSink* objects. The stream sink objects receive individual data streams and various stream-related status events. They are also used to send out various commands to other components. Each stream sink object must implement the *IMFStreamSink* interface for configuration and receiving of samples. The *IMFStreamSink* interface inherits from the *IMFMediaEventGenerator*—its functions are used to send out stream-specific commands to the MF session and the rest of the topology.

> **Note** The *CAviStream*, just like the *AVFStream* in Chapter 6, uses a built-in MF queue in the implementation of the *IMFMediaEventGenerator* functions and will not be discussed in this chapter.

The *IMFStreamSink* interface has three functions used to facilitate data flow in the stream.

- **ProcessSample()**   Receive a new sample.
- **PlaceMarker()**   Receive a stream marker with a notification about the data stream status.
- **Flush()**   Drop all of the samples from this data stream.

These methods are used by the media sink to receive samples, events, and commands. The stream sink interface also has several extra methods used to configure the stream object:

- **GetMediaSink()**   Retrieve a pointer to the *IMFMediaSink* object with which this stream object is associated. Implementation not shown here.
- **GetIdentifier()**   Get the stream ID. Implementation not shown here.
- **GetMediaTypeHandler()**   Get an *IMFMediaTypeHandler* object that allows a client to set the media type of the data stream. Implementation not shown here.

Of particular interest is the *GetMediaTypeHandler()* function. This function allows a stream sink client to get the *IMFMediaTypeHandler* pointer of an object that will be used to set the media type of the stream.

Unlike the source streams shown in Chapter 6, stream sink objects have to be configured with the media type. This is necessary because although source streams support only the media type of the underlying data streams, some stream sinks may be configured to accept data streams in different formats. For example, a stream for an audio renderer might receive data in uncompressed PCM format, in several compressed formats that will be consumed by a digital SPIDIF link to another device, or in protected DRM audio formats.

In MF this type of configuration is often handled by special objects exposing the *IMFMediaTypeHandler* interface. This interface contains methods that allow a caller to enumerate the media types supported by an object, and to set a specific media type. Here are the methods contained in the *IMFMediaTypeHandler* interface:

- **IsMediaTypeSupported()**   Check whether a specified media type is supported, and extract a different media type that is closest to the one passed in.
- **GetMediaTypeCount()**   Get the number of supported media types.
- **GetMediaTypeByIndex()**   Get a supported media type from the object based on its index.
- **SetCurrentMediaType()**   Set the media type on the object represented by the media type handler.
- **GetCurrentMediaType()**   Get the media type set on the object represented by the handler.
- **GetMajorType()**   Get the major type of the media type currently set on the underlying object.

For simplicity, the AVI stream class implements the *IMFMediaTypeHandler* class directly instead of utilizing an external handler object. Because AVI is just a container and does not prescribe or require any specific media types, the *CAviStream* class supports all media types. As a result, all of the media type handler function implementations are quite obvious—they either return the currently set media type, or the standard *MF_E_NOT_INITIALIZED* error code. Therefore, the *IMFMediaTypeHandler* implementation is not shown in this chapter.

The *CAviStream* class has several major responsibilities in this sink design:

- Support stream configuration.
- Receive samples and store them in a queue for later processing.
- Notify the sink when new samples have arrived.
- Support extraction of the samples by the sink with various helper functions.
- Receive and handle marker objects with stream information.
- Send out various stream events when the sink starts, pauses, and stops.

In the following sections, you will see how each of these responsibilities is implemented.

Stream Playback Control Functions

In MF each individual stream sink object must request samples and report its status through the use of events. The mechanism for this is the same as in the source streams presented in Chapter 6—the *IMFStreamSink* interface inherits from the *IMFMediaEventGenerator* interface. The stream sinks use the media event system to fire events requesting samples and notifying clients of various stream conditions.

Here is the *CAviStream::OnStarted()* helper function called by the media sink to start playback. This function is used to start pulling data through the stream object.

```
//
// Start playback - member method called by the sink.
//
HRESULT CAviStream::OnStarted(void)
{
    HRESULT hr = S_OK;

    do
    {
        // fire an event indicating that this stream has started processing data
        hr = QueueEvent(MEStreamSinkStarted, GUID_NULL, S_OK, NULL);
        BREAK_ON_FAIL(hr);

        // request a sample
        hr = QueueEvent(MEStreamSinkRequestSample, GUID_NULL, S_OK, NULL);
        BREAK_ON_FAIL(hr);

        // request another sample - we will store two samples in the queue
        hr = QueueEvent(MEStreamSinkRequestSample, GUID_NULL, S_OK, NULL);
        BREAK_ON_FAIL(hr);
    }
    while(false);

    return hr;
}
```

All the function does is fire several events that start the data flow. First of all, the function fires an event that indicates that the stream sink object has started operating—the *MEStreamSinkStarted* event. This is a notification event that informs the registered MF components that the stream sink has been initialized and is ready to receive data. Then the *OnStarted()* method fires two sample request events. These request events are received by the MF media session, which starts pulling in samples. Because the function fires two of these *MEStreamSinkRequestSample* events, the maximum length of the sample queue in the AVI sink object will be two samples.

When the stream sink object receives the stop event, its behavior is quite similar—it fires the *MEStreamSinkStopped* event, notifying the sink client that the stream has stopped and will not be requesting any more samples for the foreseeable future.

Stream Sample Functions

The *CAviStream* class does not do much sample processing on its own. As shown in the previous section, most of the sample analysis is done inside the media sink itself. The sample-related responsibilities of the stream sink objects in this design are confined to storing individual samples, sending notification events to the media sink when samples arrive, and retrieving sample data on request.

The *CAviStream* class stores samples in a queue. Strictly speaking, the queue is somewhat redundant, because the AVI sink writes to a file, and therefore does not need sample buffering that could be used to smooth playback of rendering media sinks. However, the queue does not add any complexity and provides additional advantages that will become obvious after you consider stream markers.

Here is the *IMFStreamSink::ProcessSample()* function. This function is called by the client of the sink to deliver a sample to the stream sink object, after the client receives a *MEStreamSinkRequestSample* event. The client is usually the media session that receives the various events and passes samples between Media Foundation components in the topology. Each *MEStreamSinkRequestSample* event will result in a new sample being delivered to the *ProcessSample()* function while there are any samples left in the data stream.

```
//
// Receive a sample for this stream sink, store it in the sample queue, and call
// the media sink, notifying it of the arrival of a new sample.
//
HRESULT CAviStream::ProcessSample(IMFSample* pSample)
{
    HRESULT hr = S_OK;
    CComPtr<IMFSample> pMediaSample = pSample;

    do
    {
        CComCritSecLock<CComAutoCriticalSection> lock(m_critSec);

        BREAK_ON_NULL(pSample, E_POINTER);
        BREAK_ON_NULL(m_pSinkCallback, E_UNEXPECTED);

        // add the sample to the internal sample queue
        EXCEPTION_TO_HR( m_sampleQueue.AddTail(pMediaSample) );

        // schedule an asynchronous work item on the sink that will cause it to pull out
        // the new sample that has just arrived
        hr = m_pSink->ScheduleNewSampleProcessing();
    }
    while(false);

    return hr;
}
```

In this implementation, the *ProcessSample()* function stores the sample in the sample queue and calls the sink's *ScheduleNewSampleProcessing()* helper method. That helper method will internally schedule a work item on the sink, which will eventually result in an asynchronous call to the *CAviSink::ProcessStreamSamples()* function shown earlier.

```
//
// Add a work item to the thread that indicates that a new sample is available in a stream
// and needs to be processed.
//
HRESULT CAviSink::ScheduleNewSampleProcessing(void)
{
    return MFPutWorkItem(MFASYNC_CALLBACK_QUEUE_STANDARD, this, NULL);
}
```

As you can see, there isn't much to the helper *ScheduleNewSampleProcessing()* method. All it does is schedule a work item callback to the AVI stream sink object. The only reason that this call is in a separate method is that the same call needs to also be made from the *CAviStream* class when it has a new sample.

To process the next sample in the stream queue, the sink will call three helper *CAviStream* methods:

1. *GetNextSampleTimestamp()*, which retrieves the time stamp of the sample at the head of the stream internal queue. This function is used by the sink to decide which stream has the earliest sample. The sink uses this information to write samples to the file in presentation order.

2. *GetNextSampleLength()*, which gets the amount of data in the sample at the head of the queue. This helper function is used to ensure that there is enough space in the internal sink buffer, in preparation for a call to the *GetNextSample()* function.

3. *GetNextSample()*, which removes the sample at the head of the stream sample queue and copies its data into the provided buffer.

The first function called by the sink during sample processing is the *GetNextSampleTimestamp()* function. The function is quite simple, although it needs to return one of several *HRESULT*s in cases where the stream is out of samples temporarily or permanently.

```
//
// Get the time stamp on the sample that's at the head of the queue
//
HRESULT CAviStream::GetNextSampleTimestamp(LONGLONG* pTimestamp)
{
    HRESULT hr = S_OK;
    LONGLONG sampleDuration = 0;
    DWORD sampleSize = 0;
    DWORD subsamplesInSample = 0;
```

```
    do
    {
        CComCritSecLock<CComAutoCriticalSection> lock(m_critSec);
        BREAK_ON_NULL(pTimestamp, E_POINTER);

        // see if the next sample is a marker object - if it is, fire the corresponding
        // event and remove the sample from the queue
        hr = TryFireMarkerEvent(S_OK);
        BREAK_ON_FAIL(hr);

        // make sure the queue is not empty - if it is, return a result code indicating
        // whether data for this sample will still arrive, or whether the sink should not
        // wait for data from this stream, and proceed regardless.
        if(m_sampleQueue.IsEmpty())
        {
            if(m_endOfSegmentEncountered)
            {   // data for this stream won't be available for a while
                hr = S_FALSE;
            }
            else
            {   // no data available on this stream yet, but is expected to arrive shortly
                hr = E_PENDING;
            }
            break;
        }

        // get the time stamp
        EXCEPTION_TO_HR( hr = m_sampleQueue.GetHead()->GetSampleTime(pTimestamp) );
    }
    while(false);

    return hr;
}
```

More Info The *TryFireMarkerEvent()* function will be described later in this chapter, in the "Stream Markers" section.

After some parameter verifications, the *GetNextSampleTimestamp()* function checks whether the sample queue is empty. If the queue is empty, then the function needs to return an *HRESULT* indicating the current state. If the *CAviStream* has encountered an end-of-segment message, the stream is probably not going to receive new data any time soon—thus the function returns *S_FALSE*. If the end-of-segment flag is not set, then this must be a temporary condition, and the next sample simply has not gotten to the stream yet—thus the function returns the *E_PENDING* error code.

More Info The end-of-segment event is similar to the end-of-stream messages sent out by the source. It will be discussed in more detail in the "Stream Markers" section later in this chapter.

After the media sink has determined from which stream sink object it wants to retrieve the next sample, it calls the *CAviStream::GetNextSampleLength()*. This function is extremely simple and basically passes the call to the *IMFMediaSample::GetTotalLength()* method. The next call made by the media sink is more interesting, however. The *CAviStream::GetNextSample()* method does several things—it copies the sample data into a provided buffer, checks for a key frame flag in the sample, removes the sample from the queue, and fires a new *MEStreamSinkRequestSample* event.

```
//
// Get the data in the sample at the head of the queue, removing it from the queue
//
HRESULT CAviStream::GetNextSample(BYTE* pBuffer, DWORD* pBufferSize, bool* pIsKeyFrame)
{
    HRESULT hr = S_OK;
    CComPtr<IMFMediaBuffer> pMediaBuffer;
    BYTE* internalBuffer = NULL;
    DWORD bufferMaxLength = 0;
    DWORD bufferCurrentLength = 0;
    LONG result = 0;
    UINT32 isKeyFrame = 0;

    do
    {
        CComCritSecLock<CComAutoCriticalSection> lock(m_critSec);
        BREAK_ON_NULL(pBufferSize, E_POINTER);
        BREAK_ON_NULL(pBuffer, E_INVALIDARG);

        if(m_sampleQueue.IsEmpty())
        {
            hr = E_UNEXPECTED;
            break;
        }

        // Copy data in the next sample into the provided buffer
        hr = CopyNextSampleData(pBuffer, pBufferSize);
        BREAK_ON_FAIL(hr);

        // check the sample for the CleanPoint variable - if it's there and set to 1, then
        // this is a keyframe.
        EXCEPTION_TO_HR(
            m_sampleQueue.GetHead()->GetUINT32(MFSampleExtension_CleanPoint, &isKeyFrame) );
        if(isKeyFrame != 0)
        {
            *pIsKeyFrame = true;
        }
        else
        {
            *pIsKeyFrame = false;
        }

        // if we got here, then we successfully got data from the sample - remove the sample
        // from the queue
        EXCEPTION_TO_HR( m_sampleQueue.RemoveHeadNoReturn() );
```

```
        // we processed a sample - ask for another one
        hr = QueueEvent(MEStreamSinkRequestSample, GUID_NULL, S_OK, NULL);
        BREAK_ON_FAIL(hr);
    }
    while(false);

    if(FAILED(hr))
    {
        *pBufferSize = 0;
    }

    return hr;
}
```

This function is called by the sink to extract data from the next sample. The AVI file writer is interested in three pieces of data about the sample—the internal data buffer, the amount of data in the buffer, and the key frame flag. The buffer and its size are extracted and copied in the same way as in the last couple of chapters—that work is done inside of the *CopyNextSampleData()* helper function. The key frame flag, however, is a bit more interesting. The key frame flag is a *UINT32* attribute that's attached to the sample and is associated with the *MFSampleExtension_CleanPoint* GUID. If the attribute is present and is set to 1, then the sample contains a key frame. In that case, the AVI file writer will set an equivalent flag in the file, which will facilitate faster seeking.

Finally, the function removes the sample from the head of the sample queue and fires a new sample request event. The sample request event is delivered to any event clients registered with the stream sink object.

Stream Markers

Just like Microsoft DirectShow sink filters, MF sinks support several in-band events that notify them of various stream conditions. In MF stream sink objects, in-band events are known as *stream markers* and are delivered through an interface parallel to the *IMFStreamSink::ProcessSample()* function. The stream markers are instead sent to the stream in the *PlaceMarker()* function calls.

There are four predefined marker types, each of which serves a different purpose. Some of the markers can have extra data associated with them, and the data must be returned to the client after the marker has been processed.

- **MFSTREAMSINK_MARKER_ENDOFSEGMENT**   A stream marker notifying the stream sink object of the end of the current data stream. Note that this does not indicate that no more data will arrive through the stream sink. If you use a segmented source, you can have several pieces of content queued up, in which case additional data can be sent after the current segment has finished playing. There is no additional data associated with this event.

- **MFSTREAMSINK_MARKER_TICK**   A flag that indicates that there is a gap in the data stream, with one or more samples missing. This notifies the media sink that there may not be any data coming for a while, and it should not wait for more samples before processing the samples queued in this stream sink object. This event comes with an extra value indicating the presentation time of the missing sample.

- **MFSTREAMSINK_MARKER_EVENT**   A custom, extended in-band event that contains a pointer to an *IMFMediaEvent* object.

- **MFSTREAMSINK_MARKER_DEFAULT**   A custom user-defined event that can contain any data.

Stream markers must be inserted into the queue together with samples and must be processed only after all of the samples that came before the marker have been dealt with. When the stream sink object reaches the marker, it must fire the *MEStreamSinkMarker* event.

A marker can contain two pieces of information associated with it—marker value and context value. *Marker value* is some additional data that the stream sink will need to understand and process the marker. *Context value* is an additional, unspecified value that must be attached to the *MEStreamSinkMarker* event and returned back to the client after the marker has been processed. The context value lets the client know when the marker—and all the samples that came before that marker—has been processed.

To illustrate the expected behavior of the stream sink object when it receives stream markers, consider the following scenario. The stream sink first receives a sample, then a marker, then two more samples, and finally another marker. In this case, the sample queue will look something like the following illustration.

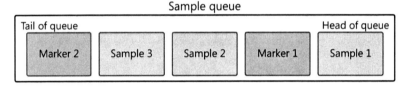

When the stream sink is processing this queue, it must first deal with Sample 1, then with Marker 1, then with Samples 2 and 3, and finally with Marker 2. Each time it processes a marker, it must fire the *MEStreamSinkMarker* event through the stream sink's *IMFMediaEventGenerator* interface, and attach whatever context value arrived with the marker.

> **Note** The markers don't actually have to be stored in the same queue as the media samples, but the order of execution shown here must be preserved. The stream markers are defined in relation to the stream of samples and must be processed together with the data stream.

To preserve the marker processing order, the *CAviStream* class stores individual markers inside dummy MF samples. The dummy samples don't have any media data but hold only attributes that indicate that they contain marker information and the marker context value. This way, the markers can be inserted directly into the media sample queue, and you don't need to implement a special container object to temporarily hold marker parameters.

Here is the *CAviStream* implementation of the *IMFStreamSink::PlaceMarker()* method that receives the markers.

```cpp
//
// Place a marker in the queue of samples, to track how the stream processes
// samples.  CAviStream ignores the marker value parameter.
//
HRESULT CAviStream::PlaceMarker(
            MFSTREAMSINK_MARKER_TYPE eMarkerType,     // marker type
            const PROPVARIANT* pvarMarkerValue,       // marker value
            const PROPVARIANT* pvarContextValue)      // context information for the event
{
    HRESULT hr = S_OK;
    CComPtr<IMFSample> pSample;
    PROPVARIANT contextCopy = {};

    do
    {
        CComCritSecLock<CComAutoCriticalSection> lock(m_critSec);

        // Use a fake empty sample to queue marker information.
        hr = MFCreateSample(&pSample);
        BREAK_ON_FAIL(hr);

        // Store the marker type in the sample.
        hr = pSample->SetUINT32(MFSTREAMSINK_MARKER_FLAG, eMarkerType);
        BREAK_ON_FAIL(hr);

        // if the marker was sent with a context value, store that value in the sample
        if(pvarContextValue != NULL)
        {
            // Deep copy the context data into the temporary PROPVARIANT value.
            hr = PropVariantCopy(&contextCopy, pvarContextValue);
            BREAK_ON_FAIL(hr);

            // Store a copy of the PROPVARIANT structure with context information in the
            // dummy sample as a memory blob.
            hr = pSample->SetBlob(
                        MFSTREAMSINK_MARKER_CONTEXT_BLOB,    // GUID identifying value
                        (UINT8*)&contextCopy,                // store the context copy
                        sizeof(contextCopy));                // size of the blob
        }

        // store the fake container sample on the queue
        hr = ProcessSample(pSample);
    }
    while(false);

    // Don't call PropVariantClear() on the marker context blob since it is stored in the
    // sample - it will be cleared after the marker data is fired in the MEStreamSinkMarker
    // event.

    return hr;
}
```

As you can see, the *PlaceMarker()* function simply creates a new MF sample and stores the marker ID and context value inside of it. The context value is provided to the function in a *PROPVARIANT* structure—therefore, the *PlaceMarker()* method creates a new copy of that structure and stores that copy in the media sample as a binary blob. Note that the context parameter may be *NULL*—in which case the value is not stored.

The *PlaceMarker()* method uses the library *PropVariantCopy()* function to create a deep copy of the *PROPVARIANT* data structure. This is needed to ensure that even if the structure contains a pointer to a memory location, and the caller of *PlaceMarker()* clears the structure with *PropVariantClear()*, the copied context data remains valid. *PlaceMarker()* is not calling *PropVariantClear()* at the end to ensure that the copy of the structure placed in the sample remains valid. To clear out the copied memory, *PropVariantClear()* will be called by the *TryFireMarkerEvent()* function after the context value has been copied into the *MEStreamSinkMarker* event.

Background As you can see, *PlaceMarker()* stores the *PROPVARIANT* in a rather indirect way—the structure is stored as a binary blob. This method is necessary because the *IMFAttributes::SetItem()* method is incapable of storing some data types that may be placed in a *PROPVARIANT*. The *SetItem()* method is designed to store only objects that can be safely copied across process boundaries. This limitation is present because the *IMFAttributes* objects may be asked to cross process boundaries while passing from the application process into a Protected Media Path (PMP) process.

The *pvarMarkerValue* parameter to the *PlaceMarker()* method is ignored because *CAviStream* does not expect any special parameters to be passed in with the marker. For the value to be useful, both the caller of the *IMFStreamSink::PlaceMarker()* function and the sink stream itself must agree on specific values that will be meaningful to the stream sink.

Note The *CAviStream* ignores the *MFSTREAMSINK_MARKER_TICK* marker signaling a gap in the data stream because the AVI sink is designed to stream from a file and not from a live source. In a sparse stream (a stream that contains large gaps between samples), the only thing different is that some samples will have non-monotonously increasing presentation time stamps, and the gaps between samples may be very large. A rendering sink in such a scenario might block waiting for a sample to arrive to every input stream object so that it can synchronize the presentation of samples from all streams. The AVI sink, however, will never block waiting for the data gap in a stream to pass, because the data source is not a real-time source, and all the stream data is available at all times. Therefore, samples for all streams will be available at all times, and the sink will be able to select the earliest sample that it will write to the AVI file.

The markers are processed and fired in the *CAviStream::TryFireMarkerEvent()* function that is called from the *GetNextSampleTimestamp()* method. Remember that *GetNextSampleTimestamp()* is the first method called by the sink when it is trying to get the next sample from the stream. Therefore, the

TryFireMarkerEvent() will be called before every attempt to extract a media sample from the queue, which means that the stream will always deal with the markers that may appear at the head of the sample queue.

Here is the flowchart that demonstrates how the *GetNextTimestamp()* function operates when we take into account stream marker extraction.

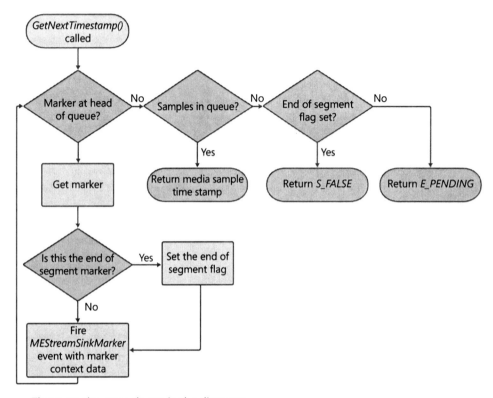

These are the steps shown in the diagram:

1. *CAviStream::GetNextTimestamp()* is called by the sink.

2. The *GetNextTimestamp()* function calls the helper *TryFireMarkerEvent()* function.

3. *TryFireMarkerEvent()* checks whether the next sample on the queue is a dummy container sample with stream marker data. If the sample at the head of the queue is not a marker sample, skip to step 6.

4. If the sample at the head of the queue is a marker container sample, extract the marker, get its corresponding context data, and fire the *MEStreamSinkMarker* event with the context data attached.

    a. If the container sample holds the *MFSTREAMSINK_MARKER_ENDOFSEGMENT* marker, set the end-of-segment flag.

5. Go back to step 3.

6. The *TryFireMarkerEvent()* returns. If there are samples in the queue, *GetNextTimestamp()* returns the time stamp of the first sample.

7. If there are no samples in the queue, check whether the end-of-segment flag was encountered.

8. If the end-of-segment flag is set, *GetNextTimestamp()* returns *S_FALSE* to indicate that this stream should be ignored by the sink.

9. If the end-of-segment flag is not set, *GetNextTimestamp()* returns *E_PENDING* to signal to the sink that more data is forthcoming.

As you can see, the *TryFireMarkerEvent()* method is responsible for detecting markers at the head of the sample queue, extracting them, and firing the corresponding *MEStreamSinkMarker* event. Here is the *TryFireMarkerEvent()* implementation.

```
//
// See if a marker is at the top of the queue, and if it is, fire an event and remove
// the marker from the queue.  Loop until all of the markers have been extracted from
// the top of the queue.
//
HRESULT CAviStream::TryFireMarkerEvent(HRESULT markerResult)
{
    HRESULT hr = S_OK;
    UINT32 markerId = 0;
    UINT32 blobSize = 0;
    PROPVARIANT markerContextData = {};
    CComPtr<IMFSample> pHeadSample;

    do
    {
        // if the sample queue is empty, just exit
        if(m_sampleQueue.IsEmpty())
        {
            break;
        }

        // get the sample from the head of the queue, making sure to check for exceptions
        EXCEPTION_TO_HR( pHeadSample = m_sampleQueue.GetHead() );
        BREAK_ON_NULL(pHeadSample, E_UNEXPECTED);

        // check for the marker value that would indicate this is a marker dummy sample
        hr = pHeadSample->GetUINT32(MFSTREAMSINK_MARKER_FLAG, &markerId);

        // if this is a normal sample, it won't have the marker flag attribute - just exit
        if(hr == MF_E_ATTRIBUTENOTFOUND)
        {
            hr = S_OK;
            break;
        }
        BREAK_ON_FAIL(hr);
```

```
            // if this is an end-of-segment marker, then it indicates the end of the current
            // stream - save a flag so that the sink can keep pulling samples from other streams
            // and ignore the fact that this one is empty
            if(markerId == MFSTREAMSINK_MARKER_ENDOFSEGMENT)
            {
                m_endOfSegmentEncountered = true;
            }
            BREAK_ON_FAIL(hr);

            // get the data stored in the dummy marker sample and associated with the event
            hr = pHeadSample->GetBlob( MFSTREAMSINK_MARKER_CONTEXT_BLOB, // GUID of the context
                    (UINT8*)&markerContextData,       // pointer to the destination
                    sizeof(markerContextData),        // size of the destination
                    &blobSize);                       // number of bytes copied

            // If the context was sent with the marker and stored in the sample, fire a marker
            // event with the context data in it.  Otherwise if the context was not found, fire
            // an event with NULL instead of context pointer.
            if(hr == S_OK)
            {
                hr = QueueEvent(MEStreamSinkMarker, GUID_NULL, markerResult, &markerContextData);
            }
            else if(hr == MF_E_ATTRIBUTENOTFOUND)
            {
                hr = QueueEvent(MEStreamSinkMarker, GUID_NULL, markerResult, NULL);
            }
            BREAK_ON_FAIL(hr);

            // remove the marker sample from the head of the queue
            m_sampleQueue.RemoveHeadNoReturn();
        }
    // loop until we break out because the event at the head of the queue is not a marker
    while(true);

    // clear the local copy of the context data object (this is necessary since it wasn't
    // cleared after PropVariantCopy() call in the PlaceMarker() function).
    PropVariantClear(&markerContextData);

    return hr;
}
```

The *TryFireMarkerEvent()* function first determines whether the event at the head of the queue is a marker container by checking for the custom *MFSTREAMSINK_MARKER_FLAG* attribute. This is a custom value that is known only inside of the stream class, because this GUID is known and used only by the AVI stream sinks. If this is a marker sample, the function tries to extract the marker context data from the sample. Then the *TryFireMarkerEvent()* method fires the *MEStreamSinkMarker* event, attaching the marker context data to it if the context object was found in the dummy sample.

Notice that like all the standard events, the *MEStreamSinkMarker* event is fired with an *HRESULT* value. The value indicates whether the marker was processed successfully or not. The only time that the markers are not processed properly is during a flush operation. The flush operation forces the sink to discard any unprocessed data, and that includes any stream markers. Therefore, during a flush, the *MEStreamSinkMarker* events are fired with the *E_ABORT* result.

After the *TryFireMarkerEvent()* method fires the marker event, it clears out any data that may be left in the *markerContextData PROPVARIANT* by calling the library *PropVariantClear()* function. This function ensures that any pointers to COM objects or arrays that might have been copied into the structure by *PropVariantCopy()* in the *PlaceMarker()* method are properly released and deleted.

Here is the *CAviStream* implementation of the *IMFStreamSink::Flush()* function.

```
//
// Flush the sink - process all of the samples in the queue
//
HRESULT CAviStream::Flush(void)
{
    HRESULT hr = S_OK;

    do
    {
        CComCritSecLock<CComAutoCriticalSection> lock(m_critSec);

        // loop through all of the items on the queue - drop regular samples and send
        // on the markers immediately with the E_ABORT result
        while(!m_sampleQueue.IsEmpty())
        {
            // try firing all of the markers at the head of the queue
            hr = TryFireMarkerEvent(E_ABORT);
            BREAK_ON_FAIL(hr);

            // if there are any samples in the queue, the head sample will NOT be a marker,
            // since the TryFireMarkerEvent() already processed all of the markers at the
            // head.  Therefore it's a normal sample.  Drop it.
            if(!m_sampleQueue.IsEmpty())
            {
                EXCEPTION_TO_HR( m_sampleQueue.RemoveHeadNoReturn() );
            }
        }
    }
    while(false);

    return hr;
}
```

The function simply loops while there are any samples left in the queue. If there are any samples, it calls the *TryFireMarkerEvent()* method, passing in *E_ABORT HRESULT*, which will be fired with any *MEStreamSinkMarker* events. That takes care of any markers at the head of the queue. If there are any samples left in the queue, the head sample is now guaranteed to be a media sample—so the *Flush()* function removes the head of the queue.

Conclusion

In this chapter, you have seen the implementation of a standard Media Foundation archival sink. The architecture of the archival file-writing sink presented here is only one of the many possible designs that can be used for sinks, but it allows you to understand the required components for all sinks. MF rendering sinks are implemented in a manner very similar to the archival sink and have very few conceptual differences.

Class Listings

For reference and to simplify your reading of this chapter, this section contains the class definitions of the main classes used in the AVI sink sample.

The *CAviSink* class represents the main class of the media sink and holds the functions necessary to start the sink and to configure the individual stream sink objects associated with the sink.

```
class CAviSink :
    public IMFFinalizableMediaSink,
    public IMFClockStateSink,
    public IMFAsyncCallback
{
    public:

        //CAviSink(void);
        CAviSink(const WCHAR* pFilename, HRESULT* pHr);
        ~CAviSink(void);

        // IUnknown interface implementation
        STDMETHODIMP QueryInterface(REFIID riid, void **ppvObject);
        virtual ULONG STDMETHODCALLTYPE AddRef(void);
        virtual ULONG STDMETHODCALLTYPE Release(void);


        // IMFMediaSink interface implementation
        STDMETHODIMP GetCharacteristics(DWORD *pdwCharacteristics);
        STDMETHODIMP AddStreamSink(DWORD dwStreamSinkIdentifier, IMFMediaType* pMediaType,
            IMFStreamSink** ppStreamSink);
        STDMETHODIMP RemoveStreamSink(DWORD dwStreamSinkIdentifier);
        STDMETHODIMP GetStreamSinkCount(DWORD* pcStreamSinkCount);
        STDMETHODIMP GetStreamSinkByIndex(DWORD dwIndex, IMFStreamSink** ppStreamSink);
        STDMETHODIMP GetStreamSinkById(DWORD dwStreamSinkIdentifier,
            IMFStreamSink** ppStreamSink);
        STDMETHODIMP SetPresentationClock(IMFPresentationClock* pPresentationClock);
        STDMETHODIMP GetPresentationClock(IMFPresentationClock** ppPresentationClock);
        STDMETHODIMP Shutdown(void);
```

```cpp
    // IMFClockStateSink interface implementation
    STDMETHODIMP OnClockStart(MFTIME hnsSystemTime, LONGLONG llClockStartOffset);
    STDMETHODIMP OnClockStop(MFTIME hnsSystemTime);
    STDMETHODIMP OnClockPause(MFTIME hnsSystemTime);
    STDMETHODIMP OnClockRestart(MFTIME hnsSystemTime);
    STDMETHODIMP OnClockSetRate(MFTIME hnsSystemTime, float flRate);

    // IMFFinalizableMediaSink interface implementation
    STDMETHODIMP BeginFinalize(IMFAsyncCallback* pCallback, IUnknown* punkState);
    STDMETHODIMP EndFinalize(IMFAsyncResult* pResult);

    // IMFAsyncCallback interface implementation
    STDMETHODIMP GetParameters(DWORD *pdwFlags, DWORD *pdwQueue);
    STDMETHODIMP Invoke(IMFAsyncResult* pAsyncResult);

    HRESULT ScheduleNewSampleProcessing(void);

private:

    enum SinkState
    {
        SinkStarted,
        SinkPaused,
        SinkStopped,
        SinkShutdown
    };


    volatile long m_cRef;                       // reference count
    CComAutoCriticalSection m_critSec;          // critical section

    WCHAR* m_pFilename;
    BYTE* m_pSampleData;
    DWORD m_dwSampleData;

    SinkState m_sinkState;
    HANDLE m_unpauseEvent;

    CComPtr<IMFPresentationClock> m_pClock;     // pointer to the presentation clock

    vector<CAviStream*> m_streamSinks;

    CAviFileWriter* m_pFileWriter;

    HRESULT ProcessStreamSamples(void);
    HRESULT GetEarliestSampleStream(int* pEarliestStream);
    HRESULT WriteSampleFromStream(DWORD nEarliestSampleStream);

    HRESULT CheckBufferSize(DWORD streamId);
    HRESULT CheckShutdown(void);
};
```

The *CAviStream* class implements the *IMFStreamSink* interface for the AVI sink sample. The stream sink objects are responsible for receiving and storing the samples received for each data stream.

In addition, this listing demonstrates two custom GUIDs used inside of the AVI stream sink to store stream markers in dummy sample objects.

```cpp
// {6DBB0806-D2F5-41A2-8CC2-32923CFE5BDA}
DEFINE_GUID(MFSTREAMSINK_MARKER_FLAG, 0x6dbb0806, 0xd2f5, 0x41a2, 0x8c, 0xc2, 0x32, 0x92, 0x3c,
    0xfe, 0x5b, 0xda);

// {C61841B8-9A1B-4845-A860-8086DB0C3F3A}
DEFINE_GUID(MFSTREAMSINK_MARKER_CONTEXT_BLOB, 0xc61841b8, 0x9a1b, 0x4845, 0xa8, 0x60, 0x80,
    0x86, 0xdb, 0xc, 0x3f, 0x3a);


class CAviStream :
    public IMFStreamSink,
    public IMFMediaTypeHandler
{
    public:

        static HRESULT CreateInstance(DWORD id, IMFMediaType* pMediaType,
            CAviSink* pSink, CAviStream** ppStream);

        CAviStream(DWORD id, IMFMediaType* pMediaType, CAviSink* pSink);
        ~CAviStream(void);

        // IUnknown interface implementation
        STDMETHODIMP QueryInterface(REFIID riid, void **ppvObject);
        virtual ULONG STDMETHODCALLTYPE AddRef(void);
        virtual ULONG STDMETHODCALLTYPE Release(void);

        // IMFStreamSink interface implementation
        STDMETHODIMP GetMediaSink(IMFMediaSink** ppMediaSink);
        STDMETHODIMP GetIdentifier(DWORD* pdwIdentifier);
        STDMETHODIMP GetMediaTypeHandler(IMFMediaTypeHandler** ppHandler);
        STDMETHODIMP ProcessSample(IMFSample* pSample);
        STDMETHODIMP PlaceMarker(MFSTREAMSINK_MARKER_TYPE eMarkerType,
            const PROPVARIANT* pvarMarkerValue, const PROPVARIANT* pvarContextValue);
        STDMETHODIMP Flush(void);

        // IMFMediaEventGenerator interface implementation
        STDMETHODIMP BeginGetEvent(IMFAsyncCallback* pCallback, IUnknown* punkState);
        STDMETHODIMP EndGetEvent(IMFAsyncResult* pResult, IMFMediaEvent** ppEvent);
        STDMETHODIMP GetEvent(DWORD dwFlags, IMFMediaEvent** ppEvent);
        STDMETHODIMP QueueEvent(MediaEventType met, REFGUID guidExtendedType, HRESULT hrStatus,
            const PROPVARIANT* pvValue);

        // IMFMediaTypeHandler interface implementation
        STDMETHODIMP IsMediaTypeSupported(IMFMediaType* pMediaType, IMFMediaType** ppMediaType);
        STDMETHODIMP GetMediaTypeCount(DWORD* pdwTypeCount);
        STDMETHODIMP GetMediaTypeByIndex(DWORD dwIndex, IMFMediaType** ppType);
        STDMETHODIMP SetCurrentMediaType(IMFMediaType* pMediaType);
        STDMETHODIMP GetCurrentMediaType(IMFMediaType** ppMediaType);
        STDMETHODIMP GetMajorType(GUID* pguidMajorType);
```

```cpp
        HRESULT GetNextSampleTimestamp(LONGLONG* pTimestamp);
        HRESULT GetNextSampleLength(DWORD* pSize);
        HRESULT GetNextSample(BYTE* pBuffer, DWORD* pBufferSize, bool* pIsKeyFrame);

        HRESULT OnStarted(void);
        HRESULT OnPaused(void);
        HRESULT OnStopped(void);

    private:
        volatile long m_cRef;                       // reference count
        CComAutoCriticalSection m_critSec;          // critical section

        DWORD m_streamId;

        CAviSink* m_pSink;
        CComPtr<IMFMediaType> m_pMediaType;
        CComPtr<IMFMediaEventQueue> m_pEventQueue;

        CInterfaceList<IMFSample> m_sampleQueue;
        CComPtr<IMFAsyncCallback> m_pSinkCallback;

        bool m_endOfSegmentEncountered;

        HRESULT CopyNextSampleData(BYTE* pBuffer, DWORD* pBufferSize);
        HRESULT TryFireMarkerEvent(HRESULT markerResult = S_OK);
        HRESULT GetMarkerContextData(PROPVARIANT** ppPropVariant);
};
```

Finally, the *CAviFileWriter* class encapsulates the VFW file-writing functions used by the AVI sink to write the AVI file to the disk.

```cpp
class CAviFileWriter
{
    public:
        CAviFileWriter(const WCHAR* pFilename);
        ~CAviFileWriter(void);

        HRESULT AddStream(IMFMediaType* pMediaType, DWORD id);
        HRESULT WriteSample(BYTE* pData, DWORD dataLength, DWORD streamId,
            bool isKeyframe = false);

    private:
        struct AviStreamData
        {
            IAVIStream* pStream;
            ULONG nNextSample;
            bool isAudio;
        };

        IAVIFile* m_pAviFile;
        hash_map<DWORD, AviStreamData*> m_streamHash;
        WAVEFORMATEX*  m_pAudioFormat;

        HRESULT AddAudioStream(IMFMediaType* pMT, IAVIStream** pStream);
        HRESULT AddVideoStream(IMFMediaType* pMT, IAVIStream** pStream);
};
```

CHAPTER 8

Custom Media Sessions

The Custom MP3 Media Session 250
Building an MP3 Topology 251
The Custom Session Data Pipeline. 261
The Session Clock. 279

In the previous chapters, you have seen the design and internal workings of various standard Microsoft Media Foundation (MF) components. The chapters demonstrated how to create a playback topology, as well as the internal structure of MF sources, MFTs, and sinks. During normal MF operations, these work with each other to display video on the screen, play audio, or change one media format to another.

In this chapter, you will see how all of these components actually pass data from one to another. This will be done by examining a custom media session that will replace the default Media Foundation media session in the sample player shown in Chapter 3, "Media Playback." The media session is the object that actually receives events from individual MF components, gets samples from one component, and passes them to another.

Up until now, all topology diagrams have shown data flowing directly from the source to the MFT, and then to the sink. The lines have connected these MF components directly, as if the individual objects call each other with synchronous function calls. This is the design of Microsoft DirectShow media graphs, and it brings across the general idea of how the components interoperate with each other. However, that is not a completely accurate representation of the data flow in Media Foundation topologies.

Remember that, in MF, individual components do not know anything about each other. Even though they are loaded into the same topology, they cannot communicate with each other directly, because there is no way for them to discover what other components are next to them. Therefore, MF uses a special object to facilitate data flow between components—the media session. The media session is a generic object that holds the topology, receives events from the objects in the topology, retrieves new samples from the objects, and passes them to the next object downstream.

Here is a diagram that more accurately represents the dataflow in a standard MF topology.

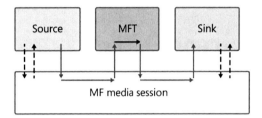

The solid arrows represent sample flow, and the dashed lines represent media events sent and received through the components' *IMFMediaEventGenerator* interface. As you can see, although the data flow does indeed proceed from the source to the MFT and then to the sink, there are actually quite a few extra steps involved. The media session needs to receive sample-ready events from the source, get the samples from it, pass the samples to the MFT, get the processed samples from the MFT, and finally pass the samples to the sink.

In Chapter 3, you saw how to create a default MF media session with the *MFCreateMediaSession()* function call. The session created in that case was a general-purpose component provided by MF—it handled all of the complexities described earlier. In almost all scenarios, the default MF session is all that you require to build your applications. By creating various custom sources, sinks, and MFTs, you can implement virtually any functionality that you may need. However, there are a handful of scenarios in which you may need to create your own custom media session. Some of those scenarios are listed here:

- Advanced file playback in which the data resides in several segmented files and the source needs to keep a single, consistent timeline and transition seamlessly between individual files

- Custom Digital Rights Media (DRM) implementation independent from the MF Protected Media Path technology and Windows Media DRM (WMDRM)/Microsoft PlayReady

- Unit tests that require tracking of individual events and samples as they flow between individual components and through the pipeline

- Integration of MF components with non-MF media sources, or processing units without media source and MFT wrappers

In this chapter, you will see a custom media session implementation, which will allow you to see exactly how all of the disparate MF components from previous chapters work together to display video. Although the sample session presented here does not do anything beyond the default session, it will demonstrate how data flows through the pipeline and how media events are used to trigger various actions.

The sample in this chapter is based on the basic MF playback application from Chapter 3. The CustomSession application uses the same UI and keeps the underlying topology-building functionality. The only change is that while playing MP3 files, the application instantiates the custom *CMP3Session* object instead of the default MF-provided media session. This object implements the generic *IMFMediaSession* interface but is designed solely for MP3 audio file playback.

The custom session plays only MP3 files to simplify the topology and clearly demonstrate all of the ideas and behaviors necessary to play back any media file. A topology for playing an MP3 file contains the Media Foundation components present in any topology but is much simpler than many other topologies. Therefore, the topology contains only the MP3 file source, MP3 decoder, an audio resampler object, and the standard audio renderer. Here is what this topology looks like when loaded in TopoEdit.

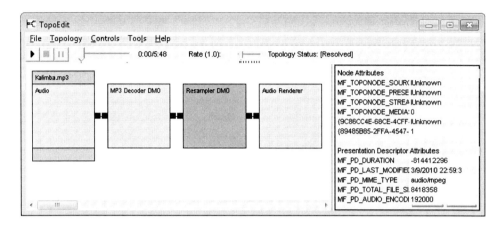

Note The Resampler DirectX Media Object (DMO) shown here is a helper component that is automatically loaded into standard topologies. This MFT is used to modify the raw audio stream for playback on your current audio setup. For example, it can reduce the number of channels in the audio if you have a mono or stereo sound system, or it can increase the audio sample rate to what the audio driver expects.

To simplify things, the resampler MFT is omitted from many of the diagrams in this chapter.

As you can see, this topology is very simple and contains only four components. Because the MP3 file playback topology is always going to be the same, and because the custom media session is designed solely for MP3 playback, the sample does not implement a full-featured topology loader. Instead, the custom media session always instantiates the same four MF components and hooks them up in the same order. This is done because MF component discovery and partial topology rendering have already been discussed in Chapter 3.

Here are the two major classes that are used in this sample:

- **CMP3SessionTopoBuilder** This is the base class for the custom MP3 session. As the name suggests, this base class contains all of the functions necessary for instantiating and negotiating the media types between the four MF components of the topology.

- **CMP3Session** This is the class that implements the functionality necessary to send data through the topology. The methods in this class are used to receive events from the MF components and pass samples between them.

Other than that, the player in the sample is nearly identical to the basic MF player in Chapter 3. If the URL passed in ends with the .mp3 extension, the player instantiates the *CMP3Session*. For all other files, the sample uses the *MFCreateMediaSession()* API to instantiate a default media session.

The Custom MP3 Media Session

An object that passes data between MF components doesn't really need to implement the *IMFMediaSession* interface. The class shown in this chapter implements this interface because it plugs into the existing MF playback sample from Chapter 3. In reality, however, the individual MF components do not know how they were instantiated, what kind of object holds references to them, or who is calling them.

As mentioned earlier, the custom session class consists of two parts—a base class concerned with constructing an MP3 topology, and a child class that actually constitutes the data pipeline, receives events, passes samples between components, and so on. Although the custom session implements the *IMFMediaSession* interface, many of its methods are left unimplemented:

- **SetTopology()**   Used to set the topology. Because the custom session uses a static internal topology, this function simply receives a pointer to an *IMFTopology* object and stores it internally. This topology is subsequently ignored and not used.

- **ClearTopologies()**   Resets the internal topology *IMFTopology* pointer.

- **GetFullTopology()**   This function is left unimplemented, only returning *E_NOTIMPL*.

- **Start()**   Starts playback.

- **Pause()**   Pauses playback.

- **Stop()**   Stops playback.

- **Close()**   Closes the session and releases all of the internal resources. This function is left unimplemented for simplicity.

- **Shutdown()**   Shuts down the media source, sink, and event queue. For simplicity, the shutdown methods of the internal components are called in the *CMP3SessionTopoBuilder* destructor, and this function is left unimplemented.

- **GetClock()**   Returns a pointer to the current presentation clock.

- **GetSessionCapabilities()**   Returns a combination of flags indicating the capabilities of the media session.

In addition to *IMFMediaSession*, the custom session implements several other interfaces that it needs to properly function:

- **IMFMediaEventGenerator**   Interface inherited from *IMFMediaSession*. This interface is used only to asynchronously report failures and error conditions.

- **IMFAsyncCallback**   The interface required for receiving asynchronous callbacks.

- **IMFGetService** Implemented only for compatibility with the default session. The player uses this interface to extract a pointer to the video renderer and the rate control object. Because the MP3 topology does not contain a video renderer, *IMFGetService::GetService()* returns E_NOINTERFACE when asked for a renderer, and returns an interface to the presentation clock when asked for the rate control.

The implementation of all of these interfaces is either trivial or has been demonstrated before. Therefore, many of the functions will be omitted from this chapter. For example, the *IMFMediaEventGenerator* interface implementation is identical to that presented in Chapter 6, "Media Foundation Sources," and Chapter 7, "Media Foundation Sinks"—all of the functions simply call into an MF-provided *IMFMediaEventQueue* object.

Building an MP3 Topology

One of the purposes of this chapter is to demonstrate how various interface methods of Media Foundation components presented earlier can be used in a viable MF implementation. Therefore, this section shows how the *CMP3SessionTopoBuilder* instantiates and connects the components required to play back an MP3 file.

Because instantiation of sources is asynchronous, the process of creating the topology is also broken up into several parts. The class first calls *IMFByteStreamHandler::BeginCreateObject()*, and then finishes rendering the topology on the callback from the byte stream handler. Here is a sequence diagram that demonstrates this process.

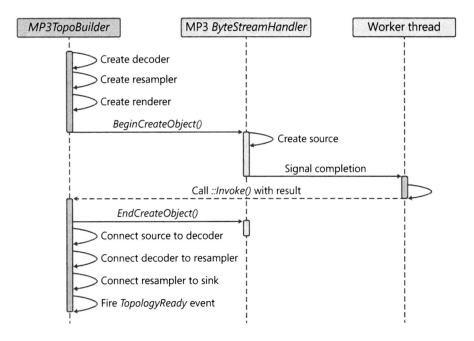

Essentially, the topology-building process is broken up into two parts—before creation of the source, and after. Remember that creation of the source requires you to call the *IMFByteStreamHandler::BeginCreateObject()* method. The method completes asynchronously. After it is done, the byte stream handler calls back the *CMP3TopoBuilder* object and passes in the result. The topology builder then gets the actual source from the byte stream handler by calling the *IMFByteStreamHandler::EndCreateObject* method, and then starts hooking up individual components. Unlike in DirectShow, in which filters are explicitly connected to each other, in MF the only thing you need to do is ensure that both components can agree on a media type, and set that media type.

Here is the function that starts the first half of the topology-building process.

```
//
// Load the custom topology for decoding MP3 files
//
HRESULT CMP3SessionTopoBuilder::LoadCustomTopology(void)
{
    HRESULT hr = S_OK;

    do
    {
        // directly instantiate the MP3 decoder MFT
        hr = m_pDecoder.CoCreateInstance(CLSID_CMP3DecMediaObject);
        BREAK_ON_FAIL(hr);

        // instantiate the helper audio resampler MFT
        hr = m_pResampler.CoCreateInstance(CLSID_CResamplerMediaObject);
        BREAK_ON_FAIL(hr);

        // create the audio renderer
        hr = MFCreateAudioRenderer(NULL, &m_pSink);
        BREAK_ON_FAIL(hr);

        // as the last step begin asynchronously creating the media source through its
        // IMFByteStreamHandler - do this last so that after the source is created we can
        // negotiate the media types between the rest of the components
        hr = BeginCreateMediaSource();
        BREAK_ON_FAIL(hr);
    }
    while(false);

    return hr;
}
```

The *CMP3SessionTopoBuilder::LoadCustomTopology()* function instantiates the topology. As you can see, the decoder and audio resampler are created directly, by calling *CoCreateInstance()* with their class IDs (CLSIDs). This is done because the procedure for searching for matching MFTs among all of the MFTs registered on the system is tedious, not interesting, and is thus not implemented in this class. The audio renderer (which shows up as *SAR*—Streaming Audio Renderer—in TopoEdit) is created with the built-in MF function *MFCreateAudioRenderer()*. After the decoder, resampler, and renderer sink objects are instantiated, the *LoadCustomTopology()* function calls a helper method that begins asynchronous MP3 source instantiation.

Here is the *BeginCreateMediaSource()* function, which essentially calls *BeginCreateObject()* on the MP3 byte stream handler.

```
//
// Create a media source for the cached file URL.
//
HRESULT CMP3SessionTopoBuilder::BeginCreateMediaSource(void)
{
    HRESULT hr = S_OK;
    CComPtr<IMFByteStream> pByteStream;
    CComPtr<IAsyncState> pState;

    do
    {
        // create an IMFByteStreamHandler object for the MP3 file
        hr = m_pByteStreamHandler.CoCreateInstance(CLSID_MP3ByteStreamPlugin);
        BREAK_ON_FAIL(hr);

        // open the file and get its IMFByteStream object
        hr = MFCreateFile(
            MF_ACCESSMODE_READ,                 // open the file for reading
            MF_OPENMODE_FAIL_IF_NOT_EXIST,      // fail if file does not exist
            MF_FILEFLAGS_NONE,                  // default behavior
            m_pFileUrl,                         // URL to the file
            &pByteStream);                      // get result here
        BREAK_ON_FAIL(hr);

        // create a state object that will identify the asynchronous operation to the Invoke
        pState = new (std::nothrow) CAsyncState(AsyncEventType_ByteStreamHandlerEvent);
        BREAK_ON_NULL(pState, E_OUTOFMEMORY);

        // create the media source from the IMFByteStreamHandler for the MP3 file
        hr = m_pByteStreamHandler->BeginCreateObject(
            pByteStream,                        // byte stream to the file
            m_pFileUrl,                         // URL-style path to the file
            MF_RESOLUTION_MEDIASOURCE,          // create a media source
            NULL,                               // no custom configuration properties
            NULL,                               // no cancel cookie
            this,                               // IMFAsyncCallback that will be called
            pState);                            // custom state object indicating event type
    }
    while(false);

    return hr;
}
```

The byte stream handler itself is again instantiated directly. You can search the registry for a matching file extension, and get the MP3 byte stream handler's CLSID that way, but this process is also not very interesting and is therefore omitted. Instead, the CLSID of the MP3 byte stream handler is hard-coded into the sample application.

Remember that *IMFByteStreamHandler::BeginCreateObject()* ordinarily takes an *IMFByteStream* object as a parameter. Though the AVFSource sample shown in Chapter 6 ignored this parameter, here it is required. Therefore, the *BeginCreateMediaSource()* method uses the *MFCreateFile()* function to get a byte stream object that corresponds to the specified URL. Despite its name, the *MFCreateFile()* function does not actually create the file here—its behavior is controlled by the access mode flags. In this case, the file is opened for read-only access, and *MFCreateFile()* is used to get the corresponding byte stream object. After this, the method finally calls the *BeginCreateObject()* function, passing in the byte stream object that will load the MP3 file and pass it to the source. Note, however, that the method also passes a custom *CAsyncState* object to the *BeginCreateObject* function.

The *CAsyncState* is a helper COM object defined in this sample project. *CAsyncState* is used to identify the asynchronous operation that caused the *Invoke()* call—it holds the ID of the operation that called the session. This object is necessary because the will receive events from several different objects, and for several reasons. Therefore, the session's *IMFAsyncCallback::Invoke()* method may be called for many reasons. The only way to distinguish between those reasons is to set and check the asynchronous call state variable and store in that variable the ID of the operation. In this case, the *CAsyncState* object receives the *AsyncEventType_ByteStreamHandlerEvent* value in the constructor. The session's *Invoke()* method will check for this value and use it to figure out that the call was made to notify the session that the byte stream handler has finished creating the media source.

Here is the corresponding *IMFAsyncCallback::Invoke()* method that is called whenever an asynchronous event calls back to the session object.

```
//
// Asynchronous worker function - called when the source has finished initializing, and when
// an event has occurred.
//
HRESULT CMP3Session::Invoke(IMFAsyncResult* pResult)
{
    HRESULT hr = S_OK;
    CComPtr<IUnknown> pUnkState;
    CComQIPtr<IAsyncState> pAsyncState;

    do
    {
        // see if the event indicates a failure - if so, fail and return the MEError event
        hr = pResult->GetStatus();
        BREAK_ON_FAIL(hr);

        // get the IAsyncState state from the result
        hr = pResult->GetState(&pUnkState);
        BREAK_ON_FAIL(hr);

        pAsyncState = pUnkState;
        BREAK_ON_NULL(pAsyncState, E_UNEXPECTED);

        // figure out the type of the operation from the state, and then proxy the call to
        // the right function
        if(pAsyncState->EventType() == AsyncEventType_ByteStreamHandlerEvent)
        {
            hr = HandleByteStreamHandlerEvent(pResult);
        }
```

```cpp
        else if(pAsyncState->EventType() == AsyncEventType_SinkStreamEvent)
        {
            hr = HandleSinkStreamEvent(pResult);
        }
        else if(pAsyncState->EventType() == AsyncEventType_SourceEvent)
        {
            hr = HandleSourceEvent(pResult);
        }
        else if(pAsyncState->EventType() == AsyncEventType_SourceStreamEvent)
        {
            hr = HandleSourceStreamEvent(pResult);
        }
        else if(pAsyncState->EventType() == AsyncEventType_SyncMftSampleRequest)
        {
            hr = HandleSynchronousMftRequest(pResult);
        }
    }
    while(false);

    // if we got a failure, queue an error event
    if(FAILED(hr))
    {
        hr = m_pEventQueue->QueueEventParamVar(MEError, GUID_NULL, hr, NULL);
    }

    return hr;
}
```

The *Invoke()* function should look pretty familiar by now. This implementation is fairly standard and almost self-explanatory. The function extracts the *CAsyncState* object stored as a state variable in an asynchronous call and gets the event type from it. Then the function checks the event type and calls the appropriate handler function. Finally, if there was an error, the *Invoke()* method queues an *MEError* event with the error code.

In this case, the call is made with the state object holding the *AsyncEventType_ByteStreamHandler-Event* enumeration value. This means that after the byte stream handler has finished executing and created the source, the worker thread eventually enters the *HandleByteStreamHandlerEvent()* function.

```cpp
//
// Negotiate media types between MF components after the IMFByteStreamHandler has created
// the source.
//
HRESULT CMP3SessionTopoBuilder::HandleByteStreamHandlerEvent(IMFAsyncResult* pResult)
{
    HRESULT hr = S_OK;
    MF_OBJECT_TYPE objectType = MF_OBJECT_INVALID;
    CComPtr<IUnknown> pUnkSource;

    do
    {
        // get the actual source by calling IMFByteStreamHandler::EndCreateObject()
        hr = m_pByteStreamHandler->EndCreateObject(pResult, &objectType, &pUnkSource);
        BREAK_ON_FAIL(hr);
```

```
        // make sure that what was created was the media source
        if(objectType != MF_OBJECT_MEDIASOURCE)
        {
            hr = E_UNEXPECTED;
            break;
        }

        // get the IMFMediaSource pointer from the IUnknown we got from EndCreateObject
        m_pSource = pUnkSource;
        BREAK_ON_NULL(m_pSource, E_UNEXPECTED);

        // call a function to negotiate the media types between each MF component in the
        // topology
        hr = NegotiateMediaTypes();
        BREAK_ON_FAIL(hr);

        // fire the MESessionTopologyStatus event with a pointer to the topology
        hr = FireTopologyReadyEvent();
    }
    while(false);

    return hr;
}
```

The *CMP3SessionTopoBuilder::HandleByteStreamHandlerEvent()* function first extracts the actual *IMFMediaSource* object from the byte stream handler and then calls another helper function to negotiate the media types between individual components. If everything succeeded, the function fires an *MFSessionTopologyStatus* event with a message indicating that the topology is ready. The player listens for that event and starts playback only after the topology is ready.

Negotiating Media Type

One of the key steps in building the topology is negotiating the media types that the components in the topology will produce and consume. This process is necessary to ensure that all of the components are configured correctly and that each upstream component is capable of producing data in the right format for its downstream component.

Media type negotiation in MF works essentially the same way as in DirectShow—each media type supported by the two components is tried in turn, until one is found on which everyone can agree. In DirectShow, the matching is usually done by the graph object. In MF this is most commonly done by the topology builder and the session. Therefore, in this sample, the custom session must do this job.

Because the MP3 topology is well known, the custom session does not need to search for MFTs that will allow it to decode and play the data stream. The custom session does not use the MFT search algorithm commonly invoked by topology builders. The MP3 session already has all the necessary MFTs instantiated at this point. Instead, the session directly connects the four components to each other, without looking for any intermediate MFTs. The media type negotiation process is driven by the *CMP3SessionTopoBuilder::NegotiateMediaTypes()* method.

```cpp
//
// Find matching media types between each MF component, and set them
//
HRESULT CMP3SessionTopoBuilder::NegotiateMediaTypes(void)
{
    HRESULT hr = S_OK;

    do
    {
        // find matching type between source and the decoder
        hr = ConnectSourceToMft(m_pDecoder);
        BREAK_ON_FAIL(hr);

        // set the media type between the decoder and the resampler
        hr = ConnectMftToMft(m_pDecoder, m_pResampler);
        BREAK_ON_FAIL(hr);

        // set the media type between the resampler and the audio sink
        hr = ConnectMftToSink(m_pResampler);
        BREAK_ON_FAIL(hr);
    }
    while(false);

    return hr;
}
```

As you can see, the session needs to establish three connections—the MP3 source must be connected to the decoder, the decoder to the resampler, and the resampler to the audio sink.

Here is the function that establishes the source-decoder connection.

```cpp
//
// Negotiate media type between source and the specified MFT.
//
HRESULT CMP3SessionTopoBuilder::ConnectSourceToMft(IMFTransform* pMft)
{
    HRESULT hr = S_OK;
    CComPtr<IMFStreamDescriptor> pStreamDescriptor;
    CComPtr<IMFMediaTypeHandler> pMediaTypeHandler;
    CComPtr<IMFMediaType> pMediaType;
    BOOL streamSelected = FALSE;
    DWORD decoderInputStreamId = 0;

    DWORD sourceTypesCount = 0;

    do
    {
        BREAK_ON_NULL(pMft, E_UNEXPECTED);

        // get the presentation descriptor for the source
        hr = m_pSource->CreatePresentationDescriptor(&m_pPresentation);
        BREAK_ON_FAIL(hr);
```

```cpp
        // get the stream descriptor for the first stream
        hr = m_pPresentation->GetStreamDescriptorByIndex(0, &streamSelected,
            &pStreamDescriptor);
        BREAK_ON_FAIL(hr);

        // get the media type handler for the source
        hr = pStreamDescriptor->GetMediaTypeHandler(&pMediaTypeHandler);
        BREAK_ON_FAIL(hr);

        // get the number of media types that are exposed by the source stream
        hr = pMediaTypeHandler->GetMediaTypeCount(&sourceTypesCount);
        BREAK_ON_FAIL(hr);

        // go through every media type exposed by the source, and try each one with the sink
        for(DWORD x = 0; x < sourceTypesCount; x++)
        {
            pMediaType = NULL;

            // get a media type from the source by index
            hr = pMediaTypeHandler->GetMediaTypeByIndex(x, &pMediaType);
            BREAK_ON_FAIL(hr);

            // try to set the input media type on the decoder - assume that the input stream
            // ID is 0, since this is a well-known MFT
            hr = pMft->SetInputType(0, pMediaType, 0);
            if(SUCCEEDED(hr))
            {
                // if the decoder accepted the input media type, set it on the source
                hr = pMediaTypeHandler->SetCurrentMediaType(pMediaType);
                BREAK_ON_FAIL(hr);
                break;
            }
        }

        // if the type was found, hr will be S_OK - otherwise hr will indicate a failure to
        // either get the media type by index, set it on the decoder, or set it on the
        // media type handler
        BREAK_ON_FAIL(hr);

        // if the source stream is not activated, activate it
        if(!streamSelected)
        {
            hr = m_pPresentation->SelectStream(0);
        }
    }
    while(false);

    return hr;
}
```

This source-MFT connection function first of all creates a presentation descriptor for the source. The presentation descriptor is needed to extract the stream descriptor for the one stream produced by the MP3 source. The stream descriptor is in turn needed to activate (select) the media stream object, and to extract the media type handler object that will be used to enumerate through all of the supported media types.

After the *IMFMediaTypeHandler* for the media stream object exposed by the source is extracted, the function loops through every media type exposed by the media stream. It then tries to set that type on the input stream of the MFT. If the MFT accepts the input type, the type is also set on the media type handler itself, and by extension on the media stream object exposed by the source.

The same approach is also used for the decoder-to-resampler connection, as well as the resampler-to-sink connection. The only difference is that the MFTs do not expose media type handlers, which means that the media types must be extracted directly, by calling the *IMFTransform::GetOutputAvailableType()* on the upstream component.

```
//
// Find matching media type for two MFTs, and set it
//
HRESULT CMP3SessionTopoBuilder::ConnectMftToMft(IMFTransform* pMft1, IMFTransform* pMft2)
{
    HRESULT hr = S_OK;
    CComPtr<IMFMediaType> pMediaType;
    DWORD mft1OutputStreamId = 0;
    DWORD mft2InputStreamId = 0;

    DWORD mft1TypeIndex = 0;

    do
    {
        BREAK_ON_NULL(pMft1, E_UNEXPECTED);
        BREAK_ON_NULL(pMft2, E_UNEXPECTED);

        // loop through all of the available output types exposed by the upstream MFT, and
        // try each of them as the input type of the downstream MFT.
        while(true)
        {
            pMediaType = NULL;

            // get the type with the mftTypeIndex index from the upstream MFT
            hr = pMft1->GetOutputAvailableType(mft1OutputStreamId, mft1TypeIndex++,
                &pMediaType);
            BREAK_ON_FAIL(hr);

            // try to set the input type on the downstream MFT
            hr = pMft2->SetInputType(mft2InputStreamId, pMediaType, 0);
            if(SUCCEEDED(hr))
            {
                // if we succeeded, set the output type on the upstream component
                hr = pMft1->SetOutputType(mft1OutputStreamId, pMediaType, 0);
                break;
            }
        }
        BREAK_ON_FAIL(hr);
    }
    while(false);

    return hr;
}
```

Again, the function loops through all of the available media types exposed by the upstream component and tries to set the media type on the downstream object. If the *IMFTransform::SetInputType()* succeeds, the function knows that it found the matching media type. It therefore sets that type on the upstream MFT and exits the loop.

The procedure for connecting the MFT to the sink is virtually identical to that for connecting the source to the MFT—one object exposes a media type handler, while the other does not. Therefore, because the technique used for the *CMP3SessionTopoBuilder::ConnectMftToSink()* function is so similar to the *ConnectSourceToMft()* method, it is omitted from this chapter.

When the media type negotiation is complete, the topology building is done. All of the components at this point are initialized and connected. Therefore, the MP3 session fires an event notifying the player that the topology is ready, after which the player will start session playback. Here is the function that actually fires the event.

```
//
// Fire the MESessionTopologyStatus event signaling that the topology is ready
//
HRESULT CMP3SessionTopoBuilder::FireTopologyReadyEvent(void)
{
    HRESULT hr = S_OK;
    PROPVARIANT variantStatus;
    CComPtr<IMFMediaEvent> pEvent;

    do
    {
        // initialize the structure
        PropVariantInit(&variantStatus);

        // initialize the PROPVARIANT with the pointer to the topology
        variantStatus.vt = VT_UNKNOWN;
        variantStatus.punkVal = m_pTopology.p;

        // create an IMFMediaEvent object that will hold MESessionTopologyStatus event
        // and a pointer to the new topology
        hr = MFCreateMediaEvent(
            MESessionTopologyStatus,    // event type
            GUID_NULL,                  // no extended event type
            hr,                         // result of operations
            &variantStatus,             // pointer to the topology
            &pEvent);
        BREAK_ON_FAIL(hr);

        // set the topology status to indicate that the topology is ready
        hr = pEvent->SetUINT32(MF_EVENT_TOPOLOGY_STATUS, MF_TOPOSTATUS_READY);
        BREAK_ON_FAIL(hr);

        // queue the event
        hr = m_pEventQueue->QueueEvent(pEvent);
    }
```

```
    while(false);

    // free any internal variables that can be freed in the PROPVARIANT
    PropVariantClear(&variantStatus);

    return hr;
}
```

The function first creates the *IMFMediaEvent* object and stores the topology pointer inside of the event. The topology pointer is again stored as part of the *PROPVARIANT* structure, as a *VT_UNKNOWN* parameter. Then the function sets the topology status *UINT32* attribute on the event, after which the event is queued on the session's *IMFMediaEventGenerator* queue.

At this point, the topology is considered complete. When the player receives the topology ready event, it immediately calls *IMFMediaSession::Start()* to start playback.

The Custom Session Data Pipeline

The second half of the custom media session object is implemented in the *CMP3Session* class, which is a child of the topology building component. The class contains several functions that are concerned with sending data through the pipeline.

The playback process begins when the player calls the *Start()* method of the custom session. The start method initializes the presentation clock, starts listening to the *IMFMediaEventGenerator* interfaces exposed by the sink and source, and finally sends the start command to the clock. Internally in the sink, this triggers its *IMFClockStateSink::OnClockStart()* method, which begins the playback process—the stream sink object starts firing media sample request events, which propagate to downstream components.

Because MF is based on the pull architecture, all of the actions in the pipeline are triggered by the sink. Specifically, the sink sends out one or more *MEStreamSinkRequestSample* events, at which point the session starts trying to pull data from the rest of the components in the pipeline. The following is an abstract diagram that demonstrates the order of operations. The diagram demonstrates how data flows through the pipeline, starting with the sink sample request in the lower-right corner, and continuing clockwise.

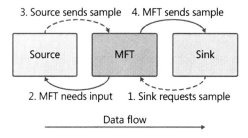

Here is a more in-depth description of this process:

1. The sink requests a sample asynchronously, by firing the *MEStreamSinkRequestSample* event.

2. The session tries to get data out of the MFT but discovers that the MFT needs more input. Therefore, the session sends a sample request to the source by calling *IMFMediaStream::RequestSample()* on the source stream.

3. The source generates a new sample and sends it asynchronously by firing the *MEMediaSample* event. The session picks up the sample and sends it to the MFT.

4. The MFT produces an output sample, and the session sends it to the sink by calling the *IMFStreamSink::ProcessSample()* method on the stream sink object.

This is the bird's-eye view of how the custom session pipeline operates. The sample request comes out of the sink, and then "percolates" upstream to the source. Then the source produces a new sample, which basically floats back downstream to the sink. In some cases there could be loops if an MFT requires more than one input sample to produce a single output sample, or if an MFT produces more than one output sample for an input sample, but this is the general idea.

Synchronous and Asynchronous MFTs

The data request process is actually a bit more complex than what was shown in the previous section. The complexity arises from the access model of the MFTs. MF in Windows 7 supports two types of MFTs—synchronous and asynchronous. The synchronous MFTs signal their need for input samples by returning the *MF_E_TRANSFORM_NEED_MORE_INPUT* error code from *IMFTransform::ProcessOutput()* calls. Asynchronous MFTs signal that they need input samples or have output samples by firing events.

The original version of MF that shipped in Windows Vista supported only synchronous MFTs. You will see soon why this model is called synchronous. Synchronous MFTs are slightly simpler than asynchronous MFTs, but they cannot easily support multithreaded components—MFTs with multiple internal threads. Therefore, in Windows 7, Microsoft introduced the asynchronous MFT model. Unlike in the synchronous model, in asynchronous processing mode, the status of an MFT is signaled by events. Just like sources and sinks, asynchronous MFTs expose the *IMFMediaEventGenerator* interface and fire events when they have new data or when they need more input.

To contrast the synchronous and asynchronous MFTs, let's take a look at how you would get data from each.

Here is the order of steps that you need to take to extract data from the synchronous model:

1. Call the MFT's *IMFTransform::ProcessOutput()* function.

2. If the MFT returns the *MF_E_TRANSFORM_NEED_MORE_INPUT* error code, go to the upstream component and request more data. Then feed that data into the transform's *ProcessInput()* and go back to step 1.

3. If the MFT returns data, you are done.

This procedure is more complex than it first appears due to the fact that sources and sinks in MF are still asynchronous. The only way the synchronous MFT can retrieve data is if it waits for the upstream component—the source—to send out a new sample. In other words, the thread that is handling the synchronous MFT request needs to block, waiting for data from the source. Which in turn means that the synchronous MFT processing must be done on a separate thread from the rest of operations—it must be done on a separate work queue from the one on which the source is delivering data.

Here is a flowchart diagram of the synchronous MFT request loop in the MP3 topology. For simplicity, the topology is ignoring the resampler MFT.

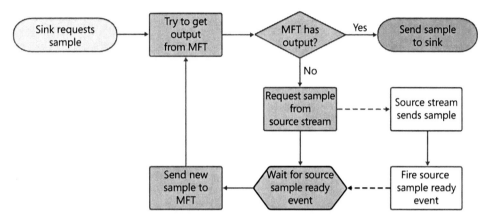

Here is a more detailed description of the steps in this flowchart.

1. The sink requests a new sample.

2. The session starts a special synchronous MFT work thread. All of the operations on this synchronous thread are shown in medium-gray (the two middle columns of the flowchart).

3. The session calls *IMFTransform::ProcessOutput()* on the synchronous MFT work thread and tries to get data from the MFT.

4. If the MFT returns a new sample, go to step 12.

5. If the MFT doesn't have data, it returns *MF_E_TRANSFORM_NEED_MORE_INPUT*.

6. The session requests a new sample from the source stream by calling its *IMFMediaStream::-RequestSample()*, still on the synchronous MFT work thread. This operation is indicated by the dashed line from the medium-gray rectangle to the white rectangle.

7. The synchronous MFT thread blocks, waiting for a custom internal event signaling that the source has delivered a new sample. The block is shown as the hexagon in the diagram.

8. The source fires an *MEMediaSample* event with the new sample. The event is fired to the main work thread, signified by the white components.

9. The session, operating on the main worker thread, receives the sample, stores it internally, and fires the internal Win32 event indicating that there is a new source sample. This custom event is shown as the dashed arrow to the hexagon.

CHAPTER 8 Custom Media Sessions 263

10. The synchronous MFT worker thread receives the new source sample event and unblocks.

11. The synchronous MFT worker thread sends the new sample to the MFT by calling its *IMFTransform::ProcessInput()* method. The thread then goes back to step 3.

12. The MFT has a new sample. Therefore it is delivered to the sink in the *IMFStreamSink::ProcessSample()* call.

Again, note that the synchronous MFT must operate on a separate thread from the other components, because the thread can block waiting for a sample from the source. If the main worker queue thread blocks, then none of the events get delivered—including the event from the source with the new sample.

Of course, this same system can be implemented differently, by storing the current state of each of the synchronous MFTs (needs data/has data), but that type of implementation can be more complex and fragile, and is therefore not shown here.

Asynchronous MFTs operate on a completely different principle. An asynchronous MFT fires events when it needs data and when it has new samples that can be extracted. The pipeline in that case will behave differently, and the algorithm changes drastically.

One way of implementing an asynchronous MFT pipeline is to separate all operations into two very simple flowcharts—one for the event that signals that the component has output, and one for the event that signals the request for input. Each component in this model would hold the count of sample requests and the count of samples available for extraction.

Here is the flowchart for the case in which a component requests a sample.

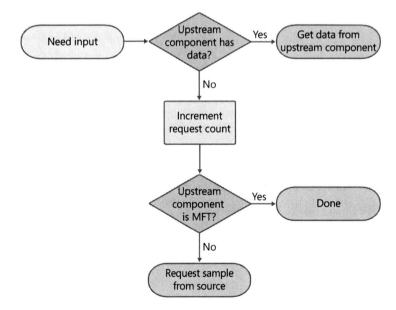

1. A component requests input.
2. Does the upstream component have data?
    a. If the upstream component has data (samples that can be extracted), get the data and exit.
    b. If the upstream component does not have data, increment the counter of sample requests. Is the upstream component an MFT?
        i. If the upstream component is an MFT, do nothing—wait for the MFT to process some data. It will fire an event when it has samples available.
        ii. If the upstream component is not an MFT, it must be a source. Send a sample request to the source and exit. The source will fire an event when it has a sample ready.

And here is the flowchart for the case in which a component fires an event signaling that it has an output sample available.

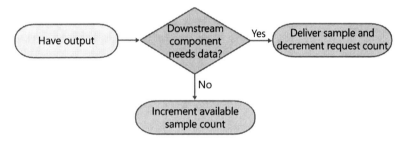

The steps that need to be executed for this event are even simpler:

1. A component signals that it has samples available.
2. Does the downstream component need data?
    a. If the downstream component needs data, deliver it and decrement the request count of the downstream component.
    b. If the downstream component does not yet need data, increment the count of available samples.

And that's it. Using this model, each component would be fed all the data it requested, and the pipeline behind it (upstream) would always be filled up. This is in some ways a push model rather than pull, because the entire pipeline will be full. However, this model is completely asynchronous, and the threads will never block.

More Info There are other peculiarities to asynchronous MFTs not listed here. For example, an asynchronous MFT will refuse to function until you set a specific attribute on it—*MF_TRANSFORM_ASYNC_UNLOCK*. See the asynchronous MFT documentation on MSDN for details at *http://msdn.microsoft.com/en-us/library/dd317909(v=VS.85).aspx*.

The sample custom session in this chapter is designed solely for synchronous MFTs, because the majority of MFTs currently available in Windows are synchronous, and because the MFTs used in the MP3 playback scenario are all synchronous.

Synchronous Media Foundation Pipeline Events

This section presents the MF data pipeline implemented in the custom MP3 session. This pipeline is designed for synchronous MFTs and therefore utilizes an extra worker queue. The worker queue is created in the constructor of the initialization function of the *CMP3Session* class.

```
//
// Initialize the CMP3Session class
//
HRESULT CMP3Session::Init(void)
{
    HRESULT hr = S_OK;

    do
    {
        // allocate a special worker thread for the blocking synchronous MFT operations
        hr = MFAllocateWorkQueue(&m_syncMftWorkerQueue);
        BREAK_ON_FAIL(hr);

        // create the event queue
        hr = MFCreateEventQueue(&m_pEventQueue);
        BREAK_ON_FAIL(hr);

        // create an event that will signal the waiting synchronous MFT thread that the source
        // has a new sample ready
        m_sourceSampleReadyEvent = CreateEvent(NULL, TRUE, FALSE, NULL);
        BREAK_ON_NULL(m_sourceSampleReadyEvent, E_UNEXPECTED);

        // crate the custom MP3 topology
        hr = LoadCustomTopology();
    }
    while(false);

    return hr;
}
```

The *CMP3Session::Init()* function initializes several key constructs necessary for the synchronous MFT pipeline. The first one is the custom work queue (with its own worker thread). The custom work queue is created by the *MFAllocateWorkQueue()* function. The function returns a *DWORD* with the queue ID. In subsequent calls, you can use this queue ID to identify which thread should process an event or callback. The queue ID is stored in the *m_syncMftWorkerQueue* class member variable. After you are done with the worker queue, you must release it by calling the *MFUnlockWorkerQueue()* function.

In addition to the synchronous MFT worker queue, this method also creates the event that the synchronous MFT will use to detect that a source has delivered samples. This is a basic Win32 event primitive created with the *CreateEvent()* API. You should release this event when you are done with it by calling *CloseHandle()* and passing in the event handle.

Besides allocating those two constructs, the *Init()* function also creates the event queue that is behind the *CMP3Session*'s *IMFMediaEventGenerator* interface implementation and calls the *LoadCustomTopology()* method to load and connect the components that constitute the MP3 topology.

As you saw earlier, after the topology has been initialized, the session calls the *MESessionTopologyStatus* event indicating that the topology is ready. When the player receives this event, it immediately calls the *IMFMediaSession::Start()* function to start playback. Here is how the MP3 session implements the *Start()* method.

```
//
// Start playback
//
HRESULT CMP3Session::Start(const GUID* pguidTimeFormat, const PROPVARIANT* pvarStartPosition)
{
    HRESULT hr = S_OK;
    CComPtr<IAsyncState> pState;

    // QI the IMFPresentationTimeSource from the sink - the audio renderer
    CComQIPtr<IMFPresentationTimeSource> pTimeSource = m_pSink;

    do
    {
        // start the session only once - all subsequent calls must be because the session is
        // paused, so there is no need to reinitialize the various parameters
        if(!m_sessionStarted)
        {
            m_sessionStarted = true;

            // start the source and pass in the presentation descriptor initialized earlier
            hr = m_pSource->Start(m_pPresentation, pguidTimeFormat, pvarStartPosition);
            BREAK_ON_FAIL(hr);

            // begin receiving events from the stream sink
            pState = new (std::nothrow) CAsyncState(AsyncEventType_StreamSinkEvent);
            BREAK_ON_NULL(pState, E_OUTOFMEMORY);

            hr = m_pStreamSink->BeginGetEvent(this, pState);
            BREAK_ON_FAIL(hr);

            // begin receiving events from the source
            pState = new (std::nothrow) CAsyncState(AsyncEventType_SourceEvent);
            BREAK_ON_NULL(pState, E_OUTOFMEMORY);
```

```
            // start getting the next event from the source
            hr = m_pSource->BeginGetEvent(this, pState);
            BREAK_ON_FAIL(hr);

            // the audio renderer is supposed to be the time source - make sure we got the
            // IMFPresentationTimeSource pointer for the audio renderer
            BREAK_ON_NULL(pTimeSource, E_UNEXPECTED);

            // create the presentation clock
            hr = MFCreatePresentationClock(&m_pClock);
            BREAK_ON_FAIL(hr);

            // set the time source on the presentation clock - the audio renderer
            hr = m_pClock->SetTimeSource(pTimeSource);
            BREAK_ON_FAIL(hr);

            // set the presentation clock on the sink
            hr = m_pSink->SetPresentationClock(m_pClock);
            BREAK_ON_FAIL(hr);

            // start the clock at the beginning - time 0
            hr = m_pClock->Start(0);
        }
        else
        {
            // unpause the clock from the old position
            hr = m_pClock->Start(PRESENTATION_CURRENT_POSITION);
        }
    }
    while(false);

    return hr;
}
```

After the topology is instantiated, the *Start()* function completes initialization of the components, starting playback. Here are the tasks done in this function:

1. Start the source—tell the source to start processing data, and pass in the starting offset and the presentation descriptor cached earlier, during topology creation.

2. Start listening to events from the source, providing a state variable that indicates that the events came from the source (*AsyncEventType_SourceEvent*).

3. Start listening to events from the stream that is exposed by the sink, providing a state variable that indicates that the events came from the sink (*AsyncEventType_StreamSinkEvent*).

4. Initialize the presentation clock—the clock that is used to determine when each sample needs to be rendered. The steps required for presentation clock instantiation are:

    a. Get the time source for the topology—the clock on which all of the sinks will synchronize. In A/V playback topologies, this is usually the audio renderer, so the renderer exposes the *IMFPresentationTimeSource* interface. Query for that interface from the sink object.

b. Create a new *IMFPresentationClock* object by calling the *MFCreatePresentationClock()* function.

c. Set the time source on the presentation clock by calling *IMFPresentationClock::SetTimeSource()*.

d. Set the presentation clock on all of the sinks. In this case there is only one sink—the audio renderer, once again. However, you still need to give it a pointer to the presentation clock.

e. Start the clock by calling *IMFPresentationClock::Start()* and pass in the starting time—zero.

This lengthy procedure should be done only once, the first time the presentation is started. If you want to unpause the presentation, all you need to do is again call *IMFPresentationClock::Start()*, but this time pass in the *PRESENTATION_CURRENT_POSITION* value as the starting time.

After the *Start()* function has been called, all events from the source and the sink will be sent to the *CMP3Session*'s *Invoke()* method. The *Invoke()* method was already shown previously—all it does is figure out who sent the event and pass the call to the appropriate event-handling function. Here is the standard sequence of events that happen during normal playback. The order of some of the events may be different in some situations, but you will get the general idea of what is happening:

1. **Source event—*MENewStream*** Signals that a new source stream has been created and provides a pointer to this stream. Store the pointer to this source stream and start listening to events from it.

2. **Sink event—*MEStreamSinkStarted*** Indicates that the stream sink has started. There is nothing to do here, although the regular session notes the state and starts obeying other events from the stream sink object. If the stream sink is not in the right state, the default session ignores unexpected events.

3. **Source event—*MESourceStarted*** Indicates that the source has started operating. Nothing to do here.

4. **Source stream event—*MEStreamStarted*** Indicates that the source stream has started. Nothing to do here.

5. **Stream sink event—*MEStreamSinkRequestSample*** This event is fired by the stream sink object to request a sample. Note that this event may fire multiple times in a row, because a sink will often buffer several samples to avoid glitches and improve quality of playback.

In essence, during initialization, various components in the topology send signals indicating that they have started, after which the source instantiates an output stream and sends an event with the pointer to that *IMFMediaStream* object. From that point on, all of the key events necessary for playback come from the source and stream sinks.

Here are several of the key event handlers that deal with the individual events sent by the various components. First is the event handler function for the MF media source object.

```cpp
//
// Handle the event coming from the source
//
HRESULT CMP3Session::HandleSourceEvent(IMFAsyncResult* pResult)
{
    HRESULT hr = S_OK;
    CComPtr<IMFMediaEvent> pEvent;
    MediaEventType eventType;
    CComPtr<IAsyncState> pState;
    PROPVARIANT eventVariant;

    do
    {
        // clear the PROPVARIANT
        PropVariantInit(&eventVariant);

        // Get the event from the event queue.
        hr = m_pSource->EndGetEvent(pResult, &pEvent);
        BREAK_ON_FAIL(hr);

        // Get the event type.
        hr = pEvent->GetType(&eventType);
        BREAK_ON_FAIL(hr);

        // request the next event immediately
        pState = new (std::nothrow) CAsyncState(AsyncEventType_SourceEvent);
        BREAK_ON_NULL(pState, E_OUTOFMEMORY);

        // start getting the next event from the media source object
        hr = m_pSource->BeginGetEvent(this, pState);
        BREAK_ON_FAIL(hr);

        // Handle the new stream event that is fired when a new stream is added to the
        // source.  Get the stream pointer and store it.
        if(eventType == MENewStream)
        {
            // get the data stored in the event
            hr = pEvent->GetValue(&eventVariant);
            BREAK_ON_FAIL(hr);

            // get the IMFMediaStream pointer from the stored IUnknown pointer
            m_pSourceStream = eventVariant.punkVal;
            BREAK_ON_NULL(m_pSourceStream, E_UNEXPECTED);

            // we got a new source stream - start listening for events coming from it
            pState = new (std::nothrow) CAsyncState(AsyncEventType_SourceStreamEvent);
            BREAK_ON_NULL(pState, E_OUTOFMEMORY);

            // start getting an event from the source's media stream object
            hr = m_pSourceStream->BeginGetEvent(this, pState);
        }
```

```cpp
        else if(eventType == MESourceStarted)
        {
            // source started
        }
    }
    while(false);

    // free any internal values that can be freed in the PROPVARIANT
    PropVariantClear(&eventVariant);

    return hr;
}
```

The most interesting event fired by the source is the one that signals the creation of a new source stream—the *MENewStream* event. The event object contains a *PROPVARIANT* variable, which holds a pointer to the newly created *IMFMediaStream* source stream object. After the media stream object pointer is extracted and stored in the *CMP3Session*'s member variable, the function registers the session as a receiver for the subsequent events coming from that media stream. This is again done by calling the *IMFMediaEventGenerator::BeginGetEvent()* method on the media stream and passing in a state object with the *AsyncEventType_SourceStreamEvent* flag. The flag allows the *CMP3Session::Invoke()* function to determine which component fired the event and which function needs to be called to handle that event.

After the stream sink has started, it fires events with requests for more samples. The stream sink events are handled by the *CMP3Session::HandleStreamSinkEvent()* method.

```cpp
//
// Handle an event from the stream sink
//
HRESULT CMP3Session::HandleStreamSinkEvent(IMFAsyncResult* pResult)
{
    HRESULT hr = S_OK;
    CComPtr<IMFMediaEvent> pEvent;
    MediaEventType eventType;
    CComPtr<IAsyncState> pState;

    do
    {
        // Get the event from the event queue.
        hr = m_pStreamSink->EndGetEvent(pResult, &pEvent);
        BREAK_ON_FAIL(hr);

        // Get the event type.
        hr = pEvent->GetType(&eventType);
        BREAK_ON_FAIL(hr);

        // request the next event immediately
        pState = new (std::nothrow) CAsyncState(AsyncEventType_StreamSinkEvent);
        BREAK_ON_NULL(pState, E_OUTOFMEMORY);
```

```
        // start getting the next event from the stream sink
        hr = m_pStreamSink->BeginGetEvent(this, pState);
        BREAK_ON_FAIL(hr);

        if(eventType == MEStreamSinkStarted)
        {
            // the sink has started
        }
        else if(eventType == MEStreamSinkRequestSample)
        {
            // create a state object that indicates that this is a synchronous MFT work item
            // that should be executed on the resampler on a separate queue
            pState = new (std::nothrow) CAsyncState(AsyncEventType_SyncMftSampleRequest);
            BREAK_ON_NULL(pState, E_OUTOFMEMORY);

            // schedule the synchronous MFT work on its own separate worker queue, since
            // that work item can block - and we want to continue to use the main queue
            hr = MFPutWorkItem(m_syncMftWorkerQueue, this, pState);
        }
    }
    while(false);

    return hr;
}
```

When the *HandleStreamSinkEvent()* function receives the *MEStreamSinkStarted* event, it must immediately start the process of retrieving the next sample. This is done by scheduling a work item on the synchronous MFT worker queue that was created earlier, in the *Init()* function. Therefore, the *HandleStreamSinkEvent()* method again creates a *CAsyncState* object, but this time it uses the *AsyncEventType_SyncMftSampleRequest* flag. Then the work item is placed on the special work queue with the ID stored in *m_syncMftWorkerQueue*, by calling the *MFPutWorkItem()* function.

MP3 Session Data Flow

After the sink has been initialized, it starts sending events requesting samples. Although these events can be honored only after all of the other components in the topology have been initialized, the custom session does not track component states. Strictly speaking, in a rigorous and robust implementation, the session would not try to process sample requests until the source has finished initialization. However, for simplicity, state tracking is omitted from this sample.

Therefore, after *Invoke()* is called by the special worker thread with the *AsyncEventType_SyncMftSampleRequest* flag, it in turn calls the *CMP3Session::HandleSynchronousMftRequest()* function, assuming that the source stream has already been started. The synchronous MFT request function gets the data from the resampler MFT, which in turn gets data from the decoder, which requests data from the source stream.

Here is the sequence of events that happen on the synchronous MFT worker thread.

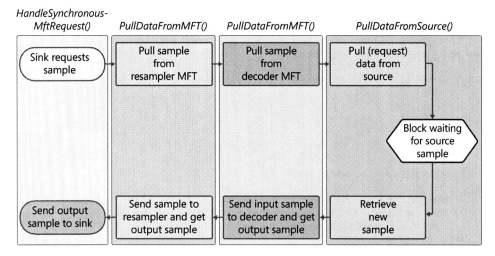

1. The sink requests a sample, which causes the *HandleSynchronousMftRequest()* function to be called.

2. *PullDataFromMft()* is called for the resampler. The function discovers that it needs more data and calls *PullDataFromMft()* for the decoder.

3. *PullDataFromMft()* for the decoder discovers that it needs more data and calls *PullDataFromSource()*.

4. *PullDataFromSource()* requests a sample from the source.

5. *PullDataFromSource()* blocks, waiting for the source sample to arrive asynchronously.

6. *PullDataFromSource()* retrieves the new sample sent by the source stream.

7. *PullDataFromMft()* for the decoder sends the new sample to the MFT and retrieves the resulting output.

8. *PullDataFromMft()* for the resampler sends the sample received from the decoder to the resampler MFT and extracts the resulting output.

9. *HandleSynchronousMftRequest()* sends the output sample received from the resampler to the sink.

As you can see, the worker thread starts and ends in the *HandleSynchronousMftRequest()* function. Here is the listing for that function.

```
//
// Synchronous MFT work item - this is run off of a separate work queue/thread and will
// block while the source is fetching data.
//
HRESULT CMP3Session::HandleSynchronousMftRequest(IMFAsyncResult* pResult)
{
    HRESULT hr = S_OK;
    CComPtr<IMFSample> pSample;

    do
    {
        CComCritSecLock<CComAutoCriticalSection> lock(m_critSec);

        // get data from the resampler - this function will call itself in order to get data
        // from the decoder MFT and then will block while waiting for data from the source
        hr = PullDataFromMFT(m_pResampler, &pSample);
        BREAK_ON_FAIL(hr);

        // send the received sample to the sink
        hr = m_pStreamSink->ProcessSample(pSample);
        BREAK_ON_FAIL(hr);
    }
    while(false);

    return hr;
}
```

This helper, of course, first extracts a sample from the component upstream of the sink—in this case, the resampler MFT—and then sends that sample to the stream sink object by calling its *IMFStreamSink::ProcessSample()* method.

Here is how the *PullDataFromMFT()* function looks.

```
//
// Get a sample from the specified MFT
//
HRESULT CMP3Session::PullDataFromMFT(IMFTransform* pMft, IMFSample** ppNewSample)
{
    HRESULT hr = S_OK;
    MFT_OUTPUT_DATA_BUFFER outputDataBuffer;
    DWORD processOutputStatus = 0;
    CComPtr<IMFSample> pMftInputSample;
    DWORD inputStreamId = 0;                        // assume the input stream ID is zero

    do
    {
        BREAK_ON_NULL(pMft, E_POINTER);
        BREAK_ON_NULL(ppNewSample, E_POINTER);

        // initialize the MFT_OUTPUT_DATA_BUFFER for the MFT
        hr = InitOutputDataBuffer(pMft, &outputDataBuffer);
        BREAK_ON_FAIL(hr);
```

```cpp
        // Try to get output data from the MFT.  If the MFT returns that it needs input,
        // get data from the upstream component, send it to the MFT's input, and try again.
        while(true)
        {
            // try to get an output sample from the MFT
            hr = pMft->ProcessOutput(0, 1, &outputDataBuffer, &processOutputStatus);

            // if ProcessOutput() did not say that it needs more input, then it must have
            // either succeeded or failed unexpectedly - in either case, break out of the
            // loop
            if(hr != MF_E_TRANSFORM_NEED_MORE_INPUT)
            {
                break;
            }

            // Pull data from the upstream MF component.  If this is the resampler, then its
            // upstream component is the decoder.  If this is the decoder, then its upstream
            // component is the source.
            if(pMft == m_pResampler)
            {
                hr = PullDataFromMFT(m_pDecoder, &pMftInputSample);
            }
            else
            {   // this is the decoder - get data from the source
                hr = PullDataFromSource(&pMftInputSample);
            }
            BREAK_ON_FAIL(hr);

            // once we have a new sample, feed it into the current MFT's input
            hr = pMft->ProcessInput(inputStreamId, pMftInputSample, 0);
            BREAK_ON_FAIL(hr);
        }
        BREAK_ON_FAIL(hr);

        // if we got here, then we must have successfully extracted the new sample from the
        // MFT - store it in the output parameter
        *ppNewSample = outputDataBuffer.pSample;
    }
    while(false);

    return hr;
}
```

The *CMP3Session::PullDataFromMFT()* method first initializes the *MFT_OUTPUT_DATA_BUFFER* structure by calling the internal *InitOutputDataBuffer()* helper function. The primary purpose of that function is to determine whether the MFT in question provides its own samples. If it does not provide its own samples, then a new sample needs to be generated and inserted into the data buffer structure—the MFT's *ProcessOutput()* function will fill in the data buffer of that sample.

After getting an initialized output data buffer structure, the *PullDataFromMFT()* method operates in a loop. It keeps trying to extract data from the MFT. If the MFT returns an error code indicating that it requires more input, the function calls the upstream component, gets a sample from it, sends that sample to the MFT's *IMFTransform::ProcessInput()* method, and then tries to get output again.

Here is the logic flow of the *PullDataFromMFT()* method.

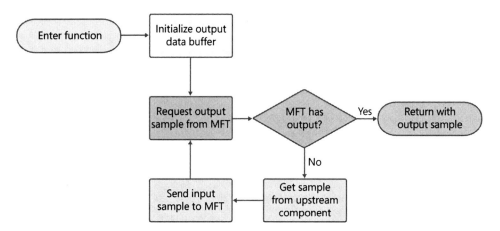

Here are the steps that the function takes, in a little more detail:

1. Enter the function.
2. Initialize the *MF_OUTPUT_DATA_BUFFER* buffer, adding a sample to it if the MFT requires that.
3. Call the MFT's *IMFTransform::ProcessOutput()* function to try to get the next output sample.
4. If the MFT has output, go to step 8.
5. If the MFT returns *MF_E_TRANSFORM_NEED_INPUT*, the transform needs input. Get a sample from the upstream component. This operation may require the function either to call itself with another MFT as a parameter or call the *PullDataFromSource()* method to get data from the source.
6. When the function has a new sample from the upstream component, send the sample to the MFT's input stream by calling *IMFTransform::ProcessInput()*.
7. Go back to step 3.
8. Done—return with the MFT's output sample.

Note that if *PullDataFromMFT()* is trying to pull a sample from the resampler MFT, then its upstream component will be the decoder. In that case, the function will call itself, but with the decoder's *IMFTransform* pointer as a parameter. If the function is being called for the decoder, however, then the only component upstream from it is the source. Therefore, it needs to call a different helper function—*PullDataFromSource()*.

Here is the listing for the function that synchronously extracts data from the source.

```
//
// Get output from the source - first request a sample from the source, and then block,
// waiting for an event that will notify us that the source has a new sample for us.
//
HRESULT CMP3Session::PullDataFromSource(IMFSample** ppNewSample)
{
    HRESULT hr = S_OK;

    do
    {
        // signal to the source stream that we need a new sample
        hr = m_pSourceStream->RequestSample(NULL);
        BREAK_ON_FAIL(hr);

        // wait forever for a new sample to arrive from the source - this event is set in
        // the HandleSourceStreamEvent() function, when it receives a MEMediaSample event
        WaitForSingleObject(m_sourceSampleReadyEvent, INFINITE);

        // at this point we should have a sample from the source ready for consumption
        BREAK_ON_NULL(m_pReadySourceSample, E_UNEXPECTED);

        // grab the sample produced by the source and consume it
        *ppNewSample = m_pReadySourceSample.Detach();

        // reset the event
        ResetEvent(m_sourceSampleReadyEvent);
    }
    while(false);

    return hr;
}
```

The function first sends a sample request to the source stream by calling its *IMFMediaStream::-RequestSample()* method, and then blocks, waiting for somebody to signal the Win32 *m_sourceSampleReadyEvent* event. The event is triggered by the *HandleSourceStreamEvent()* function when it asynchronously receives a new sample from the source sample. When the source-sample-ready event is triggered, the *PullDataFromSource()* function unblocks, resets the event for the next time it gets called, and returns the new sample.

Note again that this procedure is called on a separate thread from the main operations. If it was called on the main asynchronous event thread, the source's *MEMediaSample* event would never be received, because the thread that would process it would be stuck in this function. Therefore, the sample-ready Win32 event would never be fired, and the application would be in a deadlock.

Here is the *CMP3Session::HandleSourceStreamEvent()* function that actually fires the sample-ready Win32 event.

```cpp
//
// Handle an event sent by the source stream.
//
HRESULT CMP3Session::HandleSourceStreamEvent(IMFAsyncResult* pResult)
{
    HRESULT hr = S_OK;
    CComPtr<IMFMediaEvent> pEvent;
    MediaEventType eventType;
    CComPtr<IAsyncState> pState;
    PROPVARIANT eventVariant;

    do
    {
        // clear the PROPVARIANT
        PropVariantInit(&eventVariant);

        // Get the event from the event queue.
        hr = m_pSourceStream->EndGetEvent(pResult, &pEvent);
        BREAK_ON_FAIL(hr);

        // Get the event type.
        hr = pEvent->GetType(&eventType);
        BREAK_ON_FAIL(hr);

        pState = new (std::nothrow) CAsyncState(AsyncEventType_SourceStreamEvent);
        BREAK_ON_NULL(pState, E_OUTOFMEMORY);

        // start getting the next event from the source stream
        hr = m_pSourceStream->BeginGetEvent(this, pState);
        BREAK_ON_FAIL(hr);

        // handle the passed-in event
        if(eventType == MEStreamStarted)
        {
        }
        else if(eventType == MEMediaSample)
        {
            // get the data stored in the event
            hr = pEvent->GetValue(&eventVariant);
            BREAK_ON_FAIL(hr);

            // get the pointer to the new sample from the stored IUnknown pointer, and cache
            // it in the m_pReadySourceSample member variable
            m_pReadySourceSample = eventVariant.punkVal;
            BREAK_ON_NULL(m_pReadySourceSample, E_UNEXPECTED);

            // set the event that signals that there is a new sample ready - the synchronous
            // MFT thread should be blocked waiting for this event in the PullDataFromSource
            // function.
            SetEvent(m_sourceSampleReadyEvent);
        }
    }
    while(false);
```

Developing Microsoft Media Foundation Applications

```
        // free any internal values that can be freed in the PROPVARIANT
        PropVariantClear(&eventVariant);

        return hr;
}
```

When the *HandleSourceStreamEvent()* function receives the *MEMediaSample* event from the source stream, it first of all extracts the sample from the event object and caches it inside of the session object. Then the function calls *SetEvent()* to set the Win32 event that notifies the waiting synchronous MFT thread that a new sample is available. The synchronous MFT thread—waiting in the *PullDataFromSource()* method shown previously—extracts the sample from the internal variable and returns it.

The Session Clock

As you saw in the previous section, all sample flow in the topology is triggered by the sample request events fired by the sink. The sink actively pulls in individual samples through the topology. Because the MP3 session uses a standard rendering sink, each of those samples is rendered in turn. The sink determines when each sample should be rendered by looking at the presentation time stamps in the sample and comparing them with the presentation clock object.

The presentation clock implements the *IMFPresentationClock* interface. The presentation clock object provides access to the clock relative to the start of the media item. As you saw in the *CMP3Session::Start()* method, the presentation clock is initialized to zero at the very beginning. Each sample in the sink is rendered only when its presentation time stamp matches the time of the presentation clock.

For example, if you pause the presentation clock at five seconds and then reset it to zero again, the audio will stop playing until the clock has reached five seconds again. In other words, samples will not render until their presentation time matches the clock time. Therefore, if you reset the clock to zero and then continue playback, you will not hear anything for five seconds, because all of the samples for seconds 0 through 5 have already been rendered.

The media session is responsible for adjusting the clock on every seek. For instance, if you seek the source to 35 seconds after the start of the media, you need to also adjust the presentation clock to 35 seconds.

If your topology has multiple data streams and multiple sinks, you will most likely want to make sure that the individual streams are synchronized among each other. That is necessary to ensure that the video frames currently playing match the audio. The presentation clock object provides this functionality, allowing each sink to use the same reference time. In a standard topology, each rendering sink usually uses the same *IMFPresentationClock* object, which means that when the sinks check the time with *IMFPresentationClock::GetTime()*, they all receive a value coming from the same source.

The *IMFPresentationClock* object is just an interface used by multiple sinks to access the underlying *IMFPresentationTimeSource* object. The presentation time source is the master clock used for the presentation. The master clock is maintained by one of the media sinks—usually by the audio renderer.

Each sink must have a reference to the presentation clock before starting playback. If you look closely at the *CMP3Session::Start()* method, you will see that a pointer to the presentation clock object is passed in to the sink with the *IMFMediaSink::SetPresentationClock()* method before playback is started.

The presentation clock is also used to control the playback rate (speed) of the media. You can increase or decrease the rate at which the media is playing by accessing the clock's *IMFRateControl* interface and using its *SetRate()* method.

To access the clock of the session, you should utilize the session's *IMFGetService* interface. For example, here is how the sample player extracts the session's *IMFRateControl* interface.

```
//
// Handler for MESessionTopologyReady event - starts session playback
//
HRESULT CPlayer::OnTopologyReady(void)
{
    HRESULT hr = S_OK;

    do
    {
        // release any previous instance of the m_pVideoDisplay interface
        m_pVideoDisplay.Release();

        // Ask the session for the IMFVideoDisplayControl interface - ignore the returned
        // HRESULT in case this is an MP3 session without a video renderer.
        MFGetService(m_pSession, MR_VIDEO_RENDER_SERVICE,  IID_IMFVideoDisplayControl,
            (void**)&m_pVideoDisplay);

        // since the topology is ready, start playback
        hr = StartPlayback();
        BREAK_ON_FAIL(hr);

        // get the rate control service that can be used to change the playback rate of the
        // service
        hr = MFGetService(m_pSession, MF_RATE_CONTROL_SERVICE, IID_IMFRateControl,
            (void**)&m_pRateControl);
    }
    while(false);

    return hr;
}
```

The player uses the utility *MFGetService()* function to access the session's *IMFGetService::GetService()* method. The *MFGetService()* function itself is virtually empty—it gets the *IMFGetService* interface from the passed-in object and then sends in the call to the corresponding function. The *IMFGetService* interface is commonly used to extract an interface pointer to one of the objects contained within the interface implementer. The session holds several MF objects and components that do different things, each of which can be exposed as a different service. For example, if you call the *GetService()* function on the session and ask for the *MR_VIDEO_RENDERER_SERVICE*, the function will query the video renderer sink for the specified interface. If you ask for the *MF_RATE_CONTROL_SERVICE*, the function will query the internal presentation clock for the *IMFRateControl* interface.

> **Note** The *IMFMediaSession* interface also exposes the *GetClock()* method. Even though in most cases this method will return a pointer to the underlying *IMFPresentationClock*, this may not always be true. Therefore, you should use the *IMFGetService* functionality to get the rate control object.

Here is the MP3 session's implementation of the *IMFGetService* method.

```
//
// Get the object that implements the requested interface from the topology - not
// implemented here, just return S_OK
//
HRESULT CMP3Session::GetService(REFGUID guidService, REFIID riid, LPVOID *ppvObject)
{
    HRESULT hr = S_OK;

    do
    {
        BREAK_ON_NULL(ppvObject, E_POINTER);

        // if the caller is asking for the rate control service, query for the
        // IMFRateControl interface from the presentation clock
        if(guidService == MF_RATE_CONTROL_SERVICE)
        {
            BREAK_ON_NULL(m_pClock, E_NOINTERFACE);

            hr = m_pClock->QueryInterface(riid, ppvObject);
        }
        else
        {
            hr = MF_E_UNSUPPORTED_SERVICE;
        }
    }
    while(false);

    return hr;
}
```

As you can see, the *CMP3Session::GetService()* will return an interface only if you query it for the rate control service. In that case, the function will call *QueryInterface()* on the clock object. In all other cases, the function will return the *MF_E_UNSUPPORTED_SERVICE* error code.

By using the *IMFRateControl* interface extracted from the session, the player can control the playback rate of the media. It can increase the playback rate, which causes video and audio to play faster than normal, or it can decrease it. Internally this just means that the clock counter in the clock moves faster or slower, which causes the samples to be rendered faster or slower than normal. In other words, as a default, the *IMFPresentationClock::GetTime()* returns the time since the presentation started playing, in 100-nanosecond units, and for each second of real time the counter in the clock will increment by 1×10^7 units (1 second / 100 nanoseconds). If you double the playback rate, then after one second of playback the *GetTime()* function will return 2×10^7. If you halve the playback rate, after one second you will get 0.5×10^7.

The sample player provided in this chapter supports playback rate change. To test this behavior, simply press the Plus Sign key (+) or the Minus Sign key (-) while media is playing back. Each time you do, the playback rate will either increase or decrease by half. Thus, after you press + twice, the playback rate will double.

> **Background** Some playback sinks and topologies support negative playback rates. For negative playback, the media plays backwards. The audio sink does not support reverse playback, however.

Here is how the player implements the *IncreaseRate()* function. This function is called by the main application when it detects that the Plus Sign key has been pressed.

```
//
// Increase the playback rate by 0.5
//
HRESULT CPlayer::IncreaseRate(void)
{
    HRESULT hr = S_OK;
    float rate = 0;
    BOOL thin = FALSE;

    do
    {
        if (m_state != Started)
        {
            return MF_E_INVALIDREQUEST;
        }

        BREAK_ON_NULL(m_pRateControl, E_UNEXPECTED);

        // get the current rate
        hr = m_pRateControl->GetRate(&thin, &rate);
        BREAK_ON_FAIL(hr);
```

```
        // increase the current rate by 0.5
        rate += 0.5;

        // set the rate
        hr = m_pRateControl->SetRate(thin, rate);
    }
    while(false);

    return hr;
}
```

The *IncreaseRate()* function simply accesses the *IMFRateControl* method and first extracts the current playback rate, then adds 0.5 to it, and then sets it. By default, media plays back at normal speed, equivalent to a rate of 1.0. If you set the rate to 1.5, the media will play at one-and-a-half times normal speed.

Note that the *GetRate()* and *SetRate()* functions also get and set one extra value—the *thin* parameter. This value indicates whether the topology components are allowed to drop samples to obey the rate commands. For example, in video playback, setting the thinning value to *TRUE* will result in the intermediate *P* and *B* frames getting dropped.

Conclusion

In this chapter, you saw the design of a basic media session. This demonstrated several of the principles used by the default media session provided by MF. You saw the functions necessary to load individual MF components, connect them, and pump data through the resulting topology. Though the sample shown here focused on synchronous MFT components, the chapter also touched on the processing model of asynchronous MFTs. In addition, the chapter also presented the basic ideas behind clocking in MF topologies. It described how sinks decide which sample to display at a particular moment, and it showed how to control the playback rate of a stream.

The ideas presented here can now be used to tie together all of the individual concepts shown in the previous chapters. You can use these concepts to build just unit tests, or to create esoteric topologies and scenarios not supported by the default media session. Using the custom media session may also help you debug your existing MF objects, because with the custom session you can simply step into the code to determine what went wrong during playback in a regular topology.

Class Listings

For reference and to simplify your reading of this chapter, here are the class definitions of the core classes presented in this chapter.

The *CMP3SessionTopoBuilder* class builds the MP3 topology by instantiating the Media Foundation components in that topology and ensuring that all of them agree on their input and output media types.

```cpp
// MP3 ByteStreamHandler CLSID
// {A82E50BA-8E92-41eb-9DF2-433F50EC2993}
DEFINE_GUID(CLSID_MP3ByteStreamPlugin, 0xa82e50ba, 0x8e92, 0x41eb, 0x9d, 0xf2, 0x43, 0x3f, 0x50,
0xec, 0x29, 0x93);

// MP3 Audio Decoder CLSID
// {bbeea841-0a63-4f52-a7ab-a9b3a84ed38a}
DEFINE_GUID(CLSID_CMP3DecMediaObject, 0xbbeea841, 0x0a63, 0x4f52, 0xa7, 0xab, 0xa9, 0xb3, 0xa8,
0x4e, 0xd3, 0x8a);

// Audio resampler CLSID
// {f447b69e-1884-4a7e-8055-346f74d6edb3}
DEFINE_GUID(CLSID_CResamplerMediaObject, 0xf447b69e, 0x1884, 0x4a7e, 0x80, 0x55, 0x34, 0x6f,
0x74, 0xd6, 0xed, 0xb3);

//
// Builds the MP3 topology
//
class CMP3SessionTopoBuilder :
    public IMFAsyncCallback,
    public IMFMediaEventGenerator
{
    public:
        CMP3SessionTopoBuilder(PCWSTR pUrl);
        ~CMP3SessionTopoBuilder(void);

        // IUnknown interface implementation
        virtual HRESULT STDMETHODCALLTYPE QueryInterface(REFIID riid, void **ppvObject);
        virtual ULONG STDMETHODCALLTYPE AddRef(void);
        virtual ULONG STDMETHODCALLTYPE Release(void);

    protected:
        volatile long m_cRef;
        CComAutoCriticalSection m_critSec;

        WCHAR* m_pFileUrl;

        CComPtr<IMFMediaEventQueue>  m_pEventQueue;
        CComPtr<IMFTopology> m_pTopology;

        CComPtr<IMFByteStreamHandler> m_pByteStreamHandler;
        CComPtr<IMFPresentationDescriptor> m_pPresentation;
        CComQIPtr<IMFMediaSource> m_pSource;
        CComPtr<IMFTransform> m_pDecoder;
        CComPtr<IMFTransform> m_pResampler;
        CComPtr<IMFMediaSink> m_pSink;

        CComQIPtr<IMFMediaStream> m_pSourceStream;
        CComPtr<IMFStreamSink> m_pStreamSink;

        HRESULT HandleByteStreamHandlerEvent(IMFAsyncResult* pResult);
        HRESULT FireTopologyReadyEvent(void);
```

```cpp
    HRESULT LoadCustomTopology(void);
    HRESULT BeginCreateMediaSource(void);
    HRESULT NegotiateMediaTypes(void);
    HRESULT ConnectSourceToMft(IMFTransform* pMFTransform);
    HRESULT ConnectMftToSink(IMFTransform* pMFTransform);
    HRESULT ConnectMftToMft(IMFTransform* pMFTransform1, IMFTransform* pMFTransform2);
};
```

The *CMP3Session* class inherits from *CMP3SessionTopoBuilder*. This class contains all the functionality necessary to receive events from the various components in the topology and to pass media samples between the components.

```cpp
//
// Main MP3 session class - receives component events and passes data through the topology
//
class CMP3Session :
    public CMP3SessionTopoBuilder,
    public IMFMediaSession,
    public IMFGetService
{
    public:
        CMP3Session(PCWSTR pUrl);
        ~CMP3Session(void);

        HRESULT Init(void);

        // IUnknown interface implementation
        virtual HRESULT STDMETHODCALLTYPE QueryInterface(REFIID riid, void **ppvObject);
        virtual ULONG STDMETHODCALLTYPE AddRef(void);
        virtual ULONG STDMETHODCALLTYPE Release(void);

        // IMFMediaSession interface implementation
        STDMETHODIMP SetTopology(DWORD dwSetTopologyFlags, IMFTopology *pTopology);
        STDMETHODIMP ClearTopologies(void);
        STDMETHODIMP Start(const GUID *pguidTimeFormat,
            const PROPVARIANT *pvarStartPosition);
        STDMETHODIMP Pause(void);
        STDMETHODIMP Stop(void);
        STDMETHODIMP Close(void);
        STDMETHODIMP Shutdown(void);
        STDMETHODIMP GetClock(IMFClock** ppClock);
        STDMETHODIMP GetSessionCapabilities(DWORD* pdwCaps);
        STDMETHODIMP GetFullTopology(DWORD dwGetFullTopologyFlags, TOPOID TopoId,
            IMFTopology **ppFullTopology);

        // IMFAsyncCallback interface implementation
        STDMETHODIMP GetParameters(DWORD* pdwFlags, DWORD* pdwQueue);
        STDMETHODIMP Invoke(IMFAsyncResult* pResult);

        // IMFGetService interface implementation
        STDMETHODIMP GetService(REFGUID guidService, REFIID riid, LPVOID *ppvObject);
```

```cpp
    // IMFMediaEventGenerator interface implementation
    STDMETHODIMP BeginGetEvent(IMFAsyncCallback* pCallback,IUnknown* punkState);
    STDMETHODIMP EndGetEvent(IMFAsyncResult* pResult, IMFMediaEvent** ppEvent);
    STDMETHODIMP GetEvent(DWORD dwFlags, IMFMediaEvent** ppEvent);
    STDMETHODIMP QueueEvent(MediaEventType met, REFGUID guidExtendedType,
        HRESULT hrStatus, const PROPVARIANT* pvValue);

private:

    DWORD m_syncMftWorkerQueue;
    bool m_sessionStarted;

    CComQIPtr<IMFSample> m_pReadySourceSample;
    HANDLE m_sourceSampleReadyEvent;

    CComPtr<IMFPresentationClock> m_pClock;

    HRESULT HandleStreamSinkEvent(IMFAsyncResult* pResult);
    HRESULT HandleSourceEvent(IMFAsyncResult* pResult);
    HRESULT HandleSourceStreamEvent(IMFAsyncResult* pResult);
    HRESULT HandleSynchronousMftRequest(IMFAsyncResult* pResult);

    HRESULT PullDataFromMFT(IMFTransform* pMFTransform, IMFSample** ppNewSample);
    HRESULT InitOutputDataBuffer(IMFTransform* pMFTransform,
        MFT_OUTPUT_DATA_BUFFER* pBuffer);
    HRESULT PullDataFromSource(IMFSample** ppNewSample);
};
```

CHAPTER 9

Advanced Media Foundation Topics

Rendering a Player UI with the EVR Mixer. 289
Streaming a Network Player 298

In the previous chapters, you saw most of the core ideas behind Microsoft Media Foundation (MF). These basic concepts give you the ability to create custom components and allow you to create many different types of applications. This chapter contains several of the more advanced topics not covered earlier. Specifically, this chapter demonstrates how you can create hardware-accelerated image overlays on top of the currently playing video and shows you some network streaming concepts.

The code in this chapter is based on the same player that you have been working on throughout this book. The player, however, contains several enhancements that will be used to demonstrate some advanced MF features:

- **An alpha-blended seek bar over the video playback**   The seek bar utilizes the Enhanced Video Renderer (EVR) mixer interface to display the current relative position in the file whenever the mouse is pointing to the currently playing video. This functionality is somewhat similar to that shown in Chapter 5, "Media Foundation Transforms," where an extra image is added on top of the playing video. The difference here is that the image insertion is performed by Microsoft DirectX instead of in the custom MFT. The DirectX mixing provides a fast and efficient image insertion, while preserving the alpha transparency color of each pixel being drawn on top of the video.

- **Network streaming**   The sample in this chapter uses a custom network-streaming *IMFByteStream* object to stream the media data in ASF format to a network client. Thus, you can use Windows Media Player or some other network-aware media player to connect to the sample player and receive a video stream being played by the sample player.

- **Tee MFT behavior**   This capability allows you to send the same data stream to several sinks. In the sample player presented here, the Tee MFTs are used to transmit data both to the network sink and the rendering sinks, giving you the ability to see the video that is currently being streamed over the network.

The sample shown here builds on the concepts shown in the previous chapters and demonstrates how you can build advanced players with good-looking user interfaces and powerful features.

Note that the seek bar code uses advanced DirectX functionality and requires several libraries not available in the standard Microsoft Visual Studio installation. The seek bar code uses this advanced DirectX primarily to load and manipulate the seek bar textures and surfaces. Therefore, you will need to download, install, and link to the latest DirectX SDK.

> **More Info** To install the DirectX SDK, go to the following page and select the latest edition of the DirectX SDK: *http://msdn.microsoft.com/en-us/directx/aa937781*.

In addition to the seek bar, the sample player presented in this chapter is also capable of building network topologies. The player can build either a pure network system, with only the network ASF sink, or a hybrid topology, with both a standard rendering and the network ASF sinks. Here is what the hybrid topology looks like.

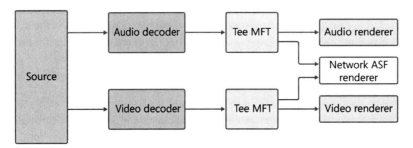

The topology shown in this chapter incorporates a new type of MFT—the Tee MFT. This MFT splits the data stream in two and sends a copy of input samples to each of its output streams. Therefore, in one of the topologies demonstrated in this chapter, the network ASF sink gets the same data that the audio and video renderers receive.

> **Note** To keep the topology simple, the player does not do any transcoding. As a result, only WMV or ASF files can be streamed over the network.

As mentioned previously, you can use Windows Media Player to connect to the network topology hosted in the sample player and receive the video. To try out the network behavior of the player, simply click Open File For Network Streaming on the File menu and select a WMV file.

To connect to the player on the same machine, you can use Windows Media Player and point it to the *http://localhost:8080/test.asf* URL as shown in the following screen shots. If you want to connect from a different machine, you will need to ensure that the right port is open in the firewall and that you use the right IP address.

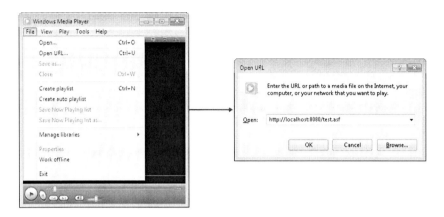

Rendering a Player UI with the EVR Mixer

The EVR—Enhanced Video Renderer—is a new generation of renderers introduced in Windows Vista. The EVR contains several improvements over the older Video Mixing Renderer (VMR) family of renderers. In this chapter, you will see how to use the mixer interface exposed by the EVR to create some interface elements for your player.

The primary purpose of the EVR is, of course, to render a video stream on the screen. The EVR uses various DirectX interfaces to connect directly to the graphics hardware of your machine and render the video while utilizing as few resources as possible.

The EVR is an extensible component that exposes several different interfaces, each of which allows you to perform various advanced operations on the EVR.

- ■ ***IMFVideoDisplayControl***   Controls how the video is displayed inside of the player window, its location, and clipping

- ■ ***IMFVideoMixerBitmap***   Allows you to add images on top of the video

- ■ ***IMFVideoMixerControl***   Allows you to add extra video streams to achieve a picture-in-picture effect

- ■ ***IMFVideoProcessor***   Controls the color and image adjustment of the video and exposes various video filter capabilities

In addition to the interfaces exposed by the video renderer, you can also replace several of the built-in components to extend the EVR capabilities. You can replace two of the major EVR components:

- **The mixer**   A component responsible for composing the final image on the screen in the video window with other, additional components. For example, you can use the mixer to enable picture-in-picture functionality, rendering an extra stream on top of the main video stream. You can also use the mixer to add extra images on top of the video, such as user interface components.

- **The presenter**   A component that draws (presents) the images on the screen and schedules when each frame should be displayed. For example, you can use the presenter to ensure the correct behavior and minimize glitches when samples in the stream are missing.

The mixer (also known as the *compositor*) component of the EVR exposes several interfaces. The sample player in this chapter uses the *IMFVideoMixerBitmap* interface exposed by the mixer to draw a seek bar on top of the video. The seek bar indicates the current playback position within the video and is displayed whenever you move the mouse pointer over the player. The player does not listen to click events, so you can't actually seek to a new location with the seek bar, but this sample functionality demonstrates how you can implement some advanced user interface features with the EVR in a player.

> **Note**   The EVR is exposed both to MF and Microsoft DirectShow graphs. You can use the EVR and all of its features with either playback technology. The only difference is that the DirectShow version of the EVR exposes several extra interfaces used for DirectShow filter manipulation and control.

The *IMFVideoMixerBitmap* interface allows you to specify an image that will be drawn on top of the video. You can specify the location of the image and control its overall transparency. The mixer is capable of using images provided either as Graphics Device Interface (GDI) device contexts (GDI DCs) or as DirectX surfaces. Though the two image formats are virtually identical, the mixer cannot use per-pixel alpha information with GDI. If you use GDI DCs, you can specify a single transparent color, but you cannot set parts of the image to be more transparent than other parts. For example, when using GDI you can set the color pink to be completely transparent, but you can't make the left half of the image 50 percent transparent and the right half 90 percent transparent.

Due to this limitation, the sample player uses DirectX surfaces to draw on top of the video. Because the default mixer can overlay only a single image on top of the video, and because the seek bar consists of several individual images that need to be blended together before they can be drawn on the video, the seek bar drawing process consists of several steps.

The player first combines the seek bar with a seek tick image that indicates the playback location relative to the seek bar length. Then the player sends that combined image to the mixer, for display over the currently playing video. The following is a diagram that demonstrates these steps.

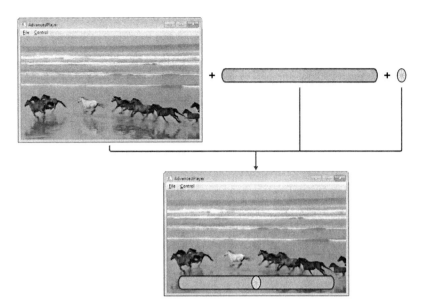

The combined seek bar with the seek tick image is passed to the mixer, which uses DirectX to draw it on top of the video. There is actually an extra step not shown in the diagram that is required to create the right type of surface that the mixer will accept. Here are the steps in a little bit more detail:

1. Initialize DirectX objects, textures, and surfaces.

2. Load the seek bar background image into an *IDirectX3DTexture9* object.

3. Load the seek "tick" image that will indicate the current location of the video into another *IDirectX3DTexture9* object.

4. Use the *ID3DXSprite* interface to draw first the seek bar and then the seek tick images onto an intermediate surface, created in the default DirectX memory pool. This surface is used to blend the two images together while preserving their per-pixel alpha information.

5. Load the intermediate default pool surface from step 4 into the final surface that is created in the system memory. This step is necessary because the *IMFVideoMixerBitmap* interface can handle only surfaces located in the system memory.

6. Send the final surface from step 5 to the *IMFVideoMixerBitmap*, specifying the rendering location.

As you probably already noticed, the first three steps of the procedure need to be done only once. You can initialize the DirectX objects and load the seek bar images only once, and then reuse everything. Therefore, the procedure is broken up into two functions—one that initializes all of the DirectX components, and another that actually sends the seek bar image to the mixer.

The seek bar initialization begins in the *CPlayer::InitializeMixer()* method. The method extracts the mixer interface from the EVR and calls other helper functions to initialize the various DirectX objects used in the player.

```
//
// Initialize the mixer pointer and DirectX objects necessary to draw the seek bar
//
HRESULT CPlayer::InitializeMixer(void)
{
    HRESULT hr = S_OK;

    do
    {
        m_pMixerBitmap = NULL;

        // get the mixer pointer from the session
        hr = MFGetService(m_pSession, MR_VIDEO_MIXER_SERVICE, IID_IMFVideoMixerBitmap,
            (void**)&m_pMixerBitmap);
        BREAK_ON_FAIL(hr);

        // load the various seek bar required objects if they have not been loaded
        if(m_pD3d9Obj == NULL)
        {
            hr = InitializeSeekbarDirectX();
        }
    }
    while(false);

    return hr;
}
```

As mentioned earlier, the mixer is one of the internal objects contained in the EVR. Therefore, it is extracted from the EVR by calling the *MFGetService()* helper function and asking for the *MR_VIDEO_MIXER_SERVICE* object. If this player instance has already been used to play a different clip, much of the internal initialization may have already happened. You still need a new pointer to the mixer itself, but the seek bar DirectX components have already been loaded. Therefore, the helper *InitializeSeekbarDirectX()* function is called only if the internal pointer to the *IDirect3D9* object is not initialized.

Here is the function that loads and initializes the seek bar DirectX components.

```
//
// Create and initialize the DirectX objects needed to draw the seek bar.
//
HRESULT CPlayer::InitializeSeekbarDirectX(void)
{
    HRESULT hr = S_OK;
    D3DDISPLAYMODE dispMode;
    D3DPRESENT_PARAMETERS d3dParams;
    WCHAR fullPath[MAX_PATH];
```

```cpp
do
{
    // create the DX9 object
    m_pD3d9Obj = Direct3DCreate9(D3D_SDK_VERSION);
    BREAK_ON_NULL(m_pD3d9Obj, E_UNEXPECTED);

    // get the current adapter display mode
    hr = m_pD3d9Obj->GetAdapterDisplayMode( D3DADAPTER_DEFAULT, &dispMode );

    // initialize the d3d parameter structure
    ZeroMemory( &d3dParams, sizeof(D3DPRESENT_PARAMETERS) );
    d3dParams.Windowed = TRUE;                    // windowed mode
    d3dParams.SwapEffect = D3DSWAPEFFECT_DISCARD;
    d3dParams.BackBufferFormat = dispMode.Format;
    d3dParams.hDeviceWindow = m_hwndVideo;

    // create a D3D9 device
    hr = m_pD3d9Obj->CreateDevice(
        D3DADAPTER_DEFAULT,                 // use the primary display adapter
        D3DDEVTYPE_HAL,
        NULL,
        D3DCREATE_SOFTWARE_VERTEXPROCESSING      // use sw processing
            | D3DCREATE_FPU_PRESERVE             // use double floating point
            | D3DCREATE_MULTITHREADED,           // multiple threads will access device
        &d3dParams,
        &m_pD3d9Device);
    BREAK_ON_FAIL(hr);

    // create the surface that will hold the render surface in system memory - that is
    // required by the mixer
    hr = m_pD3d9Device->CreateOffscreenPlainSurface(
        800, 50,                        // surface dimensions
        D3DFMT_A8R8G8B8,                // make a surface with alpha
        D3DPOOL_SYSTEMMEM,              // place surface in system memory
        &m_pD3d9RenderSurface,          // output pointer to the new surface
        NULL);                          // reserved
    BREAK_ON_FAIL(hr);

    // create a texture that will be used to blend the seek bar images
    hr = D3DXCreateTexture(m_pD3d9Device,
        1024, 64,                       // texture dimensions - factor of 2
        1,                              // MIP levels
        D3DUSAGE_RENDERTARGET,          // this texture will be a render target
        D3DFMT_A8R8G8B8,                // texture format - will have alpha
        D3DPOOL_DEFAULT,                // create texture in default pool
        &m_pTargetTexture);             // output texture ptr
    BREAK_ON_FAIL(hr);

    // get the surface behind the target texture - the render target
    hr = m_pTargetTexture->GetSurfaceLevel(0, &m_pTextureSurface);
    BREAK_ON_FAIL(hr);
```

```
            // create the sprite that will be used to blend the individual seek bar images
            hr = D3DXCreateSprite(m_pD3d9Device, &m_pDisplaySprite);
            BREAK_ON_FAIL(hr);

            // create a texture of the seek bar image
            GetLocalFilePath(L"\\seekbar.png", fullPath, MAX_PATH);
            hr = D3DXCreateTextureFromFile(m_pD3d9Device, fullPath, &m_pD3d9SeekBarTexture);
            BREAK_ON_FAIL(hr);

            // create a texture of the current location indicator image
            GetLocalFilePath(L"\\seektick.png", fullPath, MAX_PATH);
            hr = D3DXCreateTextureFromFile(m_pD3d9Device, fullPath, &m_pD3d9SeekTickTexture);
            BREAK_ON_FAIL(hr);

            // indicate that all render commands to this device will now go to the specified
            // surface
            hr = m_pD3d9Device->SetRenderTarget(0, m_pTextureSurface);
            BREAK_ON_FAIL(hr);
    }
    while(false);

    return hr;
}
```

The function uses the standard DirectX initialization procedure—first it creates the *IDirect3D9* object and the DirectX device that will be used to manage all of the explicit DirectX operations in the player. Then, the *InitializeSeekBarDirectX()* method creates the off-screen surface that will be passed in to the mixer. Note that the surface is created with the *D3DPOOL_SYSTEMMEM* flag, indicating that the surface will live in the system memory. The mixer will accept only surfaces located in the system memory. In addition to those surfaces, the function also loads each of the images into their own texture objects and creates the intermediate target texture —*m_pTargetTexture*—that will be used to blend the images together. Finally, the function extracts the top surface from the target texture and sets it on the *D3D* device created earlier. This way, whenever anything is rendered on the device, it will be drawn to the target texture.

The *CPlayer::InitializeSeekBarDirectX()* loads the two images—seekbar.png and seektick.png—from the local directory. Though the player uses PNG images because they have the additional alpha information with every pixel, you can also use JPG, BMP, and GIF images as seek bar textures.

> **Note** The *CPlayer::GetLocalFilePath()* method used in the *InitializeSeekBarDirectX()* function finds the location of the current module and adds that string to the passed-in file name.

Here is the function that is called to draw the seek bar. The *CPlayer::DrawSeekbar()* method is called from *WinMain()* on timer, once a second. This ensures that the seek bar itself is updated at least once per second. If during the call the mouse pointer is outside the window bounds of the player, this causes the *DrawSeekbar()* function to call *IMFVideoMixerBitmap::ClearAlphaBitmap*, erasing the seek bar image.

```cpp
//
// Draw the seek bar and the current position indicator on the UI
//
HRESULT CPlayer::DrawSeekbar(void)
{
    HRESULT hr = S_OK;
    MFVideoAlphaBitmap alphaBmp;

    do
    {
        // audio playback may not have initialized seek bar - just exit in that case
        BREAK_ON_NULL(m_pD3d9Device, S_OK);

        // if the seek bar is invisible just clear out the alpha bitmap from the mixer
        if(!m_isSeekbarVisible)
        {
            hr = m_pMixerBitmap->ClearAlphaBitmap();
            break;
        }

        // clear the texture of the old seek bar image
        hr = m_pD3d9Device->Clear(
            0, NULL,                    // clear the entire surface
            D3DCLEAR_TARGET,            // clear the surface set as the render target
            D3DCOLOR_RGBA(0,0,0,0),     // set to the transparency color
            1, 0 );                     // z and stencil
        BREAK_ON_FAIL(hr);

        // blend the seek bar textures together on the target surface only if the seek bar
        // is visible
        hr = RenderSeekBarSurface();
        BREAK_ON_FAIL(hr);

        // overall transparency of the seek bar image
        alphaBmp.params.fAlpha = 0.7f;

        // Initialize the structure with the alpha bitmap info
        alphaBmp.GetBitmapFromDC = FALSE;               // this is not a GDI DC
        alphaBmp.bitmap.pDDS = m_pD3d9RenderSurface;    // specify the surface
        alphaBmp.params.dwFlags =
            MFVideoAlphaBitmap_EntireDDS |              // apply alpha to entire surface
            MFVideoAlphaBitmap_Alpha |                  // use per-pixel alpha
            MFVideoAlphaBitmap_DestRect;                // specify a custom destination rect

        // specify the destination rectangle on the screen in relative coordinates
        alphaBmp.params.nrcDest.left = 0.1f;
        alphaBmp.params.nrcDest.top = 0.8f;
        alphaBmp.params.nrcDest.bottom = 0.85f;
        alphaBmp.params.nrcDest.right = 0.9f;

        // send the alpha bitmap to the mixer
        hr = m_pMixerBitmap->SetAlphaBitmap(&alphaBmp);
    }
    while(false);

    return hr;
}
```

The *DrawSeekbar()* method is called from the main window loop every second to regenerate the seek bar texture and update the location of the tick indicating the location in the file. The method first clears the surface to which the *IDirect3D9* device is rendering. This ensures that there are no afterimages of the seek bar, and that the seek bar image is cleared if the mouse pointer is not over the player window. If the mouse pointer is over the player, *DrawSeekbar()* calls the *RenderSeekBarSurface()* helper function to blend the two parts of the seek bar image and renders them onto the device's surface. After that, *DrawSeekbar()* initializes the special *MFVideoAlphaBitmap* structure with the information about the image and passes it to the mixer's *IMFVideoMixerBitmap::SetAlphaBitmap()* function.

The *DrawSeekbar()* function sets the alpha transparency of the entire seek bar image to 0.7. This means that the image will be only 70 percent visible, partially transparent. This transparency value is multiplied by the alpha value of each individual pixel, which means that pixels that were barely visible before will now be almost entirely invisible.

> **Note** The *m_isSeekbarVisible* Boolean variable is set by the *CPlayer::SetMouseVisible()* method that is called from the application's main window message loop. When the mouse pointer moves over the window, the window loop calls *SetMouseVisible()* and passes in *true*, indicating that the seek bar should be visible. When the message loop receives the *WM_MOUSELEAVE* message, it calls *SetMouseVisible()* and passes in *false*.

The process of blending the mixer components into one image and drawing them on the surface is conceptually fairly simple but takes up some space. Here is the *CPlayer::RenderSeekBarSurface()* method that actually blends the two seek bar textures together on an intermediate surface.

```
//
// Blend seek bar textures together on the intermediate surface
//
HRESULT CPlayer::RenderSeekBarSurface(void)
{
    HRESULT hr = S_OK;
    D3DXVECTOR3 tickPosition(0, 0, 0);
    LONGLONG clockTime = 0;
    MFTIME systemTime = 0;

    do
    {
        // get the current time from the presentation clock
        hr = m_pPresentationClock->GetCorrelatedTime(0, &clockTime, &systemTime);
        BREAK_ON_FAIL(hr);

        // calculate how far from the beginning of the seek bar the seek indicator should be
        tickPosition.x = (float)(960 * ((double)clockTime / (double)m_duration));
```

```cpp
        // begin drawing scene
        hr = m_pD3d9Device->BeginScene();
        BREAK_ON_FAIL(hr);

        // begin drawing the textures
        hr = m_pDisplaySprite->Begin(D3DXSPRITE_ALPHABLEND);
        BREAK_ON_FAIL(hr);

        // draw the seek bar texture on the render target of the device to which the
        // sprite object belongs to
        hr = m_pDisplaySprite->Draw(
            m_pD3d9SeekBarTexture,              // draw this texture on render target
            NULL, NULL,                         // source rectangle and center of sprite
            NULL,                               // position - use 0,0 coordinates
            D3DCOLOR_RGBA(255, 255, 255, 255)); // color modulation value - 0xffffffff
        BREAK_ON_FAIL(hr);

        // draw the current location indicator (tick) on the seek bar
        hr = m_pDisplaySprite->Draw(
            m_pD3d9SeekTickTexture,             // draw this texture on render target
            NULL, NULL,                         // source rectangle and center of sprite
            &tickPosition,                      // position - use tickPosition coords
            D3DCOLOR_RGBA(255, 255, 255, 255)); // color modulation value - 0xffffffff
        BREAK_ON_FAIL(hr);

        // end drawing the textures
        hr = m_pDisplaySprite->End();
        BREAK_ON_FAIL(hr);

        // end drawing the scene - actually draws the scene on the surface
        hr = m_pD3d9Device->EndScene();
        BREAK_ON_FAIL(hr);

        // copy the contents of the target texture's surface to the render surface - the
        // render surface is in the system memory, which is what the mixer requires
        hr = D3DXLoadSurfaceFromSurface(
                m_pD3d9RenderSurface,       // target surface
                NULL, NULL,                 // use the entire surface as the target rect
                m_pTextureSurface,          // source surface
                NULL, NULL,                 // use the entire surface as the source rect
                D3DX_DEFAULT, 0);           // image filter and special transparent color
        BREAK_ON_FAIL(hr);
    }
    while(false);

    return hr;
}
```

Here are the steps that the function takes to construct the seek bar surface:

1. Calculate the position of the seek tick image from the presentation clock.
2. Begin drawing the scene on the *D3D9* device.

   a. Begin drawing the sprite that will combine the two seek bar textures.

      - Draw the seek bar itself on the *D3D9* device through the sprite interface.
      - Draw the seek bar tick on the *D3D9* device, in the right position to indicate how much of the clip has been played.

   b. End drawing the sprite that will combine the two seek bar textures.

3. End drawing the scene on the *D3D9* device.
4. Load the surface to which the *D3D9* device was rendering into the final surface that will be passed to the mixer.

Using this mixer functionality, you can implement quite complex user interfaces. For example, by controlling the alpha of the entire image, you can create fade-in and fade-out effects, gradually fading the interface in or out in a graceful manner over a period of a second. By creating more complex bitmaps and some mouse location processing, you can also construct a UI that detects mouse movement and allows you to dynamically highlight active buttons.

If you want to support more advanced mixer behavior, you can also consider implementing a custom mixer plug-in and adding it to the EVR at run time.

Streaming a Network Player

The sample player in this chapter can build three major types of topologies—one that streams only to the screen, one that streams only to the network, and one that can stream both to the screen and the network at the same time. The main difference between these topologies is in the sink segment that comes after the Tee MFT. Compare this diagram with the one presented in the introduction to this chapter.

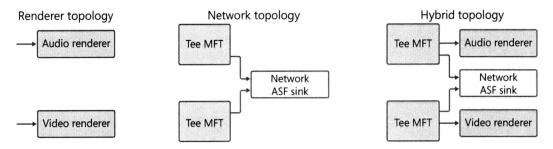

In the renderer-only topology, you don't need the Tee filter and the network sink, and the data can stream from the decoders directly to the audio and video renderers. In the network-only topology, the player adds the Tee filter for simplicity, but hooks up the Tee filters only to the network ASF sink. In the hybrid topology, the player hooks the Tee MFTs both to the network sink and the renderer sinks.

Strictly speaking, in network-only topology the Tee MFT is redundant, because there is no need to split the data streams. The *CTopoBuilder* class uses this topology structure to simplify the topology building process.

Note that the network ASF sink is rateless, and the video and audio renderers are normal rendering sinks. Whenever a rateless sink exists in the same topology as a rendering sink, the topology takes its cue from the slower rendering sink. This way, even though the rateless sink can stream as fast as the upstream topology components allow, the rendering sink controls the rate of flow, and the content is presented to the user at a normal rate. This, however, presents a problem with the hybrid topology. Because of its inherent design, the network sink will block and refuse to process samples until a network client connects to it. At the same time, the presentation clock will move forward. This can therefore result in a situation in which the on-screen content flow will glitch and skip for the amount of time that it takes for a network client to connect to the network sink.

> **Note** Though at first glance the *MF_TOPONODE_PRIMARYOUTPUT* attribute appears to be designed to solve the Tee MFT node-blocking problem, it is used only to determine which media type the Tee node will use. This attribute has no effect on the flow of samples through the Tee node.

In addition, Windows Media Player expects the network connection to close as soon as the stream is complete. However, the network sink will not close the connection until it receives an end-of-presentation message, which in turn will not be fired until the rendering sink is done rendering all of its data. Because the in-player rendering can be a few seconds behind the network stream, this stream without data that doesn't close properly can confuse Windows Media Player and cause it to display an error dialog box at the end.

One way to solve this problem would be to implement either a custom Tee MFT that will continue to stream data to one of its outputs even if the other is blocked, or a rendering sink wrapper around the rateless network sink. Another method would be to use a custom session and control how the samples flow through the topology directly. However, for simplicity, the sample demonstrated in this chapter uses the default Tee MFT, network sink, and media session implementations. Therefore, the hybrid topology shown here is only a partial and incomplete implementation of a dual network/rendering player.

CHAPTER 9 Advanced Media Foundation Topics **299**

To enable this new functionality, the player contains some new and updated code:

- **CTopoBuilder**   The topology builder class seen in Chapter 3, "Media Playback," was modified to support the creation of several different types of topologies.

- **CHttpOutputByteStream**   MF does not provide an *IMFByteStream* implementation that supports streaming to a network. Therefore, this sample contains a simple "server" byte stream class that allows a network-aware player to connect to the network sink and receive a data stream.

The sample also introduces several minor helper classes, which will be covered when they are needed.

Building the Network Topology

The process of building the topology is somewhat different from the one used in the previous chapters. This new process needs to be able to add the extra sinks on demand and correctly hook up the Tee MFTs. The player again triggers building of the topology by calling the *CTopoBuilder::RenderURL()* method. In this case, however, the method receives an extra parameter, indicating whether the network segment is needed.

```
//
// Initiates topology building from the file URL by first creating a media source, and then
// adding source and sink nodes for every stream found in the file.
//
HRESULT CTopoBuilder::RenderURL(PCWSTR fileUrl, HWND videoHwnd, bool addNetwork)
{
    HRESULT hr = S_OK;

    do
    {
        m_videoHwnd = videoHwnd;

        // The topology can have either a rendering sink (when videoHwnd is not NULL), a
        // network sink, or both.
        if(videoHwnd == NULL && !addNetwork)
        {
            hr = E_INVALIDARG;
            break;
        }

        // first create the media source for the file/stream passed in.  Fail and fall out if
        // the media source creation fails (e.g. if the file format is not recognized)
        hr = CreateMediaSource(fileUrl);
        BREAK_ON_FAIL(hr);

        // add a network sink if one was requested
        if(addNetwork)
        {
            hr = CreateNetworkSink(8080);
            BREAK_ON_FAIL(hr);
        }
```

```
        // create the actual topology
        hr = CreateTopology();
    }
    while(false);

    return hr;
}
```

Most of the changes to the topology builder are actually triggered in the new *CreateNetworkSink()* method and in the topology creation process is started when the *CreateTopology()* method is called. One additional change is that the video window handle parameter—*videoHwnd*—can be set to *NULL* if the user does not need rendering sinks. The *addNetwork* parameter, of course, indicates whether the topology created should have a network sink.

The *CreateMediaSource()* function remains unchanged from Chapter 3, and will therefore not be shown here. The *CTopoBuilder::CreateNetworkSink()* method is new, however. For simplicity, the *RenderURL()* function always calls the method with port *8080* as a parameter—that is the port on which the sink will listen for connections by clients.

```
//
// Create a network sink that will listen for requests on the specified port.
//
HRESULT CTopoBuilder::CreateNetworkSink(DWORD requestPort)
{
    HRESULT hr = S_OK;
    CComPtr<IMFPresentationDescriptor> pPresDescriptor;
    CComPtr<IMFASFProfile> pAsfProfile;
    CComQIPtr<IMFASFContentInfo> pAsfContentInfo;

    CComPtr<IMFActivate> pByteStreamActivate;
    CComPtr<IMFActivate> pNetSinkActivate;

    do
    {
        BREAK_ON_NULL(m_pSource, E_UNEXPECTED);

        // create an HTTP activator for the custom HTTP output byte stream object
        pByteStreamActivate = new (std::nothrow) CHttpOutputStreamActivate(requestPort);
        BREAK_ON_NULL(pByteStreamActivate, E_OUTOFMEMORY);

        // create the presentation descriptor for the source
        hr = m_pSource->CreatePresentationDescriptor(&pPresDescriptor);
        BREAK_ON_FAIL(hr);

        // create the ASF profile from the presentation descriptor
        hr = MFCreateASFProfileFromPresentationDescriptor(pPresDescriptor, &pAsfProfile);
        BREAK_ON_FAIL(hr);

        // create the ContentInfo object for the ASF profile
        hr = MFCreateASFContentInfo(&pAsfContentInfo);
        BREAK_ON_FAIL(hr);
```

```
        // set the profile on the content info object
        hr = pAsfContentInfo->SetProfile(pAsfProfile);
        BREAK_ON_FAIL(hr);

        // create an activator object for an ASF streaming sink
        hr = MFCreateASFStreamingMediaSinkActivate(pByteStreamActivate, pAsfContentInfo,
            &m_pNetworkSinkActivate);
        BREAK_ON_FAIL(hr);
    }
    while(false);

    return hr;
}
```

To create an ASF sink, you first need to initialize it, specifying the configuration—the number and types of input streams. Although this can be done manually, a much simpler method is to base it on the existing presentation descriptor exposed by the network source. This way, the sink will have the same number and types of streams as are present in the source that will provide the content.

Furthermore, just like all other standard MF sinks, the ASF sink needs to have an *IMFByteStream* object that will actually stream the data. Because MF does not provide a network byte stream, the sample contains a custom HTTP output byte stream. The *CHttpOutputByteStream* class will be discussed in the next section.

The initialization of the network sink therefore consists of four stages:

1. Create an output byte stream for the sink.

2. Use the presentation descriptor to create an *IMFASFProfile* object, describing the stream configuration for the ASF stream that will be generated by the sink. This is done by calling the *MFCreateASFProfileFromPresentationDescriptor()* function.

3. Use the ASF profile from step 2 to create an *IMFASFContentInfo* object that contains ASF file/stream header information. The content info object is created by the *MFCreateASF-ContentInfo()* function. Then pass the profile to the content info object by calling its *IMF-ASFContentInfo::SetProfile()* method.

4. Use the content info object from step 3 and the *IMFByteStream* object from step 1 to initialize the ASF sink.

If you have looked at the MF documentation, you may have noticed that MF provides two functions for creating a streaming (network) ASF sink—*MFCreateASFStreamingMediaSink()* and *MFCreateASFStreamingMediaSinkActivate()*. One of these obviously creates an ASF sink directly, whereas the other creates an activator object that will later be used by the topology to instantiate the actual sink. The two methods for creating the sink are essentially equivalent—the activator object simply postpones the sink creation. This type of behavior is needed primarily when you want to create a sink in a secured Protected Media Path process. The topology-building steps are slightly different, however, depending on whether you are using the actual MF object or an activator object. Here are the two sets of steps you need to take to build a branch of the playback topology, depending on whether you are using the actual sink or a deferred activation object. First are the steps for using the actual sink:

1. Instantiate the sink.
2. Instantiate the sink topology node.
3. Search the sink for an input stream with the right media type.
4. Get a sink stream from the sink with the right media type.
5. Pass the sink stream to the sink topology node.
6. Connect the source stream topology node to the sink topology node.

And here are the steps if you use a deferred activator object to instantiate the media sink:

1. Instantiate the sink activator.
2. Instantiate the sink topology node
3. Pass the sink activator object to the sink topology node.
4. Connect the source stream topology node to the sink node.

Note Some of the steps in each case need to be done for every stream—for every decoder-to-sink connection in the topology.

As you can see, if you use an activator object, then conceptually you need to take two steps fewer. You don't need to search among all of the input streams of the sink for the one with the right media type. This difference is minor, but it explains why an activator object may be preferable in some cases. The topology builder will take care of the stream selection process for you.

This is why the *CTopoBuilder::CreateNetworkSink()* method shown earlier uses the *MFCreateASF-StreamingMediaSinkActivate()* function to create an activator node for the media sink. One added complication here is that the *MFCreateASFStreamingMediaSinkActivate()* function requires an activator object for the *IMFByteStream*. Therefore, you cannot create your custom byte stream directly—instead, you need a custom activator that knows how to instantiate the *CHttpOutputByteStream* object. The activator is implemented in the *CHttpOutputStreamActivate* class described in a later section. After all of the required components have been initialized, the *CTopoBuilder::CreateNetworkSink( )* method stores the activator in a member variable for later use during the topology creation phase.

CHAPTER 9 Advanced Media Foundation Topics **303**

The topology building process is again very similar to the code presented in the earlier chapters. The primary difference is in the extra function responsible for instantiating the network topology nodes. Here is the function that adds the network branch to the topology.

```
//
// If there is a network sink, create a Tee node and hook the network sink in parallel to
// the renderer sink in the topology, then return the Tee node.
//
HRESULT CTopoBuilder::CreateTeeNetworkTwig(IMFStreamDescriptor* pStreamDescriptor,
    IMFTopologyNode*, pRendererNode IMFTopologyNode** ppTeeNode)
{
    HRESULT hr = S_OK;
    CComPtr<IMFTopologyNode> pNetworkOutputNode;
    CComPtr<IMFTopologyNode> pTeeNode;
    DWORD streamId = 0;

    do
    {
        BREAK_ON_NULL(ppTeeNode, E_POINTER);

        // if the network sink is not configured, just exit
        if(m_pNetworkSinkActivate == NULL)
            break;

        // get the stream ID
        hr = pStreamDescriptor->GetStreamIdentifier(&streamId);
        BREAK_ON_FAIL(hr);

        // create the output topology node for one of the streams on the network sink
        hr = MFCreateTopologyNode(MF_TOPOLOGY_OUTPUT_NODE, &pNetworkOutputNode);
        BREAK_ON_FAIL(hr);

        // set the output stream ID on the stream sink topology node
        hr = pNetworkOutputNode->SetUINT32(MF_TOPONODE_STREAMID, streamId);
        BREAK_ON_FAIL(hr);

        // associate the output network topology node with the network sink
        hr = pNetworkOutputNode->SetObject(m_pNetworkSinkActivate);
        BREAK_ON_FAIL(hr);

        // add the network output topology node to the topology
        m_pTopology->AddNode(pNetworkOutputNode);
        BREAK_ON_FAIL(hr);


        // create the topology Tee node
        hr = MFCreateTopologyNode(MF_TOPOLOGY_TEE_NODE, &pTeeNode);
        BREAK_ON_FAIL(hr);

        // connect the first Tee node output to the network sink node
        hr = pTeeNode->ConnectOutput(0, pNetworkOutputNode, 0);
        BREAK_ON_FAIL(hr);
```

```cpp
        // if a renderer node was created and passed in, add it to the topology
        if(pRendererNode != NULL)
        {
            // add the renderer node to the topology
            hr = m_pTopology->AddNode(pRendererNode);
            BREAK_ON_FAIL(hr);

            // connect the second Tee node output to the renderer sink node
            hr = pTeeNode->ConnectOutput(1, pRendererNode, 0);
            BREAK_ON_FAIL(hr);
        }

        // detach the Tee node and return it as the output node
        *ppTeeNode = pTeeNode.Detach();
    }
    while(false);

    return hr;
}
```

The process for creating the network branch is as follows:

1. Create an output node for the network sink stream.
2. Set the ID of the output stream that this sink stream will consume.
3. Add the network sink activator object to the sink stream topology node.
4. Create the Tee MFT node.
5. Connect one output of the Tee MFT node to the network sink node.
6. If a renderer sink topology node was passed in, connect the second output of the Tee MFT node to the renderer sink.

The HTTP Byte Stream Activator

As mentioned earlier, the topology builder needs an activator object that can instantiate the HTTP byte stream. The activator will be used during the topology resolution phase to create a new instance of the HTTP byte stream and pass it to the ASF network sink. Because the HTTP byte stream is a custom object, it needs a custom activator class.

> **Note** Instead of implementing a separate activator object, you can also have the byte stream implement the *IMFActivate* interface directly. This alternative is not used in the sample player because adding another interface to the byte stream object would increase its complexity without providing any special functionality.

Fortunately, the activator concept is very simple if you don't need to do anything fancy. An activator object simply needs to implement the *IMFActivate* interface, which inherits from the *IMFAttributes* interface. The attribute system is needed if the activator object needs to be used in a separate protected process. In this case, the activator is the simplest kind—all it needs to do is store the output port number that will be used by the byte stream, and then instantiate the byte stream object on demand. Therefore, the *IMFAttributes* methods are left unimplemented, returning the *E_NOTIMPL* error code.

The one interesting method of the HTTP byte stream activator is *IMFActivate::ActivateObject()*. Even so, there is very little code in it.

```
//
// Activate the CHttpOutputByteStream object
//
HRESULT CHttpOutputStreamActivate::ActivateObject(REFIID riid, void **ppv)
{
    HRESULT hr = S_OK;
    CComPtr<IMFByteStream> pByteStream;

    do
    {
        hr = CHttpOutputByteStream::CreateInstance(m_requestPort, &pByteStream);
        BREAK_ON_FAIL(hr);

        hr = pByteStream->QueryInterface(riid, ppv);
    }
    while(false);

    return hr;
}
```

All this method does is create an instance of the *CHttpOutputByteStream* class, pass in the stored request port, and query it for the requested interface. This method is called during the topology rendering phase, when all the other objects in the topology are instantiated and hooked up to each other.

The HTTP Output Byte Stream

Most archival or rateless sinks receive an *IMFByteStream* object as a parameter. The byte stream object is used to actually write the data to a file or send it over the network. Therefore, most archival and rateless sinks are capable of streaming data over the network, given a special network byte stream.

However, not all of the archival sinks should be used for this purpose. Most sinks are designed to write data to a file, and cannot deal with network buffering and bitrate situations. In addition, many file formats are not designed to be streamed—the player in some cases needs to be able to traverse the entire file before playing it and cannot render the data stream as it arrives on the client.

Therefore, not all sinks are suitable or should be used for network streaming. As a result, MF provides two ASF sinks—an ASF file sink, optimized for writing to a file, and an ASF streaming sink used to stream data over a network. Of course, both produce ASF network sinks that can actually be used for streaming to a file or to a network, depending on the byte stream they receive, but the streaming sink has extra internal functionality used to handle various network conditions.

Background ASF files contain a header stored at the beginning of the file, with information such as the duration and the number frames in the file. This header also specifies whether a media sample index that can be used for seeking in the file is present. Therefore, during archival, the ASF file sink creates the index, and after the archival is complete it updates the header with the final count of frames, index information, and duration.

However, when streaming an ASF data stream over HTTP, the network ASF sink cannot seek back to the beginning of the "file" to update the header, because the header has already been sent to the HTTP client. So the ASF streaming sink does not write an index, and it does not write duration information and other fields to the header. This is the main difference between the ASF file sink and the ASF streaming sink.

To create an *IMFByteStream* object for streaming data to a file, you can use the MF-provided *MFCreateFile()* function. The resulting byte stream object allows you to read or write data to the specified file and is optimized for file access. The file operations will be fast and efficient. However, MF does not contain a default implementation for a network byte stream object. Therefore, this section demonstrates the implementation of a basic network *IMFByteStream* object—the *CHttpOutputByteStream*.

Tip If you want to test your network streaming application, you can easily replace the *CHttpOutputByteStream* implementation of the *IMFByteStream* that is passed to the ASF stream writer with a version returned by the *MFCreateFile()* function. A file created in this way will be perfectly viable and can be used to verify that your topology is operating as expected without the complexity added by network streaming or custom byte streams. However, seeking within this file may not be possible because the ASF header will be missing the media sample index and will contain the wrong file duration.

The HTTP output byte stream is designed solely to stream data to a network. Upon connection, *CHttpOutputByteStream* will notify any clients that it will stream ASF data by sending the standard *video/x-ms-asf* HTTP response header before transmitting any media data. The class presents the simplest network streamer possible. It opens a port for listening, waits for a client connection, receives a request, and then blindly starts sending data on the output port. The following list describes the lifetime of the HTTP output byte stream:

1. Receive the initial synchronous *IMFByteStream::Write()* or asynchronous *BeginWrite()* request. Whether the first write request is synchronous or asynchronous depends on the sink implementation.

    a. After the write request, the sink opens a TCP listening port.

    b. Wait for a client connection.

c. When a client connects, receive the request. The idea is that a standard client will send a basic *HTTP GET* request, asking for a file. The actual contents of the request are ignored, because the byte stream is not a full-fledged server and can stream only the data that it is given.

   d. When the request is received, create an output socket.

   e. Send the HTTP response header. The response header is hard-coded in the *CHttpOutputByteStream* and notifies the client that it will receive a video stream in the *video/x-ms-asf* format.

2. Complete the initial synchronous *IMFByteStream::Write()* call.

3. Receive data from the byte stream user through the asynchronous *IMFByteStream::BeginWrite()* function.

   a. Add the data to an internal buffer. This step is necessary to avoid oversaturating the network with small data chunks, sending everything instead in large blocks.

   b. If the internal data buffer is full, send it to the network client through the output port.

   c. Use the callback to the user of the byte stream, notifying that user that the asynchronous call is complete.

4. Receive the *IMFByteStream::EndWrite()* call, and use it to notify the caller of the status of the write operation.

5. Go back to step 3.

6. Receive an *IMFByteStream::Flush()* call. Empty out the data buffer and send it regardless of how much data is in it.

7. Receive an *IMFByteStream::Close()* call, closing the output socket. Note that if Windows Media Player does not detect that the connection has closed after it received all of the ASF data, it will assume that the stream is corrupt and report an error in a message box.

CHttpOutputByteStream implements the *IMFByteStream* and the *IMFAsyncCallback* interfaces. The asynchronous callback interface is of course needed to implement the asynchronous *BeginWrite()* and *EndWrite()* methods. Though the *IMFByteStream* interface contains a lot of methods for reading and seeking within the stream, this functionality is not supported, and the functions simply return the *E_NOTIMPL* error.

Before using a byte stream object, most MF clients first call its *IMFByteStream::GetCapabilities()* method. The *GetCapabilities()* method returns a series of flags indicating what this byte stream is capable of. The following is the *CHttpOutputByteStream::GetCapabilities()* method implementation.

```
//
// Query the capabilities of this IMFByteStream object
//
HRESULT CHttpOutputByteStream::GetCapabilities(DWORD *pdwCapabilities)
{
    if(pdwCapabilities == NULL)
        return E_POINTER;

    *pdwCapabilities = MFBYTESTREAM_IS_WRITABLE;

    return S_OK;
}
```

The *CHttpOutputByteStream* supports only writing to a remote (network) stream. Therefore, it returns only the *MFBYTESTREAM_IS_WRITABLE* flag. Most clients will therefore not even try to call the read and seek *IMFByteStream* functions of this class.

As you saw earlier, the very first data-related call to the *IMFByteStream* object made by the ASF streaming sink is to the synchronous *Write()* function. Here is how the *CHttpOutputByteStream* implements this function.

```
//
// Synchronously write the data to the network
//
HRESULT CHttpOutputByteStream::Write(const BYTE *pb, ULONG cb, ULONG *pcbWritten)
{
    HRESULT hr = S_OK;

    do
    {
        BREAK_ON_NULL(pb, E_POINTER);
        BREAK_ON_NULL(pcbWritten, E_POINTER);

        // clear the written counter - if the write fails, this parameter will return 0
        *pcbWritten = 0;

        // if the output socket has not been initialized yet, initialize it - note that
        // this call will block until a network client connects
        if(m_clientSocket == INVALID_SOCKET)
        {
            hr = InitSocket(m_outputPort);
            BREAK_ON_FAIL(hr);
        }

        // send the data to the internal buffer, and eventually out to the network
        hr = SendData(pb, cb);
        BREAK_ON_FAIL(hr);

        // if we got here, the write succeeded - set the number of bytes written
        *pcbWritten = cb;
    }
    while(false);

    return hr;
}
```

The *Write()* function first checks whether the client socket has been initialized. If it has not, the function calls the internal *InitSocket()* function. Note that *InitSocket()*—and therefore *Write()*—will block until a client connects and starts requesting data. The *CHttpOutputByteStream::InitSocket()* function uses the Windows Sockets API to create a TCP socket, bind the specified port to it, and start listening for incoming TCP connections. However, because this has nothing to do with MF, its listing and description are omitted from this chapter.

The *InitSocket()* function listens for requests on the specified port and then starts streaming data whenever it receives *any* request. You can send any command to the port, and the byte stream will start streaming the file in response. For example, you can tell Windows Media Player to play *http://localhost:8080/test.asf*, *http://localhost:8080/banana.wmv*, or *http://localhost:8080/anyfile.avi*—it does not matter to the byte stream.

The network path will matter to some clients, however—some network player implementations take cues on how to render the file from the file name and network path. Windows Media Player is smart enough to detect the type of stream and render the file even if you give it the .avi extension—but it will have trouble if you remove the extension altogether and try to stream something like *http://localhost:8080/rat*.

After the byte stream has been initialized, a client of the byte stream object can use either the synchronous *IMFByteStream::Write()* function or the asynchronous *BeginWrite()/EndWrite()* methods. Though the asynchronous implementation is rather standard and should look familiar by now, it is presented here for reference.

Here is the *CHttpOutputByteStream::BeginWrite()* method implementation.

```
//
// Begin asynchronous write operation
//
HRESULT CHttpOutputByteStream::BeginWrite(const BYTE *pb, ULONG cb, IMFAsyncCallback *pCallback,
    IUnknown *punkState)
{
    HRESULT hr = S_OK;
    CComPtr<IAsyncWriteData> pWriteData;

    do
    {
        BREAK_ON_NULL(pb, E_POINTER);
        BREAK_ON_NULL(pCallback, E_POINTER);

        // create an async call state object
        pWriteData = new (std::nothrow) CByteStreamWriteData((BYTE*)pb, cb, pCallback,
            punkState);
        BREAK_ON_NULL(pWriteData, E_OUTOFMEMORY);

        // schedule the asynchronous operation on the private worker queue
        hr = MFPutWorkItem(m_netWorkQueue, this, pWriteData);
    }
    while(false);

    return hr;
}
```

This function simply stores a pointer to the passed-in data buffer in a custom state object and schedules work on the private network work queue. The work queue was created during construction of the byte stream object. Just as in earlier cases, this custom work queue is needed to ensure that other asynchronous operations in the topology are not blocked by this single component.

Here is the corresponding *IMFAsyncCallback::Invoke()* implementation.

```
//
// Asynchronous worker function - called when an asynchronous write has been scheduled.
//
HRESULT CHttpOutputByteStream::Invoke(IMFAsyncResult* pResult)
{
    HRESULT hr = S_OK;
    HRESULT sendResult = S_OK;
    CComPtr<IUnknown> pUnkState;
    CComQIPtr<IAsyncWriteData> pWriteData;
    BYTE* pData = NULL;
    DWORD dataLength = 0;

    do
    {
        // get the state object from the result
        hr = pResult->GetState(&pUnkState);
        BREAK_ON_FAIL(hr);

        // cast the IUnknown state object to IAsyncWriteData to extract the write data
        pWriteData = pUnkState;
        BREAK_ON_NULL(pWriteData, E_UNEXPECTED);

        // make sure the output port has been initialized
        if(m_clientSocket == INVALID_SOCKET)
        {
            hr = InitSocket(m_outputPort);
            BREAK_ON_FAIL(hr);
        }

        // get the data that will be sent to the client from the state object
        hr = pWriteData->GetWriteData(&pData, &dataLength);
        BREAK_ON_FAIL(hr);

        // send the data to the internal buffer, and eventually to the client
        sendResult = SendData(pData, dataLength);
    }
    while(false);

    // always call a helper function to send the result of the write operation to the caller
    SendAsyncWriteResult(pWriteData, sendResult);

    return hr;
}
```

The *Invoke()* function simply extracts the data that needs to be written from the asynchronous state object and then sends the data to the internal data buffer. As mentioned earlier, the data is not sent directly over the network, but is first stored in the internal data buffer in *CHttpOutputByteStream*. This is necessary because you can easily overload the socket functions by sending a lot of small packets continuously. It is much more efficient to use larger buffers, and send them periodically. Therefore, the *SendData()* call first writes the data to the buffer, and sends the entire buffer to the network client only after the entire buffer is full.

After calling the *SendData()* function, *Invoke()* calls the helper *SendAsyncWriteResult()* method to notify the caller of the result.

```
//
// Send the result of the asynchronous write operation to the caller
//
HRESULT CHttpOutputByteStream::SendAsyncWriteResult(IAsyncWriteData* pWriteData,
    HRESULT sendResult)
{
    HRESULT hr = S_OK;

    CComPtr<IUnknown> pBeginWriteState;
    CComPtr<IMFAsyncCallback> pBeginWriteCallback;
    CComPtr<IMFAsyncResult> pBeginWriteResult;

    do
    {
        // get the callback object passed in during BeginWrite call
        hr = pWriteData->GetCallback(&pBeginWriteCallback);
        BREAK_ON_FAIL(hr);

        // get the status object passed in during BeginWrite call
        hr = pWriteData->GetStateObject(&pBeginWriteState);
        BREAK_ON_FAIL(hr);

        // create an IMFAsyncResult object that will be used to report the operation status
        // to the caller
        hr = MFCreateAsyncResult(pWriteData, pBeginWriteCallback, pBeginWriteState,
            &pBeginWriteResult);
        BREAK_ON_FAIL(hr);

        // store the send operation result in the IMFAsyncResult for the caller
        pBeginWriteResult->SetStatus(sendResult);

        // schedule a callback to the caller
        MFInvokeCallback(pBeginWriteResult);
    }
    while(false);

    return hr;
}
```

The *SendAsyncWriteResult()* method is also fairly standard. It constructs a new *IMFAsyncResult* object by calling the *MFCreateAsyncResult()* function, stores the result of the send operation in the object, and finally sends it asynchronously to the caller of *BeginWrite()*. The asynchronous result also contains the state object passed into the *Invoke()* call earlier. This state object is needed because the *IMFByteStream::EndWrite()* call needs to know how many bytes were successfully sent. Because the number of bytes is already stored in the *IAsyncWriteData* state object, the same object is sent with the result.

The corresponding *IMFByteStream::EndWrite()* call will contain the result object created in the *SendAsyncWriteResult()* function. The *EndWrite()* function will then extract the number of bytes sent over the network and return it to the caller. Here is the implementation of the *EndWrite()* method.

```
//
// End the asynchronous write operation and return the number of bytes written
//
HRESULT CHttpOutputByteStream::EndWrite(IMFAsyncResult* pResult, ULONG* pcbWritten)
{
    HRESULT hr = S_OK;
    CComPtr<IUnknown> pUnkState;
    CComQIPtr<IAsyncWriteData> pWriteData;
    BYTE* pData = NULL;
    DWORD dataLength = 0;

    do
    {
        BREAK_ON_NULL(pcbWritten, E_POINTER);
        BREAK_ON_NULL(pResult, E_POINTER);

        // see if this asynchronous call failed - if it did set the number of bytes written
        // to zero
        hr = pResult->GetStatus();
        if(FAILED(hr))
        {
            *pcbWritten = 0;
        }
        BREAK_ON_FAIL(hr);

        // get the IAsyncWriteData state object from the result
        hr = pResult->GetObject(&pUnkState);
        BREAK_ON_FAIL(hr);

        // Get the IAsyncWriteData pointer from the IUnknown pointer of the state object
        pWriteData = pUnkState;
        BREAK_ON_NULL(pWriteData, E_UNEXPECTED);

        // get the number of bytes that were stored in this state object, and return it
        pWriteData->GetWriteData(&pData, &dataLength);
        *pcbWritten = dataLength;
    }
    while(false);

    return hr;
}
```

The *EndWrite()* function first extracts the *IAsyncWriteData* state object from the result. The *IMF-AsyncResult* object also contains the *HRESULT* returned from the send operation. If the earlier send succeeded, then the function gets the number of bytes written by calling *IAsyncWriteData::GetWriteData()* and then stores that number in the *pcbWritten* output parameter.

After the user has sent all of the data to the byte stream, it calls the *IMFByteStream::Flush()* method to flush any internal buffers and send all remaining data to the network client. The following explains how this works.

```
//
// Flush the byte stream, emptying the internal buffer and sending the data to the client
//
HRESULT CHttpOutputByteStream::Flush(void)
{
    HRESULT hr = S_OK;
    int sendResult = 0;

    do
    {
        CComCritSecLock<CComAutoCriticalSection> lock(m_critSec);

        // if there is data, send it out
        if(m_dwOutputDataCollected > 0)
        {
            // send whatever is collected in the buffer
            sendResult = send( m_clientSocket, (const char*)m_pOutputBuffer,
                m_dwOutputDataCollected, 0 );
            if (sendResult == SOCKET_ERROR)
            {
                hr = HRESULT_FROM_WIN32(WSAGetLastError());
                break;
            }

            // reset the counter indicating that the buffer is now empty
            m_dwOutputDataCollected = 0;
        }
    }
    while(false);

    return hr;
}
```

The *Flush()* function underscores and demonstrates the internal design of the *CHttpOutputByteStream* class. If there is any data in the internal byte stream buffer—in other words, if the *m_dwOutputDataCollected* variable is not zero—then the function sends the remaining data out over the network. When the send is complete, the function zeroes out the counter with the amount of collected data by resetting the counter to zero.

Conclusion

In this chapter, you learned about several of the more advanced concepts of MF that you can use to build professional Media Foundation player applications. The chapter described how to add user interface elements on top of currently playing video, showed how to split the playing streams by using the Tee MFT, and demonstrated network streaming to a remote client.

The chapter also showed the basic design of an *IMFByteStream* object needed to send media streams over the network. Similar byte stream objects can also be used to load a data stream from locations not supported by MF by default, such as ISO or compressed files.

Class Listings

This section contains the class listings for the major classes used in this sample. These classes are presented here as a reference and for completeness.

The *CPlayer* class is the main media player class object. It is responsible for assembling all of the Media Foundation pieces necessary to play the video and for rendering the seek bar on top of the video window. The *PlayerState* enumeration is used inside of the player to keep track of the current state of the player object.

```
enum PlayerState
{
    PlayerState_Closed = 0,      // No session.
    PlayerState_Ready,           // Session was created, ready to open a file.
    PlayerState_OpenPending,     // Session is opening a file.
    PlayerState_Started,         // Session is playing a file.
    PlayerState_Paused,          // Session is paused.
    PlayerState_Stopped,         // Session is stopped (ready to play).
    PlayerState_Closing          // Application is waiting for MESessionClosed.
};

//
// The CPlayer class wraps MediaSession functionality and hides it from a calling
// application.
//
class CPlayer : public IMFAsyncCallback
{
    public:
        CPlayer(HWND videoWindow);
        ~CPlayer(void);

        // Playback control
        HRESULT OpenURL(PCWSTR sURL, HWND renderHwnd, bool network);
        HRESULT Play(void);
        HRESULT Pause(void);
        HRESULT Stop(void);
        PlayerState  GetState() const { return m_state; }
```

```cpp
        HRESULT IncreaseRate(void);
        HRESULT DecreaseRate(void);
        HRESULT DrawSeekbar(void);
        void SetMouseOver(bool m) { m_isSeekbarVisible = m; }

        // Video functionality
        HRESULT     Repaint();
        BOOL        HasVideo() const { return (m_pVideoDisplay != NULL); }



        //
        // IMFAsyncCallback implementation.
        //
        // Skip the optional GetParameters() function - it is used only in advanced players.
        // Returning the E_NOTIMPL error code causes the system to use default parameters.
        STDMETHODIMP GetParameters(DWORD *pdwFlags, DWORD *pdwQueue)   { return E_NOTIMPL; }

        // Main MF event handling function
        STDMETHODIMP Invoke(IMFAsyncResult* pAsyncResult);

        //
        // IUnknown methods
        //
        STDMETHODIMP QueryInterface(REFIID iid, void** ppv);
        STDMETHODIMP_(ULONG) AddRef();
        STDMETHODIMP_(ULONG) Release();

    protected:

        // internal initialization
        HRESULT Initialize(void);

        // private session and playback controlling functions
        HRESULT CreateSession(void);
        HRESULT CloseSession(void);
        HRESULT StartPlayback(void);

        HRESULT InitializeMixer(void);
        HRESULT InitializeSeekbarDirectX(void);
        HRESULT RenderSeekBarSurface(void);
        HRESULT DetermineDuration(void);

        // MF event handling functionality
        HRESULT ProcessEvent(CComPtr<IMFMediaEvent>& mediaEvent);

        // Media event handlers
        HRESULT OnTopologyReady(void);
        HRESULT OnPresentationEnded(void);

        void GetLocalFilePath(WCHAR* filename, WCHAR* fullPath, DWORD fullPathLength);

        volatile long               m_nRefCount;           // COM reference count.

        CTopoBuilder                m_topoBuilder;
```

```
        CComPtr<IMFMediaSession>          m_pSession;
        CComPtr<IMFVideoDisplayControl>   m_pVideoDisplay;
        CComPtr<IMFRateControl>           m_pRateControl;

        CComPtr<IDirect3D9>               m_pD3d9Obj;
        CComPtr<IDirect3DDevice9>         m_pD3d9Device;
        CComPtr<IDirect3DTexture9>        m_pD3d9SeekBarTexture;
        CComPtr<IDirect3DTexture9>        m_pD3d9SeekTickTexture;
        CComPtr<IDirect3DSurface9>        m_pD3d9RenderSurface;

        CComPtr<IDirect3DTexture9>        m_pTargetTexture;
        CComPtr<IDirect3DSurface9>        m_pTextureSurface;

        CComPtr<ID3DXSprite>              m_pDisplaySprite;


        CComPtr<IMFVideoMixerBitmap>      m_pMixerBitmap;
        CComPtr<IMFClock>                 m_pPresentationClock;

        LONGLONG m_duration;

        HWND                              m_hwndVideo;      // Video window.
        PlayerState                       m_state;   // Current state of the media session.

        // event fired when session close is complete
        HANDLE                            m_closeCompleteEvent;

        bool m_isSeekbarVisible;
};
```

The *CTopoBuilder* class builds the topologies for the player. The class receives parameters indicating whether it should add rendering and network components to the topology, passes the requested output port to the network ASF sink, and assembles all of the data processing components into the needed configuration.

```
class CTopoBuilder
{
    public:
        CTopoBuilder(void)  { m_addRenderers = false; m_addNetworkSink = false; };
        ~CTopoBuilder(void) { ShutdownSource(); };

        HRESULT RenderURL(PCWSTR fileUrl, HWND videoHwnd, bool addNetwork);

        IMFTopology* GetTopology(void) { return m_pTopology; }

        HRESULT ShutdownSource(void);

    private:
        CComQIPtr<IMFTopology>            m_pTopology;       // the topology itself
        CComQIPtr<IMFMediaSource>         m_pSource;         // the MF source
        CComQIPtr<IMFVideoDisplayControl> m_pVideoDisplay;   // pointer to the mixer
        HWND                              m_videoHwnd;       // the target window
```

```cpp
    CComPtr<IMFActivate> m_pNetworkSinkActivate;
    DWORD m_nextNetworkSinkStreamIndex;

    bool m_addRenderers;
    bool m_addNetworkSink;

    HRESULT CreateMediaSource(PCWSTR sURL);
    HRESULT CreateNetworkSink(DWORD requestPort);
    HRESULT CreateTopology(void);

    HRESULT AddBranchToPartialTopology(
        CComPtr<IMFPresentationDescriptor> pPresDescriptor,
        DWORD iStream);

    HRESULT CreateSourceStreamNode(
        CComPtr<IMFPresentationDescriptor> pPresDescriptor,
        CComPtr<IMFStreamDescriptor> pStreamDescriptor,
        CComPtr<IMFTopologyNode> &ppNode);

    HRESULT CreateOutputNode(
        CComPtr<IMFStreamDescriptor> pSourceSD,
        HWND hwndVideo,
        IMFTopologyNode* pSourceNode,
        IMFTopologyNode** ppOutputNode);

    HRESULT CreateTeeNetworkTwig(IMFStreamDescriptor* pStreamDescriptor,
        IMFTopologyNode* pRendererNode, IMFTopologyNode** ppTeeNode);
};
```

The *CHttpOutputStreamActivate* class is used to store the parameters necessary to instantiate the HTTP output byte stream object. The only parameter necessary in this case is the output port—therefore, the class leaves the required *IMFAttributes* interface empty, and all of its functions return *E_NOTIMPL*.

```cpp
class CHttpOutputStreamActivate :
    public IMFActivate
{
    public:
        CHttpOutputStreamActivate(DWORD requestPort);
        ~CHttpOutputStreamActivate(void);

        // IUnknown interface implementation
        STDMETHODIMP QueryInterface(REFIID riid, void **ppvObject);
        virtual ULONG STDMETHODCALLTYPE AddRef(void);
        virtual ULONG STDMETHODCALLTYPE Release(void);

        // IMFActivate interface implementation
        STDMETHODIMP  ActivateObject(REFIID riid, void **ppv);
        STDMETHODIMP  ShutdownObject(void) { return S_OK; }
        STDMETHODIMP  DetachObject(void) { return S_OK; }

        // IMFAttributes interface implementation - all not implemented
        STDMETHODIMP GetItem(REFGUID guidKey, PROPVARIANT *pValue) { return E_NOTIMPL; }
        STDMETHODIMP GetItemType(REFGUID guidKey, MF_ATTRIBUTE_TYPE *pType)
        { return E_NOTIMPL; }
        STDMETHODIMP CompareItem(REFGUID guidKey, REFPROPVARIANT Value, BOOL *pbResult)
```

```cpp
        { return E_NOTIMPL; }
        STDMETHODIMP  Compare(IMFAttributes *pTheirs, MF_ATTRIBUTES_MATCH_TYPE MatchType,
            BOOL *pbResult) { return E_NOTIMPL; }
        STDMETHODIMP  GetUINT32(REFGUID guidKey, UINT32 *punValue) { return E_NOTIMPL; }
        STDMETHODIMP  GetUINT64(REFGUID guidKey, UINT64 *punValue) { return E_NOTIMPL; }
        STDMETHODIMP  GetDouble(REFGUID guidKey, double *pfValue) { return E_NOTIMPL; }
        STDMETHODIMP  GetGUID(REFGUID guidKey, GUID *pguidValue) { return E_NOTIMPL; }
        STDMETHODIMP  GetStringLength(REFGUID guidKey, UINT32 *pcchLength)
        { return E_NOTIMPL; }
        STDMETHODIMP  GetString(REFGUID guidKey, LPWSTR pwszValue, UINT32 cchBufSize,
            UINT32 *pcchLength) { return E_NOTIMPL; }
        STDMETHODIMP  GetAllocatedString(REFGUID guidKey, LPWSTR *ppwszValue,
            UINT32 *pcchLength) { return E_NOTIMPL; }
        STDMETHODIMP  GetBlobSize(REFGUID guidKey, UINT32 *pcbBlobSize)
        { return E_NOTIMPL; }
        STDMETHODIMP  GetBlob(REFGUID guidKey, UINT8 *pBuf, UINT32 cbBufSize,
            UINT32 *pcbBlobSize) { return E_NOTIMPL; }
        STDMETHODIMP  GetAllocatedBlob(REFGUID guidKey, UINT8 **ppBuf, UINT32 *pcbSize)
        { return E_NOTIMPL; }
        STDMETHODIMP  GetUnknown(REFGUID guidKey, REFIID riid, LPVOID *ppv)
        { return E_NOTIMPL; }
        STDMETHODIMP  SetItem(REFGUID guidKey, REFPROPVARIANT Value) { return E_NOTIMPL; }
        STDMETHODIMP  DeleteItem(REFGUID guidKey) { return E_NOTIMPL; }
        STDMETHODIMP  DeleteAllItems(void) { return E_NOTIMPL; }
        STDMETHODIMP  SetUINT32(REFGUID guidKey, UINT32 unValue) { return E_NOTIMPL; }
        STDMETHODIMP  SetUINT64(REFGUID guidKey, UINT64 unValue) { return E_NOTIMPL; }
        STDMETHODIMP  SetDouble(REFGUID guidKey, double fValue) { return E_NOTIMPL; }
        STDMETHODIMP  SetGUID(REFGUID guidKey, REFGUID guidValue) { return E_NOTIMPL; }
        STDMETHODIMP  SetString(REFGUID guidKey, LPCWSTR wszValue) { return E_NOTIMPL; }
        STDMETHODIMP  SetBlob(REFGUID guidKey, const UINT8 *pBuf, UINT32 cbBufSize)
        { return E_NOTIMPL; }
        STDMETHODIMP  SetUnknown(REFGUID guidKey, IUnknown *pUnknown) { return E_NOTIMPL; }
        STDMETHODIMP  LockStore(void) { return E_NOTIMPL; }
        STDMETHODIMP  UnlockStore(void) { return E_NOTIMPL; }
        STDMETHODIMP  GetCount(UINT32 *pcItems) { return E_NOTIMPL; }
        STDMETHODIMP  GetItemByIndex(UINT32 unIndex, GUID *pguidKey, PROPVARIANT *pValue)
        { return E_NOTIMPL; }
        STDMETHODIMP  CopyAllItems(IMFAttributes *pDest) { return E_NOTIMPL; }

    private:
        volatile long m_cRef;

        DWORD m_requestPort;
};
```

The *CHttpOutputByteStream* class is a custom *IMFByteStream* object designed to allow a sink to write data to an HTTP output port. The class uses the Windows Socket APIs to open a TCP socket, bind it to the specified port, and start listening for incoming requests. As soon as a request is received, the class starts sending out data that it has buffered internally.

```cpp
class CHttpOutputByteStream :
    public IMFByteStream,
    public IMFAsyncCallback
{
    public:
        static HRESULT CreateInstance(DWORD requestPort, IMFByteStream** ppByteStream);
```

```cpp
    // IUnknown interface implementation
    STDMETHODIMP QueryInterface(REFIID riid, void **ppvObject);
    virtual ULONG STDMETHODCALLTYPE AddRef(void);
    virtual ULONG STDMETHODCALLTYPE Release(void);

    // IMFByteStream interface implementation
    STDMETHODIMP  GetCapabilities(DWORD *pdwCapabilities);
    STDMETHODIMP  GetLength(QWORD *pqwLength);
    STDMETHODIMP  SetLength(QWORD qwLength);
    STDMETHODIMP  GetCurrentPosition(QWORD *pqwPosition);
    STDMETHODIMP  SetCurrentPosition(QWORD qwPosition);
    STDMETHODIMP  IsEndOfStream(BOOL *pfEndOfStream);
    STDMETHODIMP  Read(BYTE *pb, ULONG cb, ULONG *pcbRead);
    STDMETHODIMP  BeginRead(BYTE *pb, ULONG cb, IMFAsyncCallback *pCallback,
        IUnknown *punkState);
    STDMETHODIMP  EndRead(IMFAsyncResult *pResult, ULONG *pcbRead);
    STDMETHODIMP  Write(const BYTE *pb, ULONG cb, ULONG *pcbWritten);
    STDMETHODIMP  BeginWrite(const BYTE *pb, ULONG cb, IMFAsyncCallback *pCallback,
        IUnknown *punkState);
    STDMETHODIMP  EndWrite(IMFAsyncResult *pResult, ULONG *pcbWritten);
    STDMETHODIMP  Seek(MFBYTESTREAM_SEEK_ORIGIN SeekOrigin, LONGLONG llSeekOffset,
        DWORD dwSeekFlags, QWORD *pqwCurrentPosition);
    STDMETHODIMP  Flush(void);
    STDMETHODIMP  Close(void);

    // IMFAsyncCallback interface implementation
    STDMETHODIMP GetParameters(DWORD* pdwFlags, DWORD* pdwQueue);
    STDMETHODIMP Invoke(IMFAsyncResult* pResult);

private:
    volatile long m_cRef;
    CComAutoCriticalSection m_critSec;          // critical section

    WSADATA m_wsaData;
    SOCKET m_clientSocket;
    SOCKET m_listenSocket;
    DWORD m_outputPort;

    HANDLE m_testThread;

    DWORD m_netWorkQueue;

    BYTE* m_pOutputBuffer;
    DWORD m_dwOutputBuffer;
    volatile DWORD m_dwOutputBufferNewSize;
    DWORD m_dwOutputDataCollected;
    bool m_bIsStopping;

    CHttpOutputByteStream(void);
    ~CHttpOutputByteStream(void);

    HRESULT InitSocket(DWORD port);
    HRESULT SendData(const BYTE* data, DWORD dataLength);
    HRESULT SendAsyncWriteResult(IAsyncWriteData* pWriteData, HRESULT sendResult);
};
```

The *CByteStreamWriteData* class is used to pass asynchronous write requests sent to the byte stream to its internal worker thread.

```cpp
struct __declspec(uuid("BF1998FC-9CFE-4336-BF07-50B10F9A9AFE")) IAsyncWriteData;

DEFINE_GUID(IID_IAsyncWriteData, 0xBF1998FC, 0x9CFE, 0x4336, 0xbf, 0x07, 0x50, 0xb1, 0x0f,
    0x9a, 0x9a, 0xfe);

struct IAsyncWriteData : public IUnknown
{
    public:
        virtual HRESULT GetWriteData(BYTE** pWriteData, DWORD* dataLength) = 0;
        virtual HRESULT SendCallback(HRESULT status) = 0;
        virtual HRESULT GetStateObject(IUnknown** ppState) = 0;
        virtual HRESULT GetCallback(IMFAsyncCallback** ppCallback) = 0;
};

class CByteStreamWriteData :
    public IAsyncWriteData
{
    public:
        CByteStreamWriteData(BYTE* pData, DWORD dwData, IMFAsyncCallback* callback,
            IUnknown* pState);

        // IUnknown interface implementation
        virtual HRESULT STDMETHODCALLTYPE QueryInterface(REFIID riid, void **ppvObject);
        virtual ULONG STDMETHODCALLTYPE AddRef(void);
        virtual ULONG STDMETHODCALLTYPE Release(void);

        virtual HRESULT GetWriteData(BYTE** pWriteData, DWORD* dataLength);
        virtual HRESULT SendCallback(HRESULT status);
        virtual HRESULT GetStateObject(IUnknown** ppState);
        virtual HRESULT GetCallback(IMFAsyncCallback** ppCallback);

    private:
        ~CByteStreamWriteData(void);

        volatile long m_cRef;

        BYTE* m_pData;
        DWORD m_dataLength;
        CComPtr<IMFAsyncCallback> m_pCallback;
        CComPtr<IUnknown> m_pStateObj;
};
```

APPENDIX A

Debugging Media Foundation Code

Microsoft Media Foundation (MF) represents a particular challenge because it is implemented with the asynchronous execution model. MF differs from standard applications and Microsoft DirectShow programs because in MF, though each API call might succeed, one of the components might fire an error event asynchronously. Often it might be difficult to determine which component fired the error and why. In addition, a lot of the underlying MF code is unavailable and cannot be easily debugged. Unlike in DirectShow, you cannot step into many of the basic functions and objects to determine why an API call returned a failing *HRESULT*.

Media Foundation Error Lookup

When an error is returned in an asynchronous event, the failing *HRESULT* will be stored in a member variable of the *IMFAsyncResult* object sent to the *IMFAsyncCallback::Invoke()* method. Here are the relevant values stored in the asynchronous result object that you may be interested in when something fails:

- **The type of the event, which provides a context to the failure**   The event type can be extracted with the *IMFAsyncResult::GetType()* method.

- **The failing *HRESULT* that signals the cause of the failure**   To get the *HRESULT*, you can use the *IMFAsyncResult::GetStatus()* function. MF *HRESULT*s are fairly specific, which means that unlike in many other applications, this *HRESULT* may provide very good clues to the failure.

Unfortunately, MF error codes are not commonly stored in various *HRESULT* lookup tools. The lookup tool that comes with Microsoft Visual Studio 2010, for example, will not recognize these error codes. The fastest way to figure out what an MF error means is to try looking it up inside of the mferror.h header file. All standard MF errors start with a *C00D* hex value—that is, all of the common MF error numbers are between *0xC00D0000* and *0xC00DFFFF*. The following table contains a list of the standard MF error ranges.

Error Range	Error Type
14000-14999	General MF errors
15000-15999	ASF parsing errors
16000-16999	Media source errors
17000-17999	MF network errors
18000-18999	MF Windows Media Container errors
19000-19999	Media sink errors
20000-20999	Renderer errors
21000-21999	Topology errors
25000-25999	Timeline errors
28000-28999	Transform errors
29000-29999	Content protection errors
40000-40999	Clock errors
41000-41999	MF quality management errors
42000-42999	MF transcode API errors

For example, general MF errors will fall in the *0xC00D0000+14000* to *0xC00D0000+14999* range (*0xC00D36B0* to *0xC00D3A97*). The mferror.h header also contains brief one-sentence descriptions of the errors.

Similarly, to map the event type from the number returned by the *IMFAsyncResult::GetType()* method, you can look in the mfobjects.h header file, in the *MediaEventType* enumeration. The media event type names are fairly descriptive and should give you some context to the error code.

The MFTrace Tool

To help with determining the cause of failures and problems in Media Foundation, Microsoft introduced the MFTrace tool in the Windows 7 software development kit (SDK). MFTrace allows you to hook up to a running application and receive detailed tracing information from it. The traces are very complete and will help you figure out what went wrong during program execution. For example, you can look through the resulting traces and search for the "fail" string to find a failed MF method, what object that method belonged to, and the failing *HRESULT*.

More Info The MFTrace tool is part of the Windows 7 SDK, and is therefore commonly located in the C:\Program Files\Microsoft SDKs\Windows\v7.1\Bin directory. The tool consists of three files—MFTrace.exe, MFDetours.dll, and Detoured.dll. For instructions on downloading and installing the Windows 7 SDK, see the Introduction.

The MFTrace tool can function in one of two modes—it can hook up to the internal functions of an MF application by using the Detours library, tracing out the return results of these functions, or it can receive Event Tracing for Windows (ETW) and Windows Preprocessor (WPP) trace events from the application. MFTrace is most often used in the tracing mode.

In addition to the newer ETW and WPP events, MFTrace also detects debug messages produced by applications calling the *OutputDebugString()* functions. Consequently, your application and MF components can use these debug text messages to output debugging information in the MFTrace log, thereby helping you read the sequence of events or any additional pertinent information that should be traced out.

> **More Info** To simplify and speed up reading of the enormous logs produced by MFTrace, you can use the TextAnalysisTool.Net. This tool allows you to quickly and efficiently filter out unneeded traces from the log file and find the messages that you are interested in. For additional information on the TextAnalysisTool.Net, go to *http://blogs.msdn.com/b/delay/archive/2007/06/21/powerful-log-file-analysis-for-everyone-releasing-textanalysistool-net.aspx*.

MFTrace uses the Microsoft Detours library to hook up to core MF and COM functions inside of an application. Detours allows MFTrace to connect to the process and wrap around and instrument all of the core functions by rewriting the relevant code in memory. This causes the modified functions to notify MFTrace when they return an error. MFTrace then logs this information to a text file for analysis.

The resulting text log may be quite large, but it provides a detailed breakdown of events and can be invaluable in figuring out the problem in an MF application. For example, in trace mode, MFTrace will give you a list of all the *CoCreateInstance()* calls that instantiate COM objects. Using this information, you can figure out whether a topology is even trying to instantiate an MFT that you expect to be loaded automatically. You can see all of the *IMFTransform::SetInputType()* and *SetOutputType()* calls made in the topology, examine the media types passed in, and confirm that the right types were accepted by various MF components.

Here are the most commonly used MFTrace parameters.

MFTrace Option	Description
-o	Allows you to specify the output file name for the trace log. All of the traces will go to that file.
-a	Attaches to the specified process. The process can be given either by process ID or by its executable file name.

If all of the interesting events occur in the application at startup, you can also tell MFTrace to start the application, passing in the executable file name and all the required parameters. For example, to start the notepad.exe application under MFTrace, you can type **MFTrace.exe -o TestLog.log notepad.exe** in an elevated command prompt. This will cause MFTrace to launch Notepad, logging all of the information it detects into the TestLog.log file. Obviously, because Notepad is not an MF application, the log won't contain much, but it will detect things such as *CoCreateInstance()* calls.

Note that you need to use the right flavor of MFTrace for your application. If you are using a 32-bit application, you can attach to it using only the 32-bit version of MFTrace. If you are debugging a 64-bit application, you must use the 64-bit version of MFTrace. You also need to run the tool in the administrator context, by launching it from a command prompt that was started with administrator credentials.

More Info For additional information on the MFTrace tool, go to *http://msdn.microsoft.com /en-us/library/ff685116(v=VS.85).aspx*.

An MFTrace Example

As an example, here's a look at how TopoEdit creates a topology for streaming an MP3 file. This example focuses on MP3s because the required playback topology is simple and easy to understand.

As a refresher, here's the image of the topology created with this process.

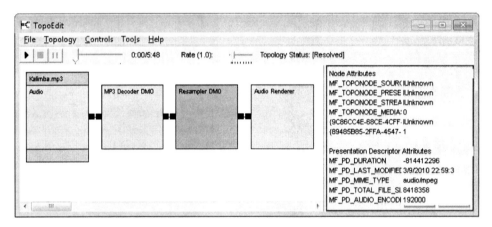

The MP3 playback topology consists of four components. The topology starts with the MP3 media source, which is connected to the MP3 decoder. The MP3 decoder is connected to the resampler MFT component—which is necessary because the audio sample rate of the audio file in this case does not match the sample rate expected by the audio renderer. Finally, the resampler MFT is connected to the audio renderer.

As mentioned earlier, you can attach the MFTrace tool to an application by using the *–a* parameter from a command prompt running in the administrator security context. For example, in this case, you would enter the following command line to attach to the TopoEdit tool.

```
MFTrace.exe -a TopoEdit.exe -o TopoEdit_trace.txt
```

This causes MFTrace to attach to a process with the TopoEdit.exe name and output the captured traces to the TopoEdit_trace.txt file. If you attach to TopoEdit and then render an MP3 file, the trace log will contain all the major steps taken by TopoEdit and MF to build the topology.

The following section provides the major steps and the traces that correspond to them. Because this is a simplified example, the traces shown omit some basic steps and do not show the process ID, thread ID, or the time at which the traces were taken.

MP3 Source Instantiation Traces

The first stage of the topology creation is instantiation of the MF media source. As you saw in Chapter 6, "Media Foundation Sources," MF media sources are created in several steps. First the source resolver creates a scheme handler, then the scheme handler creates an *IMFByteStream* object, and then you get the *IMFByteStreamHandler* object, which takes the byte stream and instantiates the actual media source.

Here are the traces that the MFTrace tool produces during these media source creation steps.

```
CMFSourceResolverDetours::CreateObjectFromURL @045DEDB8 URL: 'C:\Users\Public\Music\Sample
    Music\Maid with the Flaxen Hair.mp3'
COle32ExportDetours::CoCreateInstance @ Created {477EC299-1421-4BDD-971F-7CCB933F21AD} File
    Scheme Handler (C:\Windows\System32\mf.dll) @00203A88 - traced interfaces:
    IMFSchemeHandler @00203A88,
CMFSchemeHandlerDetours::BeginCreateObject @00203A88 URL:
    'file:///C:/Users/Public/Music/Sample%20Music/Maid%20with%20the%20Flaxen%20Hair.mp3'
CMFPlatExportDetours::MFBeginCreateFile @ URL: 'C:\Users\Public\Music\Sample Music\Maid with
    the Flaxen Hair.mp3'
CMFSchemeHandlerDetours::HandleObject @00203A88 New bytestream @04329718
COle32ExportDetours::CoCreateInstance @ Created {A82E50BA-8E92-41EB-9DF2-433F50EC2993} MP3
    Byte Stream Handler (C:\Windows\System32\mf.dll) @00205800 - traced interfaces:
    IMFByteStreamHandler @00205800,
CMFByteStreamDetours::BeginRead @04329718 buffer @076885C0 size 65536B
CMFByteStreamDetours::EndRead @04329718 read 65536B
CMFByteStreamDetours::BeginRead @04329718 buffer @04520048 size 65536B
CMFByteStreamDetours::EndRead @04329718 read 50642B
CMFByteStreamDetours::BeginRead @04329718 buffer @076885C0 size 65536B
CMFByteStreamDetours::EndRead @04329718 read 65536B
COle32ExportDetours::CoCreateInstance @ Created {275C23E2-3747-11D0-9FEA-00AA003F8646}
    Multi Language Support (C:\Windows\system32\mlang.dll) @001FCAC8 - traced interfaces:
    CMFByteStreamHandlerDetours::HandleObject @00205800 New source @045E0998
```

Note Your traces will look slightly different because your text file won't be constrained to a specific line length and will contain the application's process ID, thread ID, and the time at the beginning of each line. Also, various objects in your runs will reside at different and random memory locations.

The traces shown here take up several lines in the final log file. Each of these lines contains information that you can use to decipher what is happening during source creation and what each of the components is doing. Here is what these lines indicate:

1. The TopoEdit tool calls the *IMFSourceResolver::CreateObjectFromURL()* method to create the source and passes in the MP3 file name as the URL.

2. The source resolver instantiates a scheme handler. Because this is a file, the scheme in question is a file—therefore, the source resolver instantiates a file scheme handler. In this case, the file scheme handler object resides in memory at *0x00203A88*.

3. The source resolver calls *IMFSchemeHandler::BeginCreateObject()* on the scheme handler object stored at *0x00203A88*. The source resolver passes in the modified file name from step 1, adjusted to match the URL convention. As you can see, the URL starts with *file:///*, because the URL indicates a local file.

4. The scheme handler calls *MFBeginCreateFile()* to create an *IMFByteStream* object that will be used to load the MP3 file.

5. The scheme handler that resides in memory at *0x00203A88* receives the new byte stream object. The byte stream object is located in memory at address *0x04329718*.

6. The scheme handler uses the *CoCreateInstance()* call to create an *IMFByteStreamHandler* object that will process the byte stream from step 5. The new byte stream handler object is stored in memory at *0x00205800*. The byte stream handler object that is instantiated exposes the *IMFByteStreamHandler* interface that starts at position *0x00205800*. This indicates that the instantiated object itself implements this interface.

7. The byte stream handler reads some data from the file by calling the *IMFByteStream::BeginRead()* and *EndRead()* methods. This is the byte stream object instantiated in step 5—you can identify it by its memory location: *0x04329718*. The handler uses that data to confirm that the created media source can parse the passed-in file. This all happens before the topology starts playing, and before any other MF components are instantiated.

8. The byte stream handler instantiates a new source, which is placed in memory at *0x045E998*.

As you can see, whenever an object is instantiated, MFTrace gives you the memory address of that object. You can use this address to search through the log and figure out what each object is doing by searching for the object's memory location.

After the MP3 media source is created, TopoEdit activates its output stream. This step produces very useful tracing information, because you can see the information about the stream's output media type.

```
CMFMediaSourceDetours::TracePD @045E0998 Stream 0 (ID 0): selected 1, MT: MF_MT_MAJOR_TYPE=
    MEDIATYPE_Audio;MF_MT_AUDIO_PREFER_WAVEFORMATEX=1;MF_MT_SUBTYPE=MFAudioFormat_MP3;
    MF_MT_AUDIO_NUM_CHANNELS=2;MF_MT_AUDIO_SAMPLES_PER_SECOND=44100;
    MF_MT_AUDIO_BLOCK_ALIGNMENT=1;MF_MT_AUDIO_AVG_BYTES_PER_SECOND=24000;MF_MT_USER_DATA=01
    00 00 00 00 00 73 02 00 00 00 00
```

The source in question is still located at *0x04E0998*; this allows you to identify which source is exposing the stream. There is only one stream, and it has the audio major media type and the *MFAudioFormat_MP3* subtype. MFTrace gives you all of the information about this media type—all of the internal attributes stored in that media type object.

After the source stream is instantiated, the TopoEdit application (through the built-in topology builder) calls *MFTEnumEx* to instantiate the audio decoder that can consume the source stream media type and produce a media type that can be consumed by the audio renderer.

```
CMFPlatExportDetours::MFTEnumEx @ Category: MFT_CATEGORY_AUDIO_DECODER, Flags: 0x00000053,
    input MT:MF_MT_MAJOR_TYPE=MEDIATYPE_Audio;MF_MT_SUBTYPE=MFAudioFormat_MP3, output MT:
    MF_MT_MAJOR_TYPE=MEDIATYPE_Audio;MF_MT_SUBTYPE=MFAudioFormat_Float
CMFPlatExportDetours::MFTEnumEx @ Activate 00 @0464BEB0,MF_TRANSFORM_CATEGORY_Attribute=
    MFT_CATEGORY_AUDIO_DECODER;MFT_TRANSFORM_CLSID_Attribute=
    {BBEEA841-0A63-4F52-A7AB-A9B3A84ED38A};MFT_INPUT_TYPES_Attributes=61 75 64 73 00 00 10
    00 80 00 aa 00 38 9b 71 55 00 00 00 00 00 10 00 80 00 00 aa 00 38 9b 71;
    MFT_OUTPUT_TYPES_Attributes=61 75 64 73 00 00 10 00 80 00 00 aa 00 38 9b
COle32ExportDetours::CoCreateInstance @ New MFT @0463FF98, <NULL>
COle32ExportDetours::CoCreateInstance @ Created {BBEEA841-0A63-4F52-A7AB-A9B3A84ED38A} MP3
    Decoder DMO (C:\Windows\SysWOW64\mp3dmod.dll) @0463FF98 - traced interfaces:
    IMFTransform@0463FF98, IMediaObject @0463FFB0,
CMFActivateDetours::ActivateObject @0464BEB0 New MFT @0463FF98
```

> **Note** Some of the longer lines in these code listings have been shortened by removing extra data at the end.

The topology builder first uses the *MFTEnumEx()* function to enumerate functions with the requested input and output media types. *MFTEnumEx()* returns an activator object at *0x0464BEB0*. The topology builder then uses the *IMFActivate* object to instantiate the MFT, which is placed in memory at *0x0463FF98*. The MFT is called the MP3 Decoder DMO and is loaded from the mp3dmod.dll file.

After that, the topology builder hooks up the MP3 decoder to the media source's output stream by setting the input type on the decoder MFT. To connect, the *IMFTransform::SetInputType()* method must succeed.

```
CMFTransformDetours::SetInputType @0463FF98 Succeeded MT:MF_MT_MAJOR_TYPE=MEDIATYPE_Audio;
    MF_MT_AUDIO_PREFER_WAVEFORMATEX=1;MF_MT_SUBTYPE=MFAudioFormat_MP3;
    MF_MT_AUDIO_NUM_CHANNELS=2;MF_MT_AUDIO_SAMPLES_PER_SECOND=44100;
    MF_MT_AUDIO_BLOCK_ALIGNMENT=1;MF_MT_AUDIO_AVG_BYTES_PER_SECOND=24000;MF_MT_USER_DATA=01
    00 00 00 00 00 73 02 00 00 00 00
```

After that, the topology builder creates the resampler MFT and connects the decoder to the resampler.

```
COle32ExportDetours::CoCreateInstance @ New MFT @0023EA64, <NULL>
COle32ExportDetours::CoCreateInstance @ Created {F447B69E-1884-4A7E-8055-346F74D6EDB3}
    Resampler DMO (C:\Windows\SysWOW64\resampledmo.dll) @0023EA64 - traced interfaces:
    IMFTransform @0023EA64, IMediaObject @0023EA7C,
CMFTransformDetours::SetInputType @0023EA64 Succeeded MT:MF_MT_MAJOR_TYPE=MEDIATYPE_Audio;
    MF_MT_SUBTYPE=MFAudioFormat_Float;MF_MT_AUDIO_NUM_CHANNELS=2;
    MF_MT_AUDIO_SAMPLES_PER_SECOND=44100;MF_MT_AUDIO_BLOCK_ALIGNMENT=8;
    MF_MT_AUDIO_AVG_BYTES_PER_SECOND=352800;MF_MT_AUDIO_BITS_PER_SAMPLE=32;
    MF_MT_ALL_SAMPLES_INDEPENDENT=1;MF_MT_AUDIO_CHANNEL_MASK=3
CMFTransformDetours::SetOutputType @0463FF98 Succeeded MT:MF_MT_MAJOR_TYPE=MEDIATYPE_Audio;
    MF_MT_SUBTYPE=MFAudioFormat_Float;MF_MT_AUDIO_NUM_CHANNELS=2;
    MF_MT_AUDIO_SAMPLES_PER_SECOND=44100;MF_MT_AUDIO_BLOCK_ALIGNMENT=8;
    MF_MT_AUDIO_AVG_BYTES_PER_SECOND=352800;MF_MT_AUDIO_BITS_PER_SAMPLE=32;
    MF_MT_ALL_SAMPLES_INDEPENDENT=1;MF_MT_AUDIO_CHANNEL_MASK=3
CMFTransformDetours::SetOutputType @0023EA64 Succeeded MT:MF_MT_MAJOR_TYPE=MEDIATYPE_Audio;
    MF_MT_SUBTYPE=MFAudioFormat_Float;MF_MT_AUDIO_NUM_CHANNELS=2;
    MF_MT_AUDIO_SAMPLES_PER_SECOND=48000;MF_MT_AUDIO_BLOCK_ALIGNMENT=8;
    MF_MT_AUDIO_AVG_BYTES_PER_SECOND=384000;MF_MT_AUDIO_BITS_PER_SAMPLE=32;
    MF_MT_ALL_SAMPLES_INDEPENDENT=1;MF_MT_AUDIO_CHANNEL_MASK=3
```

The traces shown here tell you that the topology builder first creates the resampler DMO that lives at *0x0023EA64*. It then sets the input type on the resampler (which you can identify by its address) and sets the corresponding output on the decoder (identified again by its address, *0x0463FF98*). Finally, the topology builder sets the output media type on the resampler by calling its *IMFTransform::SetOutputType()* method.

In each of these steps, you can see all the key parameters passed into the functions, and examine the individual media types. If the MF components in the topology try several media types, you will see each successive *SetInputType()* and *SetOutputType()* call, together with the passed-in media types.

Whenever you get a failure in your application that you can't debug directly, one of the first steps should be to look through the MFTrace log and try to find a *"fail"* string. This message will tell you which method failed, what object that method belongs to, the failing *HRESULT*, and the key parameters of the method call. For example, here is what you might see when an *IMFTransform::SetInputType()* method fails.

```
CMFTransformDetours::SetInputType @00672C90 Failed MT:MF_MT_MAJOR_TYPE=MEDIATYPE_Video;
    MF_MT_SUBTYPE=MFVideoFormat_WMV3;MF_MT_FRAME_SIZE=3092376453600 (720,480);
    MF_MT_USER_DATA=4f d1 1a 01;MF_MT_AVG_BITRATE=1895000;MF_MT_FRAME_RATE=128849018881001
    (30000,1001);MF_MT_PIXEL_ASPECT_RATIO=34359738377(8,9);MF_MT_INTERLACE_MODE=2
```

This trace indicates that MFTrace caught a failure in the *SetInputType()* method that's part of the MFT that is located in memory at *0x00672C90*, and shows you the media type that was passed in.

APPENDIX B

COM Concepts

Component Object Model (COM) is a component interoperability technology that was introduced by Microsoft in 1993. Since then, the technology has gone through several revisions and been used and enhanced by several libraries. Microsoft Media Foundation (MF) uses COM extensively to support communication between various components. This section provides a (very) brief overview of this technology and should be used only as a refresher or a reference. To fully comprehend COM, you should use a COM textbook such as Don Box's *Essential COM* (Addison-Wesley Professional, 1998), or *Inside COM* by Dale Rogerson (Microsoft Press, 1997).

At its core, COM is a technology used by different components to expose their capabilities to any caller that doesn't need to know their exact class structure and wants to abstract the implementation. In other words, COM allows a component to call into a class without seeing its class definition. In addition, COM allows you to register an object compiled into a binary on a PC and for another component to discover the location of its binary and instantiate the object.

The *IUnknown* Interface

The most basic requirement for a COM class is that it must inherit from the *IUnknown* interface. This interface exposes three functions: one that allows somebody to query the class for other COM interfaces that it may support, one that allows you to increment the reference count of the class, and one that allows you to decrement the reference count.

Here is a simplified class definition for the *IUnknown* interface.

```
class IUnknown
{
   public:
      virtual HRESULT STDMETHODCALLTYPE QueryInterface(REFIID riid, void **ppvObject) = 0;
      virtual ULONG STDMETHODCALLTYPE AddRef(void) = 0;
      virtual ULONG STDMETHODCALLTYPE Release(void) = 0;
};
```

The functions here are as follows:

- **QueryInterface()** Used to query a class to find out if it implements an interface identified with the specified GUID value. The GUID, passed in as the *riid* parameter in this example, provides a unique identifier. All COM interfaces across all programs are guaranteed to have unique IDs.

    If the class implements the specified interface, a pointer to that interface is returned by the *QueryInterface()* method and the reference count of the object is increased by one.

- **AddRef()** Increments the reference count of the object. The reference count indicates how many other components have a pointer to this object. While the object is in use, the reference count must be more than zero.

- **Release()** Decrements the reference count of the object. When *Release()* detects that the reference count has reached zero, it deletes the object.

You will see implementations of these functions later in this section.

Here is a sample interface that inherits from the *IUnknown* interface. This example is actually a class that is used in the code sample provided with Chapter 8, "Custom Media Sessions."

```
enum AsyncEventType
{
    AsyncEventType_SourceEvent,
    AsyncEventType_SourceStreamEvent,
    AsyncEventType_SinkStreamEvent,
    AsyncEventType_ByteStreamHandlerEvent,
    AsyncEventType_SyncMftSampleRequest
};


// {88ACF5E6-2ED1-4780-87B1-D71814C2D42A}
DEFINE_GUID(IID_IAsyncState, 0x88acf5e6, 0x2ed1, 0x4780, 0x87, 0xb1, 0xd7, 0x18, 0x14, 0xc2, 0xd4, 0x2a);

// Microsoft-specific extension necessary to support the __uuidof(IAsyncState) notation.
class __declspec(uuid("88ACF5E6-2ED1-4780-87B1-D71814C2D42A")) IAsyncState;

class IAsyncState : public IUnknown
{
   public:
      virtual AsyncEventType EventType(void) = 0;
};
```

The *AsyncEventType* enumeration shown here is provided for completeness—it doesn't actually have anything to do with COM.

The GUID definition shown here is the standard declaration used throughout header files. This GUID is used to identify the *IAsyncState* interface and associates it with the *IID_IAsyncState* constant. This GUID was generated by using the Create GUID tool provided with Microsoft Visual Studio. GUIDs are simply pseudo-random 128-bit integers. You can create a GUID with any random number generator, although some algorithms look for specific non-random bit sequences in the GUID to provide additional behavior. Due to its length and the random number generator, the probability of any other machine generating the same GUID approaches zero and is essentially impossible.

> **Note** If you are getting a linker error claiming that the IID constant for an interface you created is an unresolved external, make sure that you are including the InitGuid.h header file. That file is required for the *DEFINE_GUID()* construct to function.

The GUID defined here has the name *IID_IAsyncState*—this means that it is the Interface ID (IID) of the *IAsyncState* interface. This constant is known to all classes and components that want to use an *IAsyncState* object.

After the *IID_IAsyncState* definition, you can see the custom Microsoft-specific expression that is used to associate the *IAsyncState* class with the same GUID. The *uuid()* expression allows you to use the (also Microsoft-specific) *__uuidof()* keyword to get the GUID of an object. For example, you can use *__uuidof(IAsyncState)* to get exactly the same GUID as with the *IID_IAsyncState*. This Microsoft-specific expression is necessary here because the helper Active Template Library (ATL) classes use the *__uuidof()* keyword extensively. These helper ATL classes are shown in Appendix C.

Finally, you can see the new COM interface itself. The interface inherits from the *IUnknown* interface and provides a single function.

Here is a class that inherits from and implements *IAsyncState*. Because *IAsyncState* inherits from *IUnknown*, the class also implements the *IUnknown* interface. The main purpose of this class is to pass the *AsyncEventType* value in a COM object. The reason for this requirement is explained in Chapter 8.

```
class CAsyncState :
    public IAsyncState
{
    public:
        CAsyncState(AsyncEventType type);
        ~CAsyncState(void) {};

        // IUnknown interface implementation
        virtual HRESULT STDMETHODCALLTYPE QueryInterface(REFIID riid, void **ppvObject);
        virtual ULONG STDMETHODCALLTYPE AddRef(void);
        virtual ULONG STDMETHODCALLTYPE Release(void);

        // IAsyncState interface implementation
        virtual AsyncEventType EventType(void) { return m_eventType; }

    private:
        volatile long m_cRef;                    // reference count

        AsyncEventType m_eventType;
};
```

As you can see, the implementation of the *IAsyncState::EventType()* method is so simple that it is provided in the class definition, as an inline function. Here is the implementation of the *IUnknown::QueryInterface()* function.

```
//
// Get the interface specified by the riid from the class
//
HRESULT CAsyncState::QueryInterface(REFIID riid, void** ppv)
{
    HRESULT hr = S_OK;

    if (ppv == NULL)
    {
        return E_POINTER;
    }

    if (riid == IID_IUnknown)
    {
        *ppv = static_cast<IUnknown*>(this);
    }
    else if (riid == IID_IAsyncState)
    {
        *ppv = static_cast<IAsyncState*>(this);
    }
    else
    {
        *ppv = NULL;
        hr = E_NOINTERFACE;
    }

    if(SUCCEEDED(hr))
        AddRef();

    return hr;
}
```

The *QueryInterface()* function simply checks the *riid* parameter to see if it contains an ID of an interface supported by this class. If the *riid* parameter indicates an interface exposed by the class, the *QueryInterface()* method gets a pointer to that interface and calls *IUnknown::AddRef()* to increment the reference count of the object. If the class does not implement the specified interface, the function returns the standard and well-known *E_NOINTERFACE* error code.

In this case, the class implements two interfaces—*IUnknown* and *IAsyncState*. Each of those interfaces is identified by a GUID. The *IUnknown* ID is stored in the *IID_IUnknown* constant, and the *IAsyncState* ID is stored in the *IID_IAsyncState* constant. Therefore, the function checks the *riid* parameter against both of the unique IDs in turn.

Here are the *IUnknown::AddRef()* and *Release()* functions. These functions allow an object to increment its count and to delete itself whenever it is not being used by any components.

```cpp
//
// Increment reference count of the object.
//
ULONG CAsyncState::AddRef()
{
    return InterlockedIncrement(&m_cRef);
}

//
// Decrement the reference count of the object.
//
ULONG CAsyncState::Release()
{
    ULONG refCount = InterlockedDecrement(&m_cRef);
    if (refCount == 0)
    {
        delete this;
    }

    return refCount;
}
```

The reference count is simply an integer stored in a member variable of the class—in this case, in the *CAsyncState::m_cRef* variable. In the *AddRef()* function, the variable is incremented by using the helper *InterlockedIncrement()* function. *InterlockedIncrement()* increases the value of the passed-in variable by one in an atomic fashion. This means that no other thread can interrupt the increment operation and leave the *m_cRef* variable in an unknown state.

The *IUnknown::Release()* function decreases the value of the *m_cRef* variable. When the variable hits zero, the class deletes itself. This is possible because COM classes are always allocated dynamically. Note that just like the *AddRef()* function, *Release()* uses a special atomic function to decrement the *m_cRef* variable. This eliminates the danger of race conditions and ensures that a COM object is always deleted only once, no matter how many threads are calling *Release()* concurrently.

As you can see, each call to the object's *AddRef()* function must be paired with a corresponding *Release()* call. Failing to do so will cause either access violations, and therefore crashes, or a memory leak.

For completeness, here is the *CAsyncState* class constructor.

```cpp
CAsyncState::CAsyncState(AsyncEventType type) :
    m_cRef(0),
    m_eventType(type)
{
}
```

The only interesting thing about the *CAsyncState* class constructor is that it immediately initializes the *m_cRef* variable to zero. This ensures that the reference count of the COM object is always correct.

COM Object Registration

Besides providing a method for determining the capabilities of an object, COM also gives you the ability to discover and load various components on the computer. In other words, COM object information is stored in the registry, and other applications are given the ability to discover and load these external objects at run time.

To create a registered COM object, you need to know its class ID (CLSID). The class ID is again a GUID. The registry contains a list of all registered COM objects together with their corresponding DLLs and special configuration parameters under HKEY_LOCAL_MACHINE\Software\Classes\CLSID. If you take a look at that registry key, you will see hundreds of keys with GUID names—these are the CLSIDs of the registered objects. Under that key you will find the location and name of the binary file that holds that object.

Note For backwards compatibility, the CLSID is also stored under HKCR\CLSID. In addition, on 64-bit versions of Windows, 32-bit components will be stored in some other locations, such as HKLM\Software\Classes\Wow6432Node\CLSID.

Each of these class IDs is also listed in another location—in some sort of directory in the registry. Media Foundation keeps lists of CLSIDs in a special registry location for all the objects that satisfy some sort of condition. For instance, all of the MFTs registered on the machine are listed under HKLM\Software\Classes\MediaFoundation\Transforms.

The actual procedure used to create the COM object consists of several steps. As an example, here are the steps that an application can take to instantiate an MF transform:

1. Find the transform class ID under HKLM\Software\Classes\MediaFoundation\Transforms. The transform may also hold some parameters and information such as the supported input and output types.

2. Use the CLSID found in step 1 and call *CoCreateInstance()*, passing in the CLSID and the requested IID.

    a. *CoCreateInstance()* looks up the DLL that corresponds to the specified CLSID in the registry.

    b. *CoCreateInstance()* loads the relevant DLL.

    c. *CoCreateInstance()* calls into the DLL's *DllGetClassObject()* exported function to get the helper object that implements the *IClassFactory* interface.

    d. *CoCreateInstance()* calls the *IClassFactory::CreateInstance()* method and passes in the requested COM interface ID.

        i. If the class factory knows about an object with the specified IID, it instantiates it and returns a pointer to it.

Here is a sample implementation of the *DllGetClassObject()* function. This is a standard function exposed by all binaries with public COM objects.

```
//
// Get the object with the specified IID
//
STDAPI DllGetClassObject(REFCLSID clsid, REFIID riid, void **ppObj)
{
    HRESULT hr = E_OUTOFMEMORY;
    *ppObj = NULL;

    // create a helper class factory object
    ClassFactory* pClassFactory = new ClassFactory();
    if (pClassFactory != NULL)
    {
        // get the object that implements the requested interface from the class factory
        hr = pClassFactory->QueryInterface(riid, ppObj);

        // release the class factory
        pClassFactory->Release();
    }

    return hr;
}
```

DllGetClassObject() returns a pointer to the class factory object. The class factory is a standard COM class that implements the *IClassFactory* interface and performs the actual instantiation of the published COM object.

Here is the standard implementation of the *ClassFactory::CreateInstance()* function that creates the published COM object. This example is taken from the AVF Source sample in Chapter 6, "Media Foundation Sources," which is why it instantiates the *AVFByteStreamHandler*.

```
//
// IClassFactory::CreateInstance implementation.  Attempts to create an instance of the
// specified COM object, and return the object in the ppvObject pointer.
//
HRESULT STDMETHODCALLTYPE ClassFactory::CreateInstance(
    IUnknown *pUnkOuter,     // aggregation object - used only for for aggregation
    REFIID riid,             // IID of the object to create
    void **ppvObject)        // on return contains pointer to the new object
{
    HRESULT hr = S_OK;
    AVFByteStreamHandler* pByteStreamHandler;

    // this is a non-aggregating COM object - return a failure if we are asked to aggregate
    if ( pUnkOuter != NULL )
        return CLASS_E_NOAGGREGATION;

    // create a new instance of the byte stream COM object
    pByteStreamHandler = new AVFByteStreamHandler();
```

```cpp
    // if we failed to create the object, this must be because we are out of memory -
    // return a corresponding error
    if (pByteStreamHandler == NULL)
        return E_OUTOFMEMORY;

    // Attempt to QI the new object for the requested interface
    hr = pByteStreamHandler->QueryInterface(riid, ppvObject);

    // if we failed the QueryInterface call for any reason, then this must be the wrong
    // object, delete it and make sure the ppvObject pointer contains NULL.
    if(FAILED(hr))
    {
        delete pByteStreamHandler;
        *ppvObject = NULL;
    }

    return hr;
}
```

This *IClassFactory::CreateInstance()* implementation is designed to work only with the AVF Source example. It expects to receive requests only for an object implementing the *IMFByteStreamHandler* interface that can instantiate the *AVFSource*. As a result, the function simply creates an instance of the *AVFByteStreamHandler* class and calls *QueryInterface()* on it, passing in the requested IID. If the class implements the requested interface—in this case, either *IUnknown* or *IMFByteStreamHandler*—it returns a pointer to an object that implements that interface.

Many libraries provide custom and template-based implementations for the class factory objects. The samples provided in this book do not use those implementations because they can make it more difficult to debug instantiation issues.

APPENDIX C

Active Template Library Objects

The code samples in this book utilize several useful Active Template Library (ATL) objects and wrappers. These objects simplify various operations, providing automatic handling of standard COM and Windows primitives. This appendix lists several of the ATL objects as a reference.

Most of the ATL components shown in this appendix use the same principle to operate—they call one function in the constructor of a helper class and call another function in the destructor. This allows you to ensure that both functions are called, and that for every call of the first function there is a corresponding call of the second.

ATL Smart Pointers

As you saw in Appendix B, the reference count of a COM object is extremely important. The reference count is the only way to ensure that the COM object is not freed while somebody else is still using it, and that the object is properly deleted after everyone is done with it. In other words, the object is released and deleted only when its reference count reaches zero.

Reference count issues are among the most common problems in COM applications. If an object reference count is not incremented properly, the object will be released prematurely, and some function will cause an access violation calling into now unused memory. If the reference count is incremented too much, the object will never be released, and your application will leak memory.

To help with reference count issues, the Microsoft ATL provides two special objects, the *CComPtr* and *CComQIPtr* smart pointers. These objects automatically handle most of the *IUnknown::AddRef()* and *Release()* calls, greatly simplifying the programmer's life.

First let's examine the *CComPtr* class. As you can tell from the class name, *CComPtr* is a special COM object pointer—it holds pointers to COM objects. The *CComPtr* class uses templates to hold the interface as a template parameter of the object it will represent. The interface is incremented on assignment and decremented when the class is destroyed. For all practical purposes, a *CComPtr* object can be used exactly as if it were a pointer to the interface for which it was created. You can call the interface methods, and even get a pointer to the interface, by using the ampersand (&) operator.

Here is an example function that uses *CComPtr* to hold a pointer to the object. You should increment the reference counter of a COM object if the object will be kept around after the function is finished executing.

```
//
// COM test demonstration function
//
HRESULT CTestClass::ComUsingTestFunction(void)
{
    HRESULT hr = S_OK;
    CComPtr<IAsyncState> pResult;
    CComQIPtr<IAsyncState1> pResult1;

    do
    {
        // Create one IAsyncState object using the standard CoCreateInstance call.
        hr = pResult1.CoCreateInstance(CLSID_AsyncStateObj, NULL, 0);
        BREAK_ON_FAIL(hr);

        // Create a copy of the COM pointer by using assignment, and AddRef() the pointer.
        pResult1 = pResult;
        BREAK_ON_NULL(pResult1, E_UNEXPECTED);

        // do something with pResult and pResult1
    }

    return hr;

    // pResult and pResult1 are released once the pointer objects go out of scope.
}
```

In this short example, the sample *ComUsingTestFunction()* method creates an internal COM object by using the functionality built into *CComPtr*. The *CComPtr::CoCreateInstance()* method internally calls the standard COM *CoCreateInstance()* function. The function then gets a copy of that pointer by assigning the pointer to a second smart pointer.

The *CComQIPtr* smart pointer overrides the assignment operator. Internally, the assignment operation calls the *IUnknown::QueryInterface()* method on the *IAsyncState* object stored in *pResult*. This ensures that the pointer stored in *pResult1* implements the interface for which the smart pointer object was created—the *IAsyncState1* interface. If the object does not implement that interface, the *QueryInterface()* call will fail, and *pResult1* will contain *NULL*. In addition, the assignment operation ensures that the reference count of the object is incremented as necessary, and the object will not be released and deleted while the function is executing.

When the smart pointers go out of scope—in other words, when you exit the *ComUsingTestFunction()* function—the *pResult* and *pResult1* objects are destroyed, and their destructors are called. The smart pointer class destructors call *Release()* on the object to which the smart pointer is pointing. Therefore, the object reference count is incremented when the smart pointers are created and initialized, and is decremented when the smart pointers are released.

The *CComPtr* class has a limitation: a pointer of another interface cannot be assigned to this object (unless it is also wrapped in a *CComPtr* object). You can explicitly call *QueryInterface()* on the object and get a pointer to one of its interfaces that way, but the overloaded equals operator in *CComPtr* does not call *QueryInterface()* in all situations.

The actual rules of where it is allowed to attempt to assign a pointer of a different type to the *CComPtr* and where it isn't are actually somewhat involved and are beyond the scope of this brief refresher. It's sufficient to say that some attempts to assign a pointer to a *CComPtr* object may fail at compile time.

To simplify this situation, ATL provides another smart pointer class, *CComQIPtr*. *CComQIPtr* explicitly calls *QueryInterface()* on passed-in pointers. If *QueryInterface()* succeeds and the underlying object implements the required interface, then the assignment succeeds. Otherwise, the target pointer is set to *NULL*.

Here is an example of how you can use *CComQIPtr* to implicitly call *QueryInterface()*.

```
//
// Asynchronous worker function.
//
HRESULT CTestClass::Invoke(IMFAsyncResult* pResult)
{
    HRESULT hr = S_OK;
    CComQIPtr<IMFAsyncCallback> pCallbackPtr;

    // Call QueryInterface()for the IMFAsyncCallback interface.  Assignment will
    // most likely fail since pResult probably does not implement the IMFAsyncCallback
    // interface.
    pCallbackPtr = pRslt;

    if(pCallbackPtr == NULL)
    {
        // do something - object to which pResult points to does not implement the
        // IMFAsyncCallback interface, and QueryInterface() returned E_NOINTERFACE
    }
    else
    {
        // do something else - assignment - and therefore QueryInterface() call - succeeded
    }

    return hr;
}
```

CComQIPtr is actually a child class of *CComPtr*. It adds a few special-case overloaded assignment operator functions that call *QueryInterface()* on passed-in pointers. In this case, the attempt to assign *pRslt* to the *pCallbackPtr* smart pointer causes *pCallbackPtr* to internally call *IUnknown::QueryInterface()* on the object to which *pRslt* points. If the *QueryInterface()* call succeeds, the *pCallbackPtr* pointer value will not be *NULL*.

The only inconvenience with template-based smart pointers is that you cannot pass them into a function by pointer. In other words, you cannot pass a pointer to a *CComPtr<type>* into a function. If you want to return something through the function in/out parameters, you need to either use a reference to the *CComPtr* or convert things to the underlying pointer type and use the standard pointer to the interface pointer notation. Here is an example of how this would work.

```
//
// Demonstrate extraction of a variable from a function by using a reference to a smart
// pointer and the pointer to pointer notation.
//
HRESULT CTestClass::SmartPointerCalls(void)
{
    HRESULT hr = S_OK;
    CComPtr<IUnknown> byRef;
    CComPtr<IUnknown> byPtr;

    hr = GetUnknownObjByRef(byRef);
    if(FAILED(hr))
        return hr;

    hr = GetUnknownObjByPtr(&byPtr);

    return hr;
}


//
// Use a reference to the smart pointer to return a pointer to the caller of the function
//
HRESULT CTestClass::GetUnknownObjByRef(CComPtr<IUnknown>& pUnk)
{
    // since pUnk is a reference to the smart pointer, just assign to it
    pUnk = m_internalUnknownObj;

    return S_OK;
}


//
// Use a pointer to pointer to return an object to the caller of the function
//
HRESULT CTestClass::GetUnknownObjByPtr(IUnknown** ppUnk)
{
    // dereference the pointer to pointer, and set its value
    *ppUnk = m_internalUnknownObj;

    // AddRef the pointer since now there will be two handles to the object.
    m_internalUnknownObj->AddRef();

    return S_OK;
}
```

The *SmartPointerCalls()* method is demonstrating how you would retrieve an object from a function through the use of its out parameters. The first example uses a reference to the smart pointer object. This allows the *GetUnknownObjByRef()* function to simply set the value of the smart pointer internally. In this case, the parameter used in the *GetUnknownObjByRef()* function is the actual *byRef* object from the caller function. The second example uses the standard pointer-to-pointer notation. *CComPtr* has an overloaded address-of operator (&). By getting the address of the smart pointer, you are actually getting the address of the underlying standard (not-smart) pointer that *CComPtr* represents. Therefore, you can use the standard C++ notation to assign a value to the parameter passed in to the *GetUnknownObjByPtr()* function.

This book uses both methods shown here interchangeably, because there is very little actual difference between them.

CComCritSecLock and *CComAutoCriticalSection* Thread Synchronization Helpers

The *CComCritSecLock* class and *CComAutoCriticalSection* ATL classes wrap around the standard *CRITICAL_SECTION* Windows primitive, ensuring that you never forget to exit from the critical section. These classes work in tandem, simplifying the use of critical sections, and therefore providing very simple synchronization mechanisms for ensuring that only one thread can execute in a specific function or set of functions.

A regular critical section is controlled through the standard *EnterCriticalSection()* and *LeaveCriticalSection()* Win32 APIs. These functions allow a thread to enter a critical section, blocking all other threads from accessing code blocks protected by this critical section. The *CComAutoCriticalSection* class presented here simplifies access to the critical section, initializing it in the class constructor, deleting it in the class destructor, and giving you the ability to easily lock and unlock it. In this respect, the *CComCritSecLock* and *CComAutoCriticalSection* classes are similar to the smart pointers described in earlier in this appendix—the constructor initializes some resource, and the destructor releases that resource. Therefore, the classes ensure that for each initialization of a resource (in this case the critical section) the resource is released exactly once.

Most of the classes used in this book have a *CComAutoCriticalSection* private member variable. This variable takes care of proper initialization and destruction of the Win32 critical section.

The *CComAutoCriticalSection* class is usually used in conjunction with the *CComCritSecLock* helper object. This object ensures that if you enter into a critical section, you will always leave it. This is done by calling the *CComAutoCriticalSection::Lock()* function from the class constructor, and the corresponding *CComAutoCriticalSection::Unlock()* method from the class destructor.

The *CComCritSecLock* class simplifies the use of the critical section. Here is a sample class that demonstrates how you can use the *CComCritSecLock* and *CComAutoCriticalSection* objects together to ensure that only a single thread can execute in the code blocks protected by the same section. In this case, both *TestFunction1()* and *TestFunction2()* are protected by the same critical section.

```
class CTestClass
{
    public:

        void TestFunction1(void)
        {
            // lock the function
            CComCritSecLock<CComAutoCriticalSection> lock(&m_critSec);

            // do work in a locked section

            // unlock section when the lock goes out of scope
        }
        void TestFunction2(void)
        {
            // lock the function
            CComCritSecLock<CComAutoCriticalSection> lock(&m_critSec);

            // do work in a locked section

            // unlock section when the lock goes out of scope
        }

    private:
        CComAutoCriticalSection m_critSec;
};
```

The *CTestClass::TestFunction1()* method shows how you can use a *CComCritSecLock* variable and scope to control entering and exiting from a critical section. The method is locked by the critical section that is represented by the *lock* variable. When a thread enters the function and initializes the *lock* variable, the *CComCritSecLock* constructor locks the critical section, and no other thread can execute in that area of code. As soon as the thread exits from the curly braces, the *lock* variable goes out of scope, and the thread automatically calls the *CComCritSecLock* class destructor. The destructor internally calls *CComAutoCriticalSection::Unlock()*, which unlocks the critical section. If any other thread has been waiting to enter this locked section, it is now allowed to do so.

This mechanism ensures that only a single thread can execute in all pieces of the code protected by *CTestClass::m_critSec*. In this example, both *TestFunction1()* and *TestFunction2()* are protected by the same critical section. That means that if a thread enters into *TestFunction1()*, no other threads can enter into either one of the two *CTestClass* methods until the first thread is done executing in the first function. However, the first thread can call *TestFunction2()* from within *TestFunction1()*—that is perfectly acceptable, because both functions are protected by the same critical section, and the thread is already inside of that section.

Index

Symbols

@ (at sign), 193

A

AAC format, 81, 90
activator objects, 302–303, 305–306
Active Template Library. *See* ATL (Active Template Library)
Add Audio Capture Source option (Topology menu), 20
Add button (TopoEdit), 18
Add Custom Sink option (Topology menu), 206
Add EVR option (Topology menu), 17
Add SAR option (Topology menu), 17
Add Source option (Topology menu), 16
Add Transform option (Topology menu), 18, 100
Add Video Capture Source option (Topology menu), 20
AMD Playback Decoder MFT, 18
archival sinks
    about, 205
    pausing, 211
ASF files, 70, 81, 306–315
AsyncEventType enumeration, 332
AsyncEventType_SourceStreamEvent flag, 271
AsyncEventType_SyncMftSampleRequest flag, 272
asynchronous communication
    about, 27
    asynchronous source command functions, 171–174
    MF and, 143–145
    MFTs and, 262–266
    playback sessions and, 30, 31–34
    processing data, 114
    sink writers and, 79
    source readers and, 79
    transcoding sessions and, 74

AsyncObject class
    BeginAsyncCall() method, 144, 171
    BeginAsyncWork() method, 152
    EndAsyncCall() method, 145
    Invoke() method, 145
    race conditions and, 145
ATL (Active Template Library)
    CComAutoCriticalSection class, 343–344
    CComCritSecLock class, 34, 106, 152, 343–344
    CComPtr class, 152, 339–343
    CComQIPtr class, 67, 341
    smart pointers, 339–343
    synchronization considerations, 145
ATSC format, 127
at sign (@), 193
audio files
    compression and, 2–3
    format negotiation, 84–88
    mapping sink writer streams, 81–84
    media streams and, 141
    pipeline data flow, 2–5, 7–9
    playing in TopoEdit, 14–15
    rendering, 12
audio recorders, enabling, 21
audio renderer, 17
AVFByteStreamHandler class
    about, 142, 150, 190
    BeginCreateObject() method, 151, 153
    class definition, 196–197
    concurrent clients and, 153
    GetValue() method, 193–194
    Initialize() method, 191
    Invoke() method, 151–152, 153–154
AVFFileParser class, 164–165
AVF format
    about, 142
    byte stream handlers, 149–156

AVFSource class

AVFSource class
- about, 142, 145, 150, 159
- BeginOpen() method, 150, 153, 160–161, 164
- class definition, 197–199
- CreateAudioStream() method, 167–170
- CreateVideoStream() method, 167–170
- DispatchSamples() method, 184
- EndOpen() method, 164
- GetEvent() method, 179–180
- InternalCreatePresentationDescriptor() method, 165–168
- InternalOpen() method, 163, 164
- InternalPause() method, 163, 172–173, 174
- InternalRequestSample() method, 180–182
- InternalStart() method, 163, 176–177
- Invoke() method, 151, 161–162, 170–172, 174, 180, 184
- main command functions, 171–174
- media stream objects and, 183
- ParseHeader() method, 165–166
- parsing media files, 190
- SendSampleToStream() method, 181–182, 184
- Start() method, 176
- streaming source samples, 180

AvfSource.dll file, 143, 148

AVFStream class
- about, 142, 170
- class definition, 199–200
- DeliverSample() method, 184, 189
- DispatchSamples() method, 186–187, 189
- media stream objects and, 183–185
- Pause() method, 174
- RequestSample() method, 184–185, 189
- SendSamplesOut() method, 187–189
- SetVideoMediaType() method, 170
- Stop() method, 174

AVIFileParser class
- about, 142, 159
- class definition, 202–203
- GetPropertyStore() method, 192
- GetVideoMediaType() method, 170
- streaming source samples, 180

AVI files
- about, 220
- AVI media stream, 227–241
- media sink clock functions, 216–220
- media stream sink control functions, 211–216
- parsing, 140
- sample AVI file sinks, 207–210

sink data loop, 220–227
video codec support, 18
AVIParser class, 170
AviSink.dll file, 209

B

Box, Don, 331
brightness (luma) value, 123
byte stream activator, 305–321
byte stream handlers
- AVF sources and, 149–156
- instantiating sources and, 147–149

byte stream objects, 47, 143

C

CAsyncState object, 254–255
CAviFileWriter class
- about, 208
- class definition, 245
- initializing, 217
- sink data loop, 223

CAviSink class
- about, 208
- class definition, 242–243
- GetEarliestSampleStream() method, 223, 224–225
- GetNextSampleTimestamp() method, 225–226
- GetStreamSinkById() method, 214
- GetStreamSinkByIndex() method, 213
- media stream sink control functions, 211–212
- ProcessStreamSamples() method, 222–223
- ScheduleNewSampleProcessing() method, 209, 231
- sink data loop, 221
- WriteSampleFromStream() method, 223–224

CAviStream class
- about, 208, 227
- class definition, 244–246
- Flush() method, 241
- GetNextSample() method, 231, 233
- GetNextSampleLength() method, 231, 233
- GetNextSampleTimestamp() method, 231–232, 237–239
- media type support, 228
- OnStarted() method, 219, 229–230
- PlaceMarker() method, 234–237, 236–237
- sink data loop, 223

sink design responsibilities, 228
stream markers and, 235
stream sample functions, 230
TryFireMarkerEvent() method, 232, 237–241
CBasePin::GetMediaType() method, 108
CBmpFile class
    about, 99, 123, 130
    class definition, 136–137
CBR (constant-bitrate) encoding, 67
CByteStreamWriteData class, 321–322
CComAutoCriticalSection class (ATL)
    about, 343–344
    Lock() method, 343
    Unlock() method, 343
CComCritSecLock class (ATL)
    about, 106, 152, 343–344
    instantiating objects, 34
CComPtr class (ATL)
    about, 152, 339–343
    CoCreateInstance() method, 340
CComQIPtr class (ATL), 67, 341
CFrameParser class
    about, 99, 117, 123
    class definition, 135–136
    DrawBitmap_UYVY() method, 131
    SetFrameType() method, 130–131
CheckBufferSize() function, 224
CheckShutdown() helper function, 163
chroma (color) value, 123
chroma smoothing, 128
chroma subsampling, 123
chrominance format, 123
CHttpOutputByteStream class
    about, 300, 306, 307–308
    BeginWrite() method, 310
    class definition, 319–320
    Flush() method, 314
    GetCapabilities() method, 308
    InitSocket() method, 310
    instantiating objects, 303
    SendAsyncWriteResult() method, 312
CHttpOutputStreamActivate class, 318–319
CImageInjectorMFT class
    about, 99, 108
    CheckMediaType() method, 108
    class definition, 134–136
    GetSupportedMediaType() method, 108, 109–110
    SetInputType() method, 112

CImageInjector::SetInputType() method, 128
CInterfaceList class, 187
class IDs (CLSIDs)
    renderers and, 17
    scheme handler objects, 147–148
    sinks, 206
Client class
    Invoke() method, 145–146
    race conditions and, 145
clock object, 21
CloseHandle() function, 267
CLSIDs (class IDs)
    renderers and, 17
    scheme handler objects, 147–148
    sinks, 206
CMP3Session class
    about, 248–249, 261
    class definition, 285–286
    GetService() method, 282
    HandleSourceStreamEvent() method, 277–279
    HandleStreamSinkEvent() method, 271–272
    HandleSynchronousMftRequest() function, 272–273
    Init() function, 266–267
    Invoke() method, 254–255, 269, 271, 272
    PullDataFromMft() method, 273–276
    PullDataFromSource() method, 273, 276–277
    Start() method, 279, 280
CMP3SessionTopoBuilder class
    about, 249
    BeginCreateMediaSource() method, 253
    building topology, 251–252
    class definition, 283–284
    ConnectMftToSink() method, 260
    ConnectSourceToMft() method, 260
    HandleByteStreamHandlerEvent() method, 255–256
    LoadCustomTopology() method, 252, 267
    NegotiateMediaTypes() method, 256
CoCreateInstance() function (COM)
    COM object registration, 336
    custom media sessions, 252
    instantiating objects, 23
    media foundation sinks, 206–208
    MFTrace tool and, 325
    MFT registration, 121
COINIT_APARTMENTTHREADED parameter, 24
CoInitializeEx() function (COM), 23–24, 28
color (chroma) value, 123

COM APIs

COM APIs, 23
COM (Component Object Model), 23, 331–338
COM objects
    byte stream handlers, 148
    COM API and, 23
    MFTs, 97
    registering, 336–338
    sinks as, 206, 207
compression
    in audio/video files, 2–3
    transcoding and, 87
constant-bitrate (CBR) encoding, 67
container type attributes, 70
Controls menu (TopoEdit), 14
converting RGB to YUV format, 125–128
CopyNextSampleData() function, 234
CoUninitialize() function (COM), 23, 28
CPlayer class
    about, 24–25
    class definition, 57–59, 315–317
    CloseSession() method, 36–37, 38–39
    CreateSession() method, 32
    DrawSeekbar() method, 294, 296
    GetLocalFilePath() method, 294
    IncreaseRate() method, 282–283
    InitializeMixer() method, 292
    InitializeSeekBarDirectX() method, 294
    Invoke() method, 36, 41
    OnTopologyReady() method, 41
    OpenURL() method, 26, 28–29
    ProcessMediaEvent() method, 34–35, 36, 39, 41
    RenderSeekBarSurface() method, 296
    SetMouseVisible() method, 296
    StartPlayback() method, 41–42, 42
CReaderWriterTranscoder class
    class definition, 96
    ConnectStream() method, 84
    GetTranscodeAudioType() method, 90
    GetTranscodeMediaType() method, 84, 89–90
    GetTranscodeVideoType() method, 90
    MapStreams() method, 84
    RunTranscode() function, 79
    Transcode() method, 81
CreateEvent() API, 267
Create GUID tool, 332
CTopoBuilder class
    about, 24–25, 26, 43–44, 48, 300
    class definition, 59–60, 317–318
    CreateMediaSource() method, 45, 48, 301
    CreateNetworkSink() method, 301, 303

    CreateSourceStreamNode() method, 53
    CreateTopology() method, 50–51, 54, 301
    RenderURL() method, 300
    streaming network players, 299
    transcode API and, 63
CTranscodeApi class
    class definition, 94–95
    IMFAsyncCallback interface and, 74
    Invoke() method, 74–75
    ParseMediaEvent() method, 75–77
    WaitUntilCompletion() method, 76–77
CTranscodeApiTopoBuilder class
    class definition, 95–96
    CreateTranscodeTopology() method, 64
    GetTypeAttributesFromTypeCollection() method, 67
    GetVideoOutputAvailableTypes() method, 69, 72–73
    SetAudioAttributes() method, 65
    SetContainerAttributes() method, 70
    SetVideoAttributes() method, 68–69

D

D3DPOOL_SYSTEMMEM flag, 294
data capture from external sources, 20–21
data functions, 101, 113–119
data streams. *See* media streams
debugging
    asynchronous models and, 27
    MFTrace tool support, 113, 324–330
decoding/decoders
    format negotiation, 84–88
    in rendering example, 13
    vendors shipping MFTs with drivers, 72
Digital Rights Management (DRM), , 62
digital signal processing (DSP), 97
directed acyclic graphs, 3
DirectShow, 141, 143
DirectX Media Object (DMO)
    about, 13, 249
    IMFTransform interface and, 13
DirectX objects, 291–292, 294
DivX encoder, 18
DllGetClassObject() function, 336–337
DllRegisterServer() function (COM), 121
DMO (DirectX Media Object)
    about, 13, 249
    IMFTransform interface and, 13

DRM (Digital Rights Management), , 62
DSP (digital signal processing), 97

E

E_ABORT error code, 241
E_FAIL error code, 54
encoding/encoders
    CBR, 67
    format negotiation, 84–88
    instantiating with default parameters, 73
    multipass, 62
    VBR, 62
    vendors shipping MFTs with drivers, 72
Enhanced Video Renderer (EVR)
    about, 17, 205
    IMFVideoDisplayControl interface, 42
    rendering player UI with, 289–298
E_NOINTERFACE error code, 251, 334
E_NOTIMPL error code
    about, 102–103
    IMFAsyncCallback interface and, 33
    IMFAttributes interface and, 306
    IMFByteStream interface and, 308
    IMFMediaSession interface and, 250
    IMFTransform interface and, 98, 120
E_PENDING error code, 223, 226, 232, 239
error lookup, 323–324
ETW (Event Tracing for Windows), 325
event functions, 119–121, 120–121
events. *See also* specific events
    about, 157–159
    cycle overview, 32–33
    pipeline events, 266–272
    player behavior and, 34–43
    source media event functions, 178–180
Event Tracing for Windows (ETW), 325
EVR (Enhanced Video Renderer)
    about, 17, 205
    IMFVideoDisplayControl interface, 42
    rendering player UI with, 289–298
EXCEPTION_TO_HR macro, 170, 216
external sources, data capture from, 20–21

F

file extension mappings, 46
file formats. *See also* specific formats
    audio/video processing, 2–5
    MF native support, 70

File menu (TopoEdit)
    Render File option, 100
    Render Media File option, 12
file rendering. *See* rendering media files
file scheme handlers, 147–148
filters
    DirectShow, 141
    T-splitter, 102
format negotiation, source readers, 84–88
frame format detection, 128–130
frame rate (media types), 16, 91
frame size (media types), 16
frame stride, defined, 130
FT_OUTPUT_DATA_BUFFER structure, 275
functions. *See also* specific functions
    asynchronous source command, 171–174
    data, 101, 113–119
    event, 119–121, 120–121
    media sink clock, 216–220
    media stream sink control, 211–216
    media type selection, 107–113, 108–114
    messaging, 101
    sink creation, 206
    source media event, 178–180
    status query, 119–121, 120–121
    stream configuration, 101, 101–107
    unimplemented, 102

G

GDI DCs (Graphics Device Interface device contexts), 290
GET request (HTTP), 308
GetUnknownObjByPtr() function, 343
GetUnknownObjByRef() function, 343
GPU (graphics processing unit), 61
Graphics Device Interface device contexts (GDI DCs), 290
graphics processing unit (GPU), 61
graphs. *See* pipeline
GUID_NULL parameter, 43
GUIDs
    container type, 70
    defined, 6
    IMFMediaSession interface and, 42
    mapping to string representations, 15

H.264 format

H

H.264 format, 18, 81, 87, 91
H264 Video Decoder MFT decoder, 18
HTTP
    byte stream activator, 305–306
    output byte stream, 306–314
HTTP GET request, 308

I

IAsyncState interface
    about, 333
    EventType() method, 334
    inheritance, 333
IAsyncWriteData interface
    about, 314
    GetWriteData() method, 314
IClassFactory interface
    about, 336
    CreateInstance() method, 336
ID3DXSprite interface, 291
IDirect3D9 object, 292, 294, 296
IDirectX3DTexture9 object, 291
IID_IAsyncState constant, 332–333
IIinitializeFromFile interface, 193
IInitializeWithFile::Initialize() method, 190–191
IInitializeWithStream interface, 190
image conversion, RGB to YUV, 125–128
image injection into video frames
    about, 122
    frame format detection, 128–130
    Nv12, 132–133
    RGB to YUV image conversion, 125–128
    uncompressed video formats, 123–125
    UYVY, 130–132
image reduction methods, 123
images, color and brightness format, 123
IMFActivate interface
    about, 55
    ActivateObject() method, 55
    determining target transcode format, 72–73
    inheritance, 305
    ShutdownObject() method, 55
IMFASFContentInfo::SetProfile() method, 302
IMFASFProfile interface, 302
IMFAsyncCallback interface
    about, 57, 161, 250
    byte stream handling, 150

    CPlayer class and, 57
    CTranscodeApi class and, 74
    events and, 158
    GetParameters() method, 33
    HTTP output byte stream and, 308
    Invoke() method, 27, 30, 32–34, 74–75, 150, 200, 209, 222–223, 254, 311, 323
    media stream objects and, 184
    passing pointers, 144
    sink data loop, 222
    worker queue and, 172
IMFAsyncCallbackPointer interface, 153
IMFAsyncEvent::Invoke() method, 39
IMFAsyncResult interface
    about, 75, 174
    creating objects, 153, 161
    events and, 158
    GetStatus() method, 323
    GetType() method, 323
    inserting state object into, 171
    MF error lookup, 323–324
IMFAttributes interface
    about, 53
    Compare() method, 112
    inheritance, 306
    SetItem() method, 237
IMFByteStreamHandler interface
    about, 147–148
    BeginCreateObject() method, 150, 251–254
    CancelObjectCreation() method, 153–154, 156
    EndCreateObject() method, 150, 151, 252
    EndObjectCreation() method, 155
    events and, 159
    Invoke() method, 156
IMFByteStream interface
    ASF sinks and, 302
    BeginRead() method, 328
    BeginWrite() method, 307–308
    Close() method, 308
    creating objects, 47, 146, 307
    EndRead() method, 328
    EndWrite() method, 308, 313
    Flush() method, 308
    GetCapabilities() method, 308
    HTTP output byte stream and, 308
    initalizing sinks, 209
    loading data, 143
    Write() method, 307–309
IMFClockStateSink interface
    about, 210
    OnClockPause() method, 211, 217

IMFPresentationClock interface

OnClockRestart() method, 211, 217
OnClockSetRate() method, 211, 217
OnClockStart() method, 211, 217, 261
OnClockStop() method, 211, 217, 219
IMFGetService interface
    about, 251, 280
    GetService() method, 251, 281
IMFMediaEventGenerator interface
    about, 141, 157, 250
    asynchronous MFTs and, 262
    BeginGetEvent() method, 30, 32, 157–158, 160, 178, 183, 271
    custom media sessions, 248
    custom session data pipeline, 261
    EndGetEvent() method, 32, 34, 37, 41, 157–158, 160, 183
    GetEvent() method, 157–159, 160, 183
    inheritance, 178, 183, 229
    media stream objects, 184, 189
    MEError event, 157
    QueueEvent() method, 157, 160, 183
    queueing events, 261
    sink data loop, 227
    stream markers and, 235
IMFMediaEvent interface
    about, 76, 158
    creating objects, 261
    GetStatus() method, 36, 77
IMFMediaEventQueue interface
    about, 251
    BeginGetEvent() method, 179
    EndGetEvent() method, 179
    QueueEvent() method, 179
IMFMediaSample::GetTotalLength() method, 233
IMFMediaSession interface
    about, 248
    BeginGetEvent() method, 26
    ClearTopologies() method, 250
    Close() method, 36, 39, 250
    EndGetEvent() method, 34
    GetClock() method, 43, 250, 281
    GetFullTopology() method, 250
    GetSessionCapabilities() method, 250
    Pause() method, 250
    SetTopology() method, 30–31, 250
    Shutdown() method, 37, 250
    Start() method, 42–43, 250, 261, 267
    Stop() method, 250
IMFMediaSink interface
    AddStreamSink() method, 210, 212
    GetCharacteristics() method, 211, 212
    GetPresentationClock() method, 210, 217
    GetStreamSinkById() method, 210
    GetStreamSinkByIndex() method, 210
    GetStreamSinkCount() method, 210, 214
    implementing, 210
    RemoveStreamSink() method, 210, 212
    SetPresentationClock() method, 210, 280
    Shutdown() method, 211
    sink requirements, 207
IMFMediaSource interface
    about, 141, 159
    CreatePresentationDescriptor() method, 160
    GetCharacteristics() method, 160
    inheritance, 157, 178
    Pause() method, 159, 171–174
    Shutdown() method, 160
    Start() method, 159, 174–175
    Stop() method, 159
    streaming source samples, 180
IMFMediaStream interface
    AVFStream class and, 142
    creating objects, 168, 271
    GetMediaSource() method, 183
    GetStreamDescriptor() method, 183
    inheritance, 157, 178, 183
    initializing source and, 160
    instantiating objects, 170
    pipeline events, 269
    RequestSample() method, 183, 262, 263, 277
    streaming source samples, 180
IMFMediaTypeHandler interface
    about, 54
    GetCurrentMediaType() method, 228
    GetMajorType() method, 228
    GetMediaTypeByIndex() method, 228
    GetMediaTypeCount() method, 228
    IsMediaTypeSupported() method, 228
    negotiating media type, 259
    SetCurrentMediaType() method, 228
IMFMediaType interface
    about, 89–90
    IsEqual() method, 112
IMFPresentationClock interface
    about, 216, 279–281
    AddClockStateSink() method, 217
    creating objects, 269
    GetTime() method, 279, 282
    RemoveClockStateSink() method, 217
    SetTimeSource() method, 269
    Start() method, 269

IMFPresentationDescriptor interface

IMFPresentationDescriptor interface
    about, 49, 166
    DeselectStream() method, 49
    SelectStream() method, 49, 168
IMFPresentationTimeSource interface, 268, 280
IMFRateControl interface
    about, 280, 281, 282
    GetRate() method, 283
    SetRate() method, 280, 283
IMFSchemeHandler interface
    about, 147
    BeginCreateObject() method, 328
IMFSinkWriterCallback interface, 79
IMFSinkWriter interface
    AddStream() method, 84
    WriteSample() method, 78, 79, 93
IMFSourceReaderCallback interface, 79
IMFSourceReader::ReadSample() method, 78, 79, 93
IMFSourceResolver interface
    BeginCreateObjectFromURL() method, 46
    CreateObjectFromByteStream() method, 146, 149
    CreateObjectFromURL() method, 45–47, 146, 328
    EndCreateObjectFromURL() method, 46
IMFStreamDescriptor interface, 166
IMFStreamSink interface
    about, 244
    Flush() method, 227, 241
    GetCharacteristics() method, 211
    GetIdentifier() method, 214, 227
    GetMediaSink() method, 227
    GetMediaTypeHandler() method, 227
    implementing, 210
    inheritance, 229
    PlaceMarker() method, 227, 236–237
    ProcessSample() method, 227, 230–231, 234, 262, 264, 274
    sink data loop, 227
    sink requirements, 207
IMFTopoLoader interface, 55, 57
IMFTopology interface, 250
IMFTranscodeProfile interface
    SetAudioAttributes() method, 64–66
    SetContainerAttributes() method, 64
    SetVideoAttributes() method, 64
IMFTransform interface
    about, 98, 101
    AddInputStreams() method, 103
    categories of methods, 101
    CImageInjectorMFT class and, 99
    DeleteInputStream() method, 103
    DMOs and, 13
    GetAttributes() method, 119, 120
    GetInputAvailableType() method, 108, 109
    GetInputCurrentType() method, 108, 112
    GetInputStatus() method, 119, 120
    GetInputStreamAttributes() method, 103
    GetInputStreamInfo() method, 102–105
    GetOutputAvailableType() method, 73, 108, 259
    GetOutputCurrentType() method, 108, 112
    GetOutputStatus() method, 119, 120
    GetOutputStreamAttributes() method, 103
    GetOutputStreamFormat() method, 118
    GetOutputStreamInfo() method, 103
    GetStreamCount() method, 102, 104
    GetStreamIDs() method, 103
    GetStreamLimits() method, 102, 103
    implementing, 5
    ProcessEvent() method, 119
    ProcessInput() method, 105, 115–117, 119–120, 262–263
    ProcessMessage() method, 114, 115
    ProcessOutput() method, 99, 115, 117, 118, 262–263, 275–276
    SetInputType() method, 108, 260, 325, 329, 330
    SetOutputBounds() method, 119
    SetOutputType() method, 108, 113, 325, 330
IMFVideoDisplayControl interface
    about, 41, 289
    EVR support, 42
IMFVideoMixerBitmap interface, 289–291
IMFVideoMixerControl interface, 289
IMFVideoProcessor interface, 289
InitGuid.h header file, 333
InitializeSeekbarDirectX() function, 292
injecting images into video frames
    about, 122
    frame format detection, 128–130
    Nv12 image injection, 132–133
    RGB to YUV image conversion, 125–128
    uncompressed video formats, 123–125
    UYVY image injection, 130–132
input streams
    defined, 101
    stream configuration functions, 101–107
IPropertyStore interface, 190–192
isKeyFrame Boolean flag, 224
ISourceOperation container object, 180
IStream interface, 190

IUnknown interface
    AddRef() method, 332, 334–335
    class definition, 331
    collection objects and, 72
    events and, 158
    inheritance, 332
    media stream objects, 186
    PROPVARIANT object and, 77
    QueryInterface() method, 213–214, 282, 332, 334
    Release() method, 332, 334–335

L

LifeCam Cinema USB webcam, 20–21
linking topology nodes, 19
luma (brightness) value, 123

M

major type value (media types), 6, 16
MediaEventType enumeration, 36–37
media event types, 36. *See also* specific media event types
media files. *See also* audio files; video files
    parsing, 190
    playing in TopoEdit, 14–15
    property handlers, 194
    rendering, 12–16
    rendering with EVR Mixer, 289–298
    sink writers writing to, 78
    source readers accessing, 78
media playback/players
    about, 24–25
    basic file rendering, 25–43
    building media pipeline, 43–57
    control functions, 229
    determining target transcode format, 71
    rate control, 14
    seek functionality, 14
    sources and, 174–178
    streaming network players, 298–314
    in TopoEdit, 14–15
media player application
    about, 24–25
    basic file rendering
        about, 25–27
        creating media player, 27–28
        event processing and player behavior, 34–43
        intializing media session, 28–31
        media session asynchronous events, 31–34

building media pipeline
    about, 43–44
    building partial topology, 48–55
    creating MF source, 44–48
    resolving partial topology, 55–57
media sessions
    about, 25–27
    asynchronous events, 31–34
    building custom, 247–250
    creating, 30
    custom MP3 sessions, 250–251
    custom MP3 topology, 251–261
    custom session data pipeline, 261–279
    default, 24
    initializing, 28–31
    MP3 data flow, 272–279
    negotiating media type, 256–261
    session clock, 279–283
    Transcode API and, 74–77
MEDIASINK_CANNOT_MATCH_CLOCK flag, 212
MEDIASINK_CAN_PREROLL flag, 212
MEDIASINK_FIXED_STREAMS flag, 212
MEDIASINK_RATELESS flag, 212
MEDIASINK_REQUIRE_REFERENCE_MEDIATYPE flag, 212
media stream objects, 166, 168–170, 183–189
media streams
    about, 141–143
    AVI files, 227–241
    conceptual diagram depicting, 139–140
    DirectShow and, 141
    playback control functions, 229
    resampling, 13
    sample functions, 230–234
    sink control functions, 211–216
    stream configuration functions, 101–107
    streaming network players, 298–314
    streaming source samples, 180–183
    stream markers, 234–241
media types
    defined, 5
    details provided by TopoEdit, 16
    frame rate details, 16
    frame size details, 16
    major type value, 6, 16
    minor type value, 6
    negotiating, 256–261
    selection functions for, 107–113
    subtype value, 6, 16
    transcode, 88–91

media type selection functions

media type selection functions, 107–113, 108–114
MEEndOfPresentation event, 36, 166
MEEndOfStream event, 166, 187
MEError event, 157, 181, 255
MEMediaSample event
    media stream objects and, 184, 189
    MFTs and, 263
    MP3 session data flow, 277, 279
memory, storing pixel data in, 124–125
MENewPresentation event, 166
MENewStream event, 269, 271
MESessionClosed media event type, 34, 36, 76
MESessionEnded media event type, 76
MESessionStarted media event type, 36
MESessionTopologySet media event type, 36, 77
MESessionTopologyStatus event, 36, 267
MESourceStarted event, 178, 269
messaging functions, 101
MEStreamSinkMarker event, 235, 237–241
MEStreamSinkRequestSample event, 217, 230, 233, 261–262, 269
MEStreamSinkStarted event, 229, 269, 272
MEStreamSinkStopped event, 220, 229
MEStreamStarted event, 269
metadata
    extracting, 140
    Windows property handlers and, 189–195
MFAllocateWorkQueue() function, 266
MFBeginCreateFile() function, 328
MFBYTESTREAM_IS_WRITABLE flag, 309
MFByteStream object, 287
MF components. *See also* specific components
    about, 2, 5–9
    connecting, 6, 18
    for rendering media files, 13–16
    media type support, 5
    naming conventions, 5
    in pipelines, 2
    version considerations, 11
MFCreate3GPMediaSink() function, 206
MFCreateASFContentInfo() function, 302
MFCreateASFMediaSink() function, 206
MFCreateASFProfileFromPresentationDescriptor() function, 302
MFCreateASFStreamingMediaSinkActivate() function, 302, 303
MFCreateASFStreamingMediaSink() function, 206, 302
MFCreateAsyncResult() function, 313
MFCreateAudioRendererActivate() function, 54

MFCreateAudioRenderer() function, 252
MFCreateEventQueue function, 178
MFCreateFile() function, 253, 254, 307
MFCreateMediaSession() function, 30, 57, 248–249
MFCreateMP3MediaSink() function, 206
MFCreateMPEG4MediaSink() function, 206
MFCreatePresentationClock() function, 269
MFCreatePresentationDescriptor() function, 167
MFCreateSinkWriterFromURL() function, 81
MFCreateSourceResolver() function, 45
MFCreateTopology() function, 23–24
MFCreateTranscodeProfile() function, 65
MFCreateTranscodeTopology() function, 64
MFCreateVideoRendererActivate() function, 54
MF_E_END_OF_STREAM error code, 183
MF_E_INVALIDMEDIATYPE error code, 69
MF_E_NO_EVENTS_AVAILABLE error code, 159
MF_E_NO_MORE_TYPES error code, 74, 111
MF_E_NOTACCEPTING error code, 119
MF_E_NOT_INITIALIZED error code, 228
MFEnumDeviceSources() function, 20
MF error lookup, 323–324
MF_E_STREAMSINKS_FIXED error code, 214
MF_E_TRANSFORM_NEED_INPUT code, 276
MF_E_TRANSFORM_NEED_MORE_INPUT code, 115, 118, 262, 263
MF_E_TRANSFORM_TYPE_NOT_SET error code, 73
MF_E_UNSUPPORTED_SERVICE error code, 282
MF_EVENT_FLAG_NO_WAIT parameter, 159
MFGetService() function, 42, 281, 292
MFGetStrideForBitmapInfoHeader() function, 130
MFInvokeCallback() function, 154
MFMediaType_AAC media type, 90
MF_MT_DEFAULT_STRIDE attribute, 130
mfobjects.h header file, 36
MF_OUTPUT_DATA_BUFFER buffer, 276
MF_PD_DURATION attribute, 168
MFPlay API, 25
MFPutWorkItem() function, 172, 272
MF_RATE_CONTROL_SERVICE attribute, 281
MF_RESOLUTION_CONTENT_DOES_NOT_HAVE_TO_MATCH_EXTENSION_OR_MIME_TYPE flag, 46, 149
MFSampleExtension_CleanPoint GUID, 234
MFSESSION_SETTOPOLOGY_CLEAR_CURRENT parameter, 31
MFSESSION_SETTOPOLOGY_IMMEDIATE parameter, 31
MFSESSION_SETTOPOLOGY_NORESOLUTION parameter, 31
MFSessionTopologyStatus event, 256

negotiating media type

MFShutdown() function, 28
MF_SINK_WRITER_ASYNC_CALLBACK attribute, 79
MF_SOURCE_READER_ASYNC_CALLBACK attribute, 79
MFStartup() function, 27–28
MFSTREAMSINK_MARKER_DEFAULT event, 235
MFSTREAMSINK_MARKER_ENDOFSEGMENT stream marker, 234, 238
MFSTREAMSINK_MARKER_EVENT event, 235
MFSTREAMSINK_MARKER_FLAG attribute, 240
MFSTREAMSINK_MARKER_TICK flag, 234, 237
MFTEnumEx() function, 66, 72–73, 122, 329
MFTEnum() function, 98, 121–122
MF_TIME_FORMAT_SEGMENT_OFFSET parameter, 43
MFT_INPUT_STREAM_INFO structure, 105–107
MFT_INPUT_STREAM_SINGLE_SAMPLE_PER_BUFFER flag, 105
MFT_INPUT_STREAM_WHOLE_SAMPLES flag, 105
MFT_MESSAGE_COMMAND_DRAIN event, 115
MFT_MESSAGE_COMMAND_FLUSH message, 115
MFT_MESSAGE_NOTIFY_BEGIN_STREAMING event, 114
MFT_MESSAGE_NOTIFY_END_OF_STREAM message, 115
MFT_MESSAGE_NOTIFY_END_STREAMING event, 115
MFT_MESSAGE_NOTIFY_START_OF_STREAM event, 114
MF_TOPOLOGY_OUTPUT_NODE parameter, 54
MF_TOPONODE_PRIMARYOUTPUT attribute, 299
MFT_OUTPUT_DATA_BUFFER structure, 118
MFT_OUTPUT_STREAM_CAN_PROVIDE_SAMPLES parameter, 119
MFT_OUTPUT_STREAM_FIXED_SAMPLE_SIZE flag, 107
MFT_OUTPUT_STREAM_INFO structure, 107
MFT_OUTPUT_STREAM_LAZY_READ parameter, 119
MFT_OUTPUT_STREAM_PROVIDES_SAMPLES flag, 107, 118
MFTrace tool, 113, 324–330
MF_TRANSCODE_CONTAINERTYPE attribute, 70
MFTranscodeGetAudioOutputAvailableTypes() function, 66–67, 69, 71
MF_TRANSFORM_ASYNC_UNLOCK attribute, 121, 266
MFTRegister() function, 122
MFTRegisterLocalByCLSID() function, 121
MFTRegisterLocal() function, 121
MFT_SET_TYPE_TEST_ONLY flag, 112
MFTs (Media Foundation transforms)
　accessing hardware directly, 18
　advantages of, 97
　architectural overview, 98–101
　asynchronous communication, 262–266
　defined, 4, 97
　enumerating, 72
　injecting images into video frames, 122–133
　input/output streams support, 102
　inserting in topology, 18
　life cycle steps, 98–99
　listing of registered, 18
　naming conventions, 5
　processing data, 113–119
　registering, 121–122
　in rendering example, 13
　restrictions on, 5
　synchronous communication, 262–266
　Tee, 298–299
　version considerations, 100
　writing, 101–122
MFT_SUPPORT_DYNAMIC_FORMAT_CHANGE Boolean value, 120
MFUnlockWorkerQueue() function, 267
MFVideoAlphaBitmap structure, 296
MF_VIDEO_MIXER_SERVICE object, 292
Microsoft H264 Video Decoder MFT decoder, 18
Microsoft LifeCam Cinema USB webcam, 20–21
MIME (Multipurpose Internet Mail Extension), 148
minor type value (media types), 6
motion vectors, 87
MP3 format
　building MP3 topology, 251–261
　custom media sessions, 250–251
　MP support, 70
　session data flow, 272–279
　transcoding and, 81
MPEG4 format, 70, 81
MPEG43 decoder MFT, 18
MR_VIDEO_RENDERER_SERVICE attribute, 281
multipass encoding, 62
Multipurpose Internet Mail Extension (MIME), 148

N

naming conventions
　media event types, 36
　for MF components, 5
negotiating formats (transcoding), 84–88
negotiating media type, 256–261

Index **355**

network players
 about, 298–300
 building topology, 300–305
 HTTP byte stream activation, 305–306
 HTTP output byte stream, 306–314
network streaming, 78, 287
new operator, 161, 216
NTSC format, 91, 127
NV12_CHROMA structure, 133
NV12 format
 about, 123, 124
 image injection and, 132–133
NVIDIA Video Decoder MFT, 18

O

object attributes, displaying, 14–15
OnParseHeader() function, 160
Open File dialog box, 12, 16
OTA (Output Trust Authority), 15
output byte stream, 306–314
OutputDebugString() functions, 325
output streams
 defined, 101
 stream configuration functions, 101–107
Output Trust Authority (OTA), 15

P

parameters. *See* specific parameters
Pause button (TopoEdit), 14
pipeline
 building, 9, 43–44
 building partial topology, 48–55
 components of, 2, 4
 creating MF source, 44–48
 custom session data pipeline, 261–279
 data flow through, 7–9
 defined, 3
 as directed acyclic graphs, 3
 manual topology construction, 16–20
 processing overview, 2–5
 resolving partial topology, 55–57
 synchronous events, 266–272
pixel aspect ratio, 69
pixel data, storing in memory, 124–125
PKEY_Audio_Format GUID, 195
PKEY_Audio_SampleRate GUID, 195
PKEY_Audio_SampleSize GUID, 195

PKEY_Audio_StreamNumber GUID, 195
PKEY_Media_Duration GUID, 193, 195
PKEY_Video_Compression GUID, 195
PKEY_Video_FourCC GUID, 195
PKEY_Video_FrameHeight GUID, 195
PKEY_Video_FrameRate GUID, 195
PKEY_Video_FrameWidth GUID, 195
PKEY_Video_StreamNumber GUID, 195
Play button (TopoEdit), 14
Player.cpp file, 24
Player.h file, 24
PlayerState enumeration, 58
playing media files. *See* media playback/players
Play option (Controls menu), 14
PMP (Protected Media Path), 237
presentation clock
 about, 211
 media sink clock functions, 216–220
 session clock, 279–283
PRESENTATION_CURRENT_POSITION attribute, 269
presentation descriptors
 about, 49
 creating, 166–168
presentations, defined, 166
Properties dialog box, 194
property handlers (Windows), 189–195
PropVariantClear() function, 237, 241
PropVariantCopy() function, 237, 241
PROPVARIANT structure, 42, 77, 176, 237, 261, 271
Protected Media Path (PMP), 237
PSCreateMemoryPropertyStore() method (Windows), 192

Q

queues
 inserting stream markers into, 235
 storing samples in, 230

R

race conditions, 145
rate control (playback), 14
rateless sinks, 299, 306
RegisterCOMObject() function, 122
registering
 COM objects, 336–338
 MFTs, 121–122
 sinks, 207

registry (Windows)
    byte stream handlers, 148
    file extension mappings, 46
    property handlers, 193–195
    scheme handlers, 147, 148
regsvr32 utility (Windows), 148
renderer sinks, 205
Render File option (File menu), 100
rendering media files
    defined, 12
    MF components for, 13–16
    TopoEdit tool support, 12
    with EVR Mixer, 289–298
    with media sessions, 25–43
Render Media File option (File menu), 12
resampling media streams, 13
Resolve Topology option (Topology menu), 19
RGB format
    about, 122
    converting to YUV format, 125–128
RGBTRIPLE structure, 126
Rogerson, Dale, 331

S

SAR (Streaming Audio Renderer), 17, 205, 252
scheme handlers, 147–148
seek bar, 14, 287–288
seek functionality, 14
Select Capture Device dialog box, 20
session clock, 279–283
sessions. *See* media sessions
S_FALSE code, 226, 232, 239
sink events, 269
sinks
    about, 4, 205
    AVI media sinks, 210–227
    AVI media stream, 227–241
    EVR, 17
    initializing, 209
    instantiating, 206–207
    major components, 210
    naming conventions, 5
    rateless, 299, 306
    registering, 207
    in rendering example, 13
    restrictions on, 5
    sample AVI file sinks, 207–210
    SAR, 17
    in transcoding conceptual diagram, 61
    types of, 205
sink writers
    asynchronous communication, 79
    creating, 80–81
    defined, 78
    intermediate format negotiation, 84–88
    mapping streams, 81–84
    source-reader-to-sink-writer loop, 92–93
    transcode media type, 88–91
    transcoder application diagram, 78
    transcoding with, 62
smart pointers (ATL), 339–343
S_OK code, 226
source events, 269
source media event functions, 178–180
SourceOperation class
    about, 161–162, 172
    class definition, 200–202
    instantiating objects, 174
    storing file URLs, 164
    streaming source samples, 180
SourceOperationPause enumeration, 172
source readers
    asynchronous communication, 79
    creating, 80–81
    defined, 78
    intermediate format negotiation, 84–88
    source-reader-to-sink-writer loop, 92–93
    TranscodeApp sample application, 62
    transcode media type, 88–91
    transcoder application diagram, 78
    transcoding with, 62, 78–80
source resolvers
    creating, 45
    defined, 45
    media player application, 45–48
sources
    about, 4, 141–143, 159–160
    asynchronous source command functions, 171–174
    conceptual diagram depicting, 139–140
    creating for playback, 44–48
    creating for transcoding, 64
    external, 20–21
    extracting metadata, 140
    initializing, 160–170
    inserting in topology, 16
    instantiating, 146–156
    media stream objects and, 183–189

sources (continued)

sources (continued)
  naming conventions, 5
  in rendering example, 13
  restrictions on, 5
  seek functionality and, 14
  source media event functions, 178–180
  starting playback, 174–178
  streaming samples, 180–183
  in transcoding conceptual diagram, 61
  Windows property handlers, 189–195
SourceState enumeration, 199
Standard Template Library (STL) vector, 170, 173
status query functions, 119–121, 120–121
STL (Standard Template Library) vector, 170, 173
Stop button (TopoEdit), 14
stream configuration functions, 101, 101–107
stream descriptors, 48–49, 166
Streaming Audio Renderer (SAR), 17, 205, 252
streaming sinks, 205
stream markers, 234–241
subtype value (media types), 6, 16
synchronization considerations
  ATL and, 145
  synchronization primitives, 24
synchronous communication
  MFTs and, 262–266
  pipeline events, 266–272
  processing data, 114
  sources readers and, 78
System.Audio.Format property, 195
System.Audio.SampleRate property, 195
System.Audio.SampleSize property, 195
System.Audio.StreamNumber property, 195
System.Media.Duration property, 194, 195
System.Video.Compression property, 195
System.Video.FourCC property, 195
System.Video.FrameHeight property, 195
System.Video.FrameRate property, 195
System.Video.FrameWidth property, 195
System.Video.StreamNumber property, 195

T

Tee MFTs, 298–299
TextAnalysisTool.Net tool, 325
3GP (3GPP) format, 70, 81
TopoBuilder.cpp file, 25
TopoBuilder.h file, 25

TopoEdit tool. *See also* specific menu options
  attribute pane, 15–16
  availability of, 11
  capturing data from external sources, 20–21
  displaying object attributes, 14–15
  launching, 12
  loading MFTs into, 100
  manual topology construction, 16–20
  media type details provided by, 16
  playing media files in, 14–15
  rendering media files, 12
  user interface, 12
  version considerations, 11, 100
topology. *See also* pipeline
  displaying status of, 19
  manual construction of, 16–20
  resolving explicitly, 19
  resolving partial, 55–57
  sharing clock object in, 21
topology builder/building
  about, 9
  adding extra MFTs, 19
  building partial, 48–55
  as manual process, 62
  for MP3 session, 251–261
  negotiating connections, 14, 16
  streaming network players, 300–305
topology loader, 19
Topology menu (TopoEdit)
  Add Audio Capture Source option, 20
  Add Custom Sink option, 206
  Add EVR option, 17
  Add SAR option, 17
  Add Source option, 16
  Add Transform option, 18, 100
  Add Video Capture Source option, 20
  Resolve Topology option, 19
topology nodes
  about, 14
  connecting together, 18
  linking, 19
  removing invalid links, 19
transcode API
  about, 62–64
  creating transcode profile, 64–74
  CTopoBuilder class and, 63
  generating topologies via, 62
  limitations of, 62
  process overview, 63
  transcoding session, 74–77
transcode media type, 88–91

transcode profile
    configuring, 64–65
    configuring audio settings, 65–67
    configuring target container, 70
    configuring video settings, 68–69
    defined, 64
    determining target transcode format, 70–74
transcoding
    compression and, 87
    conceptual diagram of, 61–62
    defined, 61
    intermediate format negotiation, 84–88
    with sink writers, 62, 78–93
    with source readers, 62, 78–93
    transcode API and, 62–77
transforms. *See* MFTs
T-splitter filters, 102

U

UINT32 attribute, 234, 261
UML sequence diagrams, 25
UML (Unified Modeling Language), 25
uncompressed video formats, 123–125
UNICODE standard, 28
Unified Modeling Language (UML), 25
U-V color plane, 123
UYUV uncompressed format, 111
UYVY format
    about, 124, 125
    image injection and, 130–132
UYVY_MACRO_PIXEL structure, 131

V

variable-bit-rate (VBR) encoding, 62
VBR (variable-bit-rate) encoding, 62
VC1 video format, 87
vector::push_back() function, 216
VFW (Video for Windows) interfaces, 142, 207
video codecs, 18
video files
    compression and, 2–3
    format negotiation, 84–88
    mapping sink writer streams, 81–84
    pipeline data flow, 2–5
    playing in TopoEdit, 14–15
    rendering, 12
video formats, uncompressed, 123–125
Video for Windows (VFW) interfaces, 142, 207

video frames, injecting images into, 122–133
Video Mixing Renderer (VMR), 289
video renderer, 17
VMR (Video Mixing Renderer), 289
void pointer (C++), 77
VT_UNKNOWN parameter, 261

W

Windows Explorer, 189–190, 193–194
Windows Media DRM (WMDRM), 248
Windows Media Player, 140, 288
Windows Preprocessor (WPP), 325
Windows property handlers, 189–195
Windows registry
    byte stream handlers, 148
    file extension mappings, 46
    property handlers, 193–195
    scheme handlers, 147, 148
Windows Shell, 140, 190, 194
WMA format, 81
WMDRM (Windows Media DRM), 248
WM format, 81
WM_MOUSELEAVE message, 296
WMV9 format, 69
WMV format, 81
worker thread objects
    asynchronous operation example, 144
    media player application and, 32
    sequence diagram depicting, 143
WPP (Windows Preprocessor), 325
writing MFTs
    about, 101
    event functions, 119–121
    media type selection functions, 107–113
    MFT data processing, 113–119
    MFT registration, 121–122
    status query functions, 119–121
    stream configuration functions, 101–107

Y

YCbCr format
    about, 123
    converting RGB fomat to, 123
YUV format
    about, 123
    converting RGB format to, 125–128
YUVTRIPLE structure, 126

About the Author

ANTON POLINGER has worked on the Microsoft Audio/Video pipelines and media technologies for the past eight years, owning the entire pipeline for five releases of Media Center from XP through Windows 7. He has conducted seminars that describe MS media technologies and the Media Center pipeline and taught programming classes on subjects ranging from web development to advanced C++.

What do you think of this book?

We want to hear from you!
To participate in a brief online survey, please visit:

microsoft.com/learning/booksurvey

Tell us how well this book meets your needs—what works effectively, and what we can do better. Your feedback will help us continually improve our books and learning resources for you.

Thank you in advance for your input!

CPSIA information can be obtained at www.ICGtesting.com
Printed in the USA
BVOW082233131011
273600BV00002B/6/P